History and Highlights from 35 Years of the Houston Astrodome

Edited by Gregory H. Wolf

Introductions by Tal Smith and Larry Dierker
Associate Editors: Frederick C. Bush, James Forr, Len Levin, and Bill Nowlin

Society for American Baseball Research, Inc.
Phoenix, AZ

Dome Sweet Dome: History and Highlights from 35 Years of the Houston Astrodome
Edited by Gregory H. Wolf
Introductions by Tal Smith and Larry Dierker
Associate Editors: Frederick C. Bush, James Forr, Len Levin, and Bill Nowlin

ISBN 978-1-943816-33-0
Ebook ISBN 978-1-943816-32-3

Cover and book design: Gilly Rosenthol

Front and rear cover photos courtesy of the Houston Astros Baseball Club.

Society for American Baseball Research
Cronkite School at ASU
555 N. Central Ave. #416
Phoenix, AZ 85004
Phone: (602) 496-1460
Web: www.sabr.org
Facebook: Society for American Baseball Research
Twitter: @SABR

Table of Contents

Preface and Acknowledgments

IN JULY 2014 I ATTENDED THE SABR national convention in Houston, and recall vividly the impressive organization of the event and the many engaging research sessions. Of particular interest was the session at Minute Maid Park, the Houston Astros' stadium with its retractable roof. After listening intently to former Astros players speak about the careers, and members of the club's analytics department discuss advanced sabermetrics, I thought that a SABR volume focusing on the Astros' former home, the Astrodome, known as "The Eighth Wonder of the World," would be an exciting book project. When I returned home, that idea landed on the back burner until Rick Bush called me in April 2015 and asked me if I would consider editing a volume on the iconic stadium. And if that weren't enough, Rick already had a name for the book: *Dome Sweet Dome: History and Highlights from 35 Years of the Houston Astrodome.* That was all the encouragement I needed, and the project was launched.

This book evokes memories of the Astrodome through detailed summaries of 70 games played there, and nine insightful feature essays about the history of the ballpark. It was an arduous task limiting the volume to just 70 games. Our preliminary list had probably three times that many, and had other editors chosen the games, their list might have been substantially different. Some of the games might be considered great, like Nolan Ryan's record-breaking fifth no-hitter; or historical, like the first regular-season game in the 'Dome; yet other contests might be remembered for outstanding or milestone accomplishments, such as Jim Wynn becoming the first player to hit three home runs in the Astrodome, or fantastic finishes like the Astros' 22-inning victory in 1989. It would have been easy to create a volume consisting solely of great games by Ryan, J.R. Richard, Mike Scott, Jeff Bagwell, and Craig Biggio; however, we were guided by an overarching principle to present the history of the Astrodome through the baseball games played there. For us that meant including games focusing on and showcasing as many different players as possible, some well known, others less so, from Rusty Staub, Bob Watson, and Daryl Kile to Walter Bonds, Milt May, and George Bjorkman. And no volume could be complete without the Astros' memorable, and often heartbreaking, losses in postseason games in the 1980s and 1990s. The nine feature essays contextualize the stadium's history. Included are pieces focusing on the Astrodome's engineering, the major movers and shakers in the early stages of the stadium's history, such as Roy Hofheinz, George Kirksey, and Craig Cullinan, the Astrodome as a home to nonbaseball events, and of course, an in-depth historical sketch of the Astrodome itself.

Members of the Society for American Baseball Research (SABR) made this book possible. These volunteers are united by a passion for researching and writing about baseball history. I thank all of the authors for their contributions, meticulous research, cooperation through the revising and editing process, and finally their patience. I am impressed with your dedication to preserve baseball history by combing archives, interviewing players, and telling the story of so many exciting games played in, and the history of, the Astrodome.

A special "shout-out" goes to Bill McCurdy, a member of the Larry Dierker (Houston) chapter of SABR. Not only did he write a very heartfelt personal reflection about his 35 years attending sporting events in the Astrodome, he connected me with Astro icons Tal Smith and Larry Dierker, and with the Houston Astros in my search for photos. I am forever grateful to Tal Smith and Larry Dierker for agreeing to write introductions for this volume. Their personal observations about the Astrodome lend the book an additional sense of authenticity.

We had an All-Star editorial team. The second reader, Bill Nowlin, read every submission, and can spot a missing comma or a colon a mile away. This is the sixth book we've worked on together, and I think he anticipates my questions before I ask them. Rick Bush served as the third reader. His superb and conscientious editing made every contribution better. Rick also wrote most of the photo captions. James Forr was the fact-checker. He verified every statistic and fact in every essay, and offered addition insights, suggestions, and information for authors to consider. The copy editor was Len Levin, who has served in this capacity for all of the SABR books. I am not sure what we would do without his deft touch—he made us all look good. Thanks to each of you.

This book would not have been possible without the generous support of the staff and Board of Directors of SABR, SABR Publications Director Cecilia Tan, and designer Gilly Rosenthol (Rosenthol Design).

Special thanks go to the Houston Astros Baseball Club for providing the overwhelming majority of photos for this book. I'd also like express my gratitude to the Astros' Mike Acosta, manager, authentication, and Alex Bierens de Haan, photographer, for their coordination in sending the photos to us. The Astros' support of SABR's nonprofit mission is greatly appreciated. I also extend my thanks to John Horne of the National Baseball Hall of Fame for supplying additional photos.

And finally, I wish to thank my wife, Margaret, and daughter, Gabriela, for their support. They've gotten use to my late evening working on SABR projects. Thankfully they are baseball fans who also got to see a game at Minute Maid Park during the SABR convention in Houston.

Gregory H. Wolf
March 1, 2017

A trio of stars for Astros. Jimmy Wynn, Mike Cuellar, and Rusty Staub represented the Astros at the 1967 All-Star Game at Anaheim Stadium. (Courtesy of Houston Astros Baseball Club).

Reflections on the Opening of the Astrodome

By Tal Smith

I HAVE BEEN FORTUNATE TO WORK in professional baseball for almost 60 years. It has been an interesting career with many treasured and exciting experiences, and I am frequently asked what is my fondest or greatest memory.

Most of my career (35 years over three different intervals) was spent with the Houston Astros. During the years I served as general manager or president of baseball operations, there were many thrilling games and notable accomplishments. The first divisional championship in 1980 followed by the exciting playoff series with the Phillies, and the winning of the National League pennant in 2005, which led to the first World Series in Texas, certainly stand out and will live forever among my cherished memories. Many particular games and individual performances by Astro players also come to mind when recalling past events that left an indelible mark.

But wins on the field are often short-lived. There is always another game to play or another season that follows. The joy of winning is often offset at some future point by disappointment. In my memory bank, however, there is one event of a more lasting nature: the opening of the Astrodome in April 1965.

Actually, my association with the Astrodome began when it was not much more than a hole in the ground in 1963. I had achieved my boyhood dream of a job with a major-league baseball team when I joined the Cincinnati Reds in 1958. In the fall of 1960 Houston was awarded an expansion franchise in the National League, and Gabe Paul, who had been my boss as general manager of the Reds, asked me to accompany him to Houston when he accepted a similar position as GM of the fledgling franchise. By 1963, Gabe had left and become president of the Cleveland Indians. I was on the verge of joining him

in Cleveland when Judge Roy Hofheinz summoned me to his office.

Judge Hofheinz and R.E. "Bob" Smith were the principal owners of the Houston Sports Association ("HSA"), the corporate entity that operated the ballclub (known as the Colt .45s at that time and renamed Astros just before the opening of the

Tal Smith spent 35 years in Houston's front office; at different times, he was farm director, president, and general manager. As the GM, he was recognized as Major League Executive of the Year in 1980. (Courtesy of Houston Astros Baseball Club).

Astrodome). It was Hofheinz who conceived of the then unheard-of idea of building a multipurpose stadium that would be covered and air-conditioned so as to comfort and shelter baseball fans from Houston's hot and humid atmosphere and provide a venue that would host trade shows, conventions, and other sport and entertainment attractions throughout the year regardless of the elements. The Judge was clearly the visionary who came up with the idea and the master salesman, promoter, and politician who pushed the project, overcame the skeptics and other obstacles, and made it a reality.

When I met with the Judge that day in early April 1963, I had no idea what he had in mind. Like all others with the team, I had become fascinated and somewhat mesmerized listening to his oratory about what would become the world's first air-conditioned, covered stadium, but up until that time the emphasis had been centered on raising public support and public funding. The site itself was a big hole that had been excavated and then sat dormant until a second bond issue was passed.

I was aware that construction contracts had been awarded and that there was now activity at the job site, but I was completely surprised when the Judge asked me to abandon my plans to leave and to instead stay on and serve as the liaison and project manager for the HSA during the construction period. My five years of baseball experience in Cincinnati and Houston had all been related to player development and player evaluation. I professed this to the Judge and reminded him that I was not an architect or engineer. He obviously knew this and proceeded to sell me on the idea that I could do it and that I should do it.

After some reflection it seemed to me to be an exciting challenge and a once-in-a-lifetime opportunity to become involved in such a unique project. How right I was and how thankful I am that I acceded to the Judge's request.

I did sense, though, that I was faced with a "sink or swim" situation so I quickly became immersed in the raft of architectural, structural , mechanical, and electrical drawings, the hundreds of pages of

They are all smiles. Tal Smith and Joe Morgan, who returned to the Astros in 1980. (Courtesy of Houston Astros Baseball Club).

job specifications and other documents related to the building of what was to become known as the Astrodome. There is no greater way to learn than when faced with necessity. Thus began a fascinating journey for the next 2½ years.

The construction of the Astrodome was a superb team effort. An extraordinary group of architects and engineers, most of whom were Houston firms, designed the building and its innovative features. There was obviously no similar air-conditioned, covered stadium or buildings of this magnitude to serve as a model. Consequently, there were no script or existing blueprints to guide the designers in the initial design or in coping with issues or problems that might arise in the actual construction stage.

The general contractor and the subcontractors and their suppliers all seemed to recognize what was at hand — the opportunity to participate in a historic endeavor and to add their name to what would become known as "The Eighth Wonder of the World." Job-site issues were usually quickly resolved, and demanding schedules were met.

Many sports teams played in the Astrodome in the ensuing years but none had a more profound effect than the first team that was on the site — the professionals who built this majestic stadium that went on to serve as a model for stadiums worldwide. Air-conditioned, covered stadiums with upholstered seats and unobstructed sight lines, entertaining video displays, restaurants and clubs, luxurious suites, and other amenities are the norm today, but who knows when they might have come about if not for Judge Hofheinz's novel concept and those who carried out his vision.

I obviously have a lot of memories of the process and those who were involved. Recollections of the many great events that took place in The Dome are too numerous to catalog or to rate in any order of significance without doing an injustice to others equally deserving.

For me, however, the one most memorable event in my professional life occurred in the early morning hours on April 9, 1965, a few short hours before the first public event—the exhibition game with the Yankees –when I stood in the center of the field in a silent stadium with the house lights on and marveled at what had been accomplished.

A Look Back at the Astrodome

By Larry Dierker

AS A LITTLE LEAGUER IN SOUTHERN California, I was thrilled when the Dodgers moved to Los Angeles. I saw a few games at the Coliseum, but when I went to Dodger Stadium for the first time, I thought I was in heaven.

Six years later I pitched a game at Old Colt Stadium in Houston on my 18th birthday. We could all see the Astrodome across the parking lot, the steel beams and the arching roof structure. I don't think any of us could have imagined what it would look like when we got back from spring training the next year.

Our team bus pulled into the Astrodome parking lot under the veil of darkness on April 7, 1965. The roof was aglow. We really couldn't appreciate the beauty of the outside walls until the next day. But of course, the inside was the thing anyway. We entered the stadium and walked across the concourse into the box seats. It was breathtaking. The colors of the theater-style seats on each level were eye-popping. The scoreboard was gigantic. The grass was green, the dirt brown, and the field was chalked brilliant white. Although jaws dropped, it must have been at least a minute before anyone said anything. Wow!

Dodger Stadium was a relic; it was Old Colt Stadium. We were in the 21st century.

I pitched in an intrasquad game the next day and gave up a bunch of runs because the glare of the sun through the Lucite panels of the roof made it impossible for fielders to track fly balls. The next night we hosted the Yankees and Mickey Mantle hit the first home run, off Turk Farrell. Little did we know at the time, a home run to center field (or in any other direction) would be quite an accomplishment in the Dome.

Attendance was good for the first few years as people (not all of them baseball fans), came to Houston from the four corners of the earth to see what Astros owner Roy Hofheinz proclaimed to be the Eighth Wonder of the World. Indeed, he had been inspired by the Colosseum in Rome and had returned from an excursion to Europe with many architectural elements and other furnishings that he would use to embellish the Astrodome Club, the Domeskeller behind the outfield wall, and the Sky Boxes high atop the upper deck.

As you will learn, many historic events formed a timeline of the Astrodome's history. And if efforts to restore the building are successful, there may be more to come. But what I find ironic is that, in a way, the Astrodome in Houston led businessmen and politicians in many other cities right down the primrose path.

Once it was clear that grass would not grow inside, Astroturf was invented to replace it. It was yet another wonder. Who could fail to notice that both football and baseball could be played in the same stadium without the necessity of mowing the lawn. Soon there were convertible multipurpose stadiums with Astroturf in St. Louis, Cincinnati, Pittsburgh, and Philadelphia. A few other cities built convertible bowls with natural grass. But after 20 years or so, it became obvious that these venues were not ideal for football or baseball. And they were anything but charming. Camden Yards was built to bring back the feel of the "old ballpark." Then a succession of retro-style fields began replacing the big bowls. When the 21st century actually arrived, the Astros moved out of the Astrodome and into Enron Field, a retro park, in downtown Houston.

Looking back, the Astrodome's place in baseball history is similar to that of Shibe Park in Philadelphia, which started the trend of big baseball-only stadiums in 1909. After that, nine new ballparks were built in the next six years for major-league teams. Among them, only Fenway Park and Wrigley Field remain. I got to play at Wrigley and in Crosley Field, Sportsman's Park, Forbes Field, and Connie Mack Stadium. And though I missed the Polo Grounds by a year, I feel the progress of baseball and its environs in my bones.

The Astrodome: The Eighth Wonder of the World Changed Sports and Spectatorship in America

By Robert C. Trumpbour

THE HOUSTON ASTRODOME WAS the first fully enclosed, air-conditioned major-league ballpark. It was formally unveiled in an exhibition game that pitted the Houston Astros against the American League champion New York Yankees on April 9, 1965. Unlike previous sports venues, the Astrodome was built to be a massive all-purpose, climate-controlled facility that would serve as an entertainment complex for a broad variety of events and activities. Construction costs were $31.6 million.

It was unlike any venue before it, as it reveled in luxury, with padded theater-style seating throughout and an array of posh amenities designed as part of its construction. Luxury skyboxes, themed restaurants, a video scoreboard, a barbershop, a bowling alley, a weather station, and numerous other unique features were woven into the venue. The Astrodome's amenities were so diverse that comedian Bob Hope joked, "If they had a maternity ward and a cemetery, you would never have to leave." The structure was so impressive that it prompted visits from celebrities and dignitaries alike.[1] It was sufficiently unique that it was commonly referred to as the "Eighth Wonder of the World."

As such, the Astrodome inspired similar indoor facilities, including the Louisiana Superdome, which, paradoxically, helped contribute to its eventual obsolescence and demise. Before two newer sports venues replaced the Astrodome it had hosted baseball, football, boxing, basketball, soccer, trade shows, conventions, religious events, livestock shows, rodeos, concerts, political events, and a long list of other activities. Although it remained in place as of 2016, it was unused and in danger of demolition.

The design is an example of late modernist architecture, and the first truly massive domed structure not supported by internal columns. Preservationist Cynthia Neely asserts that the Astrodome "created a whole new style of architecture … [one that] made a lot of other famous buildings possible."[2] Roy Hofheinz, a hard-charging entrepreneur who served as Houston's mayor and as Harris County judge (the county's chief administrator), supervised the construction. When it was built, the feasibility of a huge indoor sports facility was not fully certain. However, the engineers and architects were confident in their ability to follow through on a previously untested concept. The project was sufficiently ambitious that it required numerous experts to be built. The firm of Lloyd & Morgan teamed up with Wilson, Morris, Crane & Anderson to serve as architects. Hermon Lloyd, S.I. Morris, Ralph Anderson, and Robert Minchew provided much of the leadership in that area. Walter P. Moore and Associates were the structural engineers, who came under the supervision of Kenneth Zimmerman. H.A. Lott, Inc., a Houston firm, and Minneapolis-based Johnson, Drake, & Piper were general contractors. Praeger-Kavanagh-Waterbury, New York-based architects and engineers, were retained as consultants for the project.[3]

Hofheinz was inspired to build the Astrodome after he visited Rome's Colosseum while serving as mayor of Houston. He was told that on exceedingly hot days, a massive cover was pulled over that venue to shade the spectators. Before construction began, Hofheinz admitted to frequently pondering the Colosseum's history. He stated, "Looking back on those ancient days, I figured that a round facility with a cover was what we needed in the United States, and

Judge Roy Hofheinz, a former Houston mayor, wanted to mold his hometown into a prominent city. His relentless efforts helped to bring major-league baseball to Houston and turned the Astrodome from a fantasy into reality. (Courtesy of Houston Astros Baseball Club).

that Houston would be the perfect spot because of its rainy, humid weather."[4]

Hofheinz was not the first to conceive of a domed baseball venue. During the 1950s Brooklyn Dodgers owner Walter O'Malley explored the possibility of a building a dome, consulting with futurists Norman Bel Geddes and Buckminster Fuller. Those plans were scuttled by a variety of factors, prompting O'Malley to abandon his longtime Brooklyn home for Los Angeles. There he oversaw the construction of Dodger Stadium, which opened three years before the Astrodome's completion.[5]

Just as the ancient bread and circuses of the Colosseum served to showcase the majesty of the Roman Empire, Hofheinz was committed to hosting numerous forms of entertainment with grand and unprecedented flourishes as a way to demonstrate the rising stature of Houston. In describing the venue's luxurious atmosphere he boasted, "Nobody can ever see this and go back to Kalamazoo, Chicago, New York, you name it, and still think this town is bush league."[6]

Before committing to stadium construction, Hofheinz initially sought to create an indoor shopping mall that would contain a dome as part of its design. He worked closely with Buckminster Fuller

as those plans unfolded. As the two were contemplating mall designs, they were, without knowing it, formulating ideas that would contribute to the Astrodome's eventual construction. Hofheinz explained that during the fact-finding process Fuller convinced him "that it was possible to cover any size space [with a dome] if you didn't run out of money."[7] The mall proposal was undermined by the success of a competitor's project, so Hofheinz shifted his talents to stadium construction at the same time as proposals were being submitted to lure a major-league baseball club to Houston. For Hofheinz, however, hosting a team was part of a much larger vision that included construction of a grand entertainment empire.

Public-relations guru George Kirksey and oil heir Craig Cullinan were instrumental in bringing a major-league team, the Colt .45s, to Houston. In 1962 the expansion team began play in Colt Stadium, a temporary facility also built under Hofheinz's supervision. The ballpark was located near the Astrodome site, so spectators were provided informal construction updates as they visited the temporary open-air facility.

The Colt .45s played in that venue through the close of the 1964 season as the Astrodome was being built. Houston's oppressively hot and humid conditions and aggressive mosquito population offered evidence as to why an indoor facility was essential for baseball to succeed in Houston. While playing at Colt Stadium, fans, players, and umpires faced fatigue and heatstroke. The concession areas sold mosquito repellent to fend off insects that were so big Dodgers pitcher Sandy Koufax remarked, "Some of the bugs there are twin engine jobs."[8] Conditions were so brutal that the National League adjusted its schedule in Houston to allow for more night games.[9]

Kirksey and Cullinan regarded baseball as essential to the Astrodome's future, but for Hofheinz, the facility was designed to be a larger-than-life entertainment facility, with baseball as a small part of a much more expansive plan. A year after the Astrodome was unveiled, he asserted that "we had to have a stadium that would be a spectator's paradise, but also one that could be used for events other than sports."[10]

Hofheinz was not involved in the preliminary plans to build a baseball venue. As franchise relocation was under way during the 1950s, Kirksey and Cullinan sought to gain a major-league team. They collaborated with banking executive William Kirkland to prepare the initial case to build a new stadium as a way to lure a team to Houston. With the approval of the Texas Legislature and backing from Houston insiders, the three were able to arrange for a referendum to fund an open-air ballpark that would contain adjoining indoor convention space. The measure passed by a 3 to 1 ratio on July 26, 1958. After Hofheinz's mall plans fell through, he persuaded Houston's power brokers to abandon the open-air plan because a large all-purpose indoor stadium would be feasible, radically shifting the direction of the project.

Shortly after committing to stadium construction, Hofheinz worked with master carpenter Stuart Young to build a $35,000 scale model of the project, using this model to persuade baseball executives to grant Houston an expansion franchise. On January 3, 1962, when it was time for the Astrodome's groundbreaking, instead of using shovels, seven dignitaries fired rounds of wax bullets from Colt .45 pistols into the ground. Lawsuits, site-selection controversies, construction delays, and a need for additional funding slowed the construction process, but once completed, the Astrodome received immense publicity.[11]

The facility was formally named the Harris County Domed Stadium, but few used that name in reference to the edifice. Several politicians were angered when the facility was rebranded, but Hofheinz bluntly argued, "I can't sell that name. I need something I can sell." The decision to rename the facility the Astrodome, was surprisingly arbitrary, however. After the Colt Industries, the conglomerate that included the gun maker, pushed to obtain royalties for official Colt .45s team merchandise, Hofheinz decided to change the baseball team's name. He was never enthusiastic about the name anyway, feeling that it suggested more about the region's past than its future. As metropolitan Houston was emerging as a hub for the nation's space program, Hofheinz and his partner, Bob Smith, debated whether to choose the Stars or Astros, with the facility to be branded the Stardome or the Astrodome. Roy Hofheinz's son, former Houston Mayor Fred Hofheinz, recounted their discussion of the merits of both options. After considerable debate, Fred Hofheinz indicated that his father "just told Mr. Smith, 'Pick one,' and he picked the Astrodome."[12] After the decision was made, Hofheinz promptly announced the team's new name, and disposed of all Colt .45s merchandise while moving forward on plans to unveil the Astrodome.

The first public event at the Astrodome was an exhibition game between the Astros and the Yankees on April 9, 1965. That exhibition game was arguably the most ballyhooed christening of a ballpark up to that time. Among those on hand were President Lyndon Johnson and his wife, Lady Bird, Texas Governor John Connolly, 21 NASA astronauts, NBC news anchor David Brinkley, and numerous other dignitaries. Total attendance was 47,876, at the time a record for an indoor sporting event. Yankees legend Mickey Mantle began the game with a single, and in the sixth inning blasted the first indoor home run ever. In storybook fashion, the Astros won the game 2-1 in the 12th inning when Nellie Fox drove in a run with a pinch-hit single.

The event was featured prominently on sports pages across the nation. Several publications put it on the front page, ahead of other major news. The *New York Times*, as one example, offered a front-page story that focused heavily on the Astrodome, those in attendance, and reactions to the venue, while providing a panoramic four-column photograph that was taken from behind home plate. *New York Times* coverage offered a lead story in the sports section, too. The focus of that coverage was the game itself, although the article did offer numerous details about the stadium.

Although a new ballpark was christened in Atlanta on the same day, coverage of that event was significantly less detailed.[13] Locally, the *Houston Chronicle* provided front-page coverage and numerous other stories, in addition to offering a special section on April 11 that was replete with photos of the festivities.[14] The Astros indicated that 188,762 spectators entered the turnstiles for five exhibition games prior to the regular-season opener, with reports that many had come "just to see the glittering palace."[15]

Among the most prominent features of the new venue was a $2 million scoreboard. It was 474 feet wide and weighed over 300 tons. It made all other scoreboards in use at the time look puny. It could be programmed to celebrate home runs, lead fans in cheers, and run between-inning advertisements. It served as a precursor to the Jumbotron and Diamondvision, and it was met with tremendous enthusiasm as the ballpark opened. It was such an attention-grabber that *Sports Illustrated* prepared a feature story on the scoreboard alone.[16]

The first regular-season game in the Astrodome received a good deal of fanfare, too. It was the lead baseball story in several newspapers, eclipsing President Johnson's throwing out the ceremonial first pitch for the Washington Senators on that same day.[17] The Phillies beat the Astros, 2-0, with Chris Short tossing a four-hit shutout. To enhance the contest, 24 of NASA's 28 astronauts were on hand and introduced, with each receiving lifetime passes for baseball games inside the Astrodome. Baseball Commissioner Ford Frick and National League President Warren Giles were also on hand, with a total reported attendance of 48,546. (The paid attendance was 42,652.)[18]

The inaugural season in the Astrodome was a time for experimentation, and in one of the odder experiments, New York Mets announcer Lindsey Nelson provided live commentary and play-by-play on April 28 while suspended from a gondola high above the action. Nelson and his producer, Joel Nixon, were lifted into the gondola a half-hour before the game, and remained there through the completion of a contest that concluded with a 12-9 Astros victory. It was the first time ever that an announcer provided play-by-play from fair territory. Before the game Mets manager Casey Stengel expressed delight that his team's announcer would be a "ground rule" if he were to be hit by a ball, while Mets coach Yogi Berra bluntly told Nelson, "I think you're crazy." Nixon was equipped with a walkie-talkie and a phone to communicate with the regular broadcast booth. He

had a scorecard and pen, but once the game began, he stopped keeping score after realizing, "If I ever dropped the pen, it would be a dangerous missile." The experiment was not repeated, but it received abundant publicity while inspiring future use of the gondola for overhead cameras.[19]

The Astrodome revolutionized the nature of sports surfaces, ushering in the use of artificial turf. The initial plan was to maintain a natural-grass surface. A special strain of grass blends called Tifway 419 Bermuda was scientifically engineered to allow for successful indoor growth in low-light settings.[20] However, the inability of ballplayers to track fly balls under the dome's clear Lucite panels required painting the roof surfaces white. That allowed fielders to do their jobs, but blocked sunlight and prevented future indoor plant growth. As a result, the 1965 season closed out with dead grass and painted dirt, an unacceptable situation.

To resolve the problem in time for the 1966 season, Hofheinz negotiated with scientists at Chemstrand, a division of Monsanto, to produce and install an artificial grass-like surface that would not require natural light to remain green. Such a product was used sparingly in urban environments, most notably to provide play areas. In a quest for solutions, front-office executive Tal Smith visited the Moses Brown School in Providence, Rhode Island, to look at such a product, then branded as ChemGrass. After observing a field that was used for that school's sporting events, Hofheinz decided to move forward with its installation inside the Astrodome.[21] This was the first time the synthetic turf was used in a professional sports venue. The product was rebranded AstroTurf. The new surface gained widespread publicity, prompting use in other sports venues as the 1970s unfolded.[22] As installation was under way Smith asserted, "With the installation of AstroTurf, we will have eliminated the last pitfall in conjunction with the stadium."[23]

The nylon product was installed in the infield to start the 1966 season, and later was added to the outfield. The first game on an entirely artificial surface was played on July 19, with the Astros defeating the Philadelphia Phillies, 8-2. Game reports indicated that there was "no apparent effect on the play."[24] In reality, players had to adjust for changes in how the ball reacted to the surface. Numerous baseball purists responded with revulsion to the change, particularly as it was introduced to other stadiums.[25]

Six no-hitters were pitched in the Dome's history, all by the Astros. In the first, on June 18, 1967, Don Wilson, a rookie right-hander, allowed just three baserunners, all on walks, pitching the Astros to a 2-0 victory over the Atlanta Braves in the first major-league no-hitter ever pitched indoors.[26] In the second no-hit effort, Larry Dierker blanked the Montreal Expos, 6-0, on July 9, 1976. It earned front-page recognition in the *New York Times*.[27] On April 7, 1979, Ken Forsch tossed a 6-0 no-hitter against the Atlanta Braves. He and Bob Forsch became the first brothers to throw no-hitters, with Bob tossing one for the St. Louis Cardinals in 1978. On September 26, 1981, 32,115 fans watched Nolan Ryan throw his fifth career no-hitter, blanking the Dodgers, 5-0.

On September 25, 1986, after nailing San Francisco's leadoff hitter, Dan Gladden, in the back, Mike Scott settled down to toss the Astrodome's fifth no-hitter. The game clinched the National League West crown for the Astros, as Scott dominated the Giants, 2-0, in an electrifying evening for 32,808 fans. The performance solidified Scott's case to earn the 1986 Cy Young Award, and it marked the first time in National League history that a no-hitter won a division-clinching game. In the final Astrodome no-hitter, on September 8, 1993, Astros right-hander Darryl Kile struck out nine in a 7-1 victory over the New York Mets. A walk, a wild pitch, and an error provided the Mets' only run, in a contest viewed by a mere 15,684 fans.

When the Astrodome was built, its roof was generally believed to be high enough to avoid being hit by baseballs, but in the first inning on June 10, 1974, Philadelphia Phillies third baseman Mike Schmidt launched a towering center-field blast that slammed into an overhead speaker attached high above a roof truss. What would have been a certain home run fell harmlessly to the field. Instead of celebrating one of the most powerful blasts ever to be hit inside the

Fireworks display inside the cavernous Astrodome. (Courtesy of Houston Astros Baseball Club).

Astrodome, Schmidt earned no more than a single. After the game the future Hall of Famer admitted to being angry, while Astros center fielder César Cedeño speculated that the ball was slammed so powerfully that "it might have hit the flag above the electronic scoreboard." Schmidt hammered two more hits that day, including a three-run double, to pace the Phillies to a 12-0 rout over the Astros.[28] He received more publicity for the unusual and prodigious hit than if he had blasted a home run. Despite being shortchanged in this game, Schmidt led the majors with 36 home runs that season.

Although rain postponements were never supposed to be an issue inside the Astrodome, one occurred on June 15, 1976, immediately before a scheduled game against the Pittsburgh Pirates. The dome remained fully intact and had no structural damage from torrential downpours that in some locations exceeded 12 inches. However, several roadways in Houston were badly flooded, road closures were numerous, isolated power failures occurred and four people in the area died..[29] Players were at the

The 1986 Astros squad's 96–66 record was the best in franchise history to that point. They battled the Mets in the NLCS but were eliminated when they lost an epic 16-inning battle in Game Six. (Courtesy of Houston Astros Baseball Club).

Astrodome as the rains came down, but the umpires could not navigate the flooded roadways surrounding the building. An Astrodome spokesman called it a "rain in," and Astros general manager Tal Smith cited safety for the postponement, indicating that the game could have been played since conditions inside were dry, "but if we had announced it was on, we could have been inviting misfortune," since some spectators might have become stranded in the deluge. To accommodate the players, tables were moved to the infield, and the two teams enjoyed a sitdown dinner. Twenty or so fans, described as "real diehards," were treated to a free meal in the Astrodome cafeteria, as well. The umpires retreated to a nearby hotel after their car reportedly stalled out in high water. It was the first weather-related postponement at the Astrodome, though an exhibition game had been canceled in 1968 after the assassination of Dr. Martin Luther King.[30]

The Astrodome hosted the first nationally televised college basketball game. The January 20, 1968, contest pitted John Wooden's undefeated and number-one-ranked UCLA Bruins against the second-ranked University of Houston Cougars. The event was promoted as the "Game of the Century." Its attendance of 52,693 stood as a single-game record for college basketball until 2003. Dick Enberg and Bob Pettit hosted the broadcast on the TVS Television Network, a pioneer in national sports syndication. Despite not being on a major broadcast network, the game attracted 12 million viewers and resulted in a $125,000 payout for each team, an amount greater than the Cougars' earnings for the entire previous season.[31]

The event featured UCLA's Lew Alcindor, whose Hall of Fame NBA career unfolded as Kareem Abdul-Jabbar, against Elvin Hayes, whose prowess on the court in 1968 earned him recognition as *The Sporting News* College Basketball Player of the Year.[32] The Cougars beat UCLA, 71–69, snapping the Bruins' remarkable 47-game winning streak. The game received front-page coverage in *Sports Illustrated* and elsewhere.[33] Such media recognition revealed the immense commercial potential of college basketball and was a harbinger of multibillion-dollar network rights fees to broadcast the NCAA basketball tournament. Leisure historian Howard P. Chudacoff asserts that this game "launched college basketball as an entertainment product on television," but beyond that, the game marked a seminal moment in college sports.[34]

With recognition that men's basketball could be played in massive indoor venues rather than in traditional arenas, the 1971 NCAA Final Four and subsequent championship game were played in the Astrodome, culminating with UCLA defeating Villanova, 68-62, for the national crown in what was described as "the largest crowds in the history of the NCAA championships." A total of 63,193 entered the Astrodome turnstiles, with 31,765 attending the championship game.[35] Future tournaments would gradually shift from sizable arenas to bigger indoor stadiums in the decades that followed. The Final Four has not been played in a traditional basketball arena since 1996.

The Astrodome also hosted the 1989 National Basketball Association All-Star game on February 12. Karl Malone earned MVP honors as the West defeated the East by a 143-134 score. The 44,735 in attendance stood as an NBA All-Star Game record until 2010.

On September 20, 1973, the Astrodome hosted the highly publicized "Battle of the Sexes" tennis match between Billie Jean King and Bobby Riggs. *New York Times* sportswriter Neil Amdur called the match "the most talked-about event in the history of tennis."[36] Both competitors were U.S. Open and Wimbledon champions, but Riggs, at age 55, was past his prime. King, then 29, was reluctant to face Riggs, as he had beaten world-class tennis champion Margaret Court in May, but his brash taunts and insults prompted her to take up the challenge. Despite the age differential, Riggs confidently stated that "there is no way she can beat me," and then asserted that he would "put Billie Jean and all other women's libbers back where they belong—in the kitchen and the bedroom."[37]

King trained hard, while Riggs self-promoted his prowess, convincing oddsmakers to make him the favorite. Before a crowd of 30,492, many paying up to $100 for a seat, a circus-like atmosphere unfolded that was nationally televised on ABC. The event attracted 90 million viewers worldwide, with 50 million in the U.S. alone, the largest audience ever to watch live tennis on network television. The broadcast was hosted by a tuxedo-clad Howard Cosell. Network advertising for the spectacle sold out in a single day.[38] The event served as a watershed moment for feminism, with considerable venom aimed at Riggs for his many incendiary taunts. However, Riggs's bravado ensured that this event would be a national spectacle, with massive amounts of money changing hands. Both Riggs and King were guaranteed $75,000 from souvenir and program sales, while the winner of the match would take home an additional $100,000.[39]

On the day of the event, King was transported to the court on a Cleopatra-style gold litter, carried by four muscular men in togas, while Riggs was wheeled in on a rickshaw propelled by six scantily clad models. Courtside spectators sipped champagne as makeshift bars were set up on the Astrodome floor. King trounced Riggs in straight sets, 6-4, 6-3, 6-3. The event received front-page coverage in numerous newspapers.[40] King's success was touted as a victory for the feminist movement at a time when Title IX was in its infancy and not yet vigorously applied to sports. Tennis also benefited commercially, gaining increased popularity as a result of the spectacle.

Not all sports worked, however. Hofheinz brought midget auto racing to the Astrodome in March 1969. The drivers complained about the conditions, and a crash into the wall caused A.J. Foyt to lose a dental filling. Despite the $60,000 purse, the concept never gained momentum.[41] Hofheinz also tried to introduce professional soccer to the Astrodome, taking a controlling interest in the Houston Stars in 1967. The United Soccer Association team was able to draw more than 30,000 in its opening game, but after struggling with attendance it folded after the 1968 season. The Astrodome later served as home to the Houston Hurricane, a North American Soccer

League team that began play in 1978, but folded three years later.[42]

However, boxing did have a degree of success within the Astrodome, with several fights featuring Muhammad Ali. The first major bout in the Astrodome involved Houston native Cleveland Williams versus Ali on November 14, 1966. Ali knocked him out in the third round after introducing the "Ali shuffle" to the crowd of 35,460. A fight between WBC heavyweight champion Larry Holmes and Randall "Tex" Cobb on November 26, 1982, was especially memorable. Cobb took the champion the full 15 rounds, yet was brutally beaten and bloodied. After repeatedly expressing revulsion on air, Howard Cosell refused to work any future boxing broadcasts, a circumstance Cobb wryly called "my gift to boxing."[43]

The Astrodome hosted numerous trade shows and other events, including circus performances and religious revivals. A boat show, for example, was held in the Astrodome's first year of operation. The Ringling Bros. and Barnum & Bailey Circus also performed in the Dome for many seasons, with Hofheinz briefly owning that circus operation during the 1970s.

One of the most heavily publicized special events in the Astrodome's first year was Billy Graham's Crusade for Christ, a multi-day event that attracted more than 300,000 worshippers, including President Lyndon Johnson, with 61,000 packing the venue to hear Graham's final sermon.[44] To generate extra revenue, Hofheinz began offering Astrodome tours for $1, a move that brought more than 400,000 visitors into the Dome during its first year alone.

Concerts were a profound part of the Astrodome's history, too, with numerous top-tier acts coming through. Judy Garland was the first major artist to appear, performing on December 17, 1965, with the Supremes as the opening act. The unprecedented size of the venue was intimidating for some performers. Elvis Presley indicated that he looked forward to a return to Texas for live performances, committing to play at the 1970 Houston Livestock Show and Rodeo, but he bluntly confessed, "That dome has me scared."[45]

The Houston Livestock Show and Rodeo was responsible for bringing many other top musicians to the Astrodome . In addition to Presley, the organization signed deals with Alabama, Tony Bennett, Johnny Cash, Bob Dylan, Michael Jackson, Loretta Lynn, Barry Manilow, Tim McGraw, Willie Nelson, Dolly Parton, Lionel Ritchie, Roy Rogers, Shania Twain, Luther Vandross, Lee Ann Womack, Hank Williams Jr., and ZZ Top. Many of them provided several performances over a multi-year period. Of the more than 400 nationally recognized performers featured on the Houston Livestock Show and Rodeo web site since its inception, the lion's share of top acts appeared at the Astrodome.[46]

Apart from the Livestock Show concerts, numerous other major artists performed at the Dome including The Who, Madonna, Paul McCartney, and the Rolling Stones. An October 28, 1981, Rolling Stones concert was marred by a fatal stabbing. The tragedy prompted a $4.7 million settlement with the victim's family. The bulk of the settlement was to be paid by the tour promoters, Pace Concerts, though the Houston Sports Association and Harry M. Stevens, the venue's concessionaire, also had to make payments after an investigation revealed that security was less than adequate.[47]

The Houston Livestock Show and Rodeo was, and remains, a major force in south Texas. Historian Jason Chrystal asserted that even before the Astrodome was built, the executives from this organization were "some of the wealthiest, most powerful, and politically connected in Houston history."[48] Their political muscle was an important factor in getting the Astrodome constructed, and, once it was built, they were major players in bringing large crowds to its events. Their move to the Astrodome propelled the multi-week Livestock Show and Rodeo to surpass one million in attendance. They continued to bring record-breaking crowds until the event was moved to nearby NRG Stadium in 2003, where, in time, its cumulative attendance exceeded 2 million.

The organization's focus on a broad range of events meshed well with Roy Hofheinz's vision for the Astrodome as an all-purpose entertainment venue. As the Astrodome neared completion, the organization built a less elaborate structure, dubbed Astrohall, next to the Astrodome. The building housed Livestock Show offices, administrative resources, and space for several agricultural events that might not draw huge crowds. Hofheinz later constructed AstroWorld, an elaborate theme park, near the Astrodome. It attracted large and enthusiastic crowds. Nevertheless, Hofheinz struggled to manage his finances amid the economic uncertainties of the 1970s, so he sold AstroWorld to the Six Flags Corporation. The facility continued to operate under the Six Flags brand from 1975 until it was closed in 2005.

The Astrodome was expected to host professional football when it opened in 1965, but Houston Oilers owner Bud Adams instead steered clear of the Astrodome until he reached a lease agreement before the 1968 season. Adams was a founding member of the American Football League, an upstart rival to the more powerful National Football League. Hofheinz and Adams feuded over the Astrodome's lease terms, with Hofheinz setting exceedingly high rental prices while unsuccessfully attempting to lure a competing NFL team to play in the Dome.

Still, football was a major part of the venue's initial years, with the University of Houston, high-school championships, and bowl games shaping the early schedule. The Astrodome's first football game was played on September 11, 1965, with Tulsa defeating Houston, 14-0, in a nationally televised matchup. The *New York Times's* Frank Litsky covered the game, but focused as much on the stadium as he did on the game. He asserted that football "seemed strange indoors," adding, "It seemed artificial, just a bit too antiseptic." He explained that the massive scoreboard was adapted to accommodate football, and indicated that the playing surface was dead grass that was painted green, so "players had trouble getting a grip with their cleats."[49]

The University of Houston played in the Astrodome through 1997, though by 1993 the Cougars had moved some of their games elsewhere, including nearby Robertson Stadium on its campus; eventually it shifted all its home games to that location.

In 1968 Houston trounced Tulsa, 100-6, perhaps providing revenge for the opening loss in 1965, with Larry Gatlin, who would later perform in the Dome as a country music star, scoring a touchdown late in the game. Later, Houston fans were treated to Bill Yeoman's veer offense in the 1970s and 1980s and to David Klingler's record-breaking passing attack from 1988 through 1991.

The Astrodome also hosted the Bluebonnet Bowl, beginning with a rebranding of the event as the Astro-Bluebonnet Bowl in 1968. In the first contest, Southern Methodist beat the Oklahoma Sooners 28-27. In subsequent years traditional football powers including Alabama, Auburn, Michigan, Nebraska, Texas, and USC were among those invited. The game was moved to Rice Stadium in 1985 and 1986. Amid financial struggles, a swan song between Texas and Pittsburgh unfolded in the Astrodome in 1987, with the Longhorns winning 32-27. The annual game was canceled in 1988.

Despite winning league championships during the 1960 and 1961 seasons, the Oilers struggled for respectability during their first decade in the Astrodome. Their first game there was played on August 1, 1968, a 9-3 exhibition-game victory over the Washington Redskins. Three heart-transplant survivors were introduced to the crowd, showcasing cutting-edge medicine as it evolved in Houston.

The Oilers never played in a Super Bowl, but after the AFL and NFL merged, the game did come to Houston in 1974. To the disappointment of Roy Hofheinz, whose financial struggles and health issues limited his negotiating abilities, it was not played in the Astrodome. Instead Super Bowl VII was booked at Rice Stadium, the first time a Super Bowl was not played in a venue that served as home to an NFL team. Nevertheless, the Astrodome was chosen to host the NFL's Super Bowl social event, informally known as the "commissioner's party," on the Friday before the game. The facility's ample space allowed expansion of the invitation list to 2,900, then a record.[50]

The Oilers improved dramatically in 1978 when they drafted Earl Campbell, a heralded running back from the University of Texas. Before entering college or the professional ranks, Campbell played in the Astrodome in 1973, leading his John Tyler High School team to a Texas state championship. In his rookie season, Campbell was the first running back ever to score four touchdowns on *Monday Night Football*, thrilling 50,290 fans with a 199-yard performance.[51]

The Oilers advanced to the AFC Championship game on January 7, 1979, and did so again on January 6, 1980. Both times they lost to the eventual Super Bowl champion Steelers at Three Rivers Stadium in Pittsburgh. The 1980 loss, by a score of 27-13, included a controversial call on a pass by Dan Pastorini to Mike Renfro that would have tied the score at 17-17 if ruled complete and possibly shifted the momentum of the game.

After that defeat, the Oilers returned to Houston, and were led by police escort into a packed Astrodome that was filled with 60,000 appreciative supporters. (Another 15,000 who couldn't get in cheered outside. An emotional coach Bum Phillips thanked Houston's fans and told them, "One year ago we knocked on the door, the following year we beat on the door. Next year we're going to kick it in."[52] That same day, the Super Bowl-bound Los Angeles Rams were greeted by a mere 3,000 fans after their NFC championship victory.[53] Despite the emotional fan support, the Oilers lost in the AFC wild card game the following year, trounced by the Oakland Raiders, 27-7, again on the road.

Those playoff failures cost Phillips his job, and the Oilers did not return to the playoffs until January 3, 1988, when quarterback Warren Moon led the Oilers to a 23-20 overtime victory over the Seattle Seahawks in front of 50,519 Astrodome fans. However, the team lost the following week in Denver. During that season Oilers owner Bud Adams indicated that he was unhappy with the Astrodome, and he threatened to move to Jacksonville if the stadium situation did not improve. His displeasure prompted a $67 million renovation that expanded seating capacity by 10,000 and provided other amenities that Adams demanded. The original scoreboard was dismantled and removed

to make room for some of those seats. The Oilers were a competitive team, with a passionate fan base, so the expectation was that the renovation would keep Adams in the Astrodome for at least 10 years.

The Oilers next hosted a playoff game in a newly expanded Astrodome on December 31, 1989, losing again to their perennial nemesis, the Steelers, 26-23, in overtime. A crowd of 59,406 watched Gary Anderson kick a 50-yard game-winning field goal. Two seasons later, Warren Moon tossed two touchdown passes as Houston defeated the New York Jets, 17-10, in front of 61,485 in the wild card game, again in the Astrodome, but the Oilers were defeated 26-24 by the Broncos in Denver a week later. On January 3, 1993, the Oilers made the playoffs but dropped a 41-38 overtime game to the Buffalo Bills in Orchard Park, New York, after leading 35-3 in the third quarter. On January 16, 1994, the team played its last playoff game in the Astrodome, a 28-20 loss to the Kansas City Chiefs. Adams began to lobby for a new taxpayer-funded open-air stadium. The team would never make the playoffs again while in Houston.

Despite the $67 million renovations, Adams decided to move his team to Tennessee, making the announcement after a disappointing 1995 season. Adams's contract with the Astrodome ran through 1997, but after the team played to sparse crowds in 1996, with fans irritated by the Oilers' lame-duck status, Adams transferred his team to Tennessee a year early. To attract a new football team, the expansion Houston Texans, a larger retractable-roof stadium was built next to the Astrodome and completed in 2002.

Even if the Astrodome did little to satisfy Adams, the venue hosted two major-league All-Star Games, one in 1968, the other in 1986. As the 1968 All-Star Game approached, players were still trying to adjust to the novelty of Astroturf, particularly American League players. St. Louis Cardinals manager Red Schoendienst, who was piloting the NL All-Stars, said, "It takes us a couple of games to get used to it each time," suggesting that neither league would have an advantage.[54] Despite speculation that the fast surface would result in more scoring than the previous year's 2-1 finish, the 1968 game concluded with a 1-0 National League victory. Willie Mays earned Most Valuable Player honors after scoring the game's only run. After smashing a single, Mays advanced to second on a failed pickoff attempt, took third after a wild pitch, then scored on a double-play ball hit by Giants teammate Willie McCovey. The prime-time contest featured a crowd of 48,321, a record gross of $383,733, and an estimated 60 million TV viewers.[55]

The stadium was less of a focus during the 1986 All-Star Game, presumably because the sports world had adapted to indoor facilities and artificial turf. The 3-2 American League victory attracted a turnout of 45,774, the largest baseball audience at the Astrodome in seven seasons. Texas native Roger Clemens pitched to the entire National League batting order without allowing a single baserunner, a feat that earned him Most Valuable Player honors.[56]

The 1986 season was a special one for the Astros, who advanced to the National League Championship Series to face the New York Mets, a team that racked up an impressive 108 wins. The two 1962 expansion franchises treated fans to an outstanding series. After the Mets topped the Astros in a 12-inning contest in New York to take a 3-games-to-2 lead, the series moved to the Astrodome. In Game Six, on October 15, the Astros tagged Mets starter Bob Ojeda for three runs in the first inning, but then did no more damage until the 14th. Bob Knepper kept the Mets' potent offense from scoring for eight innings, but they rallied for three runs in the ninth inning to tie the score. The Mets scored a run in the top of the 14th on a single by Wally Backman, but Houston responded with a solo home run by Billy Hatcher. After a scoreless 15th, the Mets scored three runs in the top of the 16th inning. The Astros rallied for two runs, and with two outs and runners on first and second, Kevin Bass pushed Mets reliever Jesse Orosco to a full count, but then struck out on a low off-speed pitch. With Astros ace Mike Scott in the dugout and ready to pitch Game Seven, Houston's fans were devastated. The Mets went on to win the World Series. Despite attending every Super Bowl ever played, veteran sportswriter Jerry Izenberg called this the "greatest game ever played."[57]

Tall Texas millionaire Drayton McLane purchased the Astros from John McMullen in 1992. During his 19-year ownership, the Astros won four division championships, made two wild-card playoff appearances, and won the NL pennant in 2005. (Courtesy of Houston Astros Baseball Club).

The October 15 game may have been the most exciting Astrodome moment ever, and for Astros fans perhaps the most disappointing, but the Astros provided numerous other memorable moments. The 1980 team advanced to the playoffs with a starting rotation that included Joe Niekro, Nolan Ryan, and J.R. Richard. Richard's career was tragically ended by a stroke in July, but the team nonetheless advanced to the NLCS to face the Philadelphia Phillies with Games Three, Four, and Five inside the Dome. Houston won Game Three, 1-0, in an 11-inning pitching duel that included 10 scoreless innings from Niekro, putting Houston within one game of earning a World Series berth. However, the Astros dropped Games Four and Five. The clincher ended after Philadelphia's Garry Maddox drove in the deciding run with a 10th-inning double, sending most of the 44,802 fans away disappointed.

As plans to move out of the Astrodome were in the works, the Astros earned a spot in the National League Division Series in 1997, 1998, and 1999. Those teams featured Jeff Bagwell and Craig Biggio, both perennial All-Stars and, later, Hall of Fame candidates. Biggio was inducted into Cooperstown in 2015. Despite some outstanding regular seasons, the Astros again did not fare well in the postseason.

They were swept, 3-0, by the Atlanta Braves in 1997, with the final defeat unfolding in the Astrodome. They avoided a sweep in 1998, but fell to the Padres 3 games to 1 after splitting Games One and Two in the Astrodome.

In the team's final year in the Astrodome, the Astros again dropped the NLDS to the Braves. After winning Game One in Atlanta, the Astros lost the next three, despite outstanding play by third baseman Ken Caminiti. The final game, a 7-5 Astros loss, was the last major-league baseball game played inside the facility. Some fans spoke of a history of losing close games, while another fan simply said, "I hope Enron Field brings us better luck."[58] (After Enron became enmeshed in a financial scandal and declared bankruptcy, the new ballpark's naming rights were sold to Minute Maid, a beverage company.)

With both the Oilers and Astros gone, the Astrodome was still booked for entertainment. The Houston Livestock Show and Rodeo brought with it world-class exhibitions in 2001 and 2002. On April 1, 2001, the Astrodome featured WrestleMania, drawing 67,925 fans. The event was broadcast coast-to-coast and in 50 countries.[59] The 2002 Livestock Show was the last one for which the Astrodome would serve as its primary venue. On March 3 a concert by George Strait attracted 68,266, an all-time Astrodome record. When NRG Stadium (then known as Reliant Stadium) was completed in 2002, the Astrodome became expendable as a large-scale entertainment venue.

Still, the Astrodome was put into use from time to time. In 2004 a film crew moved in to produce *Friday Night Lights*, the last time a Hollywood production crew would work on a major film project inside the Astrodome. It had previously served as the location for other Hollywood projects, including *Brewster McCloud* and a *Bad News Bears* sequel. In 2005 the Astrodome became a makeshift shelter for victims of Hurricane Katrina after structural damage to the Louisiana Superdome made that facility unusable for that purpose. It was the last time that the Astrodome received widespread recognition as a publicly used facility.

The Houston Livestock Show and Rodeo moved into NRG Stadium in 2003, but still used the Astrodome for ancillary events. One was a tradition called "The Hideout," an after-hours social event that featured live music and refreshments. The Hideout continued in the Astrodome through 2008, closing with a performance on March 22 by local country artist Johnny Bush. Few realized that that would be the last public performance in the venue. Later that year, code violations were uncovered that prevented anyone from obtaining a certificate of occupancy.

From that point onward, the Astrodome was off-limits for public events, though numerous proposals to repurpose the structure emerged. Some proposals included converting it into a casino, a film studio, a hotel, a retail center, or an indoor recreation facility. Although support to repurpose the venue emerged, no ideas gained substantial private sector financing, forcing officials into a challenging conundrum. On November 5, 2013, Houston voters were presented with a proposal to invest $217 million of public funds into revitalizing the Astrodome, but the measure failed by 53 to 47 percent.

The National Trust for Historic Preservation placed the Astrodome on its list of the 11 most endangered historic structures in 2013, and by January 2014 the Astrodome was approved for inclusion on the National Register of Historic Places. Cynthia Neely, a historic preservationist, nominated the Astrodome for such recognition, asserting, "It is reprehensible to allow such a valuable asset to just fall apart." Nevertheless, the classification left the Astrodome's future in an odd state of limbo. The formal designation, authorized by the National Park Service, added political complexities to attempts to bring the structure down, but was no guarantee against its demolition. The designation provided a mechanism to allow federal and state tax credits for private investments aimed at preservation, yet the size and scope of such a renovation was an ongoing deterrent to achieve such funding.[60]

As a more economical option, Ryan Slattery, a University of Houston graduate student, suggested leaving the Astrodome's steel skeleton and roof structure in place, creating a sort of open-air park area that would retain remnants of the old structure.[61] Later, Houston Livestock Show and Rodeo officials, less enamored with preservation, proposed demolishing the structure and replacing it with parkland that would include a miniature version of the Astrodome in its center.[62] As Houston prepared to host the Super Bowl in 2017 at nearby NRG Stadium, the Astrodome's exterior was power-washed, but without a substantial investment, code violations ensured that the historic venue would remain unused.

As of 2016 the Astrodome's future was uncertain, but its legacy as a revolutionary architectural achievement remained secure. The unique structure envisioned by Roy Hofheinz changed the nature of sports spectatorship, introducing fans to previously unmatched levels of opulence and comfort. For better or worse, the Astrodome served to usher in an ideology of consumerism that influenced sports-related construction in cities throughout the world.

NOTES

1   Reid Laymance, "Astros Top 50 Moments." *Houston Chronicle*, September 30, 2012: section 2, p. 4

2   Allan Turner, "Despite National Listing, Dome Still Could be Razed," *Houston Chronicle*, February 1, 2014: A1.

3   Robert C. Trumpbour and Kenneth Womack, *The Eighth Wonder of the World: The Life of Houston's Iconic Astrodome* (Lincoln: University of Nebraska Press, 2016). Lloyd & Morgan was renamed Lloyd, Morgan, & Jones while the Astrodome construction was under way, but the initial documentation listed Lloyd & Morgan as architects of record during the planning stages.

4   Edgar Ray, *The Grand Huckster: Houston's Judge Roy Hofheinz, the Genius of the Astrodome* (Memphis: Memphis State University Press, 1980), 231.

5   James Gast, *The Astrodome: Building an American Spectacle* (Boston: Aspinwall Press, 2014), 15-21.

6   Robert Lipsyte, "Astrodome Opulent, Even for Texas," *New York Times*, April 8, 1965: 50.

7   Ray, 257.

8   Roger Kahn, *A Season in the Sun* (New York: Diversion Books, 2012), 53.

9   Bill McCurdy, "Houston's Role in the Initiation of Sunday Night Baseball," *The National Pastime*, July 2014: 5-9.

10 "The Man and the Idea," in *The Astrodome: Eighth Wonder of the World* (Houston: Houston Sports Association, 1966), 5.

11 Trumpbour and Womack.

12 John P. Lopez, "Here Domes the Judge," *Houston Chronicle*, March 26, 1995: B26.

13 Robert Lipsyte, "Johnson Attends Opening of Houston's Astrodome," *New York Times*, April 10, 1965: 1; Joseph Durso, "Astros Down Yanks, 2-1, in First Game Played Under Roof, *New York Times*, April 10, 1965: 23; "60,000 in Atlanta Welcome Braves," *New York Times*, April 10, 1965: 23.

14 Dick Peebles, "LBJ: 'Everybody Will Visit Dome,'" *Houston Chronicle*, April 10, 1965: 1. "Chronicle Cameras at the Dome: Celebrities Help Open Sparkling New Stadium," *Houston Chronicle*, April 11, 1965, special section.

15 "Phils Top Astros, 2-0, on Short's 4-Hitter Before 48,546," *New York Times*, April 13, 1965: 43.

16 Joe Jares, "The Big Screen Is Watching," *Sports Illustrated*, May 31, 1965: 30.

17 "Baseball Season Opens Today with 270,000 Expected to Attend Nine Games: Astros and Phils in Indoor Contest," *New York Times*, April 12, 1965: 46.

18 "Phils Top Astros," *New York Times*, April 13, 1965: 43.

19 Barney Kremenko, "Aircaster Perches in Gondola for Bird's-Eye View of Mets," *The Sporting News*, May 15, 1965: 20.

20 "World's Most Pampered Grass," in *Inside the Astrodome: Eighth Wonder of the World*, (Houston: Houston Sports Association, 1965), 76-77.

21 Trumpbour and Womack.

22 Barbara Moran, "Artificial Turf and How It Grew," *American Heritage of Invention and Technology*, 20.4, Spring 2005: 8-16.

23

Jason Bruce Chrystal. "The Taj Mahal of Sport: The Creation of the Houston Astrodome." Ph.D. diss., Iowa State University, 2004, 319-20.

24 "Astros Triumph Over Phillies, 8-2," *New York Times*, July 20, 1966: 64.

25 Trumpbour and Womack.

26 "Wilson, Astros Rookie, Pitches a No-Hitter in 2-0 Triumph Over Braves," *New York Times*, June 19, 1967: 48.

27 "No-Hitter for Dierker," *New York Times*, July 10, 1976: 1.

28 Ken Rappoport, "As Phils Blast Astros, Astrodome Roof Speaker Is Hit for the First Time," *Corpus Christi Times*, June 11, 1974: 13A.

29 "Rains Up to 12 Inches Soak Houston; 4 Dead," *Corpus Christi Times*, June 16, 1976: 14A.

30 B.F. Kellum, "Bucs Now History-Makers in Houston," *Franklin (Pennsylvania) News Herald*, June 16, 1976: 16. Frank Brown,

"Rainout Unique for Rooters," *Franklin News Herald*, June 16, 1976: 16.

31 Howard P. Chudacoff, *Changing the Playbook: How Power, Profit, and Politics Transformed College Sports* (Urbana: University of Illinois Press, 2016), 45-46.

32 Oscar Kahan, "Alcindor, Hayes Top All-America," *The Sporting News*, March 9, 1968: 35.

33 "Big EEE over Big Lew: Houston Upsets UCLA," *Sports Illustrated*, January 29, 1968: 1.

34 Chudacoff, 46.

35 Jerry Wizig, "UCLA Stalls Way to 5th Cage Crown," *The Sporting News*, April 10, 1971: 60.

36 Neil Amdur, "Discussed and Dissected, Billie Jean, Bobby Ready," *New York Times*, September 20, 1973: 57.

37 Richard O. Davies, *Sports in American Life: A History* (New York: John Wiley and Sons, 2012), 320.

38 "Billie Jean vs. Bobby Match Is Expected to Be the Richest," *Wall Street Journal*, August 3, 1973: 7.

39 Barry Tarshis, "A Lot Preceded the Ms.-Match," *New York Times*, September 23, 1973: 215.

40 Neil Amdur, "Mrs. King Defeats Riggs, 6-4, 6-3, 6-3, Amid a Circus Atmosphere," *New York Times*, September 21, 1973: 1.

41 Bob Ottum, "Poor Li'l Midgets, Texas Style," *Sports Illustrated*, March 17, 1969: 24.

42 "A Soccer History of Houston," U.S. National Soccer Players website. ussoccerplayers.com/a-soccer-history-of-houst.

43 Mickey Herskowitz, "Super Bowl XXXVIII—Greetings From Flat City," *Houston Chronicle*, January 25, 2004: Outlook, 1.

44 "Finale by Graham Attended by 61,000," *Galveston Daily News*, November 29, 1965: 3B.

45 "Elvis Performs Live," *Austin Daily Texan*, March 1, 1970: 11.

46 "Past RodeoHouston Performers," Houston Livestock Show and Rodeo website. rodeohouston.com/Concerts/ PastRODEOHOUSTONPerformers.aspx.

47 "Settlement Reached in Concert Slaying," *Galveston Daily News*, August 24, 1986: 4A.

48 Chrystal, 37.

49 Frank Litsky, "Tulsa Downs Houston in Astrodome, 14-0," *New York Times*, September 12, 1965: S1.

50 Michael MacCambridge, *America's Game: The Epic Story of How Pro Football Captured a Nation* (New York: Random House, 2009), 314.

51 "Campbell Leads Oilers to Win," *Galveston Daily News*, November 21, 1978: 1B.

52 "Oiler Rally Draws 75,000," *Cedar Rapids* (Iowa) *Gazette*, January 7, 1980: 3B.

53 "3,000 Fans Greet Rams," *Cedar Rapids Gazette*, January 7, 1980: 3B.

54 "Visitors Study Grass and Roof," *New York Times*, July 9, 1968: 43.

55 Leonard Koppett, "National League Wins All-Star Game 1-0 on Mays's Unearned Run in First," *New York Times*, July 10, 1968: 28.

56 Michael Martinez, "All-Star Game a Special Occasion," *New York Times*, July 17, 1986: B10.

57 Jerry Izenberg, *The Greatest Game Ever Played* (New York: Henry Holt and Company, 1988).

58 Todd Ackerman, "Astros Last Game in Dome Not So Fantastic," *Houston Chronicle*, October 10, 1999: A37.

59 Dale Lezon and Danny Perez, "Wild About Wrestlemania/ Event Draws Rigs Around All Other Entertainment, Fans Insist," *Houston Chronicle*, April 2, 2001: A15.

60 Turner, A1.

61 Kiah Collier, "Pivotal Dates Loom on Fate of Astrodome," *Houston Chronicle*, June 8, 2013: A1.

62 Kiah Collier, "Plan: Raze Dome, Build Park: County to Study $66 Million Idea Suggested by Rodeo, Texans," *Houston Chronicle*, July 11, 2014: A1.

Engineering the Eighth Wonder of the World

By Kenneth Womack

IN ORDER TO BRING THE ASTRODOME to fruition, given the project's incredible size and scope, Roy Hofheinz consulted with many of the leading architectural and engineering minds of his era. He was particularly concerned with making his original vision of a modern-day Roman Colosseum a reality.

The processes associated with the design and eventual construction of the Dome's revolutionary roof structure began in early 1962, with principal architect Robert Minchew's rendering of the stadium having been completed. At this juncture, the responsibility for engineering the Astrodome's roof and supporting structural edifices became the province of Walter P. Moore and Associates. Over the years, Moore and Kenneth E. Zimmerman would serve as the engineering minds behind a host of Houston area landmarks, including the Jesse H. Jones Hall for the Performing Arts, Rice Stadium, the Warwick Hotel, the Bates-Freeman Building at the University of Texas M.D. Anderson Cancer Center, and St. Vincent de Paul Catholic Church, among others.[1]

But the Astrodome would always be Walter P. Moore and Associates' crowning achievement. After prevailing bond issues were resolved via the election of January 31, 1961, Moore and Zimmerman were formally allowed to begin the vital work of designing and testing their plans for implementing a roof structure that was capable of withstanding seismic shifts and gale-force winds, as well as the forces of time. On February 2 excavation of the site began promptly when a "huge dragline ripped dirt from a 300-acre site off S. Main."[2] Within a matter of weeks, some 260,000 cubic yards of dirt had been removed from the site in order to accommodate a mile-long drainage ditch and the building's sublevel playing field. Construction would be delayed until 1963, due

to a series of post-bond legal, financial, and political challenges. The new timetable meant that the Dome would be ready in time for the 1965 major-league season.[3]

In the interim, teams of engineers and architects had already begun honing and testing the final design specifications for the structure. Given their background in long-span structures, Moore and Zimmerman had been carrying out the technical analysis for the project since 1960. At one point they considered Buckminster Fuller's famous Geodesic Dome designs, while also exploring the notion of wood trusses to support the roof structure. Ultimately, steel was selected, given its much higher tensile strength, in order to carry the massive load. A lamella roof structure, proposed by Roof Structures, Inc., headquartered in Webster Groves, Missouri, was chosen because of its spider-web network of trusses. The lamella structure involves a double layer of steel members to ensure the building's engineering integrity.[4]

With Roof Structures, Inc., led by G.R. Kiewitt and Louis Bass, in tow, the project shifted to the testing phase in order to ascertain what kind of loads could be hung from and supported by the Dome's eventual roof design. The construction specifications stipulated that the roof be able to handle a live load of 15 pounds per square foot; a sonic boom loading of 2 pounds per square foot; and a wind load of 40 pounds per square foot or sustained wind velocities of 135 MPH with gusts of 165 MPH.[5] Given the emergence of supersonic jet technology, the issue of being able to withstand a sonic boom was believed to be a key issue in building construction during the late 1950s and 1960s. When supersonic jets like Chuck Yeager's Bell X-1 and the former British Airways/Air France Concorde broke the sound barrier, a boom and result-

Construction on the world's first domed, multi-purpose stadium began in 1962. (Courtesy of Houston Astros Baseball Club).

ing shockwave was created. During the early 1960s, a 2-pounds-per-square-foot load was considered to be acceptable at the time, although Roof Structures prepared the building for an additional 2 pounds per square foot—or the possibility of two consecutive sonic booms—as an allowance.[6]

Perhaps even more significantly, the Dome's roof had to be able to withstand hurricane-force winds, given the building's proximity to the Gulf of Mexico and its annual assaults during the Atlantic hurricane season. For this reason, Roof Structures showed particular concern for the phenomenon of uplift in terms of high wind-resistant construction necessitated by projects such as the Astrodome. In such cases, uplift forces must be transferred down toward the foundation in order to prevent catastrophic damage associated with the powerful suction associated with hurricanes. In order to properly calibrate the design, Roof Structures conducted wind-tunnel tests in an effort to establish the kinds of pressures that would imposed on the building in the event of a full-scale hurricane. With Moore in attendance, wind-tunnel tests were undertaken on a one-eighth scale model of the Dome. Given that such a large project had never been attempted before, a number of industry professionals were on hand, including Ralph Anderson from the architectural firm of Wilson, Morris, Crain, and Anderson, along with Tom Kavanagh, a peer reviewer from New York City's Praeger, Kavanagh, and Waterbury assigned to the project.[7]

The wind-tunnel tests were carried out using the aeronautical wind tunnels housed at the McDonnell-Douglas Aircraft Corporation facilities in St. Louis. Given that the Dome would have skylights permeating the surface of its roof, the model artificially represented these undulations via sand particles applied to the model's roof with adhesives to simulate the roughness of the skylights during the wind-tunnel tests. In addition to outfitting the model with pressure points created by a series of pressure orifices, the team placed cotton tufts along the surface of the roof in order to visualize the wind's varying effects upon the building.[8]

After the technical data was captured from the wind-tunnel tests, Herbert Beckman, a Rice University professor of nautical engineering, compiled and evaluated the results. In his September 29, 1961, report, Dr. Beckman observed that "during the tests, the model is subjected to a steady air stream while hurricane winds consist of small grain turbulence with a gust diameter of usually not more than 100 or 200 feet. These gusts will result in only partial loading of the building, and as a consequence, are less effective than a steady wind would be. The wind-tunnel data can be considered to give 'conservative' loads comparative with corresponding flow conditions in hurricanes." As it turned out, the data proved to be remarkably close to the hand calculations made by Bass in advance of the wind-tunnel tests in Missouri.[9]

Having completed this phase of the project, Roof Structures assimilated the dome roof pressure contours obtained from the wind-tunnel tests into the firm's design proposal for the lamella roof structure. Roof Structures accommodated the test results by incorporating different pressure bands across the graduated expanse of their roof design. Divided into five such bands, the pressure bands included segments designed to accommodate 20, 25, 30, 35, and 45 pounds per square foot, with the apex being able to withstand the highest level of pressure. Simply put, these graduated pressure bands served to contravene the suction pressure of hurricane-force winds attempting to lift the Dome away from its foundation.[10]

With Roof Structures having carried out the firm's all-important work of testing the roof's integrity, Zimmerman's team at Walter P. Moore and Associates was left to ensure that the innovative roof structure was properly anchored to the rest of the building. This moment in the life of the Astrodome marked the design phase's most significant instance in building the stadium to last. Perhaps most importantly, engineering integrity of the highest order was required in order to address a multitude of safety concerns. Roof Structures, whose success with the Dome led to the firm's later work on the New Orleans Superdome, provided four drawings in support of a tension-ring design for the Astrodome. Working from Bass's drawings, Zimmerman created diamond-shaped lamellas separated by ring structures, which doubled as the roof's trusses. As a tension-ring formation, the Dome extended across the building's supporting structure. Given the incredible forces and thoroughgoing tensions playing upon the design, the manner in which the Dome connected to the building proper was critical to its engineering.[11]

In order to accommodate the results of the wind-tunnel tests and the structural demands of Roof Structures' tension-ring design, Zimmerman devised a pair of innovations—masterworks of engineering elegance that set the Astrodome apart from any long-span structure ever conceived. Christened by Zimmerman as the "knuckle" column and the "star" column, respectively, his deft approaches to addressing the wind-tunnel results and Roof Structures' resulting proposal were nothing short of revolutionary. The knuckle column, Narendra K. Gosain observes, "was Mr. Zimmerman's brainchild." It was a "remarkable piece of engineering" based upon the human knuckle as a means for solving a complex problem: Simply put, how do you allow for movement toward the centroid or center of the Dome to account for temperature shifts, while deflecting movement of the structure caused by horizontal wind shear?[12]

To remedy this issue, Zimmerman devised a column that flexes, much like a person's knuckle, toward the center, while remaining outwardly fixed. The knuckle columns exist along the stadium's roofline, connecting the Dome itself to the exterior superstructure. Arranged circumferentially around the interior perimeter of the Dome every 5 degrees, the apparatus consists of four-foot-diameter steel pins at the end of each column. The lower bearing of each pin was welded to a plate support, leaving the top side of the pin to rotate freely in a close-fitted plate with a milled surface. If the top side had been welded, it would have been too rigid and in high wind conditions would have broken away from the structure, given the high tensions existing at that altitude of the building. In order to prevent uplift, anchorage was created at the top of each column via massive U-bolts. As long as the building exists, the knuckle columns will continue doing their work, acting in concert with temperature changes while remaining rigid in the face of enormous wind shear—flexing inward, yet not flexing outward, like the human knuckle.[13] According to Gosain, when the Dome first opened, the knuckle columns at the top of the stadium were exposed, affording fans in the upper reaches of the stadium with a rare glimpse of engineering in action. Unfortunately, many visitors found the visible movement of the knuckle columns to be unsettling; hence, the joints were later concealed behind metal plates in order to prevent fan consternation at the sight of the Astrodome flexing in response to the elements.[14]

In addition to the knuckle column, Zimmerman utilized the innovation that he described as the star column, along with the concrete retaining wall at the Astrodome's base, in order to execute Roof Structures' tension-ring design. For Zimmerman, the star column and the retaining wall at the Dome's lower perimeter afforded the massive building with two levels of tiebacks working in tandem with the knuckle column at the roofline. In engineering parlance, tiebacks act as anchors and stabilizing mechanisms in order to balance the heavy weight load of the roof—especially in a long-span structure such as the Astrodome—against the external forces working upon the building from horizontal and vertical vantage points. Zimmerman's design called for two levels of tiebacks, including the star columns positioned at mid-height around the building's exterior, as well as the tiebacks located every 5 degrees at the base of the retaining wall. The lower-level tiebacks were reinforced by a series of dead-man anchors, located 80 feet away from the retaining wall, in order to further support the efforts of the tension ring and preserve the building's structural integrity. The building's design criteria called for structural elements that protected the stadium against lateral wind loads and "people-generated sway loads." In addition to concerns about numerous natural exterior forces, the structure had to withstand abrupt and rhythmic movements of personnel and visitors inside the building.[15]

Construction of the Dome was completed in November 1964, six months ahead of schedule. The dome's diameter was 710 feet. (Courtesy of Houston Astros Baseball Club).

For the most part, Zimmerman's deployment of X-braced steel bents from the top of the stadium's structure down to the foundation afforded the Astrodome with the requisite resistance to lateral wind loads working upon the building. Given the existence of expansion joints located around the stadium, each sector of the structure required its own system of lateral load-resistant frames. These midlevel tiebacks can be viewed on the building's exterior as a series of distinctive star columns, located circumferentially around the Astrodome's perimeter and positioned every 5 degrees. Zimmerman dubbed the features star columns, which resemble giant lower-case letter t's. He coined the name to honor of the Lone Star State, Texas's distinctive nickname in reference to its former existence as an independent republic. The tieback system was completed at the Dome's lowest level by the tiebacks arranged around the base of the foundation as part of the retaining wall. The concrete that formed the retaining wall required a maximum strength of 3,000 pounds per square inch, with the perimeter retaining wall consisting of a counterfort system, which ties the building's slab and base together. In this instance, the counterfort system serves as a buttress in order to provide rigidity and reduce the shear forces imposed on the retaining wall by the soil. The external tiebacks beyond the retaining wall consisted of steel strands placed every 2.5 degrees around the stadium. In order to protect the strands against the corrosive effects of the soil, Zimmerman's design specified a cathodic protection system as a prophylactic measure. With such a system, the steel strands are protected by encasing them in a sacrificial metal, which serves as the anode of an electromechanical cell, while the steel strand that comprises each tieback acts as the cathode.[16] Decades later, when unearthed for the purposes of renovation, the structural metal revealed no signs of corrosion during the intervening years, proving the original design to be highly effective.[17]

With the integrated design of redundant systems involving the knuckle columns, the star columns, the tiebacks, and the retaining wall in place, Zimmerman was able to satisfy, with great engineering elegance and innovation, the demands of Roof Structures' tension-ring specifications.

As nearly 10,000 tons of steel began to arrive at the construction site, the contractor, American Bridge, started the process of overseeing the preparations for building the concrete retaining wall. In order to construct the Dome's storied roof structure and connect it to the steel frameworks, crews from American Bridge fabricated 37 falsework erection towers. Each tower was placed circumferentially at the base of the building in order to provide support for the trusses that grew to span 642 feet in diameter. The towers consisted of an inner ring of 12 200-foot towers, an outer ring of 24 smaller 160-foot towers, and a 303-foot center tower. Thirty-six towers were arranged as opposing pairs in 12 pie sectors each of 30 degrees, with the 37th tower placed in the middle of the building in support of the Astrodome's geometric center.[18]

The erection of the steel trusses presented particular challenges, as the tension ring had to remain vertical at 60 degrees Fahrenheit and with the dead loads applied in order to maintain the ring's structural integrity. In order to accomplish this end, jacks were placed at the top of each tower to make incremental adjustments as the erection of the steel progressed.

Throughout the year, the project had become the focal point of local, national, and even international interest. While the media offered unremitting coverage of the building's progress, Houstonians observed the ever-rising structure from vantage points across the city's southern reaches. As the crews from American Bridge welded the trusses into place, the tension ring at the heart of the Dome's structural design began to take form. Weighing 750 tons, the tension ring consisted of 72 steel sections of articulated joints in order to allow for the expansion and contraction of the roof.[19]

During the process of constructing the tension ring, Kiewitt strongly recommended that radiographs, similar to medical x-rays, be made of the welds in the tension ring in order to ensure that they were not cracking under the extreme weight of the building materials. Indeed, as the American Bridge

crews worked to put all of the trusses and frameworks into place, a certain element of risk existed—and notwithstanding the extra protection and stability afforded by the erection towers—that a gale-force wind could topple the steel skeleton and injure the construction workers nearly 200 feet below. Kiewitt had clear reason to be concerned. During the summer of 1963, a high-force wind of 90 MPH had assaulted Victoria, Texas, some 125 miles to the southwest of the construction site. Anything along those lines would have spelled almost certain doom for Hofheinz's lofty municipal dreams.[20]

Kiewitt's insistence on regular radiograph tests may have made the difference in ensuring confidence in the incipient building's structural integrity. As it happened, Hurricane Cindy pelted the Texas coastline with a steady assault of wind and rain in late September, and the frameworks, with all of its welds fully in place, withstood the onslaught with nary any damage.[21] On December 2 the tension ring had finally been completed, along with the building's support columns. As American Bridge crews anxiously watched, the jack on the central 37th tower was lowered and the tension ring rested atop its steel pillars. To commemorate the occasion, workers placed a pair of Colt .45 pennants atop the roof. Almost immediately, the stress of so much weight on top of the frameworks began to exert its awesome might, with 220,000 pounds of pressure being transferred onto the stadium's support columns. Consequently, the columns bent slightly—and by as much as an inch in some places. To deflect the pressure, the American Bridge crews hastily erected temporary steel supports in order to deflect the load and protect the steel skeleton from suffering any damage. While the incident proved to be a momentary concern, it turned out to be a harbinger of other issues to come. As a result, engineering teams from Roof Structures and Walter P. Moore assembled in January 1964 and decided to cross-brace the columns to further enhance the structure's support. As an additional measure, gamma ray equipment was deployed in order evaluate the quality of the welds before moving further with the project. As a result, 10 welds were found to be defective and subsequently corrected before construction continued.[22]

By early 1964, all of the Dome's spans had been completed and the trusses and frameworks were fully in place. At this key juncture in the building's construction—with the connections having been welded together and the alignment confirmed—the crews began the laborious and painstaking process of lowering the jacks and eventually removing the erection towers altogether.[23] On January 16 Zimmerman announced that the columns were properly braced and could now support the roof structure without benefit of the erection towers. American Bridge predicted that it would take just under three weeks to lower the jacks and remove the towers.[24] Concerns mounted as the trusses were released from the safety net afforded by the towers, and the integrity of Zimmerman's engineering and design was ready to prove itself—or, failing that, to collapse on an international stage—branding Houston once more as a hick town in the watchful eyes of a waiting world.

Zimmerman had been known to joke with friends and family that if the structure were indeed going to founder, he wanted to be standing in the middle of the construction site, hundreds of feet below the centroid, to be spared the ultimate humiliation of seeing his work collapse in upon itself.[25] But his gambit was hardly necessary. If Zimmerman truly held any doubts, they were resolved fairly quickly as the Dome's skeleton held fast. On February 4 the roof was liberated from the erection towers, and the 7.5-million-pound lamella dome came to rest entirely on the stadium walls. After all of the towers had been removed, the stadium had sunk 4 inches, as predicted by the engineers, under the combined weight of the roof and the frameworks.[26] For the first time, Hofheinz's original vision of a modern-day Roman Colosseum was beginning to take form. The steel superstructure was finally complete, and the outline of the Astrodome's interior frameworks remained visible for miles in every direction.

But as events would show, Houston's collective sigh of relief over the building's structural soundness was short-lived. With the steel frameworks in place, Zimmerman and his engineers tested the structure's plumbness to see if it held true without benefit of the erection towers. And to their great consternation, and eventual panic, the mathematics didn't add up. Simply put, the frameworks wasn't plumb. In civil-engineering parlance, plumbness refers to a structure's state of being vertical or "true." Today, engineers test a building's plumbness using laser equipment. In the Astrodome's heyday, plumbness would have been tested by deploying a lead weight on the end of a line in order to determine verticality.

During the process of slowly retracting the jacks atop each of the 37 erection towers, Zimmerman's engineering team periodically checked the tension-ring alignment and tested the plumbness of the columns. To their growing dismay, the plumbness results shifted on a daily basis. Not surprisingly, concerns began to mount among the engineers from Walter P. Moore and Roof Structures. Eventually, those concerns spread to the County Commissioners, who became increasingly nervous at the mere thought that such a high-profile project might prove to be structurally unsound after years of careful preparation and no-holds-barred politicking. Under this level of scrutiny, Zimmerman's team reconsidered the monitoring data from the plumbness tests, while also examining the design of the supporting columns to ensure that nothing was amiss. Finding nothing of concern—save for the inconsistent plumbness data—Zimmerman gave the order to lower the jacks completely and release the frame to face the elements.[27]

Specifically, the team worked to ascertain the degree to which the columns' deviation from plumbness remained constant from day to day. Specifically, the team worked to ascertain the degree to which the columns were out of plumb remained constant from day to day. Not only did the results not remain constant, but they varied daily. As the days continued to pass, tensions on the construction site mounted and the County Commissioners began to doubt the efficacy of the design. And then it finally happened: Zimmerman's "Eureka!" moment when he discovered that the plumbness differential was due

One of a kind. The Astrodome, dubbed the "Eighth Wonder of the World," stood 18 stories tall and covered 9½ acres. (Courtesy of Houston Astros Baseball Club).

entirely to temperature effects. He realized that the columns needed to be checked at the same time on successive days in order to ensure that there were no variations in temperature. In short, the plumbness calculations would shift from morning to evening, as the frameworks moved from sunshine into shadow. Recognizing that his design allowed for temperature effects, Zimmerman exclaimed that "the old girl was behaving just as was predicted!"[28]

Zimmerman's innovative design demonstrated the vital ways in which long-span structures like the Astrodome move almost continuously. The same effects can be understood in terms of high-rise buildings like the former World Trade Center in New York City, which was engineered with a certain degree of natural sway in concert with the elements—namely, wind—in order to protect both the engineering integrity and the Twin Towers' occupants. As Gosain points out, "There is no structure that is rigid. They all move—all structures move. The wonderful thing that engineers have accomplished—and especially with such buildings as the World Trade Center or the Etihad Tower 5 in Abu Dhabi—is that they minimize structural movement so that it's not perceptible."[29]

Later calculations after the Astrodome's completion confirmed Zimmerman's hypothesis, as well as the soundness of his design. The engineers' monitoring data demonstrated a temperature differential of 20 degrees Fahrenheit between the interior and the exterior of the building, but also the exterior from east to west, north to south. Yet another calculation proved that the Dome enjoyed a dead-load deflection of 1.88 inches. The fact that the Astrodome would be air-conditioned held the possibility of an interior/exterior temperature differential of more than 70 degrees Fahrenheit. Meanwhile, for the design's wind load, the horizontal movement allowed for an incredible 5½ inches of sway. This posed a particular challenge for both the architects and engineers tasked with designing the expansion joint at the edge of the Dome's roofline. The design specifications needed to be prepared for a total movement of 11 inches in order to account for 5½ inches in either direction. To remedy this issue, the design team devised a maintenance-free solution, which consisted of a screen appended to the tension ring and extending beyond a concrete curb on the edge of the stadium roof. The screen camouflaged the expansion joint, which was afforded with the requisite space to allow for total movement not to exceed 11 inches. Through this elegant solution, the screen and the curb overlap sufficiently to not allow the rain to blow into the building's interior; at the same time, the curb's height was designed to prevent rainwater from spilling downward from the edge of the roof.[30]

With the Dome's plumbness crisis having been resolved, the project moved apace with slightly more than a year to go until Opening Day in the Astrodome in April 1965. By April 1, 1964, the crews began lodging the roof's 4,596 skylights into place, with the concrete seat risers to be installed shortly thereafter.[31] With the building's skeleton having been fully completed, the project shifted toward the activities associated with fitting out any multipurpose stadium—although the Astrodome was hardly any run-of-the-mill sports complex.

As with Zimmerman and the team from Walter P. Moore, the project's construction crews were especially enamored with the process of assembling and installing the Dome's gigantic center-field scoreboard. Four stories high and 474 feet wide, the $2 million electronic scoreboard encompassed more than 50,000 individual light bulbs. Weighing more

than 300 tons, the scoreboard, which would come to be known among sports fans as the "Home Run Spectacular," required some 1,200 miles of wiring to become operational.[32] As Gosain remarks, the scoreboard was designed, with Hofheinz's typical bravado and brash showmanship, "to put the Aurora Borealis to shame!"[33]

The Astrodome's gala opening on April 9, 1965, was punctuated by far more than Mickey Mantle's home run for the visiting New York Yankees. It marked the birth, in many ways, of Space City, Houston's long-sought recognition as a cutting-edge metropolis on a collision course with the twenty-first century. For pioneering engineers like Zimmerman, the Astrodome was, most assuredly, the highlight of his career, although he would be the first to admit that it was an engineering achievement to be shared by many, especially the building's architects and the outstanding teams assembled by Roof Structures, American Bridge, and Walter P. Moore and Associates. Over the years he would be interviewed about the project. Invariably, Zimmerman would conclude his remarks by lapsing into a sentimental fondness. "It was the biggest and finest of its kind around," he would say, thinking wistfully about his signal role in engineering what, for a time at least, some folks called the Eighth Wonder of the World.[34]

NOTES

1   Lynwood Abram, "Kenneth E. Zimmerman, Helped Create Astrodome: Worked on Many Notable Projects during Long Career," *Houston Chronicle*, December 24, 2008: B7.

2   "Dragline Rips into S. Main Stadium Site," *Houston Chronicle* February 2, 1961, section 1, 1, 2.

3   Jason Bruce Chrystal, "The Taj Mahal of Sport: The Creation of the Houston Astrodome." Ph.D. diss., Iowa State University, 2004, 226.

4   Interview with Narendra K. Gosain by Robert C. Trumpbour and Kenneth Womack on July 22, 2013, at Walter P. Moore and Associates, Houston, Texas. Note: Unless otherwise indicated, subsequent interviews with Dr. Gosain took place at the time, date, and location indicated above.

5   Kenneth E. Zimmerman and Narendra K. Gosain. "Astrodome: An Engineering Marvel of the 1960s," Presented in the Texas Section of the Annual Meeting of the American Society of Civil Engineers, Houston, Texas, September 29-October 2, 2004, 4.

6   Interview with Narendra K. Gosain, 2013.

7   Interview with Narendra K. Gosain, 2013.

8   Interview with Narendra K. Gosain, 2013.

9   Interview with Narendra K. Gosain, 2013.

10 Interview with Narendra K. Gosain, 2013.

11 Zimmerman and Gosain, 4-5.

12 Interview with Narendra K. Gosain, 2013.

13 Zimmerman and Gosain, 7.

14 Interview with Narendra K. Gosain on July 22, 2013, in the NRG Astrodome, Houston, Texas.

15 Zimmerman and Gosain, 7.

16 Zimmerman and Gosain, 8-9.

17 Interview with Narendra K. Gosain, 2013.

18 Chrystal, 231-32.

19 Chrystal, 233-35.

20 Chrystal, 233-35.

21 Chrystal, 236.

22 Chrystal, 239-40.

23 Zimmerman and Gosain, 6.

24 Chrystal, 242.

25 Correspondence from Fred Womack to the authors, April 30, 2015.

26 Chrystal, 243.

27 Zimmerman and Gosain, 6.

28 Zimmerman and Gosain, 6.

29 Interview with Narendra K. Gosain, 2013.

30 Zimmerman and Gosain, 6-7.

31 Chrystal, 243-44.

32 Chrystal, 276.

33 Interview with Narendra K. Gosain, 2013.

34 Abram.

The Rise and Fall of Artificial Turf

By Mark Armour

THERE WAS A TIME, NOT LONG AGO, when many people hoped, or feared, that artificial playing surfaces would overtake natural grass in most outdoor sports facilities. The phenomenon started indoors, for good reasons, but by the 1970s every new park had to have fake turf, and even some of the old fields were ripping up God's green grass and putting down the industrial stuff. The trend was part of a widespread belief in the middle of the 20th century that technology and chemistry could be an improvement on our natural world.

After a few short years playing baseball on artificial turf, or watching others play on it, few players or fans would admit to actually liking it, but its adoption continued for a few years more, largely in deference to football. At some point a light went on, and baseball operators decided that whatever drove them to the carpets in the first place was no longer worth it. Whereas nearly 40 percent of major-league games were played on artificial turf over a period of nearly two decades, 93 percent of all 2015 contests took place on natural grass.

Although few people weep over the demise of artificial surfaces, the game played on these fields was spectacular. The baseball of the 1970s and 1980s, whatever one might think of the uniforms, or the hairstyles, or the color of the "grass," offered a wonderful balance of offense and defense, provided a fascinating variety of ballpark experiences (home-run parks, doubles parks, speed parks, pitchers' parks), and gave us a dynamic group of stars, many of whom were defined by the places in which they starred — often as not, stadiums without a blade of natural grass.

It all started in Houston, Texas. The Astrodome served as the home of the Houston Astros for 35 seasons, and also housed the Oilers football team, college football and basketball, and assorted auto conventions, rodeos, and tractor pulls. The facility re-entered the news in September 2005 by serving as

temporary housing for thousands of evacuees from New Orleans, victims of Hurricane Katrina. But the building's principal sports legacy rests with two claims to fame: It was the first domed stadium, and the first professional facility to use an artificial playing surface.

The Houston club was awarded a National League franchise in 1960, and originally hoped to have its dome in place before its first game in 1962. Legal issues delayed the start of the project, which led to the construction of a temporary 32,000-seat stadium on adjacent land. In fact, the two stadiums were constructed simultaneously in sight of each other. The original Houston team was called the Colt .45s, and its temporary edifice was Colt Stadium, famous for its unbearable heat and giant mosquitoes. Few mourned the park's demise after the 1964 season.

The opening of the Harris County Domed Stadium in 1965 was a much anticipated event, as commentators wondered whether it was possible or practical to play baseball indoors. Judge Roy Hofheinz, the team's principal owner and the long-time champion of the dome, changed the team's name to the Astros, and its new facility to the Astrodome, both monikers in celebration of the city's role as the center of the thriving space industry of the 1960s.

Branch Rickey, in the last year of his life, visited the Dome and suggested that he had seen the future. On Opening Day, 24 actual astronauts threw out 24 first balls. A 475-foot-wide scoreboard displayed an elaborate light show after each Astro home run or victory, including two "cowboys" shooting guns whose bullets ricocheted around the scoreboard, leading to a series of loud explosions. The Astrodome showed American "progress" at its finest. The facility, without a single beam obstructing the view from a single seat, was soon called the "Eighth Wonder of the World."

The field was natural grass, carefully tested to hold up under the building's roof, which was made

The First AstroTurf in the World

This is a registered, genuine piece of the original AstroTurf, created for, and installed in the Astrodome, in Houston, Texas, in 1966.

From 1966 to 1978, when it was replaced, the Champions and the Stars of Major League Baseball, Professional Football, College Football, Professional Soccer, the Bluebonnet Bowl, Track and Field, Tennis, Boxing, Basketball, the Circus, the Major Stars of the Motion Picture and Entertainment Worlds, Astronauts, Cosmonauts, and the President of the United States, among others, have performed or appeared on this very AstroTurf.

It was the forerunner of artificial playing surfaces now in use, both indoors and outdoors, in most of the stadia throughout the world.

011634
Registered Number

Given at The Astrodome   May 19, 1978

After lack of sunlight killed the Astrodome grass in 1965, the Monsanto Company installed its synthetic turf, ChemGrass, in time for the 1966 season. The product was renamed AstroTurf and became a revolutionary playing surface. (Courtesy of Houston Astros Baseball Club).

up of over 4,000 Lucite panels to let in nature's sun. Unfortunately, the panels caused so much glare during practices in the spring that players had trouble catching pop flies. The solution was to paint the outside of the dome off-white, which caused the grass to die. The Astros played the last few weeks of the 1965 season on spray-painted dirt.

Hofheinz contacted Monsanto, a company that had installed "Chemgrass" in 1964 at Moses Brown School in Providence, Rhode Island, and got the firm to put its product in the Astrodome. Monsanto installed the turf in the infield in time for the Astros' April 18, 1966, home opener, and the outfield was converted by their July 19 contest. The first man to bat on the fake grass was Dodgers shortstop Maury Wills, who singled up the middle off Robin Roberts. The

players accepted the surface pretty quickly, perhaps partly because the field it was replacing was filled with holes and ruts. Monsanto changed the name of its product to "Astroturf," a name often used for the next two decades to describe all artificial surfaces, though there were other competing technologies and brands.

Throughout the late 1960s, many journalists were predicting—and advocating—the installation of synthetic surfaces on all grass playing fields. *The Sporting News*, the erstwhile "Bible of Baseball" but accelerating rapidly downhill toward football primacy, favored the surfaces at least for football or multipurpose fields. Football was a major impetus for the spread of artificial surfaces, as many of the new stadiums being built in this era were multipurpose.

AstroTurf became part of the overall stadium spectacle when it debuted in 1966. In between innings of games, the field was "vacuumed" by space-suit-clad "Earthmen" whose vacuum cleaners were actually just for show. (Courtesy of Houston Astros Baseball Club).

Baseball didn't really have a lot of pull—for the most part, the reason municipalities agreed to build new stadiums was *because* of football, which was booming in popularity.

The University of Houston played its home football games in the Astrodome in 1966, and many college football facilities, including those at the University of Alabama and University of Arkansas, were converted by the end of the 1960s. In 1967 Astroturf was installed at Memorial Stadium in Seattle, which hosted a pro football team, the Seattle Rangers, in the Continental League. The AFL Oilers moved over from Rice University in 1968. The Philadelphia Eagles became the first NFL convert when fake grass was installed at Franklin Field in 1969. Baseball's All-Star Game in 1968, at the Astrodome, was billed as "Monsanto meets Ron Santo."

The benefits touted by its early proponents were many: ease of maintenance, simpler conversion from baseball to football or vice-versa, better drainage. Football teams, even at the high-school level, would not practice on their main field for fear of tearing it up during the week—with artificial turf, there was no longer a need for practice fields. The biggest reason of all was that the surface reduced injuries. If you didn't believe that, you only had to read the weekly half-page articles written by Monsanto for *The Sporting News* – or the occasional four- or eight-page spread regularly appearing in the same paper. The stories boasted of the rapid, and apparently inevitable, revolution being waged—putting greens, tennis courts, welcome mats, front lawns, rooftop parks, surrounding the family swimming pool. Seemingly everywhere you turned there was a grass-like rug lying beneath your feet.

Many baseball teams, some with new stadiums in progress, seriously considered synthetic surfaces in the late 1960s, as was regularly reported in the press. The first outdoor baseball field with artificial grass was Memorial Stadium in York, Pennsylvania, home of Pittsburgh's Eastern League (Double-A) affiliate. The Pirates were considering the surface for their new facility being constructed in Pittsburgh, while Monsanto was so eager to show off its product that it agreed to install the surface at no cost.

On November 10, 1968, Chicago Bears star Gale Sayers, the best running back in football at the time, suffered a career-altering injury in a game at Chicago's Wrigley Field. In response, Cubs owner Phil Wrigley told Jerome Holtzman that he would soon be installing artificial turf at Wrigley Field, certainly within a few years. In their conversation there was an overriding understanding that it was better for the players, and that the change was inevitable. This is a man, it should be recalled, who would never install lights at his ballpark.

The Chicago White Sox became the second major-league team to forgo grass, installing a synthetic infield in White Sox Park in 1969, hoping it would lead to higher-scoring games. The first major-league outdoor game on a synthetic surface took place on April 16 when the White Sox beat the expansion Kansas City Royals, 5-2.

Vince Lombardi, coaching the Washington Redskins in 1969, wanted turf installed in RFK Stadium, but Bob Short, who owned the Senators, would not agree. In fact, two years later, when the Senators moved to Texas, Short insisted that turf not be installed at Arlington Stadium, which had been the plan. Short was one of the earliest baseball leaders willing to march against the tide. But the tide kept coming.

The next season brought four new turf fields, beginning with the conversion of the grass surfaces in San Francisco's Candlestick Park and St. Louis's Busch Stadium. The first outdoor NL game on turf saw the Astros beat the Giants, 8-5, in San Francisco on April 7. Three days later the Cardinals became the fourth team with Astroturf, and they celebrated with a 7-3 victory over the Mets.

In midsummer, two new ballparks opened with artificial surfaces. Cincinnati's Riverfront Stadium debuted on June 30, featuring (for the first time in the major leagues) dirt cutouts around the bases—a characteristic first showcased at Portland, Oregon's Civic Stadium. The next month the Pirates opened Three Rivers Stadium with Tartan Turf, 3M's rival product to Monsanto's AstroTurf. The season also showcased the new surfaces in the postseason for the first time, as Pittsburgh and Cincinnati, in their brand-new parks, met in the NLCS with the Reds advancing to the World Series. It would be 18 years until baseball had another postseason with all-grass fields.

Sometime in the mid-1970s, baseball turned its pivot foot on this issue, though we all had to wait nearly a generation for all of these parks to be replaced. In 1970, not only were all new parks being introduced with artificial surfaces, but existing parks were replacing their natural grass. Within a few years, the new turfs (and the symmetrical concrete stadiums that housed them) were no longer looked upon as progress, but as a sign that the modern world had gone seriously awry. Dick Allen, future horse breeder, remarked, "If horses can't eat it, I don't want to play on it."[1] Though his wit was typically unique, his sentiments were carrying the day.

After the two converts in 1970, no baseball park would ever again remove its natural grass in favor of an artificial surface. In fact, the White Sox became the first team to reinstall grass, in 1976, and the Giants followed suit in 1979. The last outdoor baseball facility to debut in the major leagues with an artificial surface was Toronto's Exhibition Stadium in 1977. There were three new synthetic fields built in the 1980s, but they were all under domes—in Minneapolis, Toronto (retractable), and St. Petersburg. The latter park was built in order to entice baseball to award the city a franchise, but by the time it got its team in 1998, the 10-year-old hardly-used facility was a dinosaur.

The visible effects of the shift away from fake grass had to wait for an entire generation of stadiums to be replaced, a process that began in the 1990s. The nine new stadiums completed between 1970 and 1990 (beginning with Riverfront and Three Rivers and ending with the dome in St. Petersburg, opened in 1990) all had synthetic surfaces. Starting with the new Comiskey Park (later US Cellular) in 1991, major-league baseball has christened 22 new baseball parks, every single one with real grass. There were still 10 artificial surfaces used in 1994, and nine in 1998, but today there are just two, in Toronto and St. Petersburg. Of these, Toronto probably could switch to grass, since its roof retracts and all other retractable roof fields have grass. Tampa Bay is likely stuck, though the team has been trying to get a new park built for many years.

The following chart shows the trend.

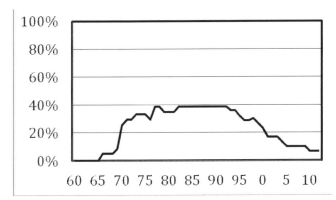

Artificial turf still lives on in pro and college football, though in reduced numbers. The surfaces have improved in many ways—many of them look more like grass than they used to, players run and cut better than in days past, and there are fewer funny turf bounces on the newer surfaces. That said, it is unlikely baseball will be returning to those days. The fans, media and players are united on that score.

Artificial turf in baseball is an anachronism today, and the mere mention of the subject is no longer considered appropriate in polite company. But make no mistake: The introduction of Astroturf in 1966 had a huge impact on the way the game was played for two decades, two of the best decades in baseball's history. Some of the more interesting teams of the era—the Big Red Machine, the "We are Family" Pirates, Herzog's Cardinals, George Brett's Royals, the 1980 Phillies—were defined by the fields they played on. In our mind's eye, when we see Brett and Ozzie Smith and Mike Schmidt, they are running, and diving, and hitting on a lime green carpet.

SOURCES

This is a revised and updated version of an article I wrote for Baseball Analysts website in 2005. In writing the original piece I used the archives of *The Sporting News* (available through Paper of Record, and free to SABR members) and retrosheet.org.

NOTES

1   greenfields.eu/artificial-grass/.

George Kirksey, Craig Cullinan, and Houston's Quest for a Major-League Team

By Robert C. Trumpbour

FOR THE ASTRODOME TO BE BUILT, many intricate pieces had to fall into place. In describing one of the most important factors, Craig Cullinan Jr. confidently asserted, "Baseball was the heart, lungs, brain, life blood of the whole thing. … Without it, there was nothing—no franchise, no stadium, no hotels."[1]

Although Roy Hofheinz is credited with supervising the planning and construction of Houston's Astrodome, without the hard work and diligence of Craig Cullinan and George Kirksey, the whole project might have gone off the rails. In the 1950s Cullinan teamed up with Kirksey, a Houston public-relations executive, to develop a plan that would lure a major-league baseball team to Houston.

Cullinan's position as a wealthy heir to the Texaco oil empire and his Ivy League pedigree helped to open doors that allowed Houston access to numerous baseball insiders, but it was Kirksey's energy, enthusiasm, and single-minded focus on bringing Houston into the major leagues that put the Bayou City into a position to build the Astrodome. In profiling Hofheinz as the Astrodome construction plans unfolded, *Sports Illustrated* writer Roy Terrell described Kirksey as a "visionary public relations man," while identifying Cullinan and Kirksey as the two most deserving of "credit for getting big league baseball interested in Houston." In explaining how Houston finally obtained a team, Kirksey described his approach as one that regarded "big league baseball as a citadel, and that we would have to take it by storm."[2]

Not surprisingly, George Kirksey was the most persistent advocate of Houston's bid to become a "major-league" city. Biographer Campbell Titchener explained that the hard-charging, enigmatic Kirksey "would say that it made him furious every time he opened up a newspaper and found Houston listed among the minor league cities."[3] However, the path he took to convince the lords of baseball to settle on Houston was circuitous, complex, and filled with disappointment. Fittingly, despite Cullinan and Kirksey having put in years of hard work, Houston's path to the major leagues ended with Hofheinz closing the deal while they agreed to look on.

Kirksey was a nationally recognized reporter for the United Press before returning to Houston. As a sports journalist, he covered teams from New York, Chicago, and elsewhere, and did nonsports reporting in Europe as well. He was assigned to the World Series, Rose Bowls, and coverage of an aging Babe Ruth and a youthful Joe DiMaggio, among others, before serving in the Air Force during World War II. After the war he moved away from reporting and headed back to Houston, where he established his own public-relations business. Although his firm had many nonsports clients, his most passionate work was focused on bringing a team to Houston.

Kirksey's first recorded attempt unfolded in 1951. Upon learning that the Philadelphia Athletics might be up for sale, he buttonholed real-estate baron Bob Smith in an impromptu meeting outside the Rice Hotel and tried to persuade him to invest $2.5 million to buy the team. Smith reportedly told Kirksey that he would put up $250,000 and instructed Kirksey to find nine other investors to make the deal work.[4] Predictably, Kirksey was unable to raise the needed funds. However, his instincts in approaching Bob Smith were not off base. Smith eventually became the principal owner of the baseball team that did come to Houston.

In the 1950s Craig Cullinan, heir to the Texaco oil empire, teamed up with George Kirksey, a Houston public-relations executive, to develop a plan that would lure a major-league baseball team to Houston. (Courtesy of Houston Astros Baseball Club).

Although Houston had a minor-league team, the Buffs, that was a respected affiliate of the St. Louis Cardinals in the Texas League, Kirksey would not be satisfied until his home city had achieved major-league stature. His next target was the Cardinals, one of the National League's most storied franchises, with six World Series victories to their credit. In 1952 Fred Saigh, the Cardinals' owner, was battling tax-evasion charges, so Kirksey explored the possibility of bringing the team to Houston. After Saigh pleaded no contest to the charges, he suggested that a sale of the team would require a $4.25 million commitment. However, with limited resources, consummating such a transaction would require creativity. Undaunted, Kirksey met with D'Arcy Advertising to try to broker a five-year, $1.25 million sponsorship deal with Anheuser Busch, the St. Louis-based brewing giant.[5]

Although such a deal might have brought in almost 30 percent of the revenue needed for the purchase, August Busch Jr., chairman of the brewery, and National League President Warren Giles did not support Kirksey's plans. Kirksey attempted to line up investors but Saigh, loyal to his Missouri roots, sold the franchise to Busch for $3.75 million, a $500,000 discount. The deal ensured that the Cardinals would remain in St. Louis, much to the dismay of Kirksey.[6]

Major League Baseball had no teams as far south as Houston, and although the South had demonstrated signs of growth, Giles' complicity in the St. Louis sale demonstrated that the lords of baseball were not ready to move away from the major population centers of the Northeast and Midwest. However, postwar demographic shifts and population increases paved the way for change in the baseball landscape.

The sudden shift of the Boston Braves to Milwaukee in 1953 ignited the fuse for further relocations. The Braves were lured by a new taxpayer-funded ballpark, offering Kirksey hope that Houston might in time acquire a team. He looked on with dismay as the St. Louis Browns moved to Baltimore in 1954 and were promptly renamed the Orioles. After making another push to acquire the Philadelphia Athletics in 1954, Kirksey was similarly disappointed when the A's moved to Kansas City in 1955.[7]

Kirksey visited both Chicago teams and made overtures to the Cincinnati Reds, too, letting all who would listen know that Houston had money and was deeply interested in joining the major leagues. On the surface, it appeared that the geography of baseball was not changing in a transformative way. Still, Kirksey ran a strong campaign that raised Houston's national profile, while the three franchise relocations offered a glimmer of hope that he might eventually succeed. Still, none of the relocation cities were anywhere near the Deep South.[8]

To succeed in such an environment, Kirksey understood that he needed more economic and political muscle than he could muster by himself. Despite previous failures, the push to bring major-league baseball to Houston gained credibility, stature, and momentum in 1956. The turning point was a meeting that included Kirksey, William A. Kirkland, and Cullinan. Houston baseball historian Robert Reed called this informal gathering "the true beginning of Major League Baseball in Houston." Kirkland was chairman of First City National Bank, Houston's largest and most prestigious financial institution. Cullinan was two decades younger than Kirksey, but Kirksey bluntly asserted that he "was looking for people with money," unapologetically indicating that Cullinan fit that profile, in addition to having "more interest and more time than anybody I had talked with before."[9]

Kirkland and Cullinan were strong supporters of baseball and each possessed unique assets. Kirkland had intimate knowledge of Houston's wealthiest power brokers, and he was respected in local baseball circles after serving as a player and manager in the Houston Bank League before rising to prominence in the financial community. Cullinan was a capable public speaker whose New England prep school and Yale University experiences allowed him to work comfortably with those connected to powerful Northeastern institutions.[10]

The Cullinan family's achievements opened doors as well. Cullinan's grandfather, Pennsylvania native Joseph Cullinan, was an acknowledged pioneer in the oil industry. His influence and reputation was so profound that he had ready access to presidents and world leaders. Among his accomplishments were bringing the ship channel, rail transportation, and other significant infrastructure projects to Houston, ensuring that the city would serve as a hub for the nation's oil industry for generations.[11]

After Kirksey, Cullinan, and Kirkland's initial collaboration, Kirkland, using his financial clout, organized a meeting at the First City National Bank's headquarters. Campbell Titchener wrote that the meeting, held on January 4, 1957, brought together 35 businessmen who by their varied achievements "represented the bulk of the city's wealth, power, and influence." After opening remarks by Kirkland, Kirksey took over, declaring that the three key elements required to succeed would be money, public support, and a modern stadium. To address these needs, shortly after the meeting, Houston Sports

Unlimited was founded, with Cullinan as its president.[12] (Its name was later changed to the Houston Sports Association.) Kirksey "used his considerable powers of persuasion" to lead Cullinan into forming the group."[13] The organization's 28 members paid $500 for the right to buy future shares of a major-league baseball franchise for $35,000 each. However, Houston leadership was reluctant to build a stadium until a major-league team was secured, creating an uncomfortable situation for Kirksey and Cullinan.[14]

Cities like Minneapolis, for example, built a new venue without a team commitment, and the proximity of Minnesota to other Midwestern franchises gave them a geographic advantage over Houston. Kirksey and Cullinan continued to meet with baseball executives, using Cullinan's wealth to fund such trips. But without a ballpark or, at a minimum, a tangible commitment to build a ballpark, Houston had less negotiating leverage in trying to lure a franchise to its city. It was a Catch-22 situation: Cullinan said that when he lobbied baseball executives, he was told, "Get a stadium and we will talk to you about a team." But in Houston, Kirksey and Cullinan were told, "Find a team and the city might talk to you about building a stadium."[15]

Kirksey and Cullinan tried to prompt local leaders to move forward on a ballpark without success. Nevertheless, in 1957, as the Giants and Dodgers prepared to move from New York to San Francisco and Los Angeles respectively, the two men sensed a seismic shift in baseball's geography. Despite facing ongoing defeat, Kirksey believed that such change might somehow work in Houston's favor. He tried to persuade Harris County Judge Bob Casey, the county's chief administrator, to allocate county funds for construction of a ballpark, but was told that the county could not act without state authorization and a subsequent referendum. Kirksey got Texas legislator Searcy Bracewell, a former client and friend, to help draft legislation that allowed the county to use public funds for "public parks and entertainment venues," while creating the Harris County Board of Park Commissioners, an organization that could oversee planning, construction, and oversight of such projects.

Senate Bill 23 was approved, giving Houston the ability to solidify ballpark planning in 1958.[16]

Kirkland was appointed chairman of the new board. He staffed it with bankers, oil barons, and Archer Romero, a former president of the influential Houston Fat Stock Show and Rodeo. This organization would serve as co-tenant, using the facility to showcase its popular event during baseball's offseason. Committee members explored what other cities had done, traveling to Milwaukee, Baltimore, and various locations in California.[17]

Kirkland hired architects to draw up plans for a new open-air ballpark, one that creatively included an attached air-conditioned arena that could be used for conventions and special events. A report released on June 20, 1958, recommended placing an $18 million construction referendum on the ballot for a July 26 election that was already in place. The report emphasized that Houston was the largest city in the United States that did not have a major-league team. It asserted that event revenues would cover the cost of the bond issue and touted the dramatic economic benefits the new venue would provide.[18]

The language was drafted for the referendum, and approval to place it on the ballot was granted three days after the report's release.[19] Media coverage suggested that Houston would gain wholesome family entertainment and dramatic economic benefits. In one example, sportswriter Mickey Herskowitz cited a Milwaukee Chamber of Commerce leader's assertion that the city gained at least $7 million in economic activity after building a less opulent ballpark to entice a major-league team.[20] With the positive drumbeat of local media and repeated assurances that the venue would be repaid in full by event revenues, taxpayers supported the referendum by a 3-to-1 ratio.[21]

With a mechanism for ballpark construction in place, Kirksey continued his push to acquire a major-league team. He never gave up on the possibility of expansion, but shortly after the election, he set his sights on the Cleveland Indians after it became known that the team had amassed $3.5 million in debt and was struggling with its finances. After a group from Minneapolis made a respectable bid that included generous attendance guarantees, Kirksey worked with wealthy Houstonians to craft his own plan. Kirksey's group offered to fully pay the debt, while agreeing to pay an additional $2.5 million to the Indians' current owners. Although the $6 million bid exceeded all other offers, Indians chairman William Daley rejected all offers, acknowledging that from a business perspective, the rejection might be unwise, but that it made sense simply "because most of the directors are Clevelanders."[22]

Kirksey was crestfallen, but he continued to look for ways to bring Houston into the major leagues. He found allies in New York City, whose anger at losing the Giants and Dodgers was palpable. After numerous attempts to coax Major League Baseball into expansion failed, William Shea, an influential New York lawyer, invited Houston and Minneapolis into an ambitious plan to launch a third major league, to be called the Continental League. Shea recruited the legendary Branch Rickey to organize the league and serve as its commissioner. Atlanta, Buffalo, Dallas, Denver, New York, and Toronto rounded out the cities that were slated to be in the new league.[23]

Major-league officials worked behind the scenes to sabotage the Continental League before it could emerge, but Rickey was sufficiently knowledgeable about the inner workings of the sport to threaten baseball's economic model. Major League Baseball continued to resist expansion, but Continental League representatives were anything but passive. Behind the scenes, they pushed for legislation that threatened baseball's antitrust exemption. Senate Bill 3483 was pushed to the floor in 1959 by Senate Majority Leader Lyndon Baines Johnson, a close friend of Roy Hofheinz. Surprisingly, it came within three votes of passage in the United States Senate. Although the legislation failed, it was sent back to committee where it might die or perhaps be rewritten in a form that might gain enough support to pass.[24]

Major League Baseball had dodged a bullet, but its officials realized that the Continental League could pose a viable threat to their future. "Every aspect of our relationship with them changed after that vote," Shea said.[25] Rickey had assembled a league that would be slated to play in new ballparks in several cities that were growing more rapidly than the traditional hotbeds for professional sports. Despite attempts to avoid expansion, the lords of baseball were finally pushed to negotiate with leaders from the upstart league.

Hofheinz, the Astrodome's maestro, was now a part of Houston's lobbying effort, and Houston had recalibrated its stadium plans to be the first fully enclosed and air-conditioned baseball stadium. On October 17, 1960, Hofheinz showcased a scale model of the planned venue as he pitched Houston's case to major-league owners during a tension-filled meeting in Chicago. After the presentation, New York and Houston were awarded National League teams to begin play in 1962.[26] Minnesota gained a franchise when Calvin Griffith decided to move his team, the Senators, from Washington to Minneapolis. Washington and Los Angeles were awarded American League expansion teams.

Although building the Astrodome was sufficiently complex that Houston's new team played in a much less opulent temporary stadium during its opening years, the efforts of George Kirksey, Craig Cullinan, and William Kirkland set the wheels in motion for the Astrodome's eventual construction. As Cullinan had suggested, without the introduction of major-league baseball to Houston, the Astrodome would not have been built.

NOTES

1   Robert Reed, *A Six Gun Salute: An Illustrated History of the Houston Colt .45s* (Houston: Gulf Publishing Company, 1999), 203.

2   Roy Terrell, "Fast Man With a .45," *Sports Illustrated*, March 26, 1962: 32-42.

3   Campbell Titchener, *The George Kirksey Story: Bringing Major League Baseball to Houston* (Austin: Eakin Press, 1989), 7.

4   John Wilson, "Kirksey, First Astro Backer, Sells His Stock," *The Sporting News*, May 21, 1966: 13

5   "Texas Group Wanted Busch to Buy Cards' Radio Rights," *The Sporting News*, March 4, 1956: 10.

6   "Prexy Giles Spends 36 Hours In St. Louis Overseeing Cards' Sale," *The Sporting News*, March 4, 1953: 10.

7   Tichener, 75.

8   Reed, 18.

9   Reed, 18-19.

10 Lee Lowenfish, *Branch Rickey: Baseball's Ferocious Gentleman* (Lincoln: University of Nebraska Press, 2007), 552.

11 John O. King, *Joseph Stephen Cullinan: A Study of Leadership in the Texas Petroleum Industry, 1897-1937* (Nashville: Vanderbilt University Press, 1970), 213-214.

12 Titchener, 74-75.

13 Reed, 19.

14 Reed, 19-20.

15 Ray, 258.

16 Reed, 20-21.

17 Dick Peebles, "Commission to Seek Information on Feasibility of Stadium Here," *Houston Chronicle*, February 12, 1998: F1.

18 Report of the Harris County Board of Parks Commissioners to Harris County Commissioners Court, June 20, 1958. Astrodome Collection, 1958-1968 files, folder 18, Houston Public Library.

19 "County Stadium Bond Issue Gets July Ballot Spot," *Houston Post*, July 24, 1958: section 4, 1.

20 Mickey Herskowitz, "Perini Says Weisbrod Rates Houston in 10-Club Possibility, *Houston Chronicle*, July 17, 1958: section 4, 1.

21 Ray, 258.

22 Hal Lebovitz, "Cleveland Is Joyful; Tribe Directors Vote to Stay Indefinitely," *The Sporting News*, October 22, 1958: 18.

23 Bob Buhite, *The Continental League* (Lincoln: University of Nebraska Press, 2014).

24 Reed, 31.

25 Reed, 32.

26 Ray, 262-263.

Bud Adams, Roy Hofheinz, and the Astrodome Feud

By Robert C. Trumpbour

WHEN ROY HOFHEINZ TOOK charge of the Astrodome project, he envisioned a venue that would host a broad range of activities. Before moving forward with the project, Hofheinz, a former state representative, judge, mayor, and entrepreneur, had worked with Buckminster Fuller to plan and design an indoor shopping mall that would feature a unique dome as part of its overall design. However, when a rival developer, Frank Sharp, edged him out in attracting anchor tenants, Hofheinz abandoned mall development entirely and immersed himself in the Astrodome's construction.

As a youngster, Hofheinz worked in radio and organized social events in Houston that included such top-tier performers as famed Louis Armstrong. From extraordinarily humble beginnings, Hofheinz acquired a vast range of creative skills that allowed him to supervise the design of a new and luxurious facility that he envisioned as a sort of entrepreneurial town square. His goal was to build a unique massive indoor venue that would bring prominence to Houston while hosting baseball, football, the Houston Livestock Show and Rodeo, concerts, large-scale exhibitions, and numerous other special events.[1]

That vision was made more complex by Kenneth "Bud" Adams. Adams owned the Houston Oilers, a professional football franchise that was expected to play its games in the Astrodome in 1965, the year it opened. However, Adams's team did not move into the facility until 1968, opting instead to play in less opulent outdoor venues.

During the lease negotiations with Hofheinz, Adams boldly proclaimed, "If the Astrodome is the eighth wonder of the world, surely its rent is the ninth wonder."[2] Needless to say, negotiations between Hofheinz and Adams did not go smoothly. The mercurial Adams tended to pinch pennies when

he could, so the high cost of moving his team into the Astrodome was something he resisted.

The philosophic gulf between Roy Hofheinz and Bud Adams was wide, and that complicated the negotiating process. Both men were influenced by the Depression. Hofheinz was prone to surround himself in luxury, an understandable reaction to years of deprivation. He regarded investment in material goods as an index of success, extending that philosophy to publicly financed civic monuments. When Hofheinz unveiled the Astrodome, he justified his desire to favor opulence by asserting that after visiting the venue, "nobody can ever go back to Kalamazoo, Chicago, New York, you name it, and still think this town is bush league."[3]

Adams was less predictable and more uneven in his spending patterns, though he tended to favor cost containment as a managerial strategy. *Houston Chronicle* sportswriter Ed Fowler asserted that Adams "couldn't settle on a style for running his organization," but when he hired staff, "the figure with the greatest say was usually a bean counter."[4]

Nevertheless, the Oilers owner could spend in luxurious and dramatic ways. Before George Steinbrenner pioneered high-stakes free agency in baseball, Bud Adams was selectively going after high-profile talent in football. In an example, he dispatched Adrian Burke, his American Football League team's attorney, to New Orleans, where he promptly signed Heisman Trophy-winning LSU running back Billy Cannon to a lucrative contract under the goalposts immediately after the 1960 Sugar Bowl game. Cannon's three-year deal, in excess of $100,000, was reported to include three gas stations and a Cadillac.[5] However, the move created instant controversy. The National Football League's Los Angeles Rams had signed Cannon before the game, but that did not deter Adams, who spent more than $73,000 on legal expenses to keep him from playing in the more established league.[6]

The signing was among the highest-profile ones in a battle between the upstart American Football League and the more prestigious National Football League. It put Adams in direct conflict with Rams general manager Pete Rozelle, who would eventually emerge as NFL commissioner, and who later would preside over the merger of the AFL and NFL. Before that merger, Adams continued to battle owners from the rival league, confidently stating, "I am going to sign all of my draft picks and any other player the other league may be after." One reporter asserted that his "persuader" when negotiating a deal was "a stack of $100 bills as thick as a Texas steak," yet Adams did not always come out the victor.[7] He made high-profile but unsuccessful bids to dissuade Donny Anderson, Tommy Nobis, and John Brodie from signing contracts with NFL teams.[8] In attempting to sign Joe Namath, Adams learned that he would not play for Houston, but that he had dreams of playing in New York, Chicago, or Los Angeles. Instead of allowing him to sign with an NFL team, Adams quietly advised the New York Jets, then owned by Sonny Werblin, to pursue the highly-touted quarterback.[9]

Yet if Adams offered top players lavish contracts, he would try to offset such signings with low-ball pay to most of the remaining roster. As one way to counter the cost of high-profile signings, Adams hired John Breen, a highly creative director of player personnel. Breen's early strategy was to park himself at Love Field, a Dallas airport and a major national hub, where he would negotiate deals with recently released and likely desperate NFL players while they were between flights home.[10] Before other teams were even aware that a player might be available, Breen had locked him into playing for the Houston Oilers.

The formula worked initially, as the Oilers won AFL championships in 1960 and 1961. They advanced to the AFL title game again in 1962, losing in double overtime to Lamar Hunt's Dallas Texans before that team moved, and was rebranded the Kansas City Chiefs. But from 1963 onward, championships eluded the Oilers, with coaching instability and penny-pinching as key factors in their on-field struggles.

When it came to renegotiating player contracts, Adams played hardball. He refused to extend a raise to wide receiver Charlie Hennigan in the year the Astrodome opened, despite Hennigan's threats to retire. Hennigan caught 101 passes in 1964, at the time a single-season pro football record, but that high-octane performance failed to get Adams to loosen his checkbook.[11]

Adams and Hofheinz were two headstrong Texans who battled each other, and the Astrodome served as a focal point for some of these skirmishes. When the Houston Sports Association was formed, Adams and Hofheinz both shared the vice-president title, but Hofheinz's insider work with real-estate mogul and oil baron Bob Smith as well as his ability to gain primary control of the Astrodome project put him in a more advantageous position among Houston's power elite.

Still, Adams made a significant splash in the newly christened American Football League. Earning AFL championships during the league's first two seasons suggested that Adams might rise as a unique national figure in sports, though subsequent struggles tempered Adams's potential for broader recognition. Hofheinz and Adams were creative pioneers on different fronts, yet each had egos that were not easily contained.

Adams was founder and CEO of ADA Oil Company. This successful company provided Adams with the deep financial resources to form the Houston Oilers as part of an upstart new football league that would compete directly with the much more powerful NFL. Adams teamed up with Lamar Hunt, a fellow Texan and the son of an exceedingly affluent oil baron, to spearhead the formation of the AFL. The two began laying the groundwork in 1959 for a league that would begin play in 1960 with Hunt in Dallas and Adams in Houston. The fledgling league pushed the more established NFL into a merger within a decade of starting play. Adams was a key figure in the league's inception and its subsequent success. However, unlike the soft-spoken, even-keeled, and reflexively humble Lamar Hunt, Adams could be brash, vocal, and highly unpredictable, particularly in his early years as the owner of the Houston Oilers football team.

While founding the AFL, Hunt was sufficiently deferential to authority that even before getting the league off the ground, he naïvely approached NFL Commissioner Bert Bell to suggest that Bell preside over both leagues. However, Bell's unexpected death in October 1959 prompted succeeding NFL officials to attempt to sabotage the new league before it took root. As plans for the AFL were unfolding, the NFL offered expansion opportunities to Hunt and Adams. Nevertheless, taking the offer would have left owners in Boston, Denver, Los Angeles, Minneapolis, and New York out in the cold, so out of a sense of loyalty Hunt rejected the offer and, to his credit, Adams did as well.

The NFL responded by extending expansion opportunities to Dallas and Minneapolis, poaching Hunt's proposed AFL market, forcing him to unveil his new league with direct competition in Dallas while pushing him to find a new team to offset the loss of Minneapolis. Despite the blow to Hunt, the extraordinarily deep financial resources of Hunt and Adams allowed the league to move forward, with a team in Oakland added to fill the void.[12]

After it became clear that Hunt had lost almost a half-million dollars in the first year of operation, H.L. Hunt, his ultra-wealthy father, quipped, "At that rate, he can't last much past the year 2135 A.D."[13] Adams, with less substantial funding, reported losing more than $700,000 in 1960.[14] A broadcast contract with ABC, then the weakest of the major television networks, helped to keep the league afloat, but legendary sports producer Roone Arledge indicated that broadcasting many of these games required creative camerawork and unorthodox production techniques to mask the sparse crowds.[15]

The stadium situation in most AFL cities did not help matters. With the Astrodome almost five years away from construction, the Oilers began play at a facility that was described by one sportswriter as "an overused high-school field." Jeppesen Stadium

was leased from the Houston Independent School District. It was initially built in 1941 as part of a federal Works Progress Administration project, and the condition of the field was so bad that when a Houston lineman once lost a shoe during a rainy game, it was never found.[16]

Yet the Oilers called Jeppesen Stadium home from 1960 to 1964, and Adams was fine with the venue despite its flaws. He reportedly spent $250,000 upgrading and expanding the facility, and he did so with a specific goal in mind.[17] Fearful that the NFL might try to expand to Houston, Adams appeared comfortable in Jeppesen Stadium because, according to *The Sporting News,* he negotiated the "sole outside playing rights in the plant, thereby shutting out the NFL."[18]

Adams's distaste for the autocratic Hofheinz likely enhanced his desire to steer clear of Colt Stadium once that venue became available in 1962. Further, his feelings about Hofheinz probably prompted a reluctance to put his team in the Astrodome in 1965. In addition, Adams's displeasure with Hofheinz's management style might have prompted an offer to sell the Oilers to the Houston Sports Association (HSA) in August 1962 for $2.5 million. While extending the offer, Adams asserted that he was unable to get specific information related to rental of Colt Stadium or the domed venue, which was then under construction.

In response, the HSA, then firmly controlled by Hofheinz, tersely indicated that "the HSA can't give Adams or anyone else a firm lease agreement on the domed stadium because the HSA does not yet have one itself," while stating that Adams, as a shareholder in the HSA, "was invited to set his own price on the rental of Colt Stadium."[19] On November 28, 1962, Adams distanced himself from Hofheinz by selling all of his HSA shares, a move that put Hofheinz and Bob Smith more firmly in control of the Astrodome and its overall operation. Of consequence, Texaco heir Craig Cullinan, one of the most influential figures in bringing major-league baseball to Houston, tendered his shares, as well.[20]

Despite evidence of acrimony, Hofheinz surged forward with the assumption that Adams would settle into the Astrodome shortly after it was unveiled. Although no formal agreement had been reached as the 1965 season approached, HSA publicity suggested that the Oilers would move into the Astrodome during its initial year of operation. Presumably to improve his negotiating position with Adams, Hofheinz attempted to charm Adams publicly, while citing the inadequacies his team faced before the Astrodome became available.

The HSA's 256-page *Inside the Astrodome* publication lauded Adams for bringing the Bluebonnet Bowl to Houston, while praising him as "a progressive business and civic leader." The publication also applauded Adams's team for bringing championships to the city and for being an "attendance leader" that "became the pace setters for the rest of the circuit." The focus on the team closed with a pointedly negative critique of Adams's prior venues, something that likely would not have occurred if the Oilers had played in Colt Stadium. According to the publication, "The Oilers can look back on five years of living through inadequate seating and parking as time well spent, and look forward to years of fruitful living in the sports showcase of the world, situated in the football hotbed of the nation."[21]

Hofheinz's public-relations tactics did not work. Those carefully studying the Houston negotiations in 1965 struggled to explain why Adams, after being slated to put his team in the Astrodome, abruptly signed a deal with Rice University instead. *The Sporting News* editor, C.C. Johnson Spink, pointedly suggested that Hofheinz might have set exceedingly high rental terms "to force the Oilers out and clear the way for a National Football League club, possibly one in which the Judge might own an interest." To support such speculation, Spink indicated that rent for Adams was reported to be "the highest any pro football team has ever been asked to meet … without any exclusive rights against an NFL team coming in at any time." Spink further asserted that Adams's sudden shift might have unfolded when an influential Rice University board member "who has little affection for Hofheinz thought this an excellent opportunity to stick a harpoon in the Judge's hide."[22]

In retracing the Oilers' early years, *The Sporting News* columnist Wells Twombly joked that the conventional wisdom from insiders was that "Rice Stadium would be open to professionals at about the same time the Baptists were permitted to hold prayer sessions on the high altar at St. Peter's in Rome."[23] Hofheinz likely felt as though Adams was severely constrained in his options. Even though his relationship with the Oilers' owner may have been icy, Hofheinz may have been convinced that the Astrodome provided Houston's fans with such a high-profile, premium venue that it could be prudently leveraged by the Oilers' owner to obtain some degree of profitability.

Adams, however, appeared to regard the high rental fees as an irretrievable expense and at the same time he seemed distrustful of Hofheinz. After a negotiation process in which Adams submitted his desired contract terms to Hofheinz, who then modified them and simply returned the document with an expectation of a signature, the Oilers owner decided that his preference was to continue showcasing his team in a less opulent and less costly venue.

In response, Hofheinz did what Spink speculated he would do. He tried to lure an NFL team, inviting Commissioner Pete Rozelle, an earlier nemesis of Adams, to visit the Astrodome. When it became clear that the NFL would not permit Hofheinz to hold a controlling interest in baseball and football teams simultaneously, he tried to coax Houston native and millionaire oil baron John Mecom into an ownership position to put a professional football tenant into the Astrodome. The NFL instead granted Mecom an expansion opportunity in New Orleans, where the team began play, like Adams, in an outdoor venue beginning in 1967. Mecom's team, the Saints, eventually moved into the Superdome, a huge indoor structure that was inspired by the Astrodome.[24]

After three years of competition away from the Astrodome, Adams finally relented, stating that "playing in the Rice Stadium rains cut crowds, so I looked forward to getting in the Dome." The Oilers became the first professional football team to play its home games indoors. Despite his frustration, Adams offered effusive praise for Hofheinz once a deal was hammered out, stating that "the people of Houston really got a bargain" with the Astrodome, while indicating, "I have the highest respect for Judge Hofheinz and what he has done for the city." Despite asserting that negotiations were "amicable," Adams admitted that he had the final stages of the process handled entirely by intermediaries, making it abundantly clear that his preference was to avoid direct negotiations with Hofheinz.[25]

The Oilers struggled in their early years at the Astrodome, but by the close of the 1970s, they had built an exciting, hard-hitting team directed by Texas native Bum Phillips. They advanced to the conference championship game in 1978 and 1979, but after they fell short in the playoffs again in 1980, Adams fired the popular Phillips. By the late 1970s, Roy Hofheinz was no longer involved with the Astrodome, but Adams's team was still locked into the venue as his home base.

Bothered that the Astrodome was no longer a premium venue, Adams in 1987 threatened to move his team to Jacksonville, Florida, if action was not taken to improve the Dome. He insisted on added seating and major renovations. He also pushed for a cap on his annual rent payments and fought for a more substantial share of advertising, parking, and concessions revenues, including a demand that would have given Adams as much as 83 percent of the parking revenues. The Houston Sports Association attempted to negotiate with him.[26] In addition, Harris County approved $50 million to expand and renovate the Astrodome, a figure that later ballooned to $67 million.[27]

Although Hofheinz died in 1982, the renovations eliminated some of the stadium infrastructure that the late judge most coveted. The luxury apartment that once served as home base to the Hofheinz empire was dismantled and most of its contents discarded, as were the massive scoreboard, the bowling alley, and several other well-publicized amenities. The all-faiths chapel was also removed; most of its contents were donated to a local hospital.[28]

The Astrodome, touted for all its luxuries and amenities, ultimately proved to be too restrictive to

Adams, whose desire for a higher percentage of stadium-based revenue could not be satisfied as long as the Houston Astros' hierarchy controlled the venue. By the 1990s the dynamic in NFL team ownership had changed. New stadiums were being built and owners, who were compelled to share a portion of their gate revenues, were getting better lease terms than in a generation prior. Of significance, owners were not required to share skybox, advertising, parking, and other stadium-based revenue streams with competing owners. Publicly financed stadiums had become a cash cow for owners more than in any previous era.[29] Football historian Michael Oriard aptly noted, "Television continued to be the largest single pot of money … but stadiums became the new economic engine driving the NFL into the financial stratosphere."[30] Adams pushed harder to gain profits that several other owners were now obtaining, aggressively attempting to grab his piece of the lucrative stadium-generated pie.

Renovations made in the 1980s pacified Adams temporarily, but he decided that the Astrodome could no longer serve his team looking forward. Thus, by the 1990s he pushed hard to get a brand-new domed stadium built for his team. Mayor Bob Lanier pushed back, citing city services as a more important priority for Houstonians, though talk of funding an open-air stadium unfolded. The popular mayor attempted to negotiate with Adams, but he was hard-nosed about protecting taxpayers. He pointedly said, "It's very hard for me to go into neighborhoods that need streetlights and sidewalks and police and parks and ask those people for money for a stadium they probably can't afford to buy tickets for."[31]

In response, Adams predictably threatened to move, and eventually carried out the threat, shifting his franchise to Tennessee, where he played in outdoor venues but on terms that he was in a better position to dictate. Adams was reviled by many of Houston's diehard football fans, but he did not move from the Houston area even after his team shifted elsewhere.

The Oilers departed after the 1996 season, a year before their Astrodome lease officially ended, and they were later renamed the Tennessee Titans. Initially, Adams expressed a willingness to stay in Houston until his Astrodome lease fully expired, but once his announced move was made, Houstonians reacted with revulsion, with many avoiding the stadium on game day. With numerous empty seats as the new reality, the NFL was glad to approve the team's departure a year earlier than expected. Houston officials hammered out a settlement that cost Adams more than $5 million, but it allowed the team to relocate immediately.[32]

Nevertheless, the football team that cost Adams $25,000 in league fees in 1959 was valued at $1.06 billion when he died in October 2013.[33] Clearly, Adams's pioneering entry into professional football was a major financial success, yet the hard-charging oil baron struggled for respectability and acceptance during his time in Houston. Stadium-related issues were often at the core of that struggle. When the Astrodome opened in 1965, Adams resisted playing in the highly touted venue. Somewhat fittingly, when his team left Houston, it was in large part because the revolutionary Astrodome failed to meet his expectations.

NOTES

1   Edgar Ray, *The Grand Huckster: Houston's Judge Roy Hofheinz — Genius of the Astrodome* (Memphis: Memphis State University Press, 1980).

2   Harry Shattuck, "Money, Intrigue, Suspense — Oilers vs. HSA Battle Heats Up," *Houston Chronicle*, September 13, 1987: Sports, 1.

3   Robert Lipsyte, "Astrodome Opulent, Even for Texas," *New York Times*, April 8, 1965: 50.

4   Ed Fowler, *Loser Takes All: Bud Adams, Bad Football, and Big Business* (Atlanta: Longstreet Press, 1997), 33.

5   "Cannon Scores After Game — Signs 100G Houston Pact," *The Sporting News*, January 13, 1960: 22.

6   "Oilers Spent $73,000 in Court Costs," *The Sporting News*, December 3, 1966: 9.

7   Joe King, "College Heroes Eye Adams' Money Tree," *The Sporting News*, January 5, 1963: section 2, 1.

8   Jack Gallagher, "New Trend in AFL: Every Team Seeks Lincoln-Style Back," *The Sporting News*, December 4, 1965: 54; Al Thomy, "Nobis, NFL Rookie of the Year, Bargain at Any Price," *The Sporting News*, January 7, 1967: 5; Joe King, "Interloop Jumps Possible, but None Did," *The Sporting News*, February 11, 1967: 9.

9   John McClain, "Remembering Bud Adams — Pioneering Owner Part of a Colorful Era," *Houston Chronicle*, October 22, 2013: Sports, 1.

10 Al Carter, "See Ya, Blue: Oilers Leave Legacy of Odd Deals, Bad Luck, and Low-Budget Absurdity," *Dallas Morning News*, June 29, 1997: 22B.

11 Ibid.

12 Michael Oriard, *Brand NFL: Making and Selling America's Favorite Sport* (Chapel Hill: University of North Carolina Press, 2010), 19.

13 Ed Gruver, *The American Football League: A Year-by-Year History, 1960-1969* (Jefferson, North Carolina: McFarland, 1997), 56.

14 Clark Nealon, "Colt Owners Shun Chance to Buy Oilers," *The Sporting News*, September 1, 1962: 20.

15 Roone Arledge, *Roone: A Memoir* (New York: Harper Collins, 2003), 64.

16 John Lopez, "Remembering the 1960-61 Oilers — Days of Glory," *Houston Chronicle*, December 15, 1991: Sports, 17.

17 Clark Nealon, "Vets Spark Oilers to Fast Start in AFL," *The Sporting News*, October 5, 1960: 23.

18 Joe King, "New League Hurls Challenge at NFL — Drafts Name Stars," *The Sporting News*, December 2, 1959: 46.

19 Nealon, "Colt Owners."

20 "Seven Houston Shareholders Sell Their Interest in Club," *The Sporting News*, December 8, 1962: 21.

21 *Inside the Astrodome: Eighth Wonder of the World* (Houston: Houston Sports Association, 1965), 208.

22 C.C. Johnson Spink, "We Believe," *The Sporting News*, June 19, 1965: 14.

23 Wells Twombly, "Ridiculous Business Starting Again," *The Sporting News*, February 16, 1976: 8.

24 Ray, 332.

25 Ray, 332-333.

26 Harry Shattuck, "Adams Details Beefs with HSA," *Houston Chronicle*, October 10, 1987: 14.

27 Bill Coulter, "$50 Million Upgrading for Dome Approved," *Houston Chronicle*, July 22, 1987: A1. For final expense totals for the Astrodome renovation, see Fowler, 152.

28 Brenda Sapino, "Hofheinz's Dome Rooms Are Doomed," *Houston Chronicle*, May 5, 1988: A1.

29 Robert Trumpbour, *The New Cathedrals: Politics and Media in the History of Stadium Construction* (Syracuse, New York: Syracuse University Press, 2007), 277-278.

30 Oriard, 153.

31 Fowler, 157.

32 Steve Brewer, "Tennessee-Saw Battle Officially Over for Oilers," *Houston Chronicle*, July 4, 1997: A1.

33 David Barron, "Bud Adams: 1923-2013—He Brought Us the Oilers, Then Took Them Away," *Houston Chronicle*, October 22, 2013: A1.

The Yankees Invade Houston for the First Game in the Astrodome

April 9, 1965: Houston Astros 2, New York Yankees 1 (12 innings), at the Astrodome

By Rory Costello

"THE OPENING NIGHT AGAINST THE Yankees was one of the most electrifying nights I've spent in baseball. The excitement was everywhere. It was incredible to see that place filled. It was hard not to look up and be just as awed as any fan."[1]

That was Rusty Staub in 1985, 20 years after professional baseball's first indoor game. In 1965, Staub—then the Astros' right fielder—was just 21. Yet many older people were just as excited about the brand-new Astrodome. Various veteran sportswriters compared it to the Taj Mahal.[2]

The most prominent amazed fan that Friday night was the president of the United States, Lyndon Baines Johnson. LBJ told Judge Roy Hofheinz, president and co-owner of the Astros, "Roy, I want to congratulate you; it shows so much imagination." He later called the edifice "massive and beautiful."[3] It was one of seven times that a US president was on hand for a major-league ballpark's debut.[4]

To conclude the 1965 exhibition season, the Astros and Yankees played a three-game series that ended on Sunday, April 11 (the Baltimore Orioles also played two games in Houston that weekend). The date with the Yankees was set at least as early as November 1964.[5] The Bronx Bombers were long established as baseball's premier franchise. They were also the reigning American League pennant winners, and their star—Mickey Mantle—was then rivaled only by Willie Mays as the sport's biggest name.

There was a good reason to hold the first game at night. During an intrasquad game that Thursday, the Astros had discovered how difficult it was to see fly balls against the dome's translucent roof when it was sunny outside. They experimented vainly with vari-ous shades of sunglasses and even different-colored baseballs.[6]

The spectacle of the new stadium fueled a standing-room crowd of 47,876 for the first game. Attendance for each of the two weekend games against the Yankees surpassed 48,000 even though, by some accounts, the Astrodome's listed seating capacity for baseball was then 46,000.[7]

Throwing out the ceremonial first ball—and wearing an Astros cap—was the governor of Texas, John Connally. He was flanked by Warren Giles, president of the National League, and Praxedis Balboa, governor of the Mexican state of Tamaulipas (which borders the southern tip of Texas).[8]

The Yankees' manager, Johnny Keane—a Houston resident—catered to the fans with his lineup selection. Mickey Mantle had not been in the lineup for several days, yet Keane not only played him but also made him the leadoff batter.[9] Mantle opened the game with a single off the Astros' starter, Dick "Turk" Farrell.

Keane also started various other "name" players, including Roger Maris, Bobby Richardson, and Tony Kubek. New York's starting pitcher was Mel Stottlemyre, who had been quite impressive in 1964 after reaching the majors in August. Hofheinz appreciated the gesture, declaring of Keane, "Johnny's a real class gentleman. He always has been."[10]

Lyndon and Lady Bird Johnson were announced in the bottom of the first inning.[11] The native Texans received a huge standing ovation from the crowd in their home state.[12] It had been up in the air whether the president would come to the game. Earlier that week he had told Hofheinz that he would not be

President Lyndon Baines Johnson and Roy Hofheinz watched the first game in the Astrodome from a luxury Skybox, one of the Astrodome's many innovations. Hofheinz also had his own private quarters in the Astrodome. (Courtesy of Houston Astros Baseball Club).

able to make it. However, Johnson's close adviser, Jack Valenti—a Houstonian who later became the long-time president of the Motion Picture Association of America—told Hofheinz, "You know how the president is: If his desk gets cleared off early enough on Friday, he might just say, 'Come on. Let's go to the ballgame.'"[13]

Even on Friday afternoon, the White House played it close to the vest, saying only that the president had left "for Texas"—it wasn't clear whether that meant Houston or the LBJ Ranch in Johnson City (about 200 miles west in Blanco County).[14] The destination was not confirmed to be Houston until Johnson had been flying for 55 minutes aboard his Air Force jet.[15]

Along with their entourage, the Johnsons sat in the owners' suite, high in right field just to the right of the giant scoreboard.[16] Hofheinz knew LBJ very well. Indeed, he had been Johnson's campaign manager in some races.

A relaxed and smiling LBJ enjoyed hors d'oeuvres, chicken, and ice cream while watching the game.[17] The White House had also ordered that nine special phone lines be ready at the stadium for the presidential party's use.[18]

The Astros did not cash in on a couple of early opportunities, notably in the third, when Ron Brand tripled with one out. In the top of the sixth inning,

Mantle hit a solo homer to score the game's first run. He later said that he hit it "pretty good," but the ball barely made it into the first row of seats, just to the right of the 406-foot mark in center field. Echoing Mantle—and prefiguring other players' sentiments for years to come –Stottlemyre said, "This ought to be a pitchers' paradise. The ball just doesn't carry the way it does outdoors. You've really got to hit one to knock it out."[19]

Mantle and Maris also remarked on other aspects of visibility for outfielders. Mantle (who played left field that night) thought that line drives to left-center and right-center would be hard to handle. "They came out of the lights out there," he said. Maris remarked, "The ball blends into the girders. Maybe not so much as it does in the daytime, but you can notice it just the same."[20]

Houston tied it with an unearned run in the bottom of the sixth. Stottlemyre issued a leadoff walk to Farrell; Yankees first baseman Joe Pepitone then overthrew second base while going for a double play on a ball hit by Joe Morgan. The bases were loaded after Al Spangler's bunt down the third-base line stayed fair. Staub hit into a fielder's choice, scoring Farrell, but Walt Bond grounded into a double play.

Farrell pitched one more scoreless inning—center fielder Jimmy Wynn threw out Johnny Blanchard at the plate—and then gave way to Hal Woodeshick. Stottlemyre pitched through the eighth; he was relieved by Hal Reniff. LBJ and his party left before the top of the ninth; a rousing Texas-themed scoreboard show saw them off.[21] When Houston did not score in its half of the ninth, it was on to extra innings.

Reniff pitched three scoreless frames for the Yankees. Meanwhile, Woodeshick allowed no runs in five innings, giving up just two hits and walking two.

Finally, facing Pete Mikkelsen in the bottom of the 12th inning, the Astros won it. (The game was played in a brisk 2 hours and 34 minutes). Wynn beat out an infield single and stole second. With two out, Nellie Fox hit a bloop single to center to bring Wynn home.[22] The 37-year-old Fox had played little in spring training. In fact, before the game he said, "I have retired as a player."[23] Although he had been

Mickey Mantle knocked 536 regular-season home runs and 18 postseason round-trippers in his Hall of Fame career. He also hit the first homer in Astrodome history in an April 9, 1965, exhibition game against Houston.

the Astros' starting second baseman in 1964, Fox was released at the end of the season and then signed as a coach. He was on standby in case Joe Morgan didn't make the grade, and he worked hard to remain in shape.[24]

The next morning, ahead of the first afternoon game, Paul Richards, then Houston's general manager, said to Hofheinz that there was no alternative but to offer a money-back guarantee to fans if the fly ball visibility situation got out of hand. Hofheinz considered for about 10 seconds and then replied, "You're right. We've had a billion dollars worth of publicity and are off to a great start. We can't jeopardize it now."[25] Fortunately, Saturday and Sunday were cloudy, and the Astrodome's roof was soon painted.

In later years the Astros continued to celebrate the inauguration of the dome, and Mickey Mantle remained a part of the pregame festivities.

• On the 10th anniversary of the first game, The Mick (then age 43) hit three home runs off Ken Johnson and Bob Bruce, two other 1965 Astros pitchers.[26]
• On the 20th anniversary, Mantle "took a few obligatory swings at the plate" in his first appearance since Commissioner Peter Ueberroth reinstated him from a 1983 ban.[27]

Mantle refused, however, to throw out the first pitch as the Astros and Yankees played on March 30, 1995. At that time, Major League Baseball's most crippling strike still had not been resolved. The rosters for that exhibition game consisted of replacement players.[28]

The Astrodome hosted its last big-league game in 1999. Nonetheless, on April 9, 2015, a 50th-anniversary party was held at Carruth Plaza, outside the dome. The public was allowed inside for photo opportunities. An estimated 23,000 to 25,000 people turned out—including former Astros star José Cruz. The crowd was roughly half that of half a century before, but it was long on loyalty and emotion.[29]

NOTES

1   Mike Tierney, "In 20 years, Astrodome matures from baseball novelty to tradition," *St. Petersburg Times*, April 9, 1985: 1C.

2   "Writers Awed by Houston's Dome," Associated Press, April 10, 1965.

3   John Wilson, "Everyone in Orbit Over Astrodome," *The Sporting News*, April 24, 1965: 9.

4   John F. Kennedy threw out the first pitch at D.C. Stadium (later Robert F. Kennedy Stadium) on April 9, 1962 (although the Washington Redskins of the NFL had played the 1961 season there). George H.W. Bush threw out the first pitch at Baltimore's Camden Yards on April 6, 1992. Bill Clinton did the same at Cleveland's Jacobs Field (later Progressive Field) on April 4, 1994. George W. Bush threw out the second pitch at Milwaukee's Miller Park on April 6, 2001 (following Commissioner Bud Selig) and the first pitch at Washington's Nationals Park on March 30, 2008. Former President Jimmy Carter threw out the first pitch at San Diego's Petco Park on April 8, 2004.

5   "Ford Visits Domed Stadium; Leaves Hospital to Go Home," *The Sporting News*, November 28, 1964. Whitey Ford, the Yankees' star pitcher, had gone to Houston for an operation performed by the renowned vascular surgeon Denton Cooley.

6   Curt Block, "Astros Top Yanks in New Stadium," United Press International, April 10, 1965. John Wilson, "Lone Star Sun Glare Gives Players Daytime Nightmare," *The Sporting News*, April 24, 1965:10. "Colored Baseballs Fizzle," Associated Press, April 10, 1965.

7   "Astrodome Opens This Weekend," Associated Press, April 4, 1965. "Astros Take Dome Opener," Associated Press, April 10, 1965. Other references cite 42,217 for the 1965 season.

8   Wilson, "Everyone in Orbit Over Astrodome."

9   "Astro Bosses Praise Keane for Using Varsity Yankees," *The Sporting News*, April 24, 1965: 9.

10 Ibid.

11 "LBJ Sees Astros," Associated Press, April 10, 1963.

12 Murray Chass, "Astrodome Dedicated," Associated Press, April 10, 1965.

13 "Nine Special Phone Lines Set Up at Stadium for LBJ," *The Sporting News*, April 24, 1965: 10.

14 Ibid.

15 "LBJ Returns to Scenes of Youth", United Press International, April 10, 1965.

16 Wilson, "Everyone in Orbit Over Astrodome."

17 "LBJ Returns to Scenes of Youth"; "Everyone in Orbit Over Astrodome."

18 "Nine Special Phone Lines Set Up at Stadium for LBJ."

19 Til Ferdenzi, "Yanks Size Up The Astrodome: 'Pitchers' Park," *The Sporting News*, April 24, 1965: 10.

20 Ibid.

21 Chass, "Astrodome Dedicated." Jimmy Wynn with Bill McCurdy, *Toy Cannon* (Jefferson, North Carolina: McFarland & Company, 2010). 62.

22 Chass, "Astrodome Dedicated."

23 "Houston, Atlanta Fields Dedicated," Associated Press, April 10, 1965.

24 "'Coach' Fox Just Kidding?," Associated Press, March 27, 1965. "Astros Activate Fox, Cut White," Associated Press, May 13, 1965. Fox played in his last 21 big-league games from May through July 1965.

25 "Judge Ready to Give Refunds If Games Had Proved Farce," *The Sporting News*, April 24, 1965: 10.

26 "Hey, Mick, how about a DH job," Associated Press, April 10, 1975.

27 "Mickey Mantle takes some swings as Astrodome celebrates anniversary," Associated Press, April 10, 1985. The prior commissioner, Bowie Kuhn, had banned Mantle and Willie Mays from all association with baseball in 1983 because of their public relations duties with Atlantic City casinos.

28 "Replacement baseball debuts for anniversary at Astrodome," Associated Press, March 31, 1995.

29 Doug Miller, Alice Barr, and Marcelino Benito, "Fans gather to celebrate Astrodome's 50th birthday," KHOU.com, April 9, 2015. Anita Hassan and Mike Tolson, "Houston celebrates 50th Astrodome Anniversary with one last party," *Houston Chronicle*, April 10, 2015.

Play Ball: The First Regular Season Game in the Astrodome

April 12, 1965: Philadelphia Phillies 2, Houston Astros 0, at the Astrodome

By Richard Riis

ON APRIL 9, 1965, THE FORMER Houston Colt .45s took the field as the Houston Astros, inaugurating indoor baseball in the Astrodome with a 2-1 exhibition win over the New York Yankees.

Three nights later, on April 12, a standing-room-only crowd of 48,546 (42,652 paid[1]), including Commissioner Ford Frick, National League President Warren Giles, and a large contingent of guests from NASA, was on hand to witness the first official contest inside the Space Age wonder of the sports world as the Houston Astros played host to the Philadelphia Phillies.

"It seemed only right that the Phils should open the league season in the spectacular Harris County Domed Stadium," cracked one scribe. "The Philadelphia Phillies, remember, are essentially the same baseball team which took off like Gemini II last summer only to lose nine of its final 10 games and crash in despair."[2]

Before the game Astros players and management assembled on the field for a ceremony to retire the number 32 worn by reliever Jim Umbricht, the only Houston pitcher to post a winning record in each of the team's first two seasons. Umbricht had died of melanoma on April 8, 1964, at the age of 33. After the funeral, his ashes had been spread from a small plane over the Astrodome construction site.[3]

Shifting from sadness to celebration, 22 of 24 NASA astronauts, each of whom was presented with a lifetime major-league pass by Giles, were introduced to throw out the first pitch, simultaneously, to 22 of the Astros.

Along with a new name, new uniforms, and a new stadium, the Astros had a (more or less) new manager in Lum Harris. Harris, who had succeeded Paul Richards as interim manager of the Baltimore Orioles when the latter stepped down in August 1961 to become general manager of the expansion Colt .45s, had followed Richards to Houston as a coach in 1962. Harris served almost three full seasons as coach under manager Harry Craft until Richards fired Craft and turned the job over to Harris on September 19, 1964.

Harris's pick for Opening Day starter was Bob Bruce, a 31-year-old right-hander who had enjoyed a breakout season in 1964, setting club records with 15 wins (against nine losses), four shutouts, and a 2.76 ERA.

Phillies manager Gene Mauch held back his number-one starter, Jim Bunning, for his club's home opener against the Giants two days later and instead gave the ball to Chris Short. The left-handed Short had enjoyed a breakout season of his own in 1964, with a 17-9 record, fanning 181 in 220⅔ innings while walking only 51, and posting the NL's third-best ERA at 2.20. It was Short who, with Bunning, had been called upon by Mauch to start eight of the Phillies' last 11 games in 1964. Despite the heavy workload, Short pitched reasonably well, giving up only six earned runs in 19 innings over his final three starts, but failed to win even one as the reeling Phillies blew a 6½-game lead and lost the pennant.

Leading off for the Phillies as the game got under way was second baseman Tony Taylor, who doubled to left for the first official hit in the Astrodome. Dick (then Richie) Allen, who'd enjoyed a phenomenal

In 1965 the Houston Colt .45s became the Astros and moved into the Harris County Domed Stadium [the Astrodome's original name]. They went 36-45 during their inaugural season in the Eighth Wonder of the World. (Courtesy of Houston Astros Baseball Club).

freshman season in 1964, winning NL Rookie of the Year honors and finishing seventh in the MVP voting, popped up to Joe Morgan at second for the first out. After Johnny Callison flied out to center, Wes Covington was caught looking for the Dome's first strikeout.

Short made short work of the Astros in the bottom of the first, issuing only a walk to the rookie Morgan, starting his first season in the majors after brief call-ups to Houston in 1963 and 1964.

After a scoreless second, Ruben Amaro opened the third inning for the Phillies with a single to left. Short sacrificed Amaro to second. Taylor tapped back to the mound for the second out, but Allen followed with a 410-foot blast over the fence in straightaway center field to put the Phillies up 2-0.[4]

Short, for his part, handcuffed the Astros inning after inning, facing the minimum three batters in the second, third, and fifth innings, and offsetting two singles with three strikeouts in the fourth.

Short ran into minor trouble in the seventh when, with one out, he walked Jim Beauchamp and Joe Gaines back-to-back. John Bateman's bunt moved

the runners to second and third, but Mike White, hitting for Bruce, struck out to end the threat.

Bruce scattered nine hits while walking one and striking out five over seven innings. Only in the second did he manage to keep the Phillies off the basepaths. In the fourth he survived a jam by fanning Short with the bases loaded.

Hal Woodeshick took the mound for the Astros in the top of the eighth, with his club still two runs down. The 6-foot-3-inch sinkerballing southpaw, after an injury-plagued 5-16 season as a starter for Houston in 1962, had become the team's relief ace in 1963, winning 11 games with a team-leading 10 saves and a 1.97 ERA and earning a selection to the All-Star Game. He also led the NL with 23 saves in 1964.

The Phillies immediately put Woodeshick to the test. Callison singled to left to open the inning, John Herrnstein, who had replaced Covington in left field in the fifth, sacrificed Callison to second. A grounder to second by Tony Gonzalez advanced Callison to third base, bringing Dick Stuart to the plate.

Manager Harris made the decision to avoid pitching to Stuart—who was acquired by Philadelphia during the offseason for his potent bat (75 home runs and 232 RBIs in two seasons for the Boston Red Sox) in exchange for pitcher Dennis Bennett—and instead ordered an intentional walk to put runners at the corners. Mauch pulled the slow-footed Stuart for the more nimble Bobby Wine, but Woodeshick struck out Clay Dalrymple looking to end the inning.

Allen's ninth-inning, two-out boot of Beauchamp's grounder to third gave a glimmer of hope to the Astros, but Allen recovered to scoop up a groundball by Gaines on the next play, tossing to first to end the game.

About the only bright spot for the Astros that day was the fine play of the 21-year-old Morgan. The future Hall of Famer and eventual runner-up for the 1965 NL Rookie of the Year Award collected a single, a double, and a walk in four trips to the plate. He recorded six putouts and nine assists as he effectively covered the right side of the infield.

Short, with a 2-0, four-hit shutout, was the winning pitcher. Bruce, who struggled in spots but essentially made only one bad pitch, was tagged with a hard-luck loss.

Short had been sharp all night, striking out 11, walking only three, and permitting but one runner to reach third base. A notoriously slow starter in springs past, he was elated. "It was the first time in my life, either in the majors or minors, that I ever pitched a season opener," said Short, "and it must be the first time I have ever won a game the first two weeks of any season in the big leagues."

Short gave a glowing review of the Astrodome. "It's an excellent park to pitch in," he said. "The mound is real good and so are the dimensions. Also, the absence of wind helps a lot."

"Another thing that surprised me was that I was able to raise a good sweat. I like to sweat when I'm working and I was afraid that because of the air-conditioning, I would not be able to perspire."[5]

Those who played the infield and outfield had a somewhat different take on the Astrodome, or, more specifically, the stadium's steel-framed, twin-layered clear plastic roof.

"The big news of that first official game ... was not Allen's homer, Short's pitching, or the Phillies winning," Astros center fielder Jimmy Wynn later recalled. "It was the fly balls that we couldn't see. ... I remember running in on a short fly ball, then looking up to see it nowhere. The next thing I knew, the ball was falling to the ground beside me for a 'lost-in-the-sky-on-the-way-up-or-down' base hit. Everybody else was having the same problem. You just couldn't see the ball a lot of times once it blended into all those clear glass panels and close-to-ball-color girders in the Astrodome roof."[6]

On April 20 the Astrodome's 4,596 plastic windows were coated with 700 gallons of a special off-white paint developed by architects, engineers, and optical experts to resolve the visibility problem, at a cost of $20,000.[7] That the painted-over roof would eventually cause the grass on the field to die would be a problem for another day.

SOURCES

In addition to the sources listed in the notes, the author also consulted:

Gast, James. *The Astrodome: Building an American Spectacle* (Boston: Aspinwall Press, 2014).

Amarillo Daily News.

Houston Chronicle.

The Sporting News.

NOTES

1   "Opening Day Attendance Off Slightly," *Corpus Christi Times*, April 13, 1965: 4B.

2   Gary Cartwright, "Phils Sink Astros, 2-0," *Dallas Morning News*, April 13, 1965: 2-1.

3   Fran Zimniuch. *Shortened Seasons: The Untimely Deaths of Major League Baseball's Stars and Journeymen* (Lanham, Maryland: Taylor Trade Publishing, 2007), 131.

4   "Phils Top Astros, 2-0, on Short's 4-Hitter Before 48,546," *New York Times*, April 13, 1965: 43.

5   "Short Finally Finds Formula to Win Early," *Corpus Christi Times*, April 13, 1965: 4B.

6   Jimmy Wynn, *Toy Cannon: the Autobiography of Baseball's Jimmy Wynn* (Jefferson, North Carolina: McFarland and Company, 2010), 63.

7   "Face-Lifting, Plus Face-Saving Is the Hope for Houston's Dome," *Newsday* (Long Island, New York), April 20, 1965: 31C.

Rusty Sends 'Em Home Happy

April 23, 1965: Houston Astros 4, Pittsburgh Pirates 3, at the Astrodome

By Norm King

THE FIRST ONE DIDN'T COUNT.

If you want to get technical about it, the Astros' first victory in the Astrodome was a 2-1 win in a 12-inning exhibition game against the New York Yankees that inaugurated the stadium on April 9, 1965. And according to Rusty Staub, that game had a Game Seven air about it.

"Mickey Mantle hit a home run and people went crazy," Staub said. "I have to say for a nonentity game, I'm wondering if there ever has been that kind of excitement the night they opened the stadium."[1]

Staub, who was four years away from being christened "Le Grand Orange" in Montreal, played a crucial role in the first Astros home victory that counted in the standings, a 4-3 win over the Pirates, two weeks after the inaugural.[2]

Houston played its first regular-season game in the "Eighth Wonder of the World" on April 12, 1965, losing 2-0 to a Philadelphia Phillies team that was still punch-drunk from its epic collapse in the 1964 pennant race.[3] After that, they went on an eight-game road trip to New York, Pittsburgh, and Philadelphia, where they went 3-5, before returning for their first official homestand in their new digs. Once back in the Astrodome, the Astros found that an inconvenient problem from their first few home games, namely, players not being able to follow fly balls, had been dealt with.

"You just couldn't see the ball a lot of the times once it blended into all those clear glass panels and close-to-ball-color girders in the Astrodome roof," wrote former Astro Jimmy Wynn in his autobiography. "During the [first] road trip, the club decided to paint the two large pie sections of clear panels behind home plate at the Astrodome as a first fix solution to the lost fly-ball vision problem."[4]

Houston starter Bob Bruce took the mound for his third start of the young season with a 1-1 record and a 1.69 ERA. He was coming off a fine 15-9 season in 1964 (when the franchise was still known as the Colt .45s), in which he posted a 2.76 ERA and a team-leading 5.5 Wins Above Replacement (WAR). Pittsburgh starter Bob Veale was also making his third start of the year, with a 1-0 record and a 1.04 ERA. He had gone 18-12 in '64, his first full year as a starter, with a 2.74 ERA and a 5.8 WAR, second on the Pirates to Roberto Clemente's 7.2.

Veale got through the meat of the Astros order in the first inning, but gave up two runs in the second, employing the time-dishonored method of walking the leadoff hitter, who in this case was Jim Beauchamp. Beauchamp moved to third on John Bateman's single, with Bateman advancing to second on the throw to the hot corner. Bob Lillis singled to score Beauchamp and send Bateman to third. After pitcher Bruce struck out, Joe Gaines made the score 2-0 with a sacrifice fly.

In the third inning Veale conducted an experiment to find out if walking a batter with two out might have the same result as giving a free pass to the leadoff hitter and, by gum, he found out that it could. After getting Bob Aspromonte on a fly ball and Beauchamp on a popup, Veale gave Bateman a free ticket to first. That led to all kinds of trouble as Bateman moved to second when Lillis walked, then scored on Bruce's double. That two-bagger ended Veale's work for the day.

The score didn't change until the eighth, as Bruce remained steady for Houston while Tommie Sisk and Wilbur Wood provided solid relief for Pittsburgh. Bruce started to tire in the top of the frame, as he gave up a leadoff double to Gene Alley, and then a one-out walk to Dick Schofield. Astros manager Luman Harris had seen enough and brought in Hal Woodeshick to face Gene Freese, who was pinch-hitting for Bill Virdon. Freese doubled, scoring Alley and sending Schofield to third. The Pirates had to like their prospects at this point because they had two on, one out, and the ever-dangerous Roberto Clemente coming up. Woodeshick induced Clemente to ground to second, but Schofield scored and Freese went to third. Woodeshick couldn't breathe any easier, because the mighty Willie Stargell was the next batter. The lumbering Stargell legged out a groundball to deep short and Freese, who was off with the crack of the bat, came around from second to tie it. Veale was off the hook.

Harris made an unusual move in the bottom of the eighth, at least by today's standards, when he allowed Woodeshick, who was due up second in the inning, to hit for himself. The move almost proved disastrous; not only did he fail to advance Lillis, who had walked, to second base (he popped up), but he almost gave the game away when he took the mound again in the ninth. After Donn Clendenon grounded to second, Woodeshick walked Jim Pagliaroni and gave up a single to Alley. With runners on first and second, in came Jim Owens, who got Manny Mota to line to right and Schofield to fly to left to end the threat.

The game went into extra innings—this was the Astros' 10th game of 1965 and already the fifth time they had gone into overtime—and the fans there that night got an oil barrel full of excitement. After getting the first two outs in the top of the 10th, Owens walked Stargell and Bob Bailey back-to-back. Next, Clendenon hit the ball deep to the second base side of the infield for a single; Stargell tried to emulate Freese's feat by scoring from second, but a perfect relay from Morgan to Walt Bond to Bateman nailed Stargell at the plate.

It was common in those days for relief pitchers to work multiple innings. The era of the one-inning specialist, which is now the norm, was still years away; in those days a set-up man worked in a bowling alley. That explains why Al McBean, who came on for

One of Houston's early stars, Rusty Staub batted .333 in 1967 and led the NL with 44 doubles. "Le Grand Orange," as he became known in Montreal, ended his career after the 1985 season with 2,716 hits. (National Baseball Hall of Fame, Cooperstown, New York).

Pittsburgh to start the eighth, was still on the mound in the extra innings. If they made a movie serial of his outing, they could have called it *The Perils of McBean* because of the close calls he had.

In the 10th, for example, Aspromonte doubled and pinch-hitter Al Spangler was walked intentionally to set up a force at third. After Bateman struck out, Lillis moved the runners up with a groundout. Pinch-hitter Mike White was unable to bring Aspromonte home from third. Houston shouted, "Curses, foiled again!" after the 11th. McBean walked Joe Morgan with one out, and then gave up a single to Wynn. Morgan got to third when Bond grounded out, but was stuck there when Aspromonte followed with a grounder of his own to end the inning.

In the movie serials, the heroine managed to get untied from the train tracks just in time. Unfortunately for McBean, the cavalry didn't arrive in time in the 12th. Spangler, who stayed in the game, singled and, one out later, moved to second when Lillis grounded to the keystone sack. There was almost a sense of inevitability when McBean hit Ron Brand, who was pinch-hitting for Dave Giusti (who had come on in the 11th) with a pitch. That brought up Staub, who had pinch-hit for Gaines way back in the third. Staub singled to left, Spangler jogged home with the winning run and joy reigned in the House That Hofheinz Built.

SOURCES

In addition to the sources listed in the notes, the author consulted the following:

Abilene Reporter-News.

Foxsports.com.

Indiana (Pennsylvania) *Gazette.*

NOTES

1 Brian McTaggart, "Game to Remember: Rusty Staub," mlb. com, May 10, 2012.

2 Staub was one of several future Montreal Expos who played with the Astros that year. The others were catchers John Bateman and Ron Brand and pitchers Carroll Sembera and Quebec-born Claude Raymond. Another Canadian, Ron Taylor, was also on the roster. The Pittsburgh lineup on the day of the game included future Expos infielders Bob Bailey and Donn Clendenon and future manager Bill Virdon.

3 The Phillies had a 6½-game lead with 12 games to go in 1964, but lost the pennant by one game to the St. Louis Cardinals.

4 Jimmy Wynn, with Bill McCurdy, *Toy Cannon: The Autobiography of Jimmy Wynn* (Jefferson, North Carolina: McFarland, 2010), 63.

Walt Bonds' Walk-Off Single Caps Comeback Win Against Drysdale

July 2, 1965: Houston Astros 4, Los Angeles Dodgers 3, at the Astrodome

By Gordon Gattie

THE LOS ANGELES DODGERS WERE coming off a 6-3 loss to the struggling Chicago Cubs when they arrived in Houston for a three-game series with the Houston Astros. Although the Dodgers held a two-game lead over the Cincinnati Reds in the National League, they had lost two of three games against the Cubs and were only 2-3 on their current road trip. After losing the Cubs series, Dodgers manager Walt Alston said, "Anything can happen in this league. How it will all come out I don't know. You might as well ask a 6-year-old boy what he thinks instead of me."[1] Slated to pitch for Los Angeles was All-Star Don Drysdale, who had lost his last four starts, lowering his record to 11-7.

The Astros, although mired in ninth place, had won five of their last six games, including a four-game sweep of the New York Mets in the Astrodome the previous weekend. The Astros started Bob Bruce, whose record was 6-9. He eventually led the Astros in games started, innings pitched, strikeouts, and losses in 1965. Bruce also had the honor this season of throwing the first pitch at the Astrodome and getting the first loss, on April 12, Opening Day, to the Philadelphia Phillies.[2] On this first Friday in July, the announced attendance of 33,044 was one of the larger crowds in 1965. (The next night the Astrodome drew its largest crowd of the season when Dodgers ace Sandy Koufax took the mound against the Astros' Larry Dierker.)

The Dodgers started quickly. Leadoff batter Maury Wills singled and Junior Gilliam tripled him home. Gilliam scored on an error by Joe Morgan. Bruce then retired the side. In the bottom of the inning Morgan walked and stole second with Lee Maye at the plate. But the Astros couldn't bring Morgan around to score: Maye struck out, Jim Gentile lined out, and Walt Bond grounded out to shortstop.

In the second inning, the Dodgers threatened to increase their lead when Wes Parker led off with a double and stole third. But Bruce got Lou Johnson and Don LeJohn to ground out to third and struck out Drysdale. Parker was the last Dodger to reach third base until the sixth inning. Drysdale was also pitching well, not allowing a hit until the bottom of the fourth inning, when Bond singled. Through six innings, the Astros had yet to reach third.

Davis started the top half of the sixth inning with a single and went to second on a bunt by Fairly. Roseboro drove Davis home with a single, and increased the Dodgers' lead to 3-0. In the bottom of the inning, Drysdale faced the heart of Houston's lineup. Maye flied out to right field, Gentile grounded out to second. Bond doubled, but Bob Aspromonte struck out looking to leave Bond in scoring position. Pitching a three-hit shutout through six innings, Drysdale appeared to be on the brink of ending his losing streak.

In the seventh inning Drysdale singled with one out, but Wills hit into a 6-4-3 double play. In the bottom of the inning, Drysdale got Jim Wynn and Ron Brand on grounders. The Astros' number-eight hitter, shortstop Bob Lillis, reached first on an error by Wills. Houston manager Lum Harris sent in Rusty Staub to pinch-hit for Bruce. Staub doubled, and Lillis scored Houston's first run. Morgan was hit by a pitch. With runners on first and second, Maye's groundball struck Staub as he ran from second to third. By rule, Maye was credited with a single but Staub was called out to end the inning.

Mike Cuellar came in to pitch the eighth for Houston. Cuellar was making his fourth appearance since coming over in a midseason swap with St. Louis. Cuellar was a year away from a breakout season and went on to a brilliant career in Baltimore, but at this point he was a 28-year-old journeyman with limited major-league experience and limited success.

Gilliam greeted Cuellar with a single and Davis sacrificed him to second. Gilliam advanced to third as Fairly grounded out to second base, then Roseboro grounded out to shortstop, stranding Gilliam. Drysdale started the eighth facing the Astros' 3-4-5 hitters. Gentile started the inning with a single and was forced at second on a grounder by Bond. Aspromonte flied out to right. Jim Wynn doubled to put runners and second and third. Ron Brand, a light-hitting rookie catcher from North Hollywood, California, singled home Bond and Wynn to tie the game, then was caught trying to steal, ending the inning. Cuellar struck out Parker to start the ninth, then walked Johnson, who reached second when Cuellar threw wild on a pickoff attempt. John Kennedy struck out. Drysdale, a good hitter, batted and grounded out to short, stranding Johnson at second.

Drysdale started the ninth inning strong, getting Lillis to ground out to second and striking out Cuellar. Morgan brought some life to the Astros with a single and his second stolen base of the game.

Drysdale intentionally walked Maye, then walked Gentile to load the bases and bring Walt Bond to the plate. On a 1-and-2 count, Bond delivered his third hit of the game, a single past the diving third baseman Kennedy into left field, plating Morgan with the winning run.[3]

Cuellar earned his first win as an Astro with two scoreless innings. Although Drysdale cruised through six innings, he gave up seven hits from the seventh on and suffered his fifth loss in a row.

The Dodgers went on to win the 1965 World Series against the Minnesota Twins, while the Astros, in their first season in the Astrodome, finished ninth in the 10-team NL, 32 games behind Los Angeles.

SOURCES

In addition to the sources cited in the Notes, the author also consulted:

AstrosDaily.com (2000-2015). astrosdaily.com/history/1965/. Accessed October 17, 2015.

Thorn, John, Pete Palmer, et al. *Total Baseball: The Official Encyclopedia of Major League Baseball* (New York: Viking Press, 2004).

NOTES

1   Associated Press, "Funny Thing Happens to Dodgers on Their Way to the Astrodome," *Corpus Christi* (Texas) *Caller-Times*, July 2, 1965: 19.

2   David Skelton, "Bob Bruce," SABR Baseball Biography Project. sabr.org/bioproj/person/d899b359.

3   Karl O'Quinn, "Astros Whip Dodgers: Bond Is Hero, Like in Movies," *San Antonio Express*, July 3, 1965: 15.

Mays Clouts Number 500

*September 13, 1965: San Francisco Giants 5,
Houston Astros, 1, at the Astrodome*

By Gregory H. Wolf

"IT WAS A FASTBALL, AND I THOUGHT I hit it good," said Willie Mays after clouting a round-tripper against Houston in the inaugural season of the Astrodome to join the rarefied company of Babe Ruth (714), Jimmie Foxx (534), Ted Williams (521), and Mel Ott (511) as the newest member of the exclusive 500-home-run club.[1] There was "never the slightest question where the ball was going" once it rocketed off Mays' bat, wrote Clark Nealon of the *Houston Post*.[2]

The Say Hey Kid was not slowing down at the age of 34. After walloping 47 home runs in 1964 to capture to his second NL home-run crown in three years and the third of his career, Mays got off to a hot start in 1965, belting 17 homers and driving in 35 runs in his first 37 games. Described by Giants beat writer Jack McDonald as a "scourge at the plate," Mays was coming off one of the most productive stretches of his storied career.[3] In August he set an NL record with 17 home runs in a month (one more than Ralph Kiner in September 1949, and since broken by Sammy Sosa's 20 in 1998); knocked in 29 runs in 31 games; batted .363; and was named unanimously the league's Player of the Month.

The Giants were hitting on all cylinders as they arrived in Houston to play a four-game set with the Astros to start a 10-game road swing. Under first-year skipper Herman Franks, the Giants (83-59) had won their previous 10 games to tie the 1962 team for the longest winning streak since the franchise relocated from New York to the Bay City in 1958, and moved into first place, two games in front of the Los Angeles Dodgers. Houston changed its name from the Colt .45s to the Astros in 1965 to inaugurate a new era in professional sports in the first domed stadium, the Astrodome. Manager Lum Harris, who had taken over for the last 13 games of the previous season, had inherited an offensively challenged squad. The league's lowest-scoring team in 1964, Houston (61-83) was in ninth place at this point in '65 and seemed primed to equal the 96 losses the team suffered in each of its first three seasons since entering the league as an expansion club in 1962.

Getting the start for the Astros was Don Nottebart, a 29-year-old right-hander with a career record of 30-42 in parts of six seasons. The Massachusetts native had struggled thus far in '65, winning only four of 18 decisions. Toeing the rubber for the Giants was 27-year-old Dominican right-hander Juan Marichal, with a mark of 21-10 and a career record of 104-49 in parts of six seasons. Marichal had been involved in one of the ugliest scenes in baseball history three weeks earlier. While batting against Sandy Koufax in a game against archrival Los Angeles at Candlestick Park, Marichal clubbed Dodgers catcher John Roseboro with a bat in what Leonard Koppett of the *New York Times* called a "burst of uncontrollable temper."[4] Marichal drew a nine-day suspension from Commissioner William Eckert, and was making his fourth start since that horrific moment.

The crowd of 19,827, well off the season average of 26,561, showed up in the Astrodome on a Monday evening to catch a glimpse of history, whether they knew it or not. The Giants squandered a golden opportunity in first inning when Mays and Willie McCovey came up empty with one out and Dick Schofield on third. In the bottom of the frame, fan favorite Jimmy Wynn, affectionately known as the Toy Cannon because of his 5-foot-10, 160-pound muscular frame, belted a towering home run to give the Astros a 1-0 lead.

As Mays, with 499 career home runs, stepped to the plate to lead off the fourth inning, a smattering of applause gradually gave way to silence. The Alabama native took three straight balls and then dropped his bat after what appeared to be the fourth, and headed to first. But the home-plate umpire, veteran Augie Donatelli, called Mays back to the box on a delayed strike call. On Nottebart's next pitch Mays hit what Bob Stevens of the *San Francisco Chronicle* described as a "monstrous, 440-foot blast into the centerfield bleachers."[5] The clout "ate its way beneath the dome and into the stands so quickly," continued Stevens, that "Wynn in centerfield didn't have time to do any more than turn a shoulder." While the Astros' faithful gave the 12-time All-Star a standing ovation, his teammates mobbed him in the dugout.

Nottebart, perhaps shaken by surrendering Mays's historic homer, loaded the bases by issuing walks to McCovey and Len Gabrielson bookending a double by slugger Jim Ray Hart, who had burst on the scene by clouting 31 home runs as a rookie the previous season. Tom Haller hit an "infield roller" to first baseman Walt Bond for the first out, as Stretch McCovey scored and Hart and Gabrielson advanced.[6] The Astros played for a double play by intentionally walking light-hitting Hal Lanier to face Marichal. No slouch at the plate, Marichal singled to center to drive in Hart and end Nottebart's day. Schofield greeted reliever Dave Giusti with a long fly ball to Wynn to send Gabrielson across the plate and give the Giants a 4-1 lead.

In the top of the sixth, the Giants scored their fifth and final run. Haller hit a one-out single to center field and scored on Marichal's first career triple, deep in the right-center-field gap.

Marichal, noted Bob Stevens, was "not as sharp as normal" and seemed to be bothered by the softness around the mound after a college football game two days earlier.[7] The Astrodome crowd voiced their displeasure with Marichal by booing him throughout the game.

The Astros threatened in the middle innings, but came up empty each time. In the fourth Houston had men on first and third with two outs; and on

second and third with two outs in the fifth. The Astros' best scoring chance was in the sixth, when Bond and Rusty Staub occupied first and second via singles with one out, but Marichal squelched that opportunity as well. "Juan reached somewhere into the centerfield seats," wrote Stevens, "kicked his leg toward the top of the dome" and retired Ron Brand and Eddie Kasko on three pitches to get out of the jam.[8]

While Giusti and Ron Taylor retired all nine Giants batters they faced in the final three frames, Marichal, the "Dominican Dandy," also faced the minimum. With his 118th pitch of the game, he induced Kasko to pop up meekly to keystone sacker Lanier to complete his league-leading 24th game in 2 hours and 10 minutes.

Even on a day without his best stuff, Marichal was superb, yielding only eight hits and no walks while striking out three to tie Sandy Koufax with his 22nd victory of the year. He lowered his ERA to 1.79, well in front of Koufax's 2.14. Nottebart, collared with his 15th loss of the season, was charged with four runs (all earned) and surrendered five of the Giants' eight hits.

Notwithstanding Marichal's workmanlike effort, the man of the hour was Willie Mays, who became the youngest slugger in NL history to reach the 500-home-run plateau. Though Mays was often considered flamboyant on the field, he was soft-spoken and reserved off it. Jack Gallagher of the *Houston Post* described Mays reverently as "simplicity itself ... a plain man, not given to flowery statement."[9] Mays was not one to toot his own horn or call attention to his statistical accomplishments. "I wasn't even looking to get 500 this year, to tell the truth," said Mays, whose 52 homers easily led the NL (and the big leagues), followed by teammate McCovey's 39.[10] Mays downplayed any notion that he'd be able to break the Sultan of Swat's record for homers. "I'll have to average 40 a year to catch up with that guy," he said. "I don't think I can do it."[11]

Mays got some good ribbing from 44-year-old teammate Warren Spahn, the longtime Boston/ Milwaukee Braves hurler whom the Giants had signed on July 19 after his release from the New York

Mets. "I saw your first one," said Spahn, in his last of 21 seasons, "and now your 500th. You're a wonder."[12] Indeed, on May 28, 1952, Mays collected his first hit off Spahn, a home run in his fourth big-league game, in the Giants' 4-1 loss to the Boston Braves at the Polo Grounds in New York.

The Giants won 10 of their final 18 games but finished runner-up to the streaking Dodgers, who went 15-3 down the stretch to capture their second pennant in three years. Mays continued his torrid hitting. In addition to his league-leading home-run totals, he also paced the majors in on-base percentage (.398) and slugging percentage (.645) and was named the NL MVP for the second time.

SOURCES

In addition to the sources cited in the Notes, the author also accessed Retrosheet.org, Baseball-Reference.com, the SABR Minor Leagues Database, accessed online at Baseball-Reference.com, SABR.org, and *The Sporting News* archive via Paper of Record.

NOTES

1   Jack Gallagher, "Mays Makes It Simple. Don Threw, Willie Hit," *Houston Post*, September 14, 1965: Section 4, 2.

2   Clark Nealon, "Mays Lashes 500th Homer. Willie, Juan Win 11th in a Row," *Houston Post*, September 14, 1965: Section 4, 1.

3   *The Sporting News*, September 25, 1965: 2.

4   Leonard Koppett, "Marichal Clubs Roseboro With a Bat," *New York Times*, August 22, 1966. nytimes.com/packages/html/sports/ year_in_sports/08.22.html.

5   Bob Stevens, "Giants Win; Mays Hits 500th," *San Francisco Chronicle*, September 14, 1965: 45.

6   Ibid.

7   Ibid.

8   Ibid.

9   Gallagher.

10 Ibid

11 Murray Chass (Associated Press), "Mays' 500th, Marichal's 22nd Boost Giants Lead," *Daily Telegram* (Eau Claire, Wisconsin), September 14, 1965: 13.

12 *The Sporting News*, September 25, 1965: 11.

Aspromonte's Walk-Off Slam Lights Up the Sky for Astros

August 26, 1966: Houston Astros 7, Chicago Cubs 4, at the Astrodome

By Thomas Rathkamp

YOU'VE HEARD IT BEFORE. A BATTER steps up to the plate in a pressure situation, humbly claims that his solitary goal is to get a bat on the ball, keep the inning alive, and hopefully give his team a chance to win. The prospect of something heroic is just gravy, perhaps even sheer luck. Just don't strike out or hit into a game-ending double play. Make contact and force the defense to make a play. Often forgotten is that the result of such a nail-biting drama might be dictated by the type of pitch and its location.

Apparently Astros third baseman Bob Aspromonte ignored such edicts and instead, cranked a game-winning grand slam off reliever Cal Koonce in the bottom of the ninth inning to give Houston a dramatic 7-4 victory. It was Aspromonte's sixth career grand slam and his second against Chicago in little more than two weeks.

In his last four games against the Cubs, Aspromonte had driven in 13 runs, 12 in the last three games. This latest slam inched Aspromonte closer to rare company. At the time, only six contemporary players had hit more than six grand slams in their career. The elite group consisted of an array of familiar names: Ernie Banks, Hank Aaron, Dick Stuart, Ken Boyer, Eddie Mathews, and Bill White.[1] Three of them– Banks, Aaron, and Mathews—became Hall of Famers.

"In that case, you are just looking for a base hit to win the game," said Aspromonte after the game. "The most important thing is you're trying to prevent the double play. And you want to try to lift the ball to get a fly to score the tying run and keep from hitting into the double play." Koonce threw Aspromonte a slider, which apparently stayed up. "I knew I had hit that one," said Aspromonte. "I knew I had hit that (so and so) and it was going out."[2]

Born Robert Thomas Aspromonte in Brooklyn, New York, in 1938, the 6-foot-2, 170-pounder signed with his hometown Brooklyn Dodgers in 1956 and had one major-league at-bat that season as an 18-year-old rookie. He worked his way back to the majors in 1960, after the team had moved to Los Angeles, and was then drafted by the Houston Colt 45s in the 1961 expansion draft—five years after his pro debut. Aspromonte would later become the last Brooklyn Dodger to retire from baseball (1971). His older brother, Ken Aspromonte, last appeared in the majors in 1963 after a seven-year career.

The victory left the Astros with a 58-70 record in what had become a disappointing season. First-year manager Grady Hatton had replaced Lum Harris, who had compiled a dismal 70-105 record over less than two seasons. Hatton would suffer Harris's fate two years later, relinquishing the reigns to Harry "The Hat" Walker in 1968. In 1966 outfielder Jimmy Wynn was lost for the season on August 1 when he crashed into the wall at Connie Mack Stadium in Philadelphia. Wynn led the Astros with 18 homers despite missing the final two months of the season.

Controlling most of the game from the mound was the Cubs' rookie starter, Ken Holtzman. The young left-hander handcuffed the Astros batters for eight innings. He had retired the Houston lineup in order in the seventh and eighth innings. Before the ninth, the last batter to reach base against him was Rusty Staub, who led off the sixth with a double and was left on second. The *Houston Chronicle* declared that Holtzman seemed to be in control and it "looked as if the Cubs had it wrapped up."[3]

Houston starter Dave Giusti lasted just 4⅓ innings, handing out seven hits, two walks, and all four Cubs runs. Chicago struck first in the third inning on Billy Williams's two-run homer. The Astros countered with a run in the bottom of the inning when Chuck Harrison knocked in Joe Morgan from third with a single to left; the ever-patient Morgan had walked to lead off the inning. The Cubs knocked Giusti from the box in the fifth. Ron Santo smacked a one-out, two-run homer and after Ernie Banks followed with a single, Hatton yanked Giusti in favor of Carroll Sembera, who would pitch 2⅔ scoreless innings.

After the fifth the combatants traded zeroes for the next few innings, and the Cubs carried their 4-1 lead into the bottom of the ninth. Then the fireworks rocked the one-year-old Astrodome. John Bateman greeted Holtzman with a solo blast to lead off the ninth, the 16th of the season for the young catcher. Dave Nicholson followed with a single to left. After Ron Davis flied out, Ron Brand batted for reliever Turk Farrell, who had hurled two scoreless innings. Brand coaxed a walk off Holtzman, which sent Cubs manager Leo Durocher into a brief—albeit not uncharacteristic—tirade. Durocher yanked the phone off the wall in the dugout and tossed it onto the field in a fit of rage. Home-plate umpire Tony Venzon, opting to forgo a vociferous response to the Lip's antics, gathered the phone and returned it to the "scene of the crime." Astros owner Roy Hofheinz witnessed the temper tantrum and swiftly announced that Durocher would be billed for the replacement of the "dismembered" phone.[4]

Play resumed after Durocher replaced Holtzman with lefty Bob Hendley. Once again the prince of walks, Morgan, drew another, his third walk of the game. Before the game Morgan had expressed dismay over his recent hitting slump—he was batting just .246 since his return from the disabled list on August 5—but he played a critical role in this game.[5] With the bases loaded, Sonny Jackson, who set a rookie record in 1966 with 49 steals, beat out a chopper to

Bob Apromonte spent seven seasons in Houston, registering the franchise's first hit and first grand slam as a Colt .45. He later hit both the first Astros homer and first grand slam in Astrodome history. (Courtesy of Houston Astros Baseball Club).

shortstop Don Kessinger, plating Nicholson and cutting the deficit to two runs. Out of the dugout again came Durocher, who replaced Hendley with right-handed changeup artist Cal Koonce.[6] Next in the batter's box came Aspromonte.

Koonce, a master of changing speeds, apparently taught to him by his father,[7] elected to throw a slider, which Aspromonte parked into the left-field seats for the game-winner. Not a slugger, in 250 previous at-bats that season in the Astrodome, he had never reached the seats. The *Houston Chronicle* opined that "hopes certainly were high, but anyone who thought he was going to hit it into the stands must have been a romanticist."[8] Farrell (6-8) got the win and Hundley (4-4) took the loss. Aspromonte entered the game batting .257, not the numbers of a prolific slugger. (He ended the season at .252.) This day, though, belonged to the eight-year player.

The *Houston Post* quipped that, before Koonce entered the game, Durocher had batted .000 with his choice of relievers, and added, "Aspromonte saw to it that Lip's average didn't change."[9] To make matters worse, Houston got another walk-off win over the Cubs the next night, when Chuck Harrison's two-out single lifted the Astros to a 5-4 victory.

Durocher, in the first of eight seasons as Cubs manager, was saddled with a team that would finish last in the 10-team National League. The Astros didn't fare much better in 1966, finishing in eighth place, 23 games short of first but 13 games superior to the lowly Cubs.

NOTES

1 John Wilson, "Aspro Slams Cubbies," *Houston Chronicle*, August 27, 1966.

2 Ibid.

3 Ibid.

4 Joe Heling, "Astros Take Two From Cubs," *Houston Post*, August 27, 1966.

5 Wilson.

6 Rob Neyer and Bill James, *Neyer/James Guide to Pitchers* (New York: Fireside Books, 2004), 269-270.

7 Ibid.

8 Wilson.

9 Heling.

The "Toy Cannon" Blasts Three Shots in the Astrodome

June 15, 1967: Houston Astros 6, San Francisco Giants 2, at the Astrodome

By Gregory H. Wolf

JUNE 15, 1967, SEEMED LIKE AN UN-likely day for the Houston Astros' 25-year-old slugger Jimmy Wynn to make history. He wasn't feeling very well, and consequently took only two turns in the batting cage in the mammoth Astrodome. "I've been feeling tired for three or four days," he said.[1] While his teammates finished BP and concluded their warm-ups, Wynn retired to the clubhouse to rest.

Toeing the rubber for the Astros was one of the bright spots for club, Mike Cuellar, who had emerged the previous season with a 12-10 record and 2.22 ERA. The 30-year-old Cuban southpaw, en route to the first of his four All-Star selections, had won his last five starts, yielding just five earned runs in 44⅓ innings and striking out 45 to push his career record to 25-21 over parts of five seasons, including a 7-2 mark to this point in the season. His opponent was 28-year-old Bobby Bolin, a sturdy right-hander who had carved out ERAs of 2.76 and 2.89 the previous two seasons. San Francisco's ace, Juan Marichal, was scheduled to start, but he was a late scratch. Bolin had struggled thus far in 1967, posting a miserable 4.96 ERA and winning just three of eight decisions to drop his career record to 53-41 over parts of seven seasons.

The Astrodome was not necessarily the biggest field in baseball, but it might have been the most intimidating to batters who were playing indoors for the first time in their career. "Some hitters have complained that the fences are so far back you need a connecting flight to reach them," wrote Mickey Herskowitz of the *Houston Post*.[3] The outfield was symmetrical—340 feet down the foul lines, 375 in the power alleys, and 406 in center. Forbes Field

in Pittsburgh, for example, measured 457 feet at its deepest point in left-center, 406 in left field and 408 tapering to 375 in right field, but had a forgiving 300-foot right-field foul line. "There is no wind to push the ball," continued Herskowitz about the uniqueness of the Astrodome, "and it comes down to brute strength."[4] Only 57 homers (25 by the Astros) were hit in the inaugural season of the Astrodome in 1965; that number rose to 96 (48 by Houston) in 1966, and then dropped to 63 (31 by the Astros) in 1967.

After two scoreless innings, the Giants struck first when Hal Lanier led off the third with a single and scored on Jesus Alou's two-out single to left field; Alou advanced to second on the throw home. Jim Davenport followed with a single that moved Alou to third, but Cuellar escaped trouble by punching out Willie Mays.

After the Giants scored their first run, "things just went lousy," wrote the *San Francisco Chronicle's* Stevens. Jimmy Wynn led off the fourth with a monstrous, high-flying home run into the mezzanine section in left field to tie the game. The ball "took off like a Cape Kennedy launch," wrote John Wilson of the *Houston Chronicle*, paying homage to Houston's aeronautical and space history.[5] Wynn's size belied his power. Standing only about 5-feet-10 and weighing 160 pounds, Wynn was built like a boxer, and was affectionately nicknamed the Toy Cannon for his explosiveness. Mickey Herskowitz opined that Wynn "consists of entirely of coil springs and muscle."[6] Despite Wynn's claims of fatigue, he had been on a tear in his last 10 games, walloping four homers, driving in 13 runs, and scoring 10. Hot-hitting 23-year-old Rusty Staub, who had collected eight hits in his last

Jimmy Wynn was not a prototypical slugger, but his power contributed to his nickname, "The Toy Cannon." He was the first Astros player to belt three homers in one game. It happened at the Astrodome in 1967. (National Baseball Hall of Fame, Cooperstown, New York).

18 at-bats, and an aging Eddie Mathews both followed Wynn's blast with singles. When it seemed as if the Astros would break the game open, Norm Miller hit into a 4-6-3 double play, though Staub scored from third to give the Astros a 2-1 lead. Bob Aspromonte popped up to end the frame.

Tito Fuentes led off the Giants' fifth with a double and subsequently scored on Davenport's two-out single to tie the game. Mays followed with a hard-hit bouncer off the Astroturf to Wynn in center field. Blessed with a strong right arm, Wynn fired a rocket to third baseman Bob Aspromonte to nail Davenport, whose attempt to go from first to third Bob Stevens described as inexplicable.[7]

The score remained tied until Wynn stepped to the plate with one out in the bottom of the sixth. The five-year veteran connected with a Bolin fastball and sent the sphere flying into the pavilion in the left-field power alley to become the first Houston player to hit home runs in consecutive plate appearances.[8] Staub, who had thus far blistered opposition for a .341 average in 1967 and this season would earn the first of five consecutive and six career All-Star berths, followed with a double to send Bolin to the showers. Bolin pitched with "studied caution rather than in his old style of gay abandon," opined Bob Stevens.[9] Mike McCormick, normally a starter who eventually led the NL with 22 victories and won the Cy Young award in 1967, retired the next two batters to keep the Giants in the game.

The Astros were yet not finished battering Giants hurlers. A career .115-hitter, Cuellar helped his own cause by smacking a one-out single to center field off Ron Herbel in the seventh to drive in Aspromonte, giving the Astros a 4-2 lead.

When Wynn stepped to the plate to lead off the eighth inning, the crowd of 21,264 enjoying a Thursday evening of baseball in Houston's architectural wonder probably had one thing on their mind. Could Wynn do it again? Facing 39-year-old veteran lefty reliever Bill Henry, Wynn took a strike and then planned the unimaginable. "On the second strike, I was thinking about bunting, but the ball was inside," said Wynn after the game.[10] Discarding the idea of bunting, Wynn subsequently belted a line drive over the left-field fence for his third consecutive homer and 14th of the season. "I didn't think either of the last two would be home runs," said Wynn after the game. "I thought they'd be hits off the wall."[11] The Astros concluded their scoring when light-hitting catcher Ron Brand hit a two-out single to drive in Jim Landis and increase Houston's lead to 6-2.

Cuellar took the mound in the ninth and continued to frustrate Giants hitters with what Herskowitz called a "skitterish screwball."[12] He retired the side in order, including striking out Dick Dietz to register his 10th punchout. Cuellar's "outstanding job was somewhat overshadowed" by Wynn's feat, suggested John Wilson.[13]

As expected, reporters focused their attention on Wynn in the clubhouse after the game. "I'm hot now, I know it," he said confidently. "Hitters have their moments. My time is coming now."[14] But he also mentioned that he had trouble with left-handers (he batted just .216 with 10 homers against lefties compared to .270 and 27 against righties in 1967) and suggested that with Atlanta's Denny Lemaster scheduled to start against Houston the following day, things could sour quickly.

Mathews, Houston 35-year-old first baseman and once one of the most feared sluggers in baseball, paid perhaps the highest compliment to Wynn. "I saw Joe Adcock hit four in Ebbets Field and I hit three, but I'd say this overshadows either of those, coming in this big park."[15]

Wynn continued bashing the ball and finished the 1967 season with a career-high 37 home runs. After hitting 223 round-trippers (including two in one game on 14 occasions) in 11 campaigns with the Astros, Wynn was traded to the Los Angeles Dodgers in December 1973. In a renaissance season (32 homers and a career-best 108 RBIs) for the pennant winners in 1974, he hit three home runs against the San Diego Padres at San Diego Stadium on May 11.

SOURCES

In addition to the sources cited in the Notes, the author also accessed Retrosheet.org, Baseball-Reference.com, the SABR Minor Leagues Database, accessed online at Baseball-Reference.com, SABR.org, and *The Sporting News* archive via Paper of Record.

NOTES

1   John Wilson, "Wynn's 3 Homers Jar Giants, 6-2," *Houston Chronicle*, June 16, 1962: section 8, 1.

2   Bob Stevens, "Wynn 3 HRs Shell Giants, 6-2," *San Francisco Chronicle*, June 16, 1967: 51.

3   Mickey Herskowitz, "A Jim Dandy: Wynn's 3 Homers Stun Giants," *Houston Post*, June 16, 1967: section 4, 1.

4   Herskowitz.

5   Wilson.

6   Herskowitz.

7   Stevens.

8   Herskowitz.

9   Stevens.

10 Joe Heiling, "Ed Changes Tune to Fit Jim's Beat," *Houston Post*, June 16, 1967: section 4, 7.

11 Wilson.

12 Herskowitz.

13 Wilson.

14 Wilson.

15 Heiling.

Unhittable: Don Wilson Tosses First No-No in Astrodome History

June 18, 1967: Houston Astros 2, Atlanta Braves 0, at the Astrodome

By Gregory H. Wolf

"I WAS AMAZED BY THE GAME HE threw," gushed Houston Astros second-year skipper Grady Hatton after rookie Don Wilson fanned 15 Atlanta Braves and tossed the first no-hitter in the history of the Astrodome.[1] "I never caught anyone who threw harder," Wilson's batterymate, Dave Adlesh, said excitely. "He wasn't afraid to challenge the hitters."[2] The Braves' pitching coach, Whitlow Wyatt, in his 40th year of professional baseball, seemed in awe in of the 22-year-old hurler: "[H]e has the easiest, smoothest motion to throw that hard as anybody I have ever seen."[3] Houston beat writers were just as excited as Astros fans about the commanding performance. Joe Heiling of the *Houston Post* described it as "champagne-popping, exhilarating excitement,"[4] while Wells Twombly of the *Houston Chronicle* opined that "few rookies have been so brilliant."[5]

The Louisiana-born and California-raised Wilson was the Astros' top pitching prospect entering the 1967 season. In the previous two campaigns in the minors, Wilson had put up gaudy numbers; first in the Class A Florida State League (1.44 ERA in 181 innings) and then in 1966 with Amarillo in the Double-A Texas League, where he posted an 18-6 record and a 2.21 ERA, and struck out more than a batter an inning. Wilson had experienced some growing pains thus far in '67, such as surrendering five hits and four runs without registering an out in his second start of the season; however, he had flashed the brilliance that made the Astros' brass hold their breath. In his previous start, on June 14, he punched out 13 San Francisco Giants while scattering eight hits and surrendering just one earned run in a complete-game

7-4 victory. Wilson tossed 155 pitches in that contest, causing Hatton to doubt whether he should start the youngster on three days' rest on June 18. With his club in ninth place (25-38), 14½ games behind the Cincinnati Reds, Grady decided to go for broke and monitor the rookie closely.

A Father's Day crowd of 19,199 was on hand in the Astrodome to see Houston take on the sixth-place Braves (31-29) in the fourth and final contest of a weekend series. After dropping the first two games, Houston picked up a win when graybeard Eddie Mathews belted a walk-off home run to lead off the ninth for an exciting 4-3 victory in the second game of a twin bill.

Wilson had some concerns facing for the first time the heavy-hitting but free-swinging Braves, who led the NL in home runs in 1967. "I had intended to throw a lot of changes," he said. "But I had a real good fastball in the first inning and decided to stick with it."[6] The 6-foot-2, 200-pound right-hander mowed down the first 14 batters he faced, seven of them by punchout.

Facing the Astros was 28-year-old right-hander Phil Niekro, making just his third career start. A reliever since he debuted with the Milwaukee Braves in 1964, the knuckleballer had baffled opponents in 24 relief appearances in '67 (1.73 ERA) before tossing a masterful two-hit shutout five days earlier against Philadelphia. The Astros tagged Niekro for two hits in the first, but he otherwise matched zeros with Wilson in the first three innings to extend his scoreless streak to 14⅔ innings.

Houston ended that streak in the fourth when Sonny Jackson led off with a single and scored on

Jimmy Wynn's double down the right-field line. It was the Toy Cannon's league-leading 48th RBI of the season. Wynn moved to third on Rusty Staub's single and scored Houston's second and final run when Mathews grounded to second, forcing the slow-footed Staub.

Wilson's perfect game ended with a walk to Denis Menke with two outs in the fifth, but the tension of a no-hitter mounted. The defensive gem of the game occurred with two outs in the sixth when third baseman Bob Aspromonte dived to his left to grab Felipe Alou's screamer. Described by Joe Heiling as "sprawled out on his stomach like a camper who has tripped on a log," Aspromonte threw a perfect strike from his knees to Mathews to end the inning.[7] "It's a do-or-die play," said Hatton after the game. "Bobby went right after it full blast. The last month Aspro has been one of the best players in the league."[8]

Wilson seemed flustered in the seventh when he issued a one-out walk to Hank Aaron on a 3-and-2 count, prompting the first and only mound visit by his skipper. Moments earlier, Adlesh had failed to hold on to a third-strike foul tip. "I just went out there to tell him to slow down," said Hatton. "Never mind Hank. Keep your concentration."[9] Wilson subsequently fanned Mack Jones and retired Mike de la Hoz on a fly to center.

"I was petrified," admitted Wilson bluntly after he game. "I knew I had it. In the eighth inning I checked to see when Aaron would come up. ... I didn't want to face him again."[10] But when Wilson issued a leadoff walk to Menke in the eighth, he was assured of facing Hammerin' Hank one more time. With the tying run at the plate, Wilson fanned the next three batters, all pinch-hitters, to set up a meeting with history.

"I could hear the fans when I walked out for the ninth," said Wilson.[11] Tuning out the screaming crowd, Wilson fired a fastball to Alou, who hit a high pop fly above the catcher. According to the *Chronicle's* John Wilson, Adlesh turned the wrong way and lost the ball against the backdrop of the Astrodome's ceiling. Aspromonte rushed in from third and made a spectacular catch "almost behind home plate" for

the first out.[12] After Wilson fanned Tito Francona, only Aaron stood between him and a no-hitter. "I got behind, then I threw my fastball," explained Wilson after the game. "It was 3-and-2 and I decided he's going to break up the no-hitter or I'm going to get him out."[13] Aaron fouled off a pitch and then took a mighty swing at the next offering and missed. Wilson "finished in a blaze glory," wrote Joe Heiling, striking out five of the last six batters he faced to complete the no-hitter in 2 hours 35 minutes as his teammates mobbed him on the mound. It was the first no-hitter in the National League since Sandy Koufax tossed his fourth and final no-hitter on September 9, 1965, and the first one by an NL rookie since Chicago's Sam Jones blanked Pittsburgh on May 12, 1955.

"He threw the last one by me," said Aaron, complimenting the rookie. "It's young guys like this that make me want to retire."[14] Hatton, so nervous in the ninth inning that he hid in the dugout puffing on a cigarette, was just as impressed by the last pitch:

DON WILSON   PITCHER   HOUSTON ASTROS

Hard-throwing Don Wilson went 104–92 in parts of nine seasons (1966–1974), all with the Astros, and tossed two no-hitters. He died tragically at the age of 29 in 1975. (Courtesy of Houston Astros Baseball Club).

"That's as hard as any pitch he threw the whole game."[15]

Wilson improved his record to 4-3 and lowered his ERA to 3.12 in 80⅔ innings. Niekro gave up eight hits in seven innings and was collared with the tough-luck loss. Braves catcher Bob Uecker provided some comic relief to the situation: "I'm having to catch Niekro and his knuckleball and hit against Wilson."[16] Uecker dropped 13 knucklers, including two on two-strike counts, and fanned once before being lifted for pinch-hitter Rico Carty in the eighth.

The mood in the Astros' clubhouse after the game was jubilant, as expected. Majority owner Roy Hofheinz, a fixture at the Astros' home games, missed the historic contest preparing for a trip; however, the former mayor of Houston, affectionately known as the Judge, had a case of champagne delivered to the players. The *Chronicle* and *Post* reported that the ecstatic Hofheinz ripped up Wilson's contract and gave him a new one with a $1,000 salary increase.

Just three days after tossing 155 pitches, Wilson fired 143 pitches. According to the *Houston Chronicle*, he threw 110 fastballs, 31 sliders, and only two off-speed pitches—one changeup and one curve. "The last three innings were almost all fastballs," said Adlesh, who caught Wilson for the first time.[17]

Wilson's no-hitter was the first in the Astrodome and the third in the franchise's history. In an odd twist, neither of the first two no-hitters resulted in a no-hit, no-run game. Both occurred in Houston when the club was called the Colt .45s and played their home games in Colt Stadium. Don Nottebart tossed a no-hitter on May 17, 1963, yet surrendered a run to Philadelphia. Ken Johnson lost his no-hitter, 1-0, to Cincinnati on April 23, 1964.

"I've never had a better fastball," said an ebullient Wilson after his no-hitter.[18] His 15 punchouts tied the team record set by Mike Cuellar a year earlier; and his 28 strikeouts in two consecutive starts were a new team record. On July 14, 1968, Wilson set a Houston record by striking out 18 against Cincinnati at Crosley Field; the following season, he tossed his second no-hitter, fanning 13 Reds at the same field, on May 1.

SOURCES

In addition to the sources cited in the Notes, the author also accessed Retrosheet.org, Baseball-Reference.com, the SABR Minor Leagues Database, accessed online at Baseball-Reference.com, SABR.org, and *The Sporting News* archive via Paper of Record.

NOTES

1 John Wilson, "Astros' Wilson Fans 15, No Hits Braves," *Houston Chronicle*, June 19, 1967: Section 2, page 1.

2 Wayne Minshew, "Don 'Changed' to Fastball," *Atlanta Constitution*, June 19, 1967: 16.

3 Ibid.

4 Joe Heiling, "Wilson Admits He Was 'Petrified,'" *Houston Post*, June 19, 1967: Section 4, page 1.

5 Wells Twombly, "Day of Greatness," *Houston Chronicle*, June 19, 1967: Section 2, page 4.

6 Minshew.

7 Joe Heiling, "Wilson Fans 15 Braves in 2-0 No-Hit Classic," *Houston Post*, June 19, 1967: 1.

8 Joe Heiling, "Wilson Admits He Was 'Petrified.'"

9 Ibid.

10 Ibid.

11 Wilson.

12 Ibid.

13 Joe Heiling, "Wilson Admits He Was 'Petrified.'"

14 Wilson.

15 Joe Heiling," Wilson Admits He Was 'Petrified.'"

16 Minshew.

17 Joe Heiling, "Wilson Admits He Was 'Petrified.'"

18 Wilson.

"Wynning" Reaction for the Winning Run

July 2, 1967: Houston Astros 5,
Los Angeles Dodgers 4, at the Astrodome

By John Bauer

WHEN THE HOUSTON ASTROS hosted the Los Angeles Dodgers for a midseason series in July 1967, struggle and disappointment were themes applicable to both clubs. For the 28-47 Astros, their 10th-place standing represented an all-too-familiar spot. *The Sporting News* cited relief pitching that failed to materialize, bad infield defense, and overall poor team play as the culprits for the Astros' low standing, noting that "[t]he Astros in the field often have worked at cross purposes and, while batting, seldom have players been able to coordinate their efforts."[1] There appeared to be glimmers of hope, however. "In winning most of its games, Houston has looked like a sharp club. ... But it has been quite inconsistent in coming up with these sharp performances."[2]

The Dodgers occupied an unusual place in the NL standings. After winning pennants in 1965 and 1966, Los Angeles resided in eighth place with a record of 33-41. The club struggled with injuries as well as the retirement of Sandy Koufax. Manager Walter Alston recognized the Dodgers' predicament but refused to concede anything. "We haven't given up hope yet, but we're getting farther behind," he said. "I knew before the season started that we were going to miss Koufax, but I thought we would score more runs than we have."[3]

Despite their lowly positions, the Astros and Dodgers had provided some measure of excitement the previous evening. With a season-high crowd exceeding 33,000, the Astros broke a 2-2 deadlock in the eighth inning with Ron Brand's tiebreaking single and a double steal that scored another run for a 4-2 win. In this day's game, Astros skipper Grady Hatton did not manage because of his brother-in-law's death, leaving coach Jim Busby in charge for the sixth time this season.[4]

Wade Blasingame, who joined the Astros from Atlanta in a June 15 trade, was making his second start for Houston. Two years removed from a 16-win season during the Braves' final campaign in Milwaukee, the 23-year-old Blasingame was working his way into the rotation.[5] The Dodgers countered with their own 23-year-old. After pitching a total of 19 major-league innings during the prior three seasons, Bill Singer had featured in the Dodgers' rotation throughout 1967.

Neither pitcher allowed a run during a relatively quiet first inning. Blasingame allowed a one-out single to Nate Oliver, but Willie Davis's double-play grounder to second baseman Joe Morgan ended the Dodgers' half. Morgan walked with one out in the bottom half, but was picked off. The inning ended with Jim Wynn's popout to Dodgers second baseman Oliver in foul territory.

The Dodgers opened the scoring in the second as the first five batters reached base against Blasingame. Jim Lefebvre walked to open the inning, and Al Ferrara and Ron Fairly singled to left and right, respectively, to load the bases. Jeff Torborg's bloop single to right field scored Lefebvre and left the bases loaded for Dick Schofield. The light-hitting shortstop singled to center field, driving in Ferrara and Fairly for a 3-0 Dodgers lead. With Singer at the plate, the Astros recorded the first out when Torborg was caught attempting to steal third base. Singer grounded back to Blasingame, Wes Parker walked, and Oliver flied out to right fielder Rusty Staub to close the Dodgers' second.

Schofield followed up his offensive success with a defensive mistake at the start the Astros' second.

Staub reached first on Schofield's error. Eddie Mathews singled to right field to give the Astros two on with no outs. It came to naught, however, as Bob Aspromonte, Ron Davis, and Ron Brand went down in order to end the second inning. The Dodgers and Astros both managed two-out singles in the third inning, but neither team scored.

Los Angeles padded its lead in the top of the fourth. Torborg led off with a double to left. Schofield followed with a single to left, plating Torborg, to make the score, 4-0. The RBI was Schofield's third of the game—he would drive in only 15 all season. Blasingame avoided further damage in the inning, and then escaped the fifth without allowing runs despite Lefebvre and Ferrara reaching base. Although Blasingame's final pitching line showed 12 baserunners and four earned runs allowed in five innings, the Astros pitcher "showed enough to sustain hopes that he will be a definite asset to the club if sufficient work will get [him] back into the rhythm [from two years ago]."[6]

Houston began chipping away at the Dodgers' lead in the bottom of the fifth. Singer walked Brand and struck out pinch-hitter Sonny Jackson, then back-to-back singles to right field by Julio Gotay and Morgan pushed Brand across. Later in the inning, Staub's single to center field scored Gotay, cutting the deficit to 4-2. For the sixth inning, Busby gave the ball to Barry Latman, who sent down Schofield, Singer, and Parker in order.

After Aspromonte led off the Astros' sixth with an infield hit, Alston brought in Bob Miller to replace Singer. Ron Davis singled to left, moving Aspromonte to second. Brand then "caught the Dodgers napping"[7] with a bunt single to load the bases. Pinch-hitter Jackie Brandt struck out; however, Gotay doubled down the right-field line with one out, scoring Aspromonte and Davis to tie the game. Alston called on Jim Brewer to face Morgan with Brand on third and Gotay on second. The confrontation ended with Morgan walking to load the bases. Wynn, who entered the game as the National League RBI leader at 56 after hitting 11 home runs and 29 RBIs during June,[8] hit a short fly to Fairly in right.

Busby, coaching at third, sent Brand after the catch, gambling that Fairly's throw would be off target.[9] It wasn't. Torborg tagged Brand at home to end the inning, but the Astros had tied the game, 4-4.

Carroll Sembera took the mound for Houston in the seventh, and set down Los Angeles in order. Brewer returned to pitch for the Dodgers. After Staub popped out to Parker, Mathews doubled to center field. With one out, Brewer intentionally walked Aspromonte to set up a possible force play. The Dodgers got what they were looking for when Ron Davis hit a double-play grounder to Schofield to end the seventh.

After a scoreless eighth, Sembera returned for the top of the ninth. Pinch-hitter Len Gabrielson singled to open the inning, but Sembera retired three straight Dodgers to complete his first three-inning stint of the season.[10] Dodger Phil Regan replaced Brewer on the mound in the bottom of the ninth, and surrendered a one-out double to Wynn. Regan gave a pass to Staub to set up a possible double play, a strategy that had worked in the seventh, but had limited effect in the ninth. Mathews grounded to Parker, who threw to Schofield to force Staub at second base. With two out and runners on first and third, Los Angeles intentionally walked Aspromonte for the second time in the game.

While Ron Davis was waiting in the on-deck circle, Wynn, at third, noted the position of the Dodgers infield. He signaled to Davis that the infield was well back, trying to keep a groundball from rolling through the carpeted infield.[11] Wynn said later, "When I saw where they were playing, I knew they couldn't get either one of us if Ronnie got the bunt down perfectly."[12] Davis had experienced trouble bunting during the series. He had popped up in the first game trying to sacrifice, and twice in the second game had forced out the lead runner while trying to get down a sacrifice bunt.[13] Despite those previous troubles, Davis bunted down the third-base line. "Actually the pitch was better than I expected, a little up and right over the plate," he said after the game.[14] Regan sprinted to the ball and flipped it toward Roseboro, but the ball was well out of the catcher's reach. Wynn scored to complete the comeback, sending 26,296 fans home happy after the 5-4 win.

In its review of the Astros' 1967 season, *The Sporting News* noted two themes cited by manager Hatton for the team's disappointing season: below-average defense and the lack of quality pitching depth.[15] On the positive side, Wynn and Staub developed into major-league stars, playing in their first All-Star Games and becoming the first Astros to challenge for league-leading offensive honors. Wynn finished among the top five in the NL in several offensive categories, including home runs, RBIs, runs scored, and extra-base hits. Staub became the first Astros regular to finish a season over .300, and his .333 average was good enough for fifth in the NL.[16]

NOTES

1 John Wilson, "Astros Still Await Midseason Blastoff," *The Sporting News*, July 15, 1967: 26.

2 Ibid.

3 Dick Peebles, "Voice of the Peebles, Old Road for Alston," *Houston Chronicle*, July 3, 1967: 1 (sports).

4 *Houston Chronicle*, July 2, 1967: 5 (sports).

5 John Wilson, "Astros Bounce Dodgers, 5-4," *Houston Chronicle*, July 3, 1967: 3 (sports).

6 Ibid.

7 Ibid.

8 "Astronotes," *Houston Chronicle*, July 2, 1967, 5 (sports); *Houston Chronicle*, July 3, 1967: 3 (sports).

9 John Wilson, "Astros Bounce Dodgers, 5-4," *Houston Chronicle*, July 3, 1967: 3 (sports).

10 Ibid.

11 Ibid.

12 Ibid.

13 Ibid.

14 Ibid.

15 *The Sporting News Official Baseball Guide*—1968, 118.

16 *The Sporting News Official Baseball Guide*—1968: 121.

Tempers Flare: Cuellar Overcomes Bench Jockeying to Toss Complete-Game Two-Hitter and Score Winning Run in the 11th

July 24, 1967: Houston Astros 2, Philadelphia Phillies 1 (11 innings), at the Astrodome

By Gregory H. Wolf

IT WAS A RECIPE FOR DISASTER. Houston's Mike Cuellar, a native of Cuba, was a fiery, intensely competitive pitcher. The Phillies skipper, Gene Mauch, was known for his abrasive and combative personality. Factor in a tight game in the ninth inning, underachieving teams needing to prove something, and a good dose of bench jockeying, and the situation was on the verge of exploding. "Twice," wrote John Wilson of the *Houston Chronicle*, Cuellar "came within a few feet of getting into a fistfight with … Gene Mauch."[1] "I got mad," said Cuellar after the game. "I wanted to hit him in the mouth."[2] Notwithstanding the flaring tempers, Cuellar prevailed in an 11-inning complete game described by *Houston Post* beat man Clark Nealon as "tremendous."[3]

Skipper Grady Hatton's Astros were reeling when they arrived at the Astrodome to begin an 11-game homestand against Philadelphia. Not only were they in the NL basement, at 38-58 they owned the worst record in baseball. Houston had suffered three humiliating losses in four games to the Pittsburgh Pirates (scoring just five runs while yielding 39 in those defeats) to conclude a miserable 13-game road trip with just five wins. Mauch's Phillies had finished in fourth place in 1966 but had played lackluster ball thus far in 1967 despite increased expectations. With his club in seventh place (45-46), nine games behind the league-leading St. Louis Cardinals, the Phillies' feisty manager was on edge.

Hatton turned to his ace, southpaw Mike Cuellar, to stabilize the team. A screwball specialist who originally signed with the Cincinnati Reds as a 20-year-old in 1957, Cuellar bounced around Triple-A ball from 1957 to 1963, and failed to stick in short stints with the Reds (1959) and St. Louis Cardinals (1964) before finding a home with the Astros, who acquired him at the trading deadline in 1965. After a breakout season (12-10, 2.22 ERA) in 1966, Cuellar was named to his first of four All-Star teams in 1967. He entered this game with a 9-6 record (3.07 ERA), but had won only once since June 15. Mauch called on steady 36-year-old right-hander Larry Jackson (7-9, 3.51 ERA), who had averaged 16 wins and 249 innings per season as one of the NL's most consistent workhorses from 1957 to 1966.

While the temperature exceeded 90 degrees outside, a crowd of 20,275 enjoyed the climate-controlled 73-degree temperature in the Astrodome as they witnessed a 1960s-style pitching duel on Monday night, July 24, 1967. Cuellar mowed down the first 14 batters he faced. At one point he struck out five straight batters, and he racked up eight punchouts by the end of the fifth inning. Cookie Rojas, a former teammate of Cuellar's and a fellow Cuban national, ended the no-hitter with a hard-hit ball to shortstop Julio Gotay. The ball took a bad hop, hit Gotay's shoulder, and caromed into left field, enabling Rojas to scamper to second for a double. The partisan crowd let out a chorus of boos when the play was ruled a hit. Not to be outdone, Jackson retired 15 consecutive batters after yielding a leadoff single to Rusty Staub in the second inning.

The Phillies mounted a threat when Gotay fumbled Bobby Wine's grounder to lead off the sixth. Wine moved to second on Jackson's sacrifice, and to third on Bill White's grounder, but Cuellar retired Tony Taylor on a weak grounder back to the mound for the third out. In the seventh inning Dick Allen drew a leadoff walk, but was left stranded at second.

Poor defense contributed to the drama in the bottom of the seventh when speedy Joe Morgan beat out what Allen Lewis of the *Philadelphia Inquirer* called a "medium-speed grounder."[4] Wynn followed with a sure double-play grounder to third base, but Allen's wild throw pulled second baseman Tony Taylor off the bag. Taylor's throw to White at first was too late to nab Wynn, and both runners were safe. Staub hit what should have been another double play, but after shortstop Wine tagged second to force Wynn, he threw a bounder to White, pulling him off the bag. The Astros finally scored the game's first run when Eddie Mathews launched a deep fly to left field to drive in Morgan. Jackson, seemingly tiring, yielded a double to Norm Miller, but Staub, a notoriously slow runner, held up at third. The Astros missed a golden opportunity to tack on more runs when Jackie Brandt grounded to short to end the frame.

Mauch's heckling and bench-jockeying had intensified as the game progressed. By the ninth inning, Cuellar had had enough. While facing leadoff hitter Bill White, Cuellar became involved in a heated exchange with Mauch when he suddenly left the mound to confront his tormentor, who swiftly popped out of the dugout. Both parties were quickly restrained as the benches cleared. After order was restored, Cuellar fanned White. The heckling and bench-jockeying did not end, however. Cuellar walked Taylor, who moved to second on Allen's grounder. Don Lock hit what appeared to be a routine hopper to third base, but Mathews' throw to first was low and in the dirt, eluding first baseman Brandt and permitting Taylor to score and tie the game.

Mike Cuellar gained notice for his performance with the Astros in 1966. He struck out 16 batters in one game against St. Louis, and his 2.22 ERA that season was second only to that of Sandy Koufax. In 1967 Cuellar won 16 games, and was named to the NL All-Star squad. (Courtesy of Houston Astros Baseball Club).

When Cuellar retired Gene Oliver on a popup to end the inning, fireworks went off again, as Cuellar vaulted toward Mauch and the Phillies dugout. Once again Mauch was restrained by Mathews (who knew a lot about brawls from his days as the enforcer with the Milwaukee Braves), while several teammates, as well as Cuellar's friend Rojas, intercepted the hurler as benches emptied. Cooler heads ultimately prevailed to avert a fight; however, time was called so that the grounds crew could clean the infield, which had been littered with paper thrown by fans. The game went into extra innings when Philadelphia reliever Turk Farrell pitched his second of three consecutive scoreless innings.

Seemingly unfazed by the ninth-inning brouhaha, Cuellar tossed a 1-2-3 10th. He was aided by Gotay's breathtaking catch of Gary Sutherland's pop fly down the left-field line. Clark Nelson described how Gotay and left fielder Norm Miller "flattened" each other in a violent collision, but both stayed in the game.[5] Cuellar began the 11th inning by whiffing pinch-hitter Chuck Hiller before yielding just his second hit of the game, a single to White. The inning ended innocuously when Taylor popped out and Allen flied out to center (just the second outfield putout of the contest for Houston).

Cuellar helped his own cause in the bottom of the inning by drawing a one-out walk on a 3-and-2 count off reliever Dick Hall, who had yielded only one non-intentional walk in 56⅔ innings thus far in the season. After Gotay's sacrifice, Bobby Wine fumbled Morgan's routine grounder to short. With runners on the corners, Jimmy Wynn, who was leading the majors with 75 RBIs, lined a single to center. ("It was a high slider," said Wynn).[6] Cuellar easily scampered home to give the Astros a hard-fought 2-1 victory in 2 hours and 38 minutes.

It was, according to *Houston Chronicle* reporter John Wilson, a "brilliant" performance. Cuellar went the distance, yielding just one unearned run and striking out 12, in addition to scoring the winning run.[7] It marked the first of 13 times in his career that Cuellar pitched at least 10 innings in a game, and was one of five times he fanned at least 10 batters in 1967. (He accomplished the feat 20 times in his career.)

Most of the press, however, focused on the confrontation between Cuellar and Mauch in the ninth inning. "That is what Mauch was trying to do, get under Mike's skin," said an irritated Mathews after the game. "He went a little too far, some of the language he was using on Mike."[8] Few players (or fans for that matter) wanted to tangle with Mathews, who still commanded respect at the tail end of his career. Cuellar told reporters that it was not one thing that Mauch said, but rather the cumulative effect of the incessant harassing that set him off. "Let me do my job," said Cuellar exasperatedly.[9] "I didn't call him anything he didn't call me," said Mauch somewhat childishly.[10]

While the players were cooling off in the clubhouse, a select group of fans were dashing wildly around the infield in a mad scramble to collect cash in a bank-night promotion. Quipped Clark Nealon, "The biggest oversight was that Cuellar didn't participate."[11]

The beleaguered Astros, whose manager was on the hot seat, seemed energized by the victory and the confrontation. "The Astros clubhouse seemed to reflect more pride and enthusiasm than it had in many days," opined John Wilson. Houston went on to win nine of the 11 games on the homestand before losing all 10 games on its subsequent road trip.

SOURCES

In addition to the sources cited in the Notes, the author also accessed Retrosheet.org, Baseball-Reference.com, the SABR Minor Leagues Database, accessed online at Baseball-Reference.com, SABR.org, and *The Sporting News* archive via Paper of Record.

NOTES

1   John Wilson, "Cuellar Tops Phillies in Night of Almosts," *Houston Chronicle*, June 25, 1967: section 2, 1.

2   Ibid.

3   Clark Nealon, "Astros Subdue Phils in 11, 2-1," *Houston Post*, July 25, 1967: section 4, 1.

4   Allen Lewis, "Cuellar's 2-Hitter Holds Phils Until Astros Win in 11th," *Philadelphia Inquirer*, July 25, 1957: 28.

5   Nealon.

6   Wilson.

7   Ibid.

8   Wilson.

9   Ibid.

10   Ibid.

11   Nealon.

Cuellar Outduels Bunning

September 27, 1967: Houston Astros 1,
Philadelphia Phillies 0, at the Astrodome

By Norm King

WHILE FANS AT BASEBALL GAMES 100 years from now watch as their starting pitcher is removed after reaching his pitch limit of 25, an old-timer will regale them with stories he heard at his pappy's knee about pitchers who actually pitched nine innings in a single game, and not just in their entire Cy Young Award-winning season. The old-timer may also talk about how sometimes, back before a surcharge was electronically added to fans' credit cards if games went to extra innings—whether they were at the game or not—pitchers would stay on the hill until a team won.

Once the gasps of incredulity dies down, the old-timer may tell them about Harvey Haddix pitching 12 perfect innings before losing in the 13th to Lew Burdette of the Milwaukee Braves, who also went all the way. He may also tell them about a game in the early days of the Houston Astrodome, when the Astros' Mike Cuellar capped off a personal four-game winning streak by outdueling and outlasting future Hall of Famer Jim Bunning of the Philadelphia Phillies in a 12-inning, 1-0 classic.

It was late September back in '67, and both teams were playing out the string, as the St. Louis Cardinals had already clinched the National League pennant. Neither team could be happy about how their seasons had gone. Houston had lost 90-plus games every year of its existence, and would finish the season at 69-93. The Phillies would finish 82-80, 19½ games behind the Cardinals.

Only 3,616 fans attended the game that night, the smallest crowd in the history of the Astrodome to that point, as two of the best pitchers in the National League faced off against one another. Cuellar was a left-hander whose out pitch was a tricky screwball that could baffle good hitters. His 15-11 record going

into the game would have been impressive on any team; on the Astros it was phenomenal. Bunning was a side-armer who threw strikes; his 17-14 record at game time was deceptive, as he had already lost four games by 1-0 scores.[1] He would lead the National League in strikeouts (253), shutouts (6), and innings pitched (302⅓), and finish second in the voting for the Cy Young Award behind Mike McCormick of the San Francisco Giants. He also had an 11-2 lifetime record against Houston, including 2-1 in 1967.

Despite the final score, this game could have gotten out of hand for either team right out of the gate. After striking out Cookie Rojas to start the game, Cuellar walked Tony Taylor and gave up a single to Tony Gonzalez. Taylor stopped at second, which was significant because had he reached third, he would have scored when Don Lock hit a fly ball to deep left-center. Taylor was still at second when Rick Joseph struck out to end the inning.

Bunning got off to a smooth start in the bottom of the first when he got Sonny Jackson and Joe Morgan on groundouts. Jimmy Wynn followed with a double, which prompted Bunning to issue an intentional walk to Astros cleanup hitter Rusty Staub, who was having a breakout year—he was an All-Star for the first time, hit a career-high .333, and led the league with 44 doubles. Maybe Bunning had all those 1-0 losses in the back of his mind, but it seems he preferred facing the next hitter, Chuck Harrison, to Staub. Anyway, the move worked as Harrison hit into a fielder's choice, forcing Wynn at third.

The decision to walk Staub was an indication of how the four-year veteran was coming into his own since arriving in the majors at age 19: "At 23, Staub is a worldly young man who has come a long way from the gangly, naïve but supremely confident teen-ager

A Texan all the way, Chuck Harrison was born in Abilene, played college baseball at Texas Tech, and signed with the Colt .45s in 1963. He registered three four-hit games for the Astros in 1966. (Courtesy of Houston Astros Baseball Club).

who came out of New Orleans just a few short years ago," wrote John Wilson in *The Sporting News.*[2]

Bunning got into some trouble again in the third. He walked Morgan with two out; Morgan stole second and moved to third on catcher Gene Oliver's throwing error. Wynn, the next batter, was in the midst of having a monster season in which he hit 37 home runs and had 107 RBIs. Fortunately for Bunning, Wynn also led the league in whiffs with 137. He struck out to end the inning.

Depending on how you look at it, this was a game of blown opportunities or of exciting baseball in which the right play was made at the right time. The top of the fifth inning was a case in point. Oliver led off with a single and was sacrificed to second by

Bobby Wine. Bunning struck out, but Philadelphia proceeded to load the bases on a single by Rojas and a walk to Taylor. But then Cuellar made the right pitches (say the Astros fans, since the Astros won) to strike out Gonzales (who blew a chance to break the game open, say the Phillies fans, since the Phillies lost).

Bunning gave Phillies fans another breath-holding opportunity in the sixth. Wynn walked with two out, then stole second. Bunning gave Staub a second intentional free pass to get to Harrison and again Harrison obliged, this time by grounding into a force play at second.

Cuellar seemed to want to widen Harrison's circle of friends in the ninth and 10th by sending over all kinds of people for his first baseman to meet. He walked Johnny Callison with two out in the ninth, and when Callison stole second, he walked Oliver to put two men on. Cuellar then induced Wine to ground into a force at second. After Bunning struck out to lead off the 10th, Rojas and Taylor hit back-to-back singles to put runners on first and second. Rojas moved to third when Gonzales forced Taylor at second, becoming only the second Philadelphia player to get that far in the game. However, the Phillies squandered yet another opportunity when Lock struck out to end the inning.

There was a degree of irony in how the Astros finally won the game in the 11th because Bunning probably should have walked Staub intentionally again with two out. Instead, the young New Orleans native smacked his last double of the year, bringing up Harrison. The first baseman had a chance to be the hero for the second night in a row—he hit a walk-off home run, his second homer of the year, the previous night for a 3-2 Astros win—and he came through again, singling to center to score Staub with the winning run.

With the defeat, Bunning tied the dubious record of five 1-0 losses in a season shared by four other players: Wild Bill Donovan (Tigers, 1903), George McQuillan (Phillies, 1908), John Warhop (Yankees, 1914), and Roger Craig (Mets, 1963). It was also his third defeat by that score in his last four decisions.

Astros manager Grady Hatton had no sympathy for the future congressman.

"I can't feel sorry for him," Hatton said with a grin. "Not with all the times he's beaten us in the past. We beat a pretty good pitcher in Bunning, but it's good to beat the Phillies any time."[3]

The game symbolized the different directions each pitcher's career was taking. Cuellar was traded to the Baltimore Orioles after having a tough year in 1968, when he went 8-11 with a 2.74 ERA. He won 20 or more games four times with the Orioles, shared the 1969 American League Cy Young Award with Denny McLain of the Detroit Tigers, and pitched the clinching game when Baltimore defeated the Cincinnati Reds in the 1970 World Series.

Bunning was on the tail end of a career that would lead him to the Hall of Fame in 1996. (He was voted in by the Veterans Committee.) He went 32-51 with a 4.14 ERA in his final four seasons before retiring in 1971 with a 224-184 record and 2,855 strikeouts, which at the time was second on the all-time list behind Walter Johnson's 3,509.

SOURCES

In addition to the sources listed below, the author consulted the following:

Chicago Tribune.

Kokomo (Indiana) *Morning Times.*

Baltimore Sun.

Baseballhall.org.

NOTES

1   He lost to Gary Nolan of Cincinnati twice, Bill Singer of the Dodgers, and Dick Hughes of the Cardinals.

2   John Wilson, "Rusty Swings Like Well-Oiled Gate," *The Sporting News,* September 9, 1967.

3   "Bunning Loses Fifth by 1-0," *Delaware County Daily Times* (Chester, Pennsylvania), September 28, 1967.

The Astrodome Marathon

April 15, 1968: Houston Astros 1, New York Mets 0 (24 innings), at the Astrodome

By Richard Riis

"WE HOPE YOU'RE ENJOYING TONIGHT'S THIRD GAME AS MUCH AS YOU DID THE FIRST TWO."—Message on the Astrodome scoreboard at the top of the 20th inning.

IT WAS THE GAME THAT WOULD NOT end. It was a game of formidable pitching and feeble hitting. It was the Year of the Pitcher in a 24-inning nutshell.

It was also, at the time, the longest night game—and the longest scoreless contest—in the major leagues.

With two young flamethrowers, Tom Seaver and Don Wilson, going head to head, the 14,219 paying fans and 5,000 Boy Scouts admitted free that night at the Astrodome might have anticipated an exciting pitching duel. What they got was an epic contest of endurance that would not be decided until the early hours of the following day.

Through nine innings the score stood tied at 0-0. Wilson had allowed just five hits and three walks in a breezy outing, the Mets bringing more than four batters to the plate in an inning only three times, with no runner advancing past second base.

Seaver, for his part, had been nearly unhittable, with Hal King's double in the second inning the only Houston baserunner through nine innings. King had advanced to third on a wild pitch, only to be gunned down at the plate as he attempted to score on a groundball. No one would come that close to scoring a run for the next 21 innings.

Seaver returned to the mound for the 10th inning, running a string of consecutive Astros retired to 25 before Rusty Staub stroked a single to right field. Staub was left stranded when King grounded to first

baseman Ed Kranepool, who tossed to shortstop Al Weis for the force at second to end the inning.

"My arm was still lively in the 10th inning but there was no use in straining it," said Seaver, acknowledging Mets manager Gil Hodges' prudence in removing his young ace.[1]

Scoring opportunities continued to be few as the game was turned over to the bullpens. Seaver was replaced by Ron Taylor, who gave way to Cal Koonce, Bill Short, Dick Selma, and Al Jackson. John Buzhardt and Danny Coombs picked up where Wilson left off, hanging up zeros on the scoreboard.

Both teams mounted threats in the extra innings, several times getting runners to third, but each time to no avail. In the 12th inning the Mets got singles by Jerry Grote, Weis, and Ken Boswell, but Tommie Agee grounded out to end the inning. The Mets put runners on third in the 17th and 19th innings, while the Astros stranded a runner there in the 22nd. The marathon of futility and frustration continued.

The score remained 0-0 as Monday night turned into Tuesday morning. In the absence of sufficient entertainment on the field, the Astrodome's Fan-O-Gram scoreboard operators began to inject a little humor between the balls and strikes. "After about the 17th inning," observed Rusty Staub, "everything sort of got funny."[2]

As fans began a steady exodus from the Astrodome following the shutting down of beer sales at midnight in compliance with Texas law, the scoreboard cracked, "I TOLD YOU BASEBALL WOULDN'T REPLACE SEX."[3]

A disputed out at first on a grounder to third by Bob Aspromonte in the Astros' 18th brought boos from the remaining faithful in the stands and a lament from the scoreboard: "I'M GOING TO THROW UP."[4]

"WE HOPE YOU'RE ENJOYING TONIGHT'S THIRD GAME AS MUCH AS YOU DID THE FIRST TWO," quipped the scoreboard as the game entered its 20th inning. "FOR THOSE OF YOU STILL HERE … YOU ARE WITNESSING THE LONGEST 0-0 NIGHT GAME IN MAJOR LEAGUE HISTORY."[5]

An inning later the scoreboard got the bleary-eyed audience on its feet for a "21st INNING STRETCH."[6]

Astros rookie fireballer Jim Ray, after entering the game in the 14th inning, pitched a remarkable seven innings of scoreless relief, yielding but two hits and one walk and fanning 11. Wade Blasingame, picking up where Ray left off, faced the minimum in the 21st, 23rd, and 24th innings, running into trouble only in the 22nd, when he allowed Grote to reach second on a single and a sacrifice by pitcher Don Cardwell, a career .135 hitter pressed into service as a pinch-hitter for Danny Frisella, who was removed after hurling five scoreless innings.

"THE JUDGE [Astros' owner Roy Hofheinz, who had an apartment in the Astrodome] SAYS HE'S READY TO GO TO BED … LET'S SCORE A RUN," implored the scoreboard in the bottom of the 22nd as rookie Les Rohr became the eighth Mets pitcher.[7]

Rohr, held back until now by Hodges after having pitched 25 minutes of batting practice before the game, was uneven as he walked two (one intentionally) and uncorked a wild pitch before striking out Julio Gotay with Staub on third to retire the side.

As the 23rd inning began, Houston team officials announced that they would provide free breakfast for the press.

The deadlock was finally broken in the bottom of the 24th inning. Norm Miller led off with a single to right. Rohr then balked when he accidentally "broke his hands" from the set position, moving Miller to second.[8] Jim Wynn was walked intentionally, putting runners on first and second. A groundout to second by Staub moved the runners to second and third and

Norm Miller debuted with the Astros at the age of 19 on September 11, 1965. He scored the winning running in Houston's marathon 24-inning, 1-0 victory over the New York Mets on April 15, 1968. (Courtesy of Houston Astros Baseball Club).

Rohr walked John Bateman intentionally to load the bases, bringing Aspromonte to the plate.

"The bat felt like eight and a half pounds when I carried it to the plate," the veteran Astro recalled.[9] Aspromonte slapped a grounder to the left of second base, directly at Weis.

"It might have been a double-play grounder ending the threat and putting everybody into the 25th inning," wrote Joseph Durso of the *New York Times*. "But the ball skidded off the chemical carpet known as the Astroturf and went right through Weis' legs into left field while Miller scored the only run of the night."[10]

"I hoped he was going for the double play," said Hodges. "It looked like it hit the edge of the turf and skidded. I think he touched it."[11]

"No, it didn't take a bad hop," said Weis, who was charged with an error. "I just blew it. It went through my legs."[12]

Miller was mobbed by his teammates as the estimated 3,000 stalwart souls who remained to the end of the 6-hour 6-minute marathon erupted along with the Astrodome's exploding scoreboard.

No game had ever gone longer than 20 innings without a run being scored. No night game had ever gone longer than a 22-inning marathon on June 12, 1967, when the Washington Senators, managed by Hodges, edged the Chicago White Sox, 6-5.

The game tied the major-league mark for the longest game ever played to a decision, matching a 24-inning, 4-1 Philadelphia Athletics victory over the Boston Americans on September 1, 1906. The longest game, 26 innings, had been played on May 1, 1920, when the Boston Braves and Brooklyn Robins battled to a 1-1 tie.

In the years since the Astrodome marathon, there have been longer games, but none (as of 2016) to challenge the 23 innings of scoreless ball played from the outset by the Mets and Astros that night in 1968. The St. Louis Cardinals beat the Mets, 4-3, in a 25-inning game on September 11, 1974, and the Chicago White Sox topped the Milwaukee Brewers, 7-6, in 25 innings in a game suspended in the 18th inning on May 8, 1984, and completed the following day.

Wade Blasingame picked up the win for Houston, pitching four scoreless innings while allowing one hit and one walk. It was his only win that season, one of 17 he accumulated in six seasons with the Astros. Rohr took the hard-luck loss. Both King and Grote, remarkably, caught all 24 innings.

As for the batters, Astros skipper Grady Hatton put it best when he said, "There were some pretty sick-sounding bats in this game."[13] Agee and Swoboda, batting third and fourth, respectively, for the Mets, went a combined 0-for-20 with nine strikeouts. Aspromonte, despite driving in the winning run, was hitless in nine at-bats.

It was a long night for one other Astro who wasn't even at the game. Pitcher Tom Dukes had been re-called from Triple-A Oklahoma City before the game when Houston put Mike Cuellar on the disabled list. Dukes was told to arrive in Houston the next day, so with his 89ers playing in Nashville, he packed his bags and spent the day driving from Tennessee to Dallas, Texas. Listening to the radio broadcast of the game in a hotel, Dukes decided he might be needed and tossed his bags back in the car to continue to Houston. He was less than an hour's drive from the Astrodome when Miller gleefully pounced on the plate to end the game.

SOURCES

In addition to the sources listed in the notes, the author also consulted:

Chicago Tribune.

The Sporting News.

NOTES

1   "Win Keeps Astros on Top in NL," *Port Arthur* (Texas) *News*, April 16, 1968: 14.

2   "Even Judge Couldn't Score," *Corpus Christi Times*, April 16, 1968: D1.

3   "Baseball Wins Over 'Sex' in 24-Inning Duel," *El Paso Post-Herald*, April 16, 1968: B4.

4   "Mets—000 000 000 000 000 000 000 000-0 11 1, Astros—000 000 000 000 000 000 000 001-1 11 1," *Newsday* [Long Island, New York], April 16, 1968: 32A.

5   Arthur Daley, "The Marathoners," *New York Times*, April 17, 1968: 55.

6   Joe Dittmar. *Baseball Records Registry: The Best and Worst Single-Day Performances and the Stories Behind Them* (Jefferson, North Carolina: McFarland and Company, 1997), 12.

7   "Even Judge Couldn't Score."

8   Joseph Durso, "Mets Will Oppose Giants in Home Opener at Shea Stadium Today," *New York Times*, April 17, 1968: 55.

9   John Wilson, "Astros Defeat Mets in 24th," *Houston Chronicle*, April 16, 1968: D1.

10   Durso.

11   "Bobble Ends Record Game," *El Paso Herald-Post*, April 16, 1968: B4.

12   "Only One Chew Left at the End," *Corpus Christi Times*, April 16, 1968: D1.

13   "Weary Astros, Mets Get Day to Recuperate," *Dallas Morning News*, April 17, 1968: B6.

A Parade of Pitchers in the "Year of the Pitcher"

July 9, 1968: National League 1, American League 0, at the Astrodome

By Richard Riis

IT WAS EXPECTED TO BE A GLITTER-
ing night of firsts.

The 1968 All-Star Game was to be the first played on artificial turf, the first played indoors, and, if not the first played at night (the wartime games of 1943 and 1944 had been played under the lights), it was to be the first played entirely in prime time before an international television audience—the final few innings of 1967's 15-inning marathon, which strayed into prime time for audiences in some time zones, notwithstanding

"This is going to be an All-Star Game they won't forget for a long time," boasted Bill Giles, the Houston Astros' vice president of publicity. "The Judge [Astros owner Roy Hofheinz] is going all-out on this one."[1]

All out, indeed. There were a host of special functions, including a banquet the night before the game and a dinner on the afternoon of the game at AstroWorld's Crystal Palace. Each member of the press corps was given an attaché case, an Astrodome tie clasp, and an All-Star button. Brass bands were hired to provide entertainment at the game, and popular singer Teresa Brewer was lined up to sing the National Anthem.

NBC equipped the Astrodome with nine color cameras, at the time the most ever used to broadcast a sporting event, including one attached to a gondola some 18 stories above second base.

At 7:15 P.M. (Houston time) on Tuesday, July 9, 1968, a sellout crowd of 48,321 packed the Dome—joined by an estimated audience of 60 million[2] watching on television in the United States and perhaps 100 million more[3] watching the Spanish-language broadcast in South and Central America and in the Caribbean—to witness the 39th annual All-Star Game.

All-Star managers Red Schoendienst and Dick Williams both predicted a low-scoring contest. "I lean toward a pitcher's game," said St. Louis Cardinals skipper Schoendienst in a pregame press conference. "This has been the year of big zero."[4] Williams of the Boston Red Sox agreed. "I would say it will be a pitcher's battle," he said. "The pitchers should predominate."[5]

Depressed batting averages on both rosters reflected a season that was lopsided in favor of pitching. The AL team batting average was .263, the NL's .279, with Boston's Carl Yastrzemski (.300), St. Louis outfielder Curt Flood (.316), and Cincinnati second baseman Tommy Helms (.302) the only starters hitting at or above .300. A handful of reserves with respectable averages aside, both teams were stocked with stars having less than stellar seasons at the plate, including the likes of Willie Mays (.271), Hank Aaron (.247), Mickey Mantle (.233), and Harmon Killebrew (.204).

Cincinnati's Pete Rose, hitting .329, had been the top vote-getter among his NL peers to start in the outfield, but was relegated to the bench with a fractured thumb.

Many expected Schoendienst to start his own star pitcher, Bob Gibson (11-5, 1.06). Citing tightness in Gibson's arm, the manager gave the ball instead to the Dodgers' Don Drysdale (10-5, 1.37), who earlier in the season had tossed six straight shutouts on the way to a major-league record 58⅔ consecutive scoreless innings.[6] For Drysdale, it was to be his fifth career

All-Star start, tying the mark held by Lefty Gomez and Robin Roberts.

Williams selected Cleveland's Luis Tiant (14-5, 1.24), a first-time All-Star, to start for the AL. Tiant would be pitching on very short rest, having hurled 6⅓ innings against the California Angels only two days before. Williams defended his decision, saying he had planned on starting Tiant before he saw the weekend box scores. "I decided on Tiant when I named him to the team," he explained. "He's a darn fine pitcher."[7] He might have added that, of the squad's seven pitchers, five had worked that Sunday, the other two on Saturday.

"I was surprised when Williams told me I would start," Tiant told reporters. He admitted his arm was tired. "I'll try to pitch two innings," he added, "maybe they're easy ones."[8]

Denny McLain, with a 16-2 record on his way to the majors' first 30-win season since 1931, had pitched nine innings on Sunday, and made it clear there was no way he was able to pitch. "I know that being named to the squad is a great honor but I just do not see how I can work Sunday and pitch again Tuesday," said McLain. Asked if he would be available for an inning or two of relief, McLain was quite firm. "No, I don't see how I can do it. My first obligation is to the Tigers and their pennant chances."[9]

Newly elected Hall of Famer Joe Medwick[10] tossed out the first ball, and team captains Mantle and Mays, named to their 20th and 19th All-Star squads respectively, exchanged lineup cards at home plate.

The Angels' Jim Fregosi doubled to deep left to lead off the game, but Drysdale set down Rod Carew,

The Astrodome hosted the All-Star Game for the first time on July 9, 1968. A crowd of 48,321 watched Willie Mays score the game's only run in the first inning of the NL's victory. (Courtesy of Houston Astros Baseball Club).

Yastrzemski, and Senators slugger Frank Howard, who was leading the majors with 25 home runs, to leave Fregosi stranded.

Mays, tying Stan Musial's record of 63 All-Star at-bats, opened the bottom of the first with a single between third and short. Leading off first, Mays drew a throw from Tiant but stepped back safely. When Mays took another long lead, Tiant threw again to first. This time, though, the toss went wide of Killebrew.

"He said the ball moved," said Tiant, quoting Killebrew. "I guess it curved."[11]

Mays thought it glanced off his back. Either way, Mays took second on the play.

Tiant fell behind to the next batter, Curt Flood. On the fourth ball he uncorked a wild pitch that flew over catcher Bill Freehan's head. Mays scampered to third as Flood jogged down to first.

With runners on first and third, the American League infield played back, hoping for a double play. Willie McCovey slashed a sharp grounder that bounced off the artificial turf into second baseman Carew's glove. Carew hesitated for a moment, but with Mays already nearing the plate, he tossed the ball to shortstop Fregosi covering second, who relayed to Killebrew for the double play. Despite the record number of television cameras, NBC's attention was fixed on the double play, so television viewers across the Western Hemisphere didn't get to see Mays score on the play.

Aaron, who had hit his 498th and 499th career home runs on Sunday, drew a walk before Tiant induced Ron Santo to ground into a force at second to end the inning.

As the game progressed, the NL threatened but failed to deliver on any further scoring opportunities. With Tiant still on the mound, Tommy Helms led off the second inning with a double to right field, but two strikeouts and a fly ball left Helms stranded. Oakland's John "Blue Moon" Odom walked Santo and Helms in the fourth, but allowed no hits or runs. A sixth-inning single and stolen base by Aaron followed by a walk to Santo stirred some excitement, but McLain, in the game despite his gloomy forecast, was able to work out of that jam without any damage.

The American League, for its part, never mounted a threat. After Fregosi's leadoff double the AL failed to put another runner on base until Tony Oliva doubled off Tom Seaver with two outs in the seventh. In between, Drysdale, Juan Marichal, Steve Carlton, and Seaver set down 20 straight batters.

Seaver struck out five in two innings of work and, over the last three innings, seven of nine AL batters retired went down on strikes. The Braves' Ron Reed and Seaver's Mets teammate Jerry Koosman shared the ninth inning, with Koosman fanning Carl Yastrzemski for the final out.

Added to the list of All-Star firsts was the first 1-0 game.

The American League was limited to just three hits. Its biggest threat, some waggish commentators said, came from Oliva, who before his seventh-inning double lost his grip on a swing, sending his bat flying into the National League dugout.

"I flattened out," Schoendienst said. "I got a strawberry on my left knee from hitting the dugout floor. The bat hit Felipe Alou on the bounce."[12]

The game's most consequential play, measured by impact on the pennant race, occurred in the bottom of the third, when Killebrew went into a full split stretching for an errant throw by Fregosi on a grounder by Flood. The muscular first baseman snagged the throw for the out but collapsed from a ruptured hamstring that would keep him sidelined until September. Without Killebrew's powerful bat, the Twins, who had come within a game of the pennant in 1967, tumbled to seventh place in 1968.

Mays was voted the game's Most Valuable Player for scoring the lone run, but the award could easily have gone to second baseman Helms, who not only collected the NL's only extra-base hit but also made several sparkling defensive plays, including going deep into the hole in the fourth to rob Yastrzemski of a base hit, and charging in to scoop up a fifth-inning grounder by Willie Horton and nip him at the bag.

The most enthusiastic receptions of the evening from the Houston fans were reserved for home- team hero Rusty Staub, who popped out to third pinch-hitting against McLain—whom Dick Williams must have persuaded to pitch—in the sixth, and for Mickey Mantle, making what would be his final All-Star Game appearance. With the cheering crowd on its feet as Mantle strode to the plate to pinch-hit in the eighth, third baseman Santo visited the mound and smiled at second-year man Seaver. "Did you ever think," he asked, "you'd pitch to Mickey Mantle in an All-Star Game?" Seaver smiled back. "I never did," he said.[13]

In a microcosm of the game and of the season, Seaver struck out Mantle swinging.

SOURCES

In addition to the sources cited in the Notes, the author also consulted:

Lenburg, Jeff. *Baseball's All-Star Game: A Game-by-Game Guide* (Jefferson, North Carolina: McFarland and Company, 1986).

Dallas Morning News.

Galveston Daily News.

New York Times.

fleersticker.blogspot.com/2011/07/1968-all-star-game-broadcast.html.

NOTES

1   Wells Twombley, "Show Time! All-Star Game in Astrodome," *The Sporting News*, July 13, 1968: 7.

2   David Vincent et al., *The Midsummer Classic: The Complete History of Baseball's All-Star Game.* (Lincoln: University of Nebraska Press, 2001), 243.

3   Twombley.

4   "Low-Scoring Pitching Duel Seen by Managers of All-Star Teams," *Houston Chronicle*, July 9, 1968: 14.

5   Ibid.

6   Drysdale's record was topped in 1988 by another Dodgers pitcher, Orel Hershiser, who pitched 59 straight scoreless innings.

7   "American League Ready; Nationals Have the Rest," *Newsday*, July 9, 1968: 29.

8   "Luis Tiant Likes Idea of Starting," *Houston Chronicle*, July 9, 1968: 14.

9   "McLain Unavailable for All-Star Work," *Corpus Christi Caller-Times*, July 4, 1968: 29.

10 Medwick had a Houston connection, having played the 1931 and 1932 seasons for the Texas League's Houston Buffalos before beginning his Hall of Fame career with the Cardinals)

11 "Willie Makes the Difference," *Abilene Reporter-News*, July 10, 1968: 8A.

12 "Flying Bat Was Biggest 'Threat,'" *El Paso Herald-Post*, July 10, 1968: B5.

13 "Thrill for Seaver Means Whiff for Mantle," *Newsday*, July 10, 1968: 34.

The Heady Heights of Seventh Place

August 23, 1968: Houston Astros 3, Chicago Cubs 2, at the Astrodome

By John Bauer

BASEBALL FANS IN HOUSTON HAD never had it so good in the short history of the Astros. After completing a sweep of the Dodgers on August 21, the Astros climbed into seventh place, one-thousandth of a percentage point ahead of Philadelphia. As John Wilson wrote in the *Houston Chronicle*, "When you've been where the Astros have been, that's Mount Everest."[1] Houston's 59-69 record was its best ever after 128 games, and this was only the second time the club had been as high as eighth at this point in the season.[2] These were heady days indeed.[3]

The Cubs faced a delay in their travel plans the morning of the game. They were 40 minutes late leaving O'Hare Airport in Chicago, due partly to air traffic and partly to catcher Randy Hundley apparently oversleeping.[4] When the Cubs arrived in Houston, they brought a 68-61 record and a four-game win streak. They were locked in a tight battle for the runner-up spot in the 10-team National League with Cincinnati and San Francisco, and all three trailed runaway leader St. Louis. Despite the Cubs' successful run, there was a feeling that "the Astros will have a further chance to exercise their recently effective muscle and strengthen their growing confidence."[5] Indeed, the Astros were enjoying a sustained run of respectable baseball. After a dismal start to the season that had cost manager Grady Hatton his job, Harry Walker had piloted the Astros to a 36-31 record since taking over.[6]

Astros starter Mike Cuellar, who battled shoulder problems during the season,[7] entered the game 6-9 with a 2.37 ERA.[8] Facing Cuellar, the Cubs' Don Kessinger opened the game with a single to center field. Billy Williams advanced Kessinger to second with a one-out infield single. With cleanup hitter Ernie Banks at the plate, Cuellar had Williams dead to rights at first base but his wild throw on the pickoff allowed both Kessinger and Williams to move into scoring position. Neither Banks nor Ron Santo could drive them home, though, and the Cubs finished their inning scoreless.

Twenty-three-year-old Joe Niekro took the mound for the Cubs. Norm Miller flied out to center fielder Adolfo Phillips, and Hector Torres lined out to second baseman Glenn Beckert. With two out, Niekro walked Jim Wynn and surrendered a double to Rusty Staub. The Astros' first baseman had recently emerged from a lengthy RBI slump by driving home eight runs during the preceding series against the Dodgers.[9] Denis Menke followed Staub by grounding out to shortstop Kessinger, ending the inning.

The game remained scoreless after the second inning as neither team could muster more than a lone single. The Cubs broke the tie by striking quickly in the top of the third. Kessinger led off by doubling to right field, and scored on Beckert's single to left, giving Chicago the lead, 1-0. Cuellar limited the damage by containing the heart of the Cubs' order. Williams struck out looking, and Banks and Santo hit groundballs to third baseman Bob Aspromonte. Niekro preserved the lead by setting down the top of the Astros' lineup in the bottom of the third.

The score remained 1-0 through the fifth inning. The Cubs managed no more than a double by Jim Hickman and a single by Beckert in the fourth and fifth innings, respectively. Niekro was in the midst of retiring 10 consecutive Astros, a streak not broken until his opposite number, Cuellar, hit a two-out single in the fifth. Santo doubled the Cubs' lead by opening the sixth with his 20th home run of the season, over the left-field wall. Hundley grounded out

Catcher Ron Brand (left, next to pitcher Gary Kroll) made Astrodome history by becoming the first Houston player to register a hit in the new stadium when he tripled in the April 9, 1965, exhibition game against the New York Yankees. (Courtesy of Houston Astros Baseball Club).

Rookie Steve Shea took over pitching duties from Cuellar in the top of the inning. He opened the inning by striking out Niekro. Kessinger flied out to Wynn in center field before Beckert's grounder to Torres ended the Cubs' ninth. To this point, Niekro had surrendered only four hits and a walk to the Astros. Houston's streak of 34 games without being shut out[11] appeared in jeopardy.

What transpired next was described by the *Houston Post*'s Joe Heiling, who wrote, "Reconstructing the Astros' unbelievable ninth-inning rally … is like gathering details at the scene of an accident. You get a lot of conflicting reports. A number of people saw it differently."[12] What was clear was that Wynn led off with a line drive past third and into left field for a double, sending Niekro to the showers.

Cubs manager Leo Durocher brought reliever Phil Regan into the game. Regan, who would be awarded *The Sporting News'* Fireman of the Year Award after the season, had been the source of recent controversy. During a game at Wrigley Field against Cincinnati the previous Sunday, a tube of Vaseline and slippery elm tablets apparently fell out of his jacket during a basepath collision with Reds catcher Pat Corrales.[13] Regan denied throwing illegal pitches and he was absolved by NL President Warren Giles before the series in Houston.[14]

Staub singled to left field against Regan, scoring Wynn and cutting the deficit to 2-1. Walker sent in Dick Simpson to run for Staub. Menke's ground-ball forced Simpson at second base for the first out. Despite a history of tormenting the Cubs with home runs, Aspromonte struck out.[15] With two outs, Bateman kept the rally alive, hitting a single to right field and advancing Menke to third base. Bateman was lifted for pinch-runner Ron Brand, the backup catcher.

With two on and two out, Walker sent Doug Rader up to hit for Shea. Rader had missed the previous game, two days earlier, with a fever and tonsillitis,[16] and Walker had planned to rest him after he felt weak and dizzy during batting practice. "We felt if Doug played a complete game or had to do any extra running, he'd get dizzy," the manager said.[17] Rader, the

to shortstop Torres, and Cuellar surrendered a single to Phillips but struck out Hickman and Niekro. In the Astros' sixth, Niekro continued his "almost flawless"[10] performance by taking down Torres, Wynn, and Staub.

Kessinger led off the seventh with a single to left field, and advanced to third on groundouts by Beckert and Williams. When catcher "Big John" Bateman squeezed Banks' popup in foul territory, the threat ended. Niekro, meanwhile, continued to keep the Astros off the bases with another three-up, three-down inning. He ran the streak to nine consecutive outs before it was broken by Miller's two-out double in the eighth. When Torres grounded out to Beckert, the game moved to the ninth with the Cubs still holding a 2-0 lead.

"Red Rooster," blooped a ball that was barely fair into right field in front of the hard-charging Hickman.[18] The hit scored Menke to even the game at 2-2. Rader went to second base on Hickman's throw to the plate, and Brand reached third base to leave Houston 90 feet from an improbable win.

Lee Thomas, who pinch-hit for Cuellar in the eighth and remained in the game, taking over left field, came to the plate with first base open. Despite Thomas's .175 batting average,[19] the Cubs intentionally walked him to load the bases. Up next was Norm Miller, who had entered the game hitting .211. Miller had been sidelined recently with an ailing back and felt compelled to make up for it. He said, "I had to hit to redeem myself for the past two weeks. What had I done? Nothing. Absolutely nothing, but sit on the bench."[20] After taking Regan's first pitch for a ball, Miller sent a bouncing ball up the middle and into center field for the decisive hit.[21] Brand scored from third, and the Astros won, 3-2, to the delight of the 16,714 in attendance.

The Astros' win was their season-high fifth in a row. After years of losing since the franchise's inception, the club and its fans were enjoying a run in which success was almost expected. "They've got the fever," said Walker after the game. "They're getting to believe something will happen. Even in a game like tonight where they hadn't had a break for eight innings, they still felt they'd win it somehow."[22] Houston extended its win streak to six by defeating the Cubs the next night, but the coming 17-game road trip would begin to bring down the Astros from their current "heights." Houston lost 17 of its final 25 games to finish 72-90. With the Mets finishing 73-89, the Astros would finish in the NL basement for the first time. After the NL split into divisions for 1969, Houston at least was assured of finishing higher than seventh in future seasons.

NOTES

1 John Wilson, "Look Where the Astros Stand Today After Ripping L.A., 6-1," *Houston Chronicle*, August 22, 1968: 1 (sports).

2 John Wilson, "Rejuvenated Astros Return to Wars Against Cubs," *Houston Chronicle*, August 23, 1968: 1 (sports).

3 The Astros did not play on Thursday, August 22, but the Phillies did. Because the Phillies won on the 22nd, the Astros "reclaimed" eighth place by game time on the 23rd.

4 Edward Prell, "Astros Score Three In Last Inning To Win," *Chicago Tribune*, August 24, 1968: 2 (sports).

5 John Wilson, "Look Where the Astros Stand Today After Ripping L.A., 6-1."

6 John Wilson, "Rejuvenated Astros Return to Wars Against Cubs," *Houston Chronicle*, August 23, 1968: 1 (sports).

7 *The Sporting News Official Baseball Guide*—1969: 125.

8 *Houston Chronicle*, August 22, 1968: 2 (sports).

9 *The Sporting News*, September 7, 1968: 12.

10 Prell.

11 "Astronotes," *Houston Chronicle*, August 22, 1968: 2 (sports).

12 Joe Heiling, "Astros Score 3 In 9th To Ease by Cubbies, 3-2," *Houston Post*: 1 (sports).

13 "Found Regan's Greasy Pitch Stuff, Bristol Says," *Chicago Tribune*, August 24, 1968 : 1 (sports).

14 Ibid.

15 Prell.

16 "Astronotes," *Houston Chronicle*, August 22, 1968, 2 (sports). While the *Chicago Tribune* also reported tonsillitis as the cause of Rader's illness, the August 24 *Houston Post* said it was bronchitis.

17 Heiling.

18 Heiling; Prell.

19 Prell.

20 Heiling.

21 Ibid.

22 Ibid.

Rader's Walk-Off Slam Sinks Phillies

May 27, 1969: Houston Astros 6, Philadelphia Phillies 2, at the Astrodome

By Thomas Rathkamp

HOUSTON ASTROS THIRD BASEMAN Doug Rader had hit two home runs in 164 at-bats over his team's first 44 games. One was a three-run bomb in a 5-2 victory over the Los Angeles Dodgers on April 13, while the other was a solo shot that aided a 4-0 win over the Cincinnati Reds on May 1. Apparently he was primed for more dramatic achievements, this time at the expense of the Philadelphia Phillies, who were in fifth place in the NL East.

A sparse crowd of 13,188 watched the Astros push their May record to 18-4. Rader delivered a game-winner off reliever Luis Peraza, a 27-year-old rookie right-hander whose eight games pitched this season constituted his entire major-league career. The clutch four-bagger was the first in Rader's young career.[1] Although they didn't call them walk-offs back then, this clout qualified as one and ended a tight battle.

Douglas Lee Rader, who was born on July 30, 1944, in Chicago, was nicknamed "Red Rooster" because of his thick bundle of red hair.[2] He had signed with the Astros as an amateur free agent out of Illinois Wesleyan University before the 1965 season, jumping the gun on the first-ever amateur draft, which didn't take place until June 1965. Rader, known mostly for his defensive prowess at the hot corner, debuted with the Astros in 1967 and did not disappoint. In 168 at-bats, he posted a .333/.360/.481 line with 10 doubles, 4 triples, and 2 home runs. Despite the presence of sparkling defensive third basemen like Ron Santo and Clete Boyer, Rader won five consecutive gold gloves starting in 1970.

This was still 1969, however, and Rader entered the game hitting just .226 with the two homers and 22 RBIs. In the second inning, with his club down 1-0 after a home run by Dick Allen, Rader hammered a long double that caromed off the glove of Phillies right fielder Johnny Callison.[3] The hit advanced Dennis Menke, who had walked, to third. Johnny Edwards followed with a sacrifice fly that tied the score at 1-1 and advanced Rader to third.

With Norm Miller batting next, Rader decided to perform his Ty Cobb imitation and try to swipe home. Not known for his speed, the risk-taking Rader was gunned down at the plate for the final out of the inning. Miller entered the game with a .305 batting average, making Rader's feeble attempt to break the tie a peculiar decision, even with two out.

After the Astros evened the score, starting pitchers Don Wilson of Houston and Grant Jackson of Philadelphia each pitched three scoreless innings. The Astros were retired without a baserunner in all three of their frames. The Phillies managed a single and walk but were also caught stealing twice during that span; Larry Hisle (in the third inning) and Cookie Rojas (in the fourth) were the victims of catcher Johnny Edwards's powerful right arm. Rojas's steal attempt came as Wilson struck out Allen, resulting in a double play.[4]

A frightening moment occurred during the third inning. As Wilson swung at one of Jackson's offerings, the bat slipped from his grasp, bounced off the Phillies dugout, and continued into the stands, where it struck a young girl in the face. The child was taken to the emergency room of a local hospital, where her injuries were determined to be minor.[5]

The Phillies botched a golden chance to break the tie in the top of the fifth inning, which began when Deron Johnson reached safely on a throwing error by Rader.[6] After Wilson walked Don Money, the Phils were in business, or so it seemed. Mike Ryan laid down a bunt, that Wilson fielded and threw out

Denis Menke spent five seasons (1968–71) with the Astros, and was an All-Star selection at shortstop in 1969 and 1970. In his second All-Star season, he batted .304 with 13 homers and 92 RBIs. (Courtesy of Houston Astros Baseball Club).

Johnson at third. With one out, Larry Hisle followed with his own bunt toward Wilson, who opted for the sure out by throwing out Hisle at first.

Hisle's decision to bunt with pitcher Jackson on deck was a curious one. Was Hisle trying to reach on a bunt single, or was he merely aiming to advance the runners? The second-year slugger was no speed demon, although he did record 18 stolen bases in 1969. Regardless, Wilson rendered this query moot by striking out Jackson to thwart the threat. The teams remained tied heading into the sixth, which would prove to be an unexpectedly dramatic inning.

After striking out the leadoff hitter, Tony Taylor, Wilson gave up three consecutive singles, coincidentally occurring from left to right, in order. Rojas singled to left field, Allen to center, and Callison to

right. Right fielder Norm Miller's quick throw on Callison's single prevented Rojas from scoring on the play. With the bases loaded, Wilson struck out Johnson and it appeared that the gritty right-hander would avoid giving up the lead run. However, with Money batting, first-base umpire Bob Engel called a balk on Wilson that allowed Rojas to score and gave the Phillies a 2–1 edge. Rojas had apparently faked a move toward home, prompting Wilson to rush a pitch to the plate, and Rojas's tactic had paid off.[7]

Houston manager Harry Walker became incensed and did not conceal his objections. Walker argued vociferously that Engel was not in position to see any balk. He said third-base umpire Augie Donatelli had the better view and chose not to make a call. The *Houston Chronicle* wrote that Walker exhibited "one of his angriest displays since he became manager." After a long, heated exchange, Walker returned to the dugout but Engel ejected him anyway. It was the first time since 1967 that Walker had been tossed from a game. "That's a long time for me," admitted Walker.[8] Coach Buddy Hancken took over the managerial duties.[9]

Possibly fired up himself after the verbal melee, Wilson recorded his third strikeout of the inning by fanning Mike Ryan to end the inning. (He would total 13 K's in the game.) Jackson retired the Astros in order in the sixth, and Wilson heaped the same fate on the Phillies in the seventh, setting down Hisle, Jackson, and Taylor, before Denis Menke led off Houston's half of the inning with a game-tying homer. The eight-year-veteran shortstop now had hit safely in 18 of his last 19 games.[10]

In the top of the eighth, Wilson issued his fourth free pass of the night, this time to Rojas. Dick Allen lined a "viciously-hit liner"[11] to Miller in right for the first out. Callison popped out to Edwards in foul territory, but the catcher then allowed a passed ball that advanced Rojas to second. However, like clockwork, strikeout artist Wilson whiffed Johnson for the second time to end the inning.

After the Astros went down quietly in the eighth and Wilson worked his way out of the ninth, Rader, who thus far had an eventful night with a double, a caught stealing, and an error, took center stage again in the bottom of the ninth. Phillies manager Bob Skinner made the first pitching change of the game, replacing Jackson with rookie hurler Bill Wilson. The decision backfired on Skinner as Wilson issued consecutive walks to Joe Morgan and Jimmy Wynn, who had scorched a long foul ball on a fastball down the middle that seemed to have rattled the young right-hander. After walking Wynn, he threw a wild pitch to advance the runners to second and third and force an intentional walk to Menke.

With the bases loaded and nobody out, Skinner replaced Wilson with Peraza, who ran the count to 3-and-1 on Rader. Rader could have attempted to take a walk to earn the game-winning RBI, but he said after the game, "I wanted to hit a fly ball." He did just that, cranking the next pitch into the screen near the left-field foul pole for a dramatic, game-winning grand slam.[12] that John Wilson of the *Houston Chronicle* called a "four-megaton explosive."[13]

Peraza had delivered four straight sliders to Rader before the walk-off swing. "I had watched him warm up and knew he threw a changeup," said Rader after the game. "I knew he wasn't going to throw me the slider again. My thinking was that it was going to be a straight ball—either the fastball or the change. So I set myself to be able to get around on the fastball and hit a fly ball or pull it if it was a change."

The Phillies had put the lead runner on base in four of the nine innings but had failed to score each time. Rader, citing his team's nine-game winning streak, offered this: "I just hope three or four guys can stay hot at one time. During the whole stretch, we never have had everybody hot at once—just enough to win and that's what I hope can continue."[14]

NOTES

1   Clark Nealon, "Rader Sparks 6-2 Victory," *Houston Post*, May 28, 1969.

2   John Wilson, "Astros Top Philly by 6-2 Count," *Houston Chronicle*, May 28, 1969.

3   Ibid.

4   Ibid

5   Nealon.

6   Wilson.

7   Ibid.

8   Ibid.

9   Nealon.

10   Ibid.

11   Wilson.

12   Nealon

13   Wilson.

14   Ibid.

On-Leave from the Army Reserve, Dierker Tosses Extra-Inning Complete Game and Hits Walk-Off Single

June 8, 1969: Houston Astros 2, St. Louis Cardinals 1 (11 innings), at the Astrodome

By Gregory H. Wolf

THE COMMUTE FOR LARRY DIERKER on Sunday, June 8, 1969, was longer than normal. He had just finished the first week of his annual two-week military obligation with the 95th Training Division of the Army Reserve at Fort Polk, Louisiana, and was given a pass to travel about 200 miles to Houston for his "day job" as a starting pitcher for the Astros. "It was a special occasion," recalled Dierker. "I had gotten quite a few tickets for friends and officers from Fort Polk. They all came down and I set them up."[1] Taking the mound for the first time in 10 days, the 22-year-old right-hander dusted off the cobwebs to toss an 11-inning complete game and belt the game-winning, walk-off hit in a 2-1 victory over St. Louis. "By the time I went back to Fort Polk, I was a big hero," continued Dierker with a laugh, noting that he was freed from some of his duties. "Larry Dierker can do it all," exclaimed teammate Doug Rader. "[H]e crawled out of a foxhole to do it."[2]

"It was a strange year," Dierker reminisced. "We started out 4-20. Jim Maloney [of the Cincinnati Reds] threw a no-hitter against us [on April 30], and then on the next day Don Wilson threw one against them." Wilson's victory was the first of 20 in the next 25 contests for skipper Harry Walker's club, which crawled back to respectability. The Astros were in fifth place (26-30) in the NL West, seven games behind the Atlanta Braves, as they prepared to play the finale of a four-game set against the two-time reigning NL pennant-winners, the Cardinals. Manager Red Schoendienst's Redbirds were struggling, mired in fourth-place (25-28), 11½ games behind the streaking Chicago Cubs in the NL East.

The pitching match-up foretold a nail-biting, low-scoring game. The Cardinals' 24-year-old southpaw Steve Carlton (6-4) was perhaps the hottest pitcher in baseball. With a 36-27 record in parts of five seasons, Carlton had tossed four consecutive complete-game victories, allowing only 18 hits and five earned runs, and led the majors with a 1.75 ERA. Dierker debuted with Houston on his 18th birthday as a September call-up in 1964, and had since amassed a record of 42-41, including 7-4 with a 2.81 ERA thus far in '69. "Dierk had great command—command of the strike zone and, most importantly, command of his mound presence," said former Astros president and general manager Tal Smith. "Even as a teenager pitching in the major leagues, he had an air of confidence and toughness on the mound."[3]

The Cardinals' hot-hitting Lou Brock quieted the Astrodome crowd of 25,824 by leading off with a triple, his 21st hit his last 42 at-bats, to extend his hitting streak to 11 games. First baseman Doug Rader fumbled Vada Pinson's one-out grounder for Houston's only error of the game, but Brock stayed at third, and Dierker wriggled out of the jam by generating a 5-4-3 inning-ending twin killing off the bat of Joe Torre. St. Louis squandered another scoring chance after Tim McCarver led off with a triple in the second. Schoendienst called for a suicide squeeze bunt, but rugged Mike Shannon, affectionately called Moonman by his teammates, missed Dierker's fastball. McCarver, who had broken for home, was easily

The Astros threatened again in the fifth when Edwards led off with a walk. He moved to third on Marty Martinez's two-out single after third baseman Shannon misplayed the throw from right fielder Pinson. Carlton intentionally walked Wynn to load the bases and then whiffed Rader to end the inning.

Dierker's streak of 15 straight batters retired ended with one out in the seventh when Pinson hit a slow chopper to shortstop Hector Torres. According to the *Houston Chronicle*, Torres "failed to charge," enabling Pinson to reach first.[5] Pinson advanced to second on Torre's hit-and-run groundout and then tallied the tying run on McCarver's single to center. "Both runs were cheap," said Dierker about each team's first tally.

Dierker surrendered his third extra-base leadoff hit when Shannon doubled to left in the eighth and moved to third on Javier's sacrifice bunt. But Dierker once again escaped unscathed when he induced pinch-hitter Dave Ricketts and Carlton to ground out to second baseman Julio Gotay. "[Dierker is] mature beyond his years and he doesn't beg out of tight spots," mused Joe Heiling of the *Houston Post*.[6]

It looked as though the Astros might pull out a dramatic victory in the ninth. With Jesus Alou on first via a single, Dierker laced a two-out single to right field. Determined to force a play at home, Alou rounded third at full speed despite a sore leg; however, he stumbled and fell to the Astroturf and was subsequently tagged out to send the game into extra innings.

Long known for fundamentally sound baseball, the Cardinals committed another blunder in the 10th after Dierker's leadoff walk to Torre. Pinch-runner Dennis Ribant, a pitcher by trade, "impersonate[d] a man trying out for the Olympic 200-meter dash," opined Neal Russo of the *St. Louis Post-Dispatch* sarcastically.[7] With his head down, Ribant failed to see that right fielder Norm Miller had caught McCarver's liner or to notice third-base coach George Kissell frantically yelling at him, and he was easily doubled up.

The Astros threatened yet again when Torres lined a leadoff single in the 10th and moved to second on Martinez's sacrifice bunt. Carlton intentionally

Larry Dierker earned his first All-Star Game selection and became the Astros' first 20-game winner in 1969. He went 20-13 with a 2.33 ERA and 232 strikeouts in a career-high 305⅓ innings pitched. (Courtesy of Houston Astros Baseball Club).

tagged by catcher Johnny Edwards after a brief rundown; the play was officially scored as McCarver caught stealing home. Dierker fanned Shannon, retired Julian Javier, and breathed a sigh of relief.

The Astros collected their first hit of the game when Jimmy Wynn doubled to lead off the fourth. Rader followed with what Jim Wilson of the *Houston Chronicle* described as a "vicious bad-hopper" to second baseman Julian Javier, which struck him in the throat.[4] As Javier went down, writhing in agony, Wynn raced home and Rader made it to second. Carlton escaped further damage by fielding Norm Miller's chopper back to the mound and firing to third baseman Mike Shannon, who tagged a sliding Rader.

walked Wynn, and both runners advanced on Rader's bunt back to the mound. Don Bryant, pinch-hitting for Miller, grounded weakly to short to end the inning.

"I don't recall ever thinking that I had to come out of a game when I was young," said Dierker, but this contest was the first time he had ever gone into extra innings.[8] The 6-foot-4, 215-pound hurler tossed a hitless 11th, issuing a two-out walk to pinch-hitter Joe Hague before fanning Brock to end the frame.

Gotay led off the Astros 11th with a single off the Cardinals' first reliever, right-hander Ron Willis. Two batters later, the former Cardinal Edwards singled off reliever Joe Hoerner, an extremely dependable left-hander with a side-arm delivery who had carved out a microscopic 1.88 ERA in the previous three seasons. The Astros had left-handers Joe Morgan and Curt Blefary on the bench to pinch-hit, but they had no right-handed hitters. "Harry Walker told me to go up and hit," remembered Dierker, who was batting .136 (5-for-36) with no RBIs entering the game. "'I'm not going to send you back out there [to the mound],' he said. 'So get a hit!'" Dierker took a mighty swing at Hoerner's first pitch and launched what John Wilson described as a "booming smash off the left-field wall" to drive in Gotay for the dramatic winning run and end the game in 2 hours and 45 minutes.[9] "I figured he'd start off me off with a fastball," said Dierker after the game. "I was looking for it and just guessed right."[10]

Dierker walked only two and fanned seven in his five-hit, extra-inning complete-game performance to emerge victorious in a hard-fought duel against Carlton, who struck out 12 and walked six in a 10-inning no decision. "I had a chance to throw to a college guy at Fort Polk to stay in shape," noted Dierker, explaining that he was not surprised by his control or stamina. He also gave credit to his backstop, Johnny Edwards, a three-time All-Star while with Cincinnati. "Edwards was the best catcher I ever threw to," Dierker later stated unequivocally. "It was the mental aspect of the game. We were always

on the same page. He was a veteran and helped me to grow up."

Tal Smith said this kind of performance captured the essence of Dierker, who won 137 games and logged almost 2,300 innings in his 13 years with Houston. "[Dierker] pitched half his games in the Astrodome. True, it was a big park which favored pitchers," said Smith, who served the Astros for five decades in various front-office capacities. "But it also meant that pitchers were not generally going to get a lot of run support. That frequently resulted in Dierk and other starting pitchers being involved in close, low-scoring games. That's where Larry was usually at his best due to his tenacity and fearlessness."

Dierker enjoyed a career year in 1969, setting personal bests in victories (20), innings (305⅓), ERA (2.33), and strikeouts (232), yet did not receive a single vote for the Cy Young Award.

SOURCES

In addition to the sources cited in the Notes, the author also accessed Retrosheet.org, Baseball-Reference.com, the SABR Minor Leagues Database, accessed online at Baseball-Reference.com, SABR.org, and *The Sporting News* archive via Paper of Record.

NOTES

1   All quotations from Larry Dierker are from the author's phone interview with him on February 10, 2016, unless otherwise noted.

2   John Wilson, "Dierker Trumps Cards in 11th," *Houston Chronicle*, June 9, 1969: Section 2, 1.

3   All quotations from Tal Smith are from the author's email interview with him on January 13, 2016, unless otherwise noted.

4   Wilson.

5   Wilson.

6   Joe Heiling, "Soldier Larry Dierker Marches Astros Past Cards, 2-1," *Houston Post*, June 9, 1969, Section 3, page 1.

7   Neal Russo, "Red Rousts Sleeping Birds," *St. Louis Post-Dispatch*, June 9, 1969: 1C.

8   Dierker pitched more than nine innings on only one other occasion. On September 13, 1969, he allowed just four hits while throwing 12 shutout innings (only to receive a no-decision) against the Atlanta Braves.

9   Wilson.

10 Heiling.

"An Overly Tame Ending to a Very Hairy Game"[1]

July 11, 1970: Houston Astros 5, San Francisco Giants 4 (14 innings), at the Astrodome

By Alan Cohen

TWO TEAMS WITH A HISTORY OF extra-inning games[2] faced each other on a Saturday evening in the Astrodome and, after 4 hours and 14 minutes the Astros emerged victorious over the San Francisco Giants in 14 innings before the remnants of a crowd announced as 27,208. Giants great Willie Mays stood atop the list of home runs by an active player, and was closing in on 3,000 career hits for his career. Though Mays had hit only 10 home runs at the Astrodome, four had been memorable. His 500th came there on September 13, 1965, off Don Nottebart and, on the very next night, number 501 tied a game in the ninth inning when the Giants were down to their last out. He had tied Mel Ott as the all-time National League home run king on April 24, 1966, with number 511, off Jim Owens, and number 550 had come off Barry Latman at the Dome on June 13, 1967.

The high-powered veteran offense of the Giants had not been performing up to expectations. In May, with a record of 19-23, the club's brass sacked manager Clyde King and replaced him with Charley Fox. The move yielded few immediate dividends. After defeating Houston 8-5 on July 10, the Giants, despite a four-game winning streak, were still in fourth place in the NL West and were 17½ games out of first. The Astros were in fifth place at the time and trailed the Giants by 7½ games.

Before the game, the only excitement figured to be that of the 39-year-old Mays chasing down posterity. But by game's end, it was one of the least likely players on the field who would garner the headlines.

The Astros broke on top with single runs in the second and third innings off Giants starter Rich Robertson. In the second inning, after two-out singles by Houston pitcher Larry Dierker and former Giant Jesus Alou, Joe Morgan singled to left field to score Dierker. As he scored, Dierker stepped on the foot of Giants catcher Dick Dietz, spiking Dietz's left toe and forcing him out of the game at the end of the inning.[3] In the third, the Astros manufactured a run. After singles by Bob Watson and Denis Menke, Cesar Cedeno hit a comebacker that Robertson mishandled, loading the bases. A sacrifice fly off the bat of catcher Johnny Edwards brought in Watson with Houston's second run.

Meanwhile, Dierker was virtually untouchable. A single by Mays in the first inning brought him within five of the magical 3,000 target, but through six innings, Dierker had allowed only one other hit and had retired 13 consecutive batters, a streak that started with the last batter in the second inning.

The Giants finally broke through in their half of the seventh inning. A leadoff single by Ron Hunt and a homer by Willie McCovey, his 23rd of the season, tied the contest, but the Giants were unable to do any further damage. Dierker got out of the inning by inducing Hal Lanier to ground out with runners on first and second.

Those spectators who hung around to get one last glimpse of Mays were not disappointed when the Giants center fielder led off the ninth inning with a home run that put the Giants in front, 3-2. The homer off Dierker was the 619th of Mays's career, and his 2,996th hit. All that remained was for Giants reliever Jerry Johnson, who had come on in the sixth inning, to put one more zero on the scoreboard.

But after Jimmy Wynn led off the inning with a fly ball to Mays, Bob Watson singled, and the managers went to work. Two players whose careers had begun on Brooklyn's sandlots entered the game. Fox removed Johnson and gave the ball to Don McMahon, who at age 40 already had four wins and seven saves this season. Joe Pepitone, who had revolutionized hair care in the clubhouse during his days with the Yankees, also entered to pinch-run for Watson.

Menke greeted McMahon with a triple to knock in Pepitone and the score was tied again. Cedeno struck out, then the Giants intentionally walked two batters to get to the pitcher's spot in the Houston lineup. The gambit worked as pinch-hitter Norm Miller, recently returned from Army Reserve duty,[4] hit into a force play to send the game into extra innings.

Jim Ray came on to pitch for the Astros while McMahon stayed in the game for the Giants. Innings 10 and 11 were scoreless. The fans also sat through a scoreless 12th inning as the Astros' Fred Gladding and the Giants' Mike Davison pitched out of difficulty. Davison struck out Cedeno with the bases loaded.

Bobby Bonds led off the top of the 13th inning with his 14th home run to give the Giants a 4-3 lead. Manager Fox entrusted the lead to Davison, a 24-year-old who came up in June and was appearing in his 10th major-league game. To this point, his major-league record was 0-2 and, even after pitching two shutout innings the prior evening, his ERA for the season stood at 9.00. Thus, nobody was particularly surprised when Doug Rader led off the inning with a double and advanced to third on a bunt single by Edwards, who was attempting to sacrifice but beat the throw to first base. Don Bryant pinch-hit for Gladding and his groundout scored Rader with the tying run and advanced Edwards to second base.

The unusual continued as Alou's groundball to the left side hit Edwards as he ran to third base and Edwards was ruled out. After that, things really got dicey. A single by Joe Morgan and a walk to Wynn resulted in Davison having his second bases-loaded situation in as many innings. He escaped

Johnny Edwards caught 151 games in 1969, an Astros franchise record that stands unbroken as of 2016. An excellent defensive backstop, Edwards gunned down 49 of 102 would-be base thieves that season, a 48 percent success rate. (Courtesy of Houston Astros Baseball Club).

again—barely—thanks to second baseman Bob Heise's leaping catch of Marty Martinez's looper to short right field and the game continued into the 14th inning.

Pitcher Jim Bouton entered the game for the Astros in the 14th. He had come back from obscurity the previous season to appear in 73 games with the Seattle Pilots and the Astros. So far in 1970, he had made 24 appearances and had posted a 3-6 record. Bouton's knuckleball danced away from the bats of John Stephenson, Al Gallagher, and Frank Johnson, each of whom made contact but were retired easily.

It was Houston's turn to bat again in a game that had already seen 18 Giant names and an equal number of Astro names scribbled on the managers' lineup cards. Houston had stranded 24 runners through 13 innings, leaving the bags full four times. Davison stayed in the game to pitch for the Giants, as he was due up second in the top of the 15th inning.

Menke, who had already gone 3-for-6 in the game to raise his team-leading batting average to .314, led off and grounded out. In keeping with the theme of the inning, the play was somewhat unusual in that Menke's line drive bounced off third baseman Gallagher and caromed to shortstop Hal Lanier, who threw Menke out. Cedeno singled to center field and advanced to third base on Rader's single, the Astros' record-breaking 21st hit in a home game. That brought up Johnny Edwards, who was in the throes of a miserable season, batting just .182. He sent a soft fly ball to Bonds in right field, and Cedeno, after tagging up at third base, dashed home with the winning run. Houston's 25 men left on base were a major-league record for a game of 14 innings or less, yet the Astros had still managed to win the game.

The win went to Bouton, his fourth and last win of the season. Any of Bouton's feats on the mound would soon be overwhelmed by the publication of *Ball Four*, his telling and sometimes irreverent look at baseball that he wrote while pitching with Seattle and Houston during the 1969 season. His good fortune in getting this win led Wells Twombly of the *San Francisco Chronicle* to note, "Mark Twain never had such luck."[5] Bouton would win only one more major-league game. He retired after 1970 but made a comeback attempt with the Braves in 1978, going 1-3 in five games.

Willie Mays, in the twilight of his career, reached the 3,000-hit plateau a week after the game in Houston. His ninth-inning homer was his final one at the Astrodome.

SOURCES

In addition to sources cited in the Notes, the author used Baseball-Reference.com and the following:

Associated Press, "Houston Whips Frisco in 14th," *Port Arthur* (Texas) *News*, July 12, 1970: 13.

Bock Hal (Associated Press). "Mays Can Celebrate in Cincinnati by Having Hot Weekend," *Idaho State Journal* (Pocatello), July 12, 1970: B-6.

Thompson, Greg. "The Sideliner," *Paris* (Texas) *News*, July 12, 1970: 13.

Twombly, Wells. "The Ageless Willie Mays, But Then … ," *San Francisco Chronicle*, September 18, 1970: C3.

NOTES

1 Wells Twombly, "Giants' Fictional Loss," *San Francisco Chronicle*, July 12, 1970: C1.

2 As of the date of this game, San Francisco and Houston had played each other in four games that went 20 innings or more. The Giants and Mets on May 31, 1964, had played a 23-inning game which was the second game of a doubleheader. The Giants and Reds had played 21 innings on September 1, 1967. The Astros and the Mets on April 15, 1968, had played 24 innings, and on June 3, 1989, the Astros and Dodgers had played 22 innings.

3 United Press International, "Giants Dietz Spiked in Game," *Twin Falls* (Idaho) *Times*, July 12, 1970: 22.

4 *Terre Haute* (Indiana) *Evening Star*, July 12, 1970: 51.

5 Twombly.

The "Toy Cannon" Wallops Two Homers and Knocks In Five

August 30, 1970: Houston Astros 9, New York Mets 5, at the Astrodome

By Chuck Johnson

SUNDAY, AUGUST 30, 1970, DAWNED as a typical late-summer day in Houston, Texas: the temperature in the high 80s, humidity in the 70s, with a thunderstorm or two almost a certainty.[1] Though the inside of the Astrodome was a cool, air-conditioned 72 degrees, the hometown Astros were hotter than the outside air.

The Astros had swept a three-game series against the Expos in Montreal on a recent road trip and then had taken their first two games against the New York Mets upon returning home. Standing in the way of consecutive victory number six was Mets manager Gil Hodges' choice to start, a hard-throwing right-hander who later became a legend in Astros history, Nolan Ryan.

The Mets, on the other hand, struggled right from Opening Day in defense of their 1969 World Series championship. Consistency was their worst enemy; a four-game winning streak in mid-May was followed almost immediately by a four-game losing streak while, conversely, an early-June four-game losing streak was backed up by a four-game winning streak.

A five-game winning streak in late June pushed the Mets past the Chicago Cubs to the top of the National League Eastern Division for the first time all season. The Cubs wouldn't back down, though; a seven-game winning streak by the Mets that began on July 3 saw them pick up only a game and a half in the standings.

The Mets' early-season pattern of streakiness once again caught up to them; they immediately lost five straight after the July winning streak ended. The negative stretch of play dropped the New Yorkers out of first place, 2½ games behind the Cubs.

Things were a bit different for the Astros. Despite the recent hot spell, they sat in fifth place in the Western Division at 59-70, 23½ games behind the first-place Cincinnati Reds, as the series with the Mets approached.

Astros manager Harry Walker chose right-hander Don Wilson to oppose Ryan in the series finale. A flamethrower himself, Wilson was now healthy after an early-season elbow injury.[2] The 25-year-old Wilson was two years older than his mound opponent. While Ryan put together a legendary career that would culminate with his election to the Baseball Hall of Fame in 1999, Wilson died from accidental carbon-monoxide poisoning at the age of 29 after winning 104 games and losing 94 in nine seasons in the big leagues.

The Astros' winning streak was put in immediate jeopardy in the first inning when Mets cleanup batter Donn Clendenon powered a three-run homer to left field after Tommie Agee doubled and Wayne Garrett singled.

Houston got right back in the game in the bottom of the first when Jesus Alou walked and Jimmy Wynn drove a Ryan offering into the left-field seats, narrow the Mets' lead to 3-2. After his three-hit shutout of the Cubs on August 4, Ryan had not pitched well the remainder of the month. Coming into the Houston start, he had lost his previous four starts while making it into the sixth inning just once and had also been charged with a blown save against Cincinnati in New York on August 22nd.

Wynn, nicknamed "The Toy Cannon" for the prodigious power coiled in his 5-foot-9, 170-pound frame, averaged 20 homers per season during his 11

In 11 seasons in Houston, Jimmy Wynn lived up to his "Toy Cannon" nickname by amassing 1,291 hits, 228 doubles, 223 home runs, and 719 RBIs. He was an All-Star for the Astros in 1967. (Courtesy of Houston Astros Baseball Club).

seasons with the Astros despite playing home games in the vast Astrodome. The 1970 season proved to be tumultuous for Wynn. Hidden behind his well-known offensive production was the fact that he was also one of the top defensive center fielders in the game. However, on July 8, Wynn's role with the team changed when he was replaced in center field by 19-year-old minor-league prospect Cesar Cedeño. Wynn would finish the season strong, posting a career-high .282 average, but he was unhappy with being moved to left field to make room for the rookie. Signed from the Dominican Republic as a 17-year-old in 1967, Cedeño made his major-league debut on June 20 and finished fourth in the National League Rookie of the Year voting despite playing just 90 games.

The Mets came right back with a run in the top of the second, and led 4-2 as the Astros came up in the third inning. As was the case in the first, Wynn came to the plate with one out and one on, this time Joe Morgan via a single. Wynn again took Ryan deep, tying the score at 4-4.

Houston took the lead for good in the fourth inning. Five-time Gold Glove-winning (1970-74) third baseman Doug Rader drew a leadoff walk and went to second when New York's Ken Singleton dropped Cedeno's blooper to right field. Then Johnny Edwards punched a single to left through the drawn-in infield, scoring Rader with an unearned run.

Houston added two more runs in the fifth. Morgan walked and Wynn followed with his third hit of the game, a single to left. After John Mayberry grounded into a double play started by the pitcher, the Astros' All-Star shortstop, Denis Menke, homered for a 7-4 lead.

Wynn drove in his fifth run of the game in the sixth inning, drawing a bases-loaded walk off relief pitcher Rich Folkers, who entered the game after Ryan was lifted for a pinch-hitter in the top of the inning.

Menke concluded the Astros' scoring in the seventh with his second homer of the game, stretching the lead to 9-4. Wynn concluded his monster day with his fourth hit, a single off Ron Taylor in the eighth inning.

The Mets got a run in the ninth inning. Art Shamsky led off with a single off Jim Ray, who had come in the seventh inning when Wilson left because of a pulled groin muscle.[3] After a passed ball, a strikeout, and walk to Wayne Garrett, Harry Walker replaced Ray with Fred Gladding. Cleon Jones greeted the Houston closer with a single to left, scoring Shamsky and bringing the tying run to the on-deck circle. But Gladding retired the next two hitters, striking out Clendenon looking and getting Singleton to ground out to Morgan at second base, making the final score 9-5 and giving the Astros their sixth straight victory.

For his career, Wynn hit .375 (9-for-24) against Ryan with four homers and a .917 slugging average. Over the legendary Ryan's illustrious career, only a dozen players hit four or more career homers off him and only one, Harold Baines, did so in fewer plate appearances (25) than did Wynn. Wynn was one of four hitters (besides Rick Cerone, Bruce Bochte, and Lonnie Smith) to hit .375 or better against Ryan with as many as 30 plate appearances.

After the game, Wynn told the reporters gathered around him, "This was the best day I've had all year. Mainly because I got fastballs and that's what I expected to see against Nolan Ryan." Then he spoke of his wish to be traded. "Nothing has changed for me," he said. "I still want to be traded. I just hope if they trade me it's to an American League team."

Wynn's desire to be traded seemed to stem from a belief that he was being disciplined for some reason. Referring to general manager Spec Richardson and manager Harry Walker, Wynn said, "All I've ever gotten from them is a bunch of static."[4]

Wynn's demand for a trade wouldn't be granted until after the 1973 season, when he was sent to the Los Angeles Dodgers. Returning to center field, Wynn finished fifth in the National League MVP race and led the Dodgers to the 1974 World Series, which they lost to the three-time champion Oakland A's.

NOTES

1   Farmersalmanac.com, Houston weather, August 30, 1970.

2   Matthew Clifford, "Don Wilson," at sabr.org/bioproj/person/1643c2b4.

3   Fred Hartman, "Astros Wynn over Mets, 9-5," *Baytown* (Texas) *Sun*, August 31, 1970.

4   Associated Press, "Astros Wynn over Mets, 9-5," *Paris* (Texas) *News*, August 31, 1970.

Trailing 4-0, Houston Scores Five Unanswered Runs, and Wins on Joe Morgan's Walk-Off Homer

September 19, 1971: Houston Astros 5,
Cincinnati Reds 4 (11 innings), at the Astrodome

By Gordon Gattie

ENTERING THEIR SEPTEMBER 19, 1971, Sunday-afternoon game against the visiting Cincinnati Reds, the Houston Astros were teetering on the brink of elimination. The previous night's 11-inning, 3-2 loss to the Reds had pushed the Astros into a virtual tie for fourth place with the Reds, 10 games behind the National League West-leading San Francisco Giants.

The Astros sent 24-year-old rookie Scipio Spinks to the mound for just his second major-league start of the season. He had spent most of the season with Triple-A Oklahoma City. His first start, on September 6, was a complete-game victory over the Atlanta Braves. Before this Sunday start, Spinks had pitched five days earlier, working 5⅔ scoreless innings in relief of starter Wade Blasingame against the San Diego Padres. The Reds' starter, seven-year veteran Jim Merritt, was struggling with a 1-11 record after enjoying a 20-win season and his only All-Star appearance in the previous season.

During pregame ceremonies, Joe Morgan, the Astros' second baseman, was honored as the Most Popular Astro this season, picked in fan voting. Morgan, who was celebrating his 28th birthday, was rewarded with a trip to Acapulco for himself and his wife.

Spinks started strong, setting down Pete Rose and Dave Concepcion on groundouts, followed by the first of three strikeouts in the game by Reds first baseman Lee May. In the bottom half of the first, Roger Metzger and Cesar Cedeno both singled, but were stranded in scoring position. The Reds then started

to put a damper on Morgan's birthday and award celebration, scoring the game's first run in the top of the second inning when Hal McRae singled home Tony Perez. Cincinnati padded its lead in the third when Johnny Bench delivered a three-run homer, his 25th round-tripper of the season, bringing home Rose and Perez.

Down four runs, the Astros threatened during the fourth inning when singles by Cedeno and Denis Menke, combined with a walk to Larry Howard, loaded the bases with two outs for Houston's eighth-place hitter, John Mayberry. However, the hulking first baseman, who entered the game batting just .185, popped out to short. The Astros finally scored in the bottom of the sixth inning when Jimmy Wynn's sacrifice fly brought home Cedeno. Spinks had settled down after Bench's homer, keeping the Reds off the basepaths through the seventh inning. In the bottom of the seventh, after Howard doubled off shortstop Darrel Chaney's glove and Mayberry struck out, Astros manager Harry Walker lifted Spinks for pinch-hitter Jesus Alou while Reds manager Sparky Anderson brought in Ed Sprague to replace Merritt. Alou singled, moving Howard to third. Metzger reached on an error by Reds second baseman Concepcion, the only error in the game; Howard scored the Astros' second run and Alou reached third base. Morgan hit a sacrifice fly, then singles by Cedeno and Bob Watson tied the game, 4-4. Cedeno's seventh-inning single was his fourth hit of the game. He was perfect, with the four hits and a walk.

In the eighth the Reds responded after two outs with a single by May and walk by Perez, but Bench flied to center field against reliever Jim Ray, ending the inning. In the bottom of the eighth, the Astros were scoreless. Both teams had runners in scoring position in the ninth inning; the Reds' McRae doubled but pinch-runner Buddy Bradford was stranded, while the Astros loaded the bases with one out on a single by Metzger, a sacrifice, and two walks, one intentional. When Wynn flied to center field, Metzger tried to score, but Bradford's throw nailed him to send the ballgame into extra innings.

The Reds went down in order in the top of the 10th while the Astros moved runners into scoring position again in the bottom of the inning. With two outs, Mayberry singled. Pinch-hitter Rich Chiles singled off the Reds' Clay Carroll, advancing pinch-runner Derrel Thomas to third, but Metzger grounded to Concepcion to send the game into the 11th inning. Fred Gladding took the mound for the Astros after Ray pitched three scoreless innings. Gladding walked Bench and hit Bradford before getting Woody Woodward to ground out to third to quell the threat.

After pitching two scoreless innings, Clay Carroll returned to the mound for the bottom of the 11th. On his first pitch, Joe Morgan delivered a game-ending home run, his 13th of the season, sending the crowd of 9,260 fans home happy. The win for Gladding evened his record at 4-4, while Carroll dropped to 9-4.[1] The game-winning shot by Morgan was his last homer of the season, and his 13 blasts led the Astros.

Houston traded Joe Morgan to Cincinnati in 1971. After he won two NL MVP Awards and two World Series with the Reds, he returned to help the Astros win their first division title in 1980. (Courtesy of Houston Astros Baseball Club).

For the year, Morgan also tied Metzger for the NL lead with 11 triples and reached his personal best, to that point in his career, with 56 RBIs.

The day after the game Morgan was quoted as saying, "I said in May that if I led the team in home runs, we'll finish fifth. I guarantee you that you can't win if you don't have home runs, despite what some people say."[2] Morgan's words were nearly prophetic; the Astros finished fourth in the NL West—tied with the Reds.

The Giants defeated the Padres, 4-1, at Candlestick Park that afternoon, eliminating both the Astros and Reds from postseason play. Although Morgan was pleased with his performance during the season, he said he wouldn't be surprised if he were traded over the winter. He explained: "We've got a ball club that should have won the pennant race or come close. And we didn't. We've got to make some changes."[3]

As measured by Wins Above Replacement (WAR), Morgan was the most valuable offensive player on the 1971 Astros, with the highest on-base plus slugging percentage among regulars (.757) and the most stolen bases (40). Only staff ace Don Wilson, with a 16-10 record and a 2.45 ERA over

268 innings, had a higher WAR (6.1) than Morgan (5.6). Morgan correctly predicted that changes to the Astros' roster would be made. On November 29 the Astros traded him along with Ed Armbrister, Jack Billingham, Cesar Geronimo, and Denis Menke to Cincinnati for Tommy Helms, Lee May, and Jimmy Stewart. The trade gave the Reds the missing pieces they needed to become one of baseball's dominant teams for the rest of the decade.

SOURCES

In addition to the sources cited in the Notes, the author also consulted:

Thorn, John, Pete Palmer, et al. *Total Baseball: The Official Encyclopedia of Major League Baseball* (New York: Viking Press, 2004).

NOTES

1   Associated Press, "Reds Blow 4-0 Margin In 5-4 Loss in 'Dome,'" *Hamilton* (Ohio) *Journal News*, September 20, 1971: 54.

2   Darrell Mack, "Little Joe Slugs Again," *Brownsville* (Texas) *Herald*, September 20, 1971: 9.

3   Associated Press, "Morgan May Be Traded," *Corpus Christi* (Texas) *Caller-Times*, September 20, 1971: 18.

Reuss Spins One-Hitter

June 18, 1972: Houston Astros 10, Philadelphia Phillies 0, at the Astrodome

By Richard A. Cuicchi

THE HOUSTON ASTROS WERE IN THE midst of their first-ever winning season in 1972 when a relative newcomer to the team, Jerry Reuss, on the eve of his 23rd birthday, spun a one-hitter against the Philadelphia Phillies on June 18. The game was among the first that brought national attention to Reuss, who wound up winning 220 games, including a no-hitter.

The Astros were looking to add an experienced left-handed starter to their rotation when they acquired Reuss in a trade with the St. Louis Cardinals on Opening Day of the strike-delayed 1972 season in exchange for pitchers Lance Clemons and Scipio Spinks. Reuss joined a young Astros staff that included Don Wilson, Larry Dierker, Dave Roberts, and Ken Forsch. In his third major-league season (and first full season) in 1971, the 6-foot-5 Reuss started 35 games with the Cardinals and began to draw comparisons to teammate Steve Carlton, another tall, hard-throwing lefty.[1] However, early in his career Reuss struggled with control problems.

Since their inaugural season in the National League in 1962, the Astros had come close to a winning season only once, when they compiled an 81-81 record in 1969. Until then they had finished in eighth, ninth, or tenth place in the National League each year.

With a lineup built around sluggers Jim Wynn, Bob Watson, Cesar Cedeno, Lee May, and Doug Rader, the Astros blasted off at the beginning of the 1972 season, holding first or second place through the month of May.

On the day of Reuss's one-hitter, the Astros entered the game in second place in the National League West Division, 2½ games behind the Cincinnati Reds. The mustachioed blond had hurled a complete game in his previous start for the Astros, on June 12, for his fourth victory of the year against five losses.

The June 18 game took place on a Sunday afternoon at the Astrodome before a crowd of 20,768. The Phillies' starting pitcher was 24-year-old right-hander Bill Champion, who had won four games and lost four to that point in the season.

Reuss had no trouble with the Phillies in the first inning, when he faced only three batters to retire the side. Champion was not as fortunate; the Astros attacked him in the bottom of the first, scoring three earned runs before Champion was replaced by Barry Lersch. Lersch allowed another run, which was charged to Champion, who recorded only one out before his exit. Run-scoring doubles by Cesar Cedeno and Bob Watson were the key hits for the Astros. Altogether, the Astros pounded out five hits in the inning.

Astros manager Harry Walker didn't have any pitching decisions to make in the game, since Reuss sailed through the next seven frames, not allowing any hits to the Phillies, although he did serve up a walk in each of the second, third, seventh, and eighth innings; however, on this day, his control issues were not a factor in the game.

Meanwhile, Houston added three more runs in the fifth inning off Lersch and one in the seventh off Ken Reynolds. Cedeno hit a solo home run and Watson drove in two more runs.

In the bottom of the eighth inning, the Astros increased their lead again on a bases-loaded groundout by Jesus Alou and a bases-loaded walk to Watson, his fourth RBI of the game.

Going into the top of the ninth inning with a 10-0 lead, Reuss had struck out seven while holding

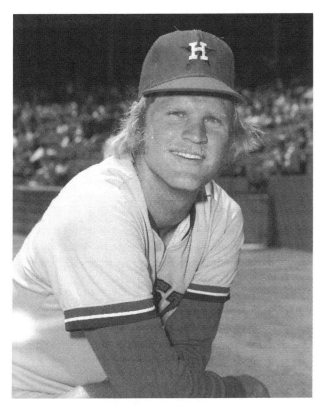

Jerry Reuss won 25 games with Houston over the 1972–73 seasons. A three-time 18-game winner, Reuss won 220 games total and captured a World Series title with the 1981 Los Angeles Dodgers. (National Baseball Hall of Fame, Cooperstown, New York).

the Phillies hitless. He had stayed with his fastball in the late innings when it became apparent a no-hitter was on the line.[2]

But it wasn't to be. Larry Bowa led off the Phillies ninth with a hard line drive between third baseman Doug Rader and the foul line for a double. It was the Phillies' first and only hit of the game. Reuss gathered himself to retire Don Money on a fly out and Greg Luzinski and Roger Freed on strikeouts to end the game. During the course of his gem, Reuss twice struck out each of the three batters (Luzinski, Freed, and Willie Montanez) in the middle of the Phillies' batting order.

Rader, a five-time Gold Glove winner during his career, was playing a few steps in front of third base, expecting that Bowa might bunt. After the game Rader said, "That was the first ball he has ever pulled hard at me in all the times we've played them. I hardly even saw it before it was by. I never expected

him to hit the ball like that and I didn't want Reuss to lose a no-hitter on a squibbler or something."[3]

Years later, Reuss recalled Rader's reaction after the game: "He apologized for not catching Bowa's smashing hit. I told him there isn't a third baseman in the history of the game that makes that play."[4]

After the game Reuss had said, "I had kind of mixed emotions after the hit. I thought, 'Well it's over.' There was kind of a relief, not that I wanted him to get a hit because I really wanted the no-hitter. But the pressure was off. I was disappointed, no question of that."[5]

Asked by a sportswriter whether he had ever pitched a no-hitter, Reuss said, "No, I've never come this close to one before. Not even in the minors. I had one or two in high school, but that was a long time ago."[6]

In a remarkably rare occurrence in baseball history, Reuss's teammate, Larry Dierker, pitched a one-hit shutout for the Astros the next day against the New York Mets. The back-to-back one-hitters tied a major-league record set by Cleveland Naps pitchers in 1907 and repeated by the Milwaukee Braves in 1965.[7] Reuss's and Dierker's efforts were indicative of the competitive nature the Astros were finally displaying in 1972.

The Astros wound up the season in second place in the West Division, one percentage point ahead of the Dodgers but 10½ games behind the division-leading Reds. Even though the season was shortened by a players' strike, the Astros' 84 wins set a team record.

Reuss finished the 1972 season with a 9-13 record in 192 innings pitched, led the team in strikeouts, and dropped his ERA to 4.17 from 4.78 in the previous year. His performance established him as a key component in the Astros' rotation, and he would go on to win 16 games in 1973.

On June 27, 1980, eight years and nine days after his one-hitter for the Astros, Reuss threw a no-hitter for the Los Angeles Dodgers against the San Francisco Giants. He just missed tossing a perfect game, with a first inning error by shortstop Bill Russell the only blemish.

Reuss is best remembered for his stints with the Pittsburgh Pirates and the Dodgers, with whom he won a World Series championship in 1981. He was only the second pitcher in baseball history, following Milt Pappas, to win 200 games without recording a 20-win season.[8]

On June 18, 1972, Reuss pitched one of the best games of his career. In the next day's edition, the *Philadelphia Inquirer* used a reference to the elite Rolls-Royce automobile as a way to illustrate the pronunciation of Reuss's surname.[9] Indeed, it was an elite performance that day for a blossoming young left-hander.

SOURCES

In addition to the sources mentioned in the notes, the author also consulted:

Eisenbath, Mike. *The Cardinals Encyclopedia* (Philadelphia: Temple Press, 1999).

Houston Astros Press/Radio/TV Guide 1973.

Hulsey, Bob. *1972 — Season Recap.* astrosdaily.com/history/. Accessed September 22, 2015.

Reuss, Jerry. *Bring In the Right-Hander!* (Lincoln: University of Nebraska Press, 2014).

NOTES

1   John Wilson. "Reuss Sidesteps Sizeup With Old Pal Steve," *The Sporting News,* February 10, 1973: 49.

2   *Houston Post,* June 19, 1972: D2.

3   *Houston Chronicle,* June 19, 1972, Section 2: 1.

4   Jerry Reuss, telephone interview with author, August 25, 2015.

5   *Houston Chronicle,* June 19, 1972, Section 2: 1.

6   *Houston Post,* June 19, 1972: D2.

7   On September 25, 1907, Addie Joss pitched a one-hitter for the Cleveland Naps against the New York Highlanders; the next day Heinie Berger threw a one-hitter for the Naps. On September 10, 1965, Wade Blasingame, Billy O'Dell, and Phil Niekro combined to pitch a one-hitter for the Milwaukee Braves against the New York Mets. The next day the Braves' Tony Cloninger threw a one-hitter against the Mets.

8   David Pietrusza, Matthew Silverman, and Michael Gershman, eds., *Baseball: The Biographical Encyclopedia* (New York: Total/Sports Illustrated, 2000).

9   Bruce Keidan. "Bowa Breaks Up No-Hitter in 9th Inning as Astros Trample Phils, 10-0," *Philadelphia Inquirer,* June 19, 1972: 13.

Home Runs, Controversies, Ejections, Home-Plate Collisions, Errors, Occasional Good Pitching and Even a Walk-Off Hit Define a Wild Double Extra-Inning Twin Bill

July 30, 1972: San Diego Padres 10, Houston Astros 7 (game one, 14 innings); Astros 4, Padres 3 (game two, 10 innings) at the Astrodome

By Gregory H. Wolf

"THINGS JUST KEPT HAPPENING, unexpected things, rare things, exciting things, dramatic things," wrote John Wilson of the *Houston Chronicle* after the Astros doubleheader split with the visiting San Diego Padres that involved everything from dramatic home runs, controversial plays at home plate, and game-interrupting disputes to stellar defensive plays and even occasionally good pitching.[1] "It was a long day of baseball at the Astrodome," he continued about the twin bill which began at 1:33 P.M. and ended at 9:06, "but it was never dull."[2]

The Astros were reeling when they took batting practice on July 30, 1972, to kick off a three-game set with the Padres as part of a season-longest 14-game homestand. Skipper Harry Walker's group had unexpectedly challenged the mighty Cincinnati Reds for first place earlier in the season and had even held the top spot in the NL West as late as June 24. But lately they had been in a freefall, having lost nine of their last 13 games to fall to 52-43, six games behind the Big Red Machine. The Padres were in familiar territory, last in the NL West (35-57), 21½ games off the pace. "[C]ollectively or individually," opined the Associated Press, "[they] make up a lousy baseball team.[3] Manager Preston Gomez was fired 11 games into the season, giving Don Zimmer, the team's third-base coach, his first opportunity to pilot a big-league club. The Padres, who finished last in runs scored and 11th of 12 teams in ERA in 1972, probably left the fiery manager wishing he was still playing for the Brooklyn Dodgers of the 1950s.

Some of the 27,388 spectators who piled into the Astrodome on the last Sunday in July probably came to see the season debut of Houston's hard-throwing 22-year-old right-hander J.R. Richard, to whom Houston newspapers still referred by his given name, James Rodney. The towering, 6-foot-8 hurler had caught the attention of the baseball world the previous September when he struck out a big-league record 15 in his major-league debut. He had thus far spent the '72 season with Oklahoma City in the Triple-A American Association, where he fanned 169 but also walked 79 in 128 innings.

In the first inning Richard displayed his heater but also his wildness, his one glaring bugaboo. He walked leadoff hitter Derrel Thomas, who stole second and subsequently scored on Curt Blefary's two-out double. Richard also fanned two. The Padres, apparently feeling no effects of their 17-inning, 4-3 victory over the Reds the previous day, tacked on another run in the second when Fred Kendall singled and later scored on Thomas's two-out single.

After the Astros picked up a run in the second when Bob Watson doubled and scored on Doug Rader's groundout, Richard imploded. Larry Stahl singled, Blefary walked, both advanced on a wild pitch, and both scored on Cito Gaston's double, which made the score 4-1 and sent the big Louisianan to the showers.

Rader, celebrating his 28th birthday, belted a two-run homer in the fourth off the Padres' starter, 29-year-old southpaw Fred Norman, to make it a game, 4-3. A foot shorter than Richard, Norman had a career 10-24 record, including 5-7 thus far in '72. He was yanked the following inning after walking pitcher George Culver, who later scored on a wild pitch to tie the game and end Norman's afternoon. The ever dangerous Jim Wynn then doubled off reliever Ed Acosta, driving in Cesar Cedeño, who had singled, to give the Astros a 5-4 lead. Wynn tallied the Astros' sixth run after he stole third and scored on Watson's sacrifice fly to center.

The Astros' 6-4 lead evaporated in the eighth when Dave Roberts belted a one-out, three-run clout to left field off reliever Jim Ray to drive in Garry Jestadt, who had reached on a bunt single to third, and Thomas, whose hot grounder shortstop Roger Metzger fumbled. "I've got to make better pitches than that in that situation," fumed Ray about his faulty slider to Roberts.[4]

The game took a bizarre turn in the bottom of the frame. The Astros loaded the bases with no outs as Rader and Tommy Helms walked and Larry Howard greeted the Padres' sixth pitcher of the day, Mike Caldwell, with a "punch single" after faking a bunt.[5] Pinch-hitter Jesus Alou followed with a chopper back to Caldwell, who immediately threw to catcher Fred Kendall.[6] The stout, 6-foot-2, 210-pound Rader barreled over Kendall, who held on to the ball, as Alou raced to first. A "king-size rhubarb" ensued, wrote Jim Wilson, when home-plate umpire Stan Landes belatedly called interference on Rader, who had already walked back to the Astros dugout.[7] Landes called Alou out and ordered him off first base, setting off an argument that interrupted the game for at least 10 minutes. "It was the worst call I've ever seen," said

Astros catcher Johnny Edwards, who, like the rest of his teammates, argued that Rader had no alternative other than run into Kendall, who had been standing on home plate.[8] Furthermore, the Astros complained that interference was rarely called on a double play. "I told Landes he was the worst umpire in the league," said Rader, who was tossed in the brouhaha. "When a man has the ball, he's fair game."[9] With tempers boiling over, Landes kept his cool, even after Helms flung his batting helmet (which normally results in an automatic ejection), missing Landes by just a foot. Second-base umpire Bruce Froemming had little sympathy: "If they want charity they should have their family umpire [at the game]."[10] When play finally resumed, Metzger grounded out to end the frame.

The "fireworks really came" in the top of the ninth, reported the AP's John Black, when Rader took the field, apparently not knowing he had been ejected.[11] When Landes told him to leave the field, Rader charged him and had to be restrained by several teammates. But in the bottom of the ninth, Houston tallied the game-tying run after consecutive one-out singles by Wynn, Lee May, and Watson. The inning ended on Watson's baserunning blunder when he was doubled off first on Bobby Fenwick's fly to left field.

Caldwell mowed down the first 12 batters he faced in extra innings despite losing his batterymate, Kendall, in the 12th with an injured finger. His replacement, Dave Roberts, just two months removed from college, had not caught since high school. An inning earlier Caldwell had benefited from left fielder Larry Stahl's athletic catch of Cedeño's fly to deep left-center. According to Jim Wilson, Stahl raced to the warning track and made a "leaping going away catch just short of the wall."[12]

The Padres' Fred Stanley led off the 14th with a single off Jim York, the Astros' fourth reliever of the game, and moved to second on Jestadt's sacrifice bunt. After York walked slugger Nate Colbert intentionally, Thomas singled to right. Stanley raced home on contact and flattened catcher Larry Howard, jarring the ball from his glove. As Howard lay dazed on the ground, Stanley was called safe. "I didn't know where

I was," said Howard, who was replaced by Johnny Edwards. "They stuck some smelling salt under me and I jerked my head around. I didn't know what was happening."[13] Roberts followed with a single, his third hit of the game, off Tom Griffin, the Astros' sixth and final hurler of the game, driving in Colbert and Thomas and giving the Padres a 10-7 lead. It would be the only five-RBI game of Roberts's 10-year career.

By this time Helms was fuming and had had enough. He was ejected by Froemming for continuing to argue Landes's eighth-inning interference call. Griffith fanned Stahl and Caldwell to end the frame.

In the bottom of the 14th Wynn gave the Astros faithful a glimmer of hope by lining a two-out single and moving to second on Caldwell's wild pitch, but Caldwell induced May to ground weakly to short to end the game in 4 hours and 30 minutes.

Caldwell held the Astros to five hits and a run over seven innings of relief to even his record at 4-4. The 22-year-old rookie southpaw's performance was in stark contrast to his start just the previous day against the Reds when he lasted just three innings, yielding three hits and two runs. Jim York was collared with the loss. It was "one of those once-in-a-season affairs," opined Jim Wilson.[14] It was a frustrating loss for the Astros in all aspects. The NL's highest-scoring team in 1972, Houston collected 11 hits and drew six walks, yet left nine men on base. The Astros committed baserunning blunders and two errors, and their pitching staff struggled against a team that batted a collective .227 for the season. Doing their best impression of Zimmer's Brooklyn Dodgers, the Padres belted out 15 hits and drew a season-high 10 walks, but also left 15 men on base.

The Second Game

The Astrodome crowd saw "every type of baseball before the second game ever started," opined John Black.[15] After an intermission of about 25 minutes, the teams took the field around 6:30. The game featured two hurlers who were involved in what was widely considered a blockbuster trade the previous December when Houston shipped a highly touted prospect, right-hander Bill Greif; infielder Derrel Thomas, who had scored three times in the first game of the doubleheader; and southpaw reliever Mark Schaeffer to San Diego in exchange for pitcher Dave Roberts.

Roberts, a 27-year-old lefty in his fourth season, was considered a rising star. In 1971 he had a breakout season, going 14-17 for a dismal Padres team, and posting a stellar 2.10 ERA that trailed only the New York Mets' Tom Seaver. Despite elevated expectations now that he was pitching half his games in the cavernous Astrodome, Roberts was not as consistent thus far in '72. Recently he had been bothered by shoulder problems and was making his first start since a dismal outing (six hits and four runs in 4⅔ innings) against the Chicago Cubs a week earlier. Though Roberts had won eight of 13 decisions for Houston to improve his career record to 30-39, his 4.29 ERA was well above the league average. Greif, a 6-foot-4, 200-pound Texan, had struggled since shutting out Atlanta in his first start of the season and entered the game with a 5-11 record and a 5.06 ERA.

Both teams threatened in the first three innings, yet unlike the first game, neither team produced a run. After Thomas drew a leadoff walk to start the game, Dave Roberts the pitcher emerged victorious when Dave Roberts the Padres third baseman hit a sharp grounder to third baseman Doug Rader, back after his first-game banishment, who initiated a 5-4-3 twin killing. Jerry Morales singled, stole second, and reached third on Johnny Edwards' errant throw to second. Cleanup hitter Nate Colbert, whose 23 homers trailed Cincinnati's Johnny Bench by one for the NL lead, flied out to end the inning.

Houston also had its chances. Hot-hitting Cesar Cedeño, who entered the doubleheader leading the majors with a .351 batting average, belted a one-out triple in the first. He broke on contact when Jim Wynn mashed a hard grounder to third, but was gunned down at the plate by third baseman Dave Roberts' strike to catcher Curt Blefary. In the third Blefary was left stranded at third following his leadoff single.

Colbert put the Padres on the board in the fourth with a towering solo shot. Acquired from the Astros in the 1968 expansion draft, Colbert was among the most feared sluggers in the league. He had belted 24, 38, and 27 homers in his first three full seasons, and had just been named to his second of three consecutive All-Star teams. After Cito Gaston walked, Johnny Jeter bounced into an inning-ending 6-4-3 double play.[16]

While this game thus far lacked the barrage of hits of the first contest, the pitching of Greif and Roberts provided an equally tense situation. Rader led off the Astros' fifth with a single and moved to third when Roberts threw Tommy Helms' sharp grounder to third out of the reach of first baseman Colbert. Houston's Roberts then helped his own cause by driving in Rader with the tying run on a sacrifice fly.

Colbert gave the Padres a 3-1 lead with one stroke of the bat when, with a man on and two outs in the sixth, he parked a Roberts offering in the seats for his second clout of the game, and the 11th in his last 94 at-bats. The two RBIs gave him 23 in his last 24 games. "Both [home runs were] well into the pavilion seats," wrote Jim Wilson of the *Houston Chronicle*.[17]

The Padres were en route to their fourth consecutive last-place finish in the NL West, and their woes affected the good-natured Greif, who had passed up multiple football scholarships to embark upon a professional baseball career in 1968. "I pretty much collapsed under the pressure of losing," he admitted candidly in an interview with the author.[18] "I had never encountered that kind of losing. I ended up internalizing it and blaming myself." Greif had lost eight straight decisions in May and June as well as his spot in the rotation. "I felt responsible for all of the losing," Greif continued about his years in San Diego during which he went 5-16, 10-17, and 9-19 from 1972 to 1974. "I'd try to tighten up the game and do something extra, but at a certain point, it became counterproductive. I got to the point that I didn't expect anything good to happen." And July 30 against the Astros was one of those days where nothing good happened. After May hit a seeing-eye single to short with one down in the sixth, Watson singled to center. Center fielder Jeter misplayed the ball, allowing it to carom past him. By the time he retrieved it, May had

Nicknamed the "Red Rooster" for his red hair as well as his feistiness, Doug Rader spent nine seasons at third base for the Houston Astros and won five consecutive Gold Gloves from 1970–1974. (Courtesy of Houston Astros Baseball Club).

scored and Watson was standing on second. Greif retired Edwards and Rader on grounders to end the inning.

The Padres maintained a 3-2 lead until the eighth, when Cedeño and Wynn opened the frame with walks that ended Greif's night. Reliever Gary Ross gave the club a big boost by inducing May to ground into a 6-4-3 double play. The inning seemed to be over when Watson hit a routine grounder to third baseman Dave Roberts, but he misplayed it, enabling the speedy Cedeño to scamper home and tie the game. The Padres' third error of the game closed the book on Greif, who finished with eight strikeouts and six hits allowed in seven innings and surrendered three unearned runs.

After Roberts retired six of the seven batters he faced in the ninth and 10th innings, Cedeño led off with a walk. One of the brightest young stars of the game, he had earlier that month been named to his first of four All-Star games in five seasons. He stole second and reached third when Blefary misplayed Wynn's sacrifice bunt for the fourth San Diego error of the game. After Ross intentionally walked May to load the bases, 33-year-old journeyman Jimmy Stewart did his impression of George Bailey in *It's a Wonderful Life* by lining a walk-off, game-winning single to right-center field off reliever Mark Schaeffer that knocked in Cedeño, and ended the game in 2 hours and 37 minutes. Ross (3-2) was charged with loss.

In his first extra-inning outing since tossing a seven-hit, 12-inning shutout against the New York Mets on August 11, 1971, Roberts picked up his team-high ninth victory while fanning seven and yielding nine hits. "We needed a win for our starters," he said after the game while applying a heat pack to his ailing shoulder, and added that the Astros bullpen needed some rest.[19] A modest player, who was just as likely to compliment players on other teams as those on his own, Roberts marveled at big Nate Colbert's power. "It's too bad that he doesn't receive the press he would if he played in New York or in other bigger cities," he said of his former teammate.[20]

After 24 innings and more than seven hours of action-packed, tense baseball on Sunday, the Astros played another nail-biter the following day. They took the rubber match on Monday evening when Johnny Edwards drew a game-ending bases-loaded walk off Padres starter Steve Arlin to preserve Larry Dierker's eight-hit complete game victory, 3-2.

SOURCES

In addition to the sources cited in the Notes, the author also accessed Retrosheet.org, Baseball-Reference.com, the SABR Minor Leagues Database, accessed online at Baseball-Reference.com, SABR.org, and *The Sporting News* archive via Paper of Record.

NOTES

1   John Wilson, "Astros Split Marathon; Never a Dull Moment," *Houston Chronicle*, July 31, 1972: Section 2, 1.

2   Ibid.

3   John Black, Associated Press, "Padres, Astros Wind-Up Dome Series Tonight," *Baytown* (Texas) *Sun*, July 31, 1972: 4.

4   Wilson, "Astros Split Marathon; Never a Dull Moment."

5   Ibid.

6   John Wilson, "Happy Birthday to Doug," *Houston Chronicle*, July 31, 1972: Section 2, 2.

7   "Wilson, Astros Split Marathon; Never a Dull Moment."

8   Wilson, "Happy Birthday to Doug."

9   Ibid.

10 Ibid.

11 Black.

12 "Wilson, Astros Split Marathon; Never a Dull Moment."

13 Ibid.

14 Wilson, "Happy Birthday to Doug."

15 Black.

16 Johnny Jeter is not related to Derek Jeter. his son Shawn briefly made it to the majors with the White Sox in 1992.

17 "Wilson, Astros Split Marathon; Never a Dull Moment."

18 Author's interview with Bill Greif on October 17, 2011. All quotations from Greif are from this interview. See Gregory H. Wolf's bio of Bill Greif on the SABR BioProject, sabr.org/bioproj/person/1946fe08.

19 Wilson, "Happy Birthday to Doug."

20 "Wilson, Astros Split Marathon; Never a Dull Moment."

Mike Schmidt Wallops a Tremendous ... Single?

June 10, 1974: Philadelphia Phillies 12, Houston Astros 0, at the Astrodome

By Chip Greene

FROM THE MOMENT THEY SELECTED Mike Schmidt in the June 1971 amateur baseball draft, the Philadelphia Phillies undoubtedly must have envisioned that one day Schmidt would become a premier major-league power hitter. "Happy and surprised"[1] were the Phillies to find Schmidt still available when their chance to pick came up in the second round. Recently named Ohio University's Most Valuable Player, Schmidt, the Bobcats' starting shortstop and a 1970 first-team All-American, was almost a lock to be accorded that honor again. In addition to his .331 batting average in 1971, Schmidt had led his team in home runs (10), doubles (13), and total bases (89), and over his three varsity seasons the senior had set several batting records, including 27 home runs. Natural sluggers like Schmidt didn't come around very often.

Schmidt proved as much during his relatively brief stay in the minor leagues. After half a season in 1971 in Double-A, where he hit a modest eight home runs, Schmidt moved up to Triple-A in '72 and blasted 26 homers to go with a .291 batting average. The Phillies had seen enough. Called up to Philadelphia at the tail end of the 1972 season, Schmidt soon hit the first of 548 career home runs. He was off and running, on the way to baseball immortality.

It took the slugger a year to truly figure things out. In his first full season, Schmidt connected for 18 home runs, yet staggered home with a batting average of just .196 and 136 strikeouts. Never again, though, would he approach such a batting nadir.

Schmidt's ascension to the elite level of home-run hitters came in 1974. In the process he delivered one of the most bizarre blasts in baseball history. On June 10 the Phillies arrived in Houston for a three-game series with the Astros. Philadelphia, whose baseball fortunes had paralleled the upward trajectory of the team's new superstar, held first place in the National League Eastern Division, with a 30-26 record. In contrast, Houston, with an almost identical 30-28 record, stood fourth in the West, 12 games behind the front-running Los Angeles Dodgers.

The confrontation offered the promise of a pretty good pitching matchup. On the mound for the Phillies was right-hander Jim Lonborg, in his second season with the team and bound for 17 wins. Making his 14th start of the campaign, Lonborg entered the game with a record of 6-5 and an impressive 2.48 ERA. Pitching for the Astros was veteran left-hander Claude Osteen, winner of 185 big-league games, who had come to Houston in an offseason trade and was making his 13th start. Thus far, Osteen had split 10 decisions for the Astros, and he took the mound with a fine 3.23 ERA. In this game, though, one of these veteran pitchers was destined for a very short evening.

Disappointingly for the Astros, only 9,487 fans were on hand in the Astrodome to witness the strange event. Perhaps those who stayed home were unaware just how torrid Schmidt's performance had been of late, otherwise they might have rushed to the ballpark hoping to see a power barrage from the slugger. Earlier in the afternoon, Schmidt had been named the National League's Player of the Week for the June 3-9 period. Over that span he'd gone 12-for-23, scored eight runs, blasted four home runs, and driven in 10 runs. In his last nine games, Schmidt had driven in 16 runs and in June he'd hit six of his season's 14 home runs; his season total placed him second for the major-league lead to the Dodgers' Jimmy Wynn (16).

"I'm just feeling good, relaxed, and swinging good and my timing is perfect now," said Schmidt of his hot streak.[2] With a .310 batting average so far, Schmidt had left 1973's dismal performance firmly behind.

It would be up to the 34-year-old Osteen to try to cool off the Phillies' hottest hitter. The veteran had quieted Schmidt's bat once before. On May 30, 1973, the only time the two had previously faced each other, Osteen, then pitching for the Dodgers, had collared the rookie, rendering him 0-for-4. This time, however, Schmidt would get the better of their battle.

Osteen found himself in trouble immediately. After leadoff hitter Dave Cash walked, Larry Bowa singled into left field, with Cash stopping at second base. That brought Schmidt to the plate. From the moment he swung, it looked as though he had launched home run number 15. As Schmidt's huge blast soared toward straightaway center field, Astros center fielder Cesar Cedeno, a two-time Gold Glove winner, retreated to the fence and looked up, hoping for a chance to make a play. Suddenly, though, as the ball rose it struck a speaker that hung from the Astrodome roof, and dropped to the turf, 50 feet in front of Cedeno. By Astrodome ground rules, the ball was in play; Schmidt was given credit for a single, and neither of the runners scored. It was the first time a player had hit a speaker in fair territory since the Astrodome opened in 1965.[3]

As anticlimaxes go, Schmidt's single was momentous; from then on, the game was a blowout. The next hitter, Bill Robinson, drilled a double, scoring Cash and Bowa, and then Mike Anderson drove in a third run with a sacrifice fly. In the second, after consecutive singles to open the frame by Willie Montanez and Bob Boone, and a Lonborg sacrifice, Cash singled home the Phillies' fourth run, which chased Osteen. Cash stole second and Bowa was walked by reliever Jim York to load the bases. Schmidt batted and scorched a double off the left-field wall to score all three runners. Anderson ended the five-run frame

by banging a single up the middle, scoring Schmidt. The Phillies' 8-0 margin held up until the ninth, when they plated four more runs on four hits, to make it 12-0.

Meanwhile, Lonborg proved masterful. Only twice were the Astros able to mount any sort of threat: in the seventh Bob Watson hit a two-out double but was stranded at second; and in the bottom of the ninth, Roger Metzger and Cedeno delivered consecutive two-out singles, only to be stranded as Watson grounded out to end the game. In all, Lonborg scattered five hits and the Phillies won, 12-0.

After the game Schmidt professed frustration at the loss of a home run. "There's no doubt it would have been a home run," he reasoned, "and I said to myself, 'That damn speaker cost me a homer.' If for some reason late in the season I'm one short [of the home run lead], I'll think back about it."[4]

He needn't have worried. Schmidt ended the season with a major-league-leading 36 home runs. It was the first of six times he led the major leagues in homers and the first of eight NL home-run titles.

So how far would Schmidt's ball have gone had it not hit the speaker 117 feet above the playing field? Some days after the game, a reporter asked Dr. Martin Wright, head of the University of Houston's department of mathematics, how far he estimated the ball would have traveled unimpeded. Wright replied: "The ball probably reached its maximum height 50 feet before it hit the speaker, or 250 feet from home plate. That would make it travel about 500 feet.[5]

Instead of a home run, Schmidt delivered one very long single.

NOTES

1   *Athens* (Ohio) *Messenger*, June 9, 1971.

2   United Press International, *Huntingdon* (Pennsylvania) *Daily News*, June 11, 1974.

3   *Gettysburg Times*, June 11, 1974.

4   United Press International, *Huntingdon* (Pennsylvania) *Daily News*, June 11, 1974.

5   *The Sporting News*, June 29, 1974: 14.

Milt May Ties Game in Ninth and Wins it in the 11th against Seaver

August 19, 1974: Houston Astros 2, New York Mets 1 (11 innings), at the Astrodome

By Gregory H. Wolf

"I JUST HAPPENED TO HIT ONE UP the middle in the right spot," said soft-spoken Milt May almost apologetically after his walk-off single in the 11th inning gave the Houston Astros a dramatic 2-1 win over Tom Seaver and the New York Mets. "I was fortunate it wasn't right at somebody."[1]

Just weeks after the 1973 season ended, the Houston Astros acquired May, a 23-year-old catcher, from the Pittsburgh Pirates in a trade widely lampooned by the local media, in exchange for sturdy left-handed hurler Jerry Reuss, who was coming off an NL-high 40 starts and a then career-best 16 wins. The Astros hoped that the highly touted May, with only 142 starts in three years of backing up All-Star Manny Sanguillen, might develop into the club's first All-Star-caliber catcher. The Pirates had moved Sanguillen to right field in the wake of Roberto Clemente's tragic death on December 31, 1972, and installed May behind the plate, but the experiment failed when Sanguillen struggled mightily in the field. Pittsburgh shifted Sanguillen back to catcher in June 1973; this made May expendable.

The Pirates appeared to have won the trade handily at first. While Reuss was en route to another fine season (16-11) as one of the NL's most consistent southpaws, May's batting average dipped to .243 on July 3. But two days later May commenced one of the hottest stretches in his 15-year big-league career. From July 5 to August 18, he batted .370 (40-for-108) and slugged .491 in 33 games. "I have been swinging the bat good," said May, the son of former Phillies All-Star third baseman Pinky May. "[I]t means a lot when you go to the plate and have confidence that you're going to hit the ball hard."[2]

The Astros entered the game in fourth place in the NL West (61-59), 13½ games behind the streaking Dodgers. First-year skipper Preston Gomez's club had struggled of late, winning just 12 of its last 30 games. The Mets had been in a season-long funk for iconic Yogi Berra, in his third year piloting the club. The reigning pennant winners were in fifth place in the NL East (52-65), trailing the Cardinals by 10½ games.

The teams sent their respective 29-year-old aces to the mound, Don Wilson and Tom Seaver, in what shaped up to be a rematch of their game on April 15, 1968, at the Astrodome. In that contest both hurlers dazzled in an eventual Astros 1-0 victory in 24 innings, the longest game in the history of either franchise and the longest shutout in major-league history. A hard-throwing right-hander, Wilson was 8-10, and sported a record of 101-89 in his nine-year career. Seaver, arguably the best hurler in the NL, if not baseball (7-7, 3.51 ERA), had thus far not pitched to his typical standards; however, the reigning Cy Young Award winner had a career record of 142-83. Recognized as the highest-paid pitcher in baseball, "Tom Terrific" had been suffering from shoulder pain since the end of the previous season, and grumblings about his demise had permeated the New York media all summer.

The 10,619 spectators in the Astrodome on Monday evening, August 19, 1974, were treated to a classic pitchers' duel in which even the slightest mistake was amplified. Through the first eight innings, the game was defined by tough pitching and failed scoring opportunities. During that time the Astros' only serious chance came in the second inning. Bob

Watson led off with a single and moved to third when Seaver unleashed two wild pitches while facing May, whose foul fly to Ken Boswell in short right was not deep enough drive in Watson. Seaver, heading toward his seventh of nine consecutive seasons with at least 200 strikeouts, whiffed Lee May and Doug Rader to end the threat.

The Mets, the league's second-lowest-scoring team, (3.53 runs per game) in 1974, failed to capitalize on men in scoring position and one out in the third, fourth, and seventh innings. After Bud Harrelson singled to advance Seaver (who had walked) to second with one out in the third, Wilson retired the next two batters on fly balls. In the fourth Boswell cracked a one-out double, then Wayne Garrett stroked a long single to right. According to UPI, Boswell "would have easily scored," but third-base coach Eddie Yost inexplicably held him up as Greg Gross's throw sailed into third.[3] With runners on second and third, Wilson ended the threat by punching out the next two batters. In the seventh, Don Hahn reached second via a walk and sacrifice bunt, but was left stranded.

Tension mounted in the ninth inning when second baseman Tommy Helms, a two-time All-Star and Gold Glove winner, muffed Garrett's grounder. Jerry Grote followed with a long single over the head of Wilbur Howard (a defensive replacement for left fielder Bob Watson, who replaced Lee May at first base) and off the wall. With runners on the corners, Mike Cosgrove relieved Wilson and yielded a bloop single to shallow right field to pinch-hitter and former Astro Rusty Staub to knock in Garrett. The Mets were on the verge on breaking the game open when Cosgrove walked Harrelson to load the bases with one out, but reliever Ken Forsch induced Felix Milan to hit a grounder to third baseman Doug Rader, who fielded it cleanly and fired a strike to Milt May at the plate to force the charging Grote; May quickly threw to Watson for the inning-ending double play.

Cesar Cedeño, Houston's fleet-footed slugger, walked to lead off the bottom of the ninth and moved to third on Watson's third hit of the game, a single, which according to *New York Times* reporter Michael Strauss, "skimmed over the edge" of first baseman Ed Kranepool's glove.[4] It was Seaver's game to win or lose as the Mets bullpen remained quiet. May tied the score on a long fly to right field; however, Watson was tagged out in a rundown between first and second in his attempt to advance. Howard then tapped one back to the mound and the game headed for extra innings.

While Forsch set down all six batters he faced in the 10th and 11th innings, Seaver began the Astros' 11th working on a six-hitter. After Gross hit a lead-off single and moved to second on Roger Metzger's sacrifice bunt, the future Hall of Famer faced the heart of the Astros batting order coming up. Seaver induced Cedeno to ground back to the mound on an offspeed pitch. With his long stride in his pitching follow-through, Seaver slipped and fell to the ground, but still managed to field the ball and throw to Kranepool in time to nab the speedy Cedeno. Assuring his skipper that he was fine, Seaver intentionally walked Watson to face Milt May. May's grounder on a 2-and-1 pitch by Seaver was described by Joe Heiling of the *Houston Post* as "just out of the reach" of second baseman Felix Millan, playing deep behind the bag.[5] Racing from second base, Gross scored easily to give the Astros an exciting 2-1 victory in 2 hours and 37 minutes. Forsch picked up the win to improve his record to 5-5, while Seaver was the tough-luck loser.

"[Seaver's] been awful tough on me the last four years," said Milt May, who entered the game with just two hits in 27 at-bats against him. "The hits have been few and far between. That's pretty common, though, with him. I don't know anyone that wears Seaver out very much."[6] The modest catcher deflected attention and lauded his pitching staff, which yielded only six hits. "You've got to give credit to Don, Kenny, and Cosy," said May. "That's the only way you're going to beat Seaver. Don pitched a great game and deserved to get a win out of it."[7]

Seaver commanded most of the attention in the Mets' clubhouse. "There was nothing wrong with me," said the future 311-game winner with an air of frustration. "The only thing that went wrong was that the pitch I tried to throw to May on the inside misfired."[8] Often perceived as cocky with a sometimes prickly relationship with the press, Seaver had no apologies for his yeoman effort, the 13th of 18 times in his 20-year career that he hurled at least 10 innings in a game. "Obviously I chose to pitch to the player I felt I could get out. I had to pitch to two of the three (Cedeño, Watson and May)."[9]

SOURCES

In addition to the sources cited in the Notes, the author also accessed Retrosheet.org, Baseball-Reference.com, the SABR Minor Leagues Database, accessed online at Baseball-Reference.com, SABR.org, and *The Sporting News* archive via Paper of Record.

NOTES

1 Joe Heiling, "Milt Melts Mets in 11th Inning," *Houston Post*, August 20, 1974: D1.

2 Dick Peebles, "Astros Win in 11th on Milt May's Hit," *Houston Chronicle*, August 20, 1974: Section 2, 5.

3 United Press International, "Mays Keys Astros by Mets, Seaver," *Valley Morning Star* (Harlingen, Texas), August 20, 1974: 10.

4 Michael Strauss, "Milt May's Single Off Seaver Wins for Astros," *New York Times*, August 20, 1974: 29.

5 Heiling.

6 Ibid.

7 Ibid.

8 Strauss.

9 Heiling.

Griffin's Unlikely RBI Single Stifles Braves in 14

September 22, 1974: Houston Astros 3, Atlanta Braves 2 (14 innings), at the Astrodome

By Thomas Rathkamp

A STARTING PITCHER'S OFFDAY routine includes — but is not limited to — stretches; warm-up tosses; advanced scouting notes; and, on occasion, batting practice. It's not often that the latter task would prove vital to the outcome of a game. On September 22, 1974, pitcher Tom Griffin pinch-hit for another pitcher, Ken Forsch, and smashed a hard grounder that knocked in Larry Milbourne with the winning run in the 14th inning. Thanks to Griffin's RBI, Forsch, who had hurled two scoreless innings of relief, earned the victory.

The two clubs were playing out the string. The 1974 campaign found the Astros hovering around .500 for the second straight season; at game time, they sat in fourth place at 77-75, 18 games back of the first-place Los Angeles Dodgers, while Atlanta (84-69) was in third place, 11½ behind. The day's starting pitchers were the Braves' Buzz Capra (15-8) and Houston hurler Don Wilson (10-13). Capra was finishing his first full year as a starter after three part-time seasons with the New York Mets. His 2.28 ERA (in 217 innings) was tops for Braves starters.[1]

Wilson, the seasoned veteran of the two, completed his ninth and final season in 1974. Tragically, his life ended mysteriously the following January, when he was found asphyxiated in his car, which was parked in his closed garage with the gas tank empty. His son Alex was also found dead of asphyxiation in his bedroom. Many suspected that Don committed suicide, although several of his teammates refused to believe it. His daughter also felt the effects of carbon monoxide poisoning but survived. Wilson's wife, Bernice, showed bruising on her face, but displayed no exposure to the carbon monoxide, leading some to ponder whether she was responsible for the deaths. A medical examiner, Dr. Joseph Jachimczyk, ruled the deaths accidental.[2]

On an afternoon marked by Houston's version of Hank Aaron Day, which commemorated what was supposed to be the Hammer's final major-league season, the marathon contest was the second consecutive extra-inning victory for the Astros and their third in four games. They had knocked off the Braves the previous day in 10 innings, 6-5. Forsch earned the victory in that game as well, shutting the door after surrendering back-to-back singles to open the 10th and then getting the victory when his teammates pushed a run across in the bottom of the inning. As if one dramatic finish were not enough, the Astros teetered on the brink of defeat a couple of times in this game before Griffin's game-winner in the series finale.

Griffin, a Los Angeles native, entered the game sporting a .286 batting average. Throughout his career, he was no slouch with the stick as pitchers go. He even had 10 career home runs, two of them in his 1969 rookie season. On the mound, his bread-and-butter pitches included a hard slider and a fastball.[3] A stalwart 6-feet-3 and 190 pounds, Griffin had the muscle to put zest into a baseball. On the mound Griffin had logged 202 innings thus far in 1974, a career high in his sixth season. He would finish the year with a career-high 14 wins against 10 defeats, and his 3.54 ERA was more than a half-run better than in the previous season.

The Braves scored first, taking a 1-0 lead in the fourth inning. Manager Clyde King's crew began the inning with consecutive singles by Mike Lum and

Frank Tepedino. Johnny Oates fanned, then shortstop Craig Robinson, a .217 hitter who would tally three hits in the game, smacked an RBI single. As Lum crossed the plate, Tepedino was thrown out at third by right fielder Greg Gross, and after applying the tag, third baseman Doug Rader whipped the ball to second to gun down Robinson. The odd 9-5-4 double play squelched a potential big inning.

The Braves clung to their 1-0 lead until the bottom of the ninth. Houston's Roger Metzger led off with a walk and was sacrificed to second by Gross. Capra walked Cesar Cedeno, then Cliff Johnson singled to score Metzger. After striking out Doug Rader, Capra was lifted for Tom House,[4] Buzz had pitched 8⅔ strong innings but had to settle for a no-decision.

Hank Aaron, a week away from his planned retirement, gave his team another chance to dispatch the Astros in the 10th. Marty Perez opened the inning with a triple off Ramon de los Santos, who had come on for Wilson to start the ninth. Darrell Evans whiffed and Dusty Baker was walked intentionally. Jim York relieved de los Santos and Aaron, pinch-hitting for Lum, smacked a grounder to shortstop Metzger, who forced Baker at second, but Aaron was safe at first as Perez scored the go-ahead run.

(Aaron batted just .268 in 1974 and had his worst slugging percentage (.491) since his rookie season. Nevertheless, he later delayed his retirement and played his last two seasons with the Milwaukee Brewers, in the city in which he began his illustrious major-league career with the Milwaukee Braves.)

The Astros lost Cedeno to injury in the 10th when he suffered a badly broken fingernail. He pleaded with manager Preston Gomez to keep him in the game, to no avail. The shuffling of players was nothing new for the veteran skipper but losing his star outfielder was a blow. "I'd have been okay this game, except for Cedeno getting hurt," said Gomez. "I just wasn't expecting that to happen."[5]

The Astros struck back against reliever Tom House with singles by Bob Watson and pinch-hitter Ray Busse, batting for the pitcher, York. Gross followed with an RBI double to plate Watson and tie the game. Both teams offered mild threats in innings 11 through 13, but the game stayed tied until the 14th. In the 11th Bob Gallagher, who had replaced Cedeno in center field, led off with a single and advanced to second on an errant pickoff attempt by House. Rader walked and was forced at second by Tommy Helms. That left Gallagher on third with two outs, and the reserve outfielder was stranded when Milbourne grounded out. In the 12th, the Braves got consecutive one-out singles by Perez and Evans off Astros reliever Mike Cosgrove but that rally died on the vine as well.

Entering the 14th inning, Gomez had one position player left on the bench, Mick Kelleher, with his paltry .161 average. But that was not the reason the skipper chose to use Griffin. "I had to save Kelleher for defensive reasons in case somebody got hurt," said Gomez. With one out in the bottom of the inning, Milbourne singled to center off diminutive reliever Max Leon and Watson followed with a single to left. Up came Griffin, who laced a grounder to short that handcuffed Craig Robinson. The ball escaped into left-center field, providing enough time for Milbourne to score easily and tag Leon with his second loss in as many days.

Griffin's last pitching start had occurred five days earlier, so fatigue was not a factor. "I wanted to go up there (to the plate)," he said. "I just knew I could hit. I like to hit."[6] Apparently Griffin was not Gomez's first choice to pinch-hit. "If Watson had led off with a hit, I would have used (pitcher) Larry Dierker to bunt because he's a better bunter than (Dave) Roberts," said Gomez. (He had used Roberts as a pinch-hitter in the 12th.) "If it had been possible, I wanted to save Roberts because I know he's played first base. Or I could have batted him later."[7] Luckily for Gomez, Griffin made his manager look smart.

"The pitchers have to get the big hits because the hitters can't," cracked Houston's pitching coach, Roger Craig, perhaps taking a free jab at the team's sluggers.[8]

Griffin was so full of jubilation after the game that his big wide smile could have been mistaken for laughter. "As much fun as throwing a complete game?" asked a reporter. "No, not that much fun," replied Griffin. "I wish that could count as a win for me. That's the first time I've ever been asked to pinch hit. I was really nervous up there. It's different from hitting in a game when you're pitching. It's tough to come off the bench and hit."[9]

Griffin finished his career in 1982 with a 77-94 record, a 4.07 ERA and a pitcher's-style .163 batting average. For one brief moment, however, Griffin overcame his nerves and delivered a victory via his bat rather than his arm.

NOTES

1 Harry Shattuck, "Griffin's Singles Tops Braves," *Houston Chronicle*, September 23, 1974.

2 Matthew Clifford, "Don Wilson," SABR BioProject, at sabr.org/bioproj/person/1643c2b4.

3 Rob Neyer and Bill James, *Neyer/James Guide to Pitchers* (New York: Fireside Books, 2004), 223.

4 John Hollis, "Griffin's Bat Turns Back Atlanta," *Houston Post*, September 23, 1974.

5 Ibid.

6 Ibid.

7 Shattuck.

8 Ibid.

9 Ibid.

Rainout in the Astrodome

June 15, 1976: Pittsburgh Pirates vs. Houston Astros

By Rick Schabowski

A RAINOUT IN THE ASTRODOME? How is that possible? It's domed, protected from the elements. The Astros don't even have the traditional rain check printed on their tickets! Yet on Tuesday, June 15, 1976, the supposedly impossible happened—a game between the Astros and the Pittsburgh Pirates was postponed because of rain.

The Astros entered the game in fourth place with a 29-33 record, 10 games behind the Cincinnati Reds. Pittsburgh had a 33-25 record but because of a red-hot start by the Philadelphia Phillies, the Pirates were 6½ games out.

The day of the game, a powerful thunderstorm had developed over the Houston area, caused by very humid, unstable atmospheric conditions along the Gulf Coast combined with a cold front that extended from the Gulf through central Texas. The storm hit shortly before noon and after it subsided seven hours later, downtown Houston had received 7.48 inches of rain. The worst flooding occurred around Market Street, the East Loop, Denver Harbor, and Reveille. The heaviest recorded rainfall was 13.06 inches at the Houston Ship Channel near 75th Street. Heavy flooding occurred around the Texas Medical Center, just north of the Astrodome, where 10.47 inches of rain was unofficially recorded.

As Astros team historian Mike Acosta described it, "It was like a tropical storm. It was raining hard, and it just kept coming down. It got to the point where the streets around the Astrodome were flooded and impassable. Fans couldn't get to the stadium. Neither could Astrodome workers. Remember, the Astrodome floor was 45 feet below ground level. So the lower ramps and entries were flooded also."[1]

Astros general manager Tal Smith recalled, "It was an absolute downpour, there was flooding all over, and people were just marooned. Houston has a low water table; we're not that far above ground, a marshy area, and when we get torrential downpours, we have flooding."[2]

How would this deluge affect the game scheduled for that night? Smith said, "At the time, it was quite a story. Obviously we could have played, but we would have done so without any umpires, without any fans. The players were there, and our offices were in the Dome, but nobody else could get there. The umpires stayed at the Shamrock Hotel, which was not that far from the Dome, maybe two miles at the most. The [crew] chief called me about 4 o'clock that afternoon and said they tried to get there and just couldn't get out, and by that time we had reports from all around the stadium about the roads being impassable and so on."[3] Later it was reported that the umpires had made a determined effort to arrive for the game, but their cars had stalled in high water and they had to wade back to their hotel.

How did the players manage to arrive for the game without major issues? Acosta said, "Players started arriving around 1 P.M., when it was still possible to get to the stadium. They had to be dressed by 3:00 or 3:30 P.M. The Pirates team bus made it through, as did the Astros coming by themselves."[4]

Indeed, the players were there, but their journey, even before the storm reached its worst stage, was not easy.

Astros pitcher Paul Siebert recalled thinking that the game would be played as he rode in. "My girlfriend dropped me off," he said. "She came back, drove through water over the hood. My 1975 Grand Prix was in the shop for a week drying out."[5]

It was a special day for Doc Medich of the Pirates. "June 16, 1976, was our seventh wedding anniversary. I was supposed to pitch. I spent the afternoon reading a Robert Ludlum book in my hotel room and remember watching it rain, and rain, and rain. It rained hard for a long time. I recall the rain lasting at least seven hours. I mean a very hard, steady rain. About 2:00 P.M., I was beginning to wonder if the game might even be called even though it was played inside. Houston is very flat, and the water doesn't run off very fast. Around 3 o'clock, I took a cab over to the Dome, it might have been with Tommy Helms. When we got there, there were a few of our players and coaches already there."[6]

Pirates pitcher Jerry Reuss recalled, "The Pirates stayed at the Shamrock Hotel that year and the bus ride to the Dome was normally 10 or 15 minutes. On the bus ride to the park, I noticed the canals that collect the runoff from the frequent Houston rainstorms were unusually high and in some cases, were spilling over their banks and into the adjacent streets. I lived in Houston for two years and never saw that happen. The trip from the hotel to the Dome that day was around a half-hour and the storm was the topic of conversation in the clubhouse. Still, we dressed and it was business as usual during our time on the field."[7]

Shirley Virdon, the wife of Astros manager Bill Virdon, had an experience she'd always remember. "I remember it well! My daughter and I were stranded in our car on top of the interstate at the Kirby exit to the Dome. I sat in the car 5½ hours waiting for the rain to subside, and the water to go away so I could get off the freeway; our daughter waded over to the Dome."[8]

The players inside the Astrodome had no knowledge of what was going on outside, or whether the game would be played or postponed. Bill Virdon remembered, "When we first got on the field we thought we would play."[9] Larry Dierker said he "didn't know,"[10] but Astros infielder Rob Andrews said, "We did have our doubts when water began to cascade over the outfield scoreboard."[11] Houston pitcher Mike Cosgrove "couldn't believe the water outside, cars were under water!"[12]

As game time approached, a decision had to be made. Tal Smith, assessing the situation, made the logical decision to postpone the game; the main reason was concern for fans and employees, and not putting them in harm's way. The decision was announced around 5:00 P.M., while the rain was still heavy and showing no sign of subsiding. The announcement of the postponement was the lead story on the local TV news.

Smith thought it was an easy decision. "Nobody could get there, and I just thought the intelligent thing to do was to call the game. There was some concern by some of our other people, some of my management associates, particularly in the nonbaseball side, that this would make us look bad. I said, to the contrary, I think it's a major news story, it's nothing we've done, that it's a question of the elements, the weather and so on. It was the responsible, prudent thing to do. On that day, June 15, it was the trading deadline, and Joe Brown was the general manager of the Pittsburgh club at the time. I conferred with him, told him what I was going to do, which was fine."[13]

An Astros spokesman told the press, "It wasn't exactly a rain-out-it was a rain-in."[14]

About 20 fans did make it to the game, and they became dinner guests of the Astros in a stadium cafeteria. The players were also treated to a meal, but rather than a cafeteria setting, they ate on the field. According to Medich, "The Astros brought food down onto the field and served it on tables out by second base."[15] Virdon said the players from both teams "were happy to be fed at that time."[16] Cosgrove thought it was "great—a great gesture by whoever put it on."[17]

None of the players could recall what was on the menu that evening. The *Houston Post* said that they were catered steak dinners, and Paul Siebert remarked, "I don't remember, more drinks than food."[18] Mike Acosta, the team historian, said, "Concession workers set up a buffet and tables behind second base, and both teams ate dinner on the field together. The players were in uniforms, but some of them were wearing shower flip-flops on their feet. The Astrodome staff ate with the players as well."[19] Jerry Reuss noted, "Since the Astros players and office personnel were in the same predicament, a decision was made to make everyone as comfortable as possible. A makeshift kitchen was set up just beyond the infield, picnic tables were placed nearby as personnel from both clubs were invited to the impromptu meal."[20]

After the meal, a few of the Astros, including Larry Dierker, decided to climb to the top of the Dome and crawl on the catwalk.

Tal Smith's decision saved many fans from a harrowing experience attempting to get to the game, but there was one last hurdle to conquer. How did the people already at the Astrodome get safely home?

Paul Siebert recalled, "We left late. My car didn't start. We got a ride with Ed Herrmann."[21]

Doc Medich's trip home began around 8:00 P.M. "I guess the rain slacked off enough for us to get a bus back to the hotel. The streets were still flooded and the bus had to go very slow through the streets."[22] Bill Virdon was able to get home in his car, but his wife, Shirley, had to abandon hers on a bridge near the ballpark. As the evening grew later, the danger decreased. Dierker recalled leaving at around 10:00, and Roger Metzger, around midnight. Rob Andrews and Mike Cosgrove chose to ride home in the morning, after spending the night in the Astrodome in a luxury suite sleeping while the waters subsided.

Even on the next morning things were still far from normal. "The drive home was surreal," said Andrews. "No one was on the roads. As I got on the interstate by the Dome I had to weave through abandoned cars left right where they stalled the night before. I couldn't shake the feeling I was in some kind of world-ending disaster flick."[23]

Tal Smith recalled another rain adventure that happened to him in 2004. "Driving home during one of these torrential downpours, I flooded my car out. Sometimes you just have no chance. You're able to drive, and all of a sudden you run into a situation where there's massive water that's risen so rapidly, there's no place to go."[24]

SOURCES

Houston Post.

Houston Chronicle.

Personal correspondence (2014):

Mike Cosgrove.

Larry Dierker.

Doc Medich.

Jerry Reuss.

Paul Siebert.

Bill Virdon.

Personal interview:

Tal Smith, telephone interview, February 3, 2014.

NOTES

1 Ken Hoffmann, "Astros made history with a rainout," *Houston Chronicle*, June 17, 2009.

2 Personal interview Tal Smith, February 3, 2014.

3 Smith interview.

4 Hoffmann.

5 Personal correspondence with Paul Siebert.

6 Personal correspondence with Doc Medich.

7 Personal correspondence with Jerry Reuss.

8 Personal correspondence with Bill Virdon.

9 Virdon.

10 Personal correspondence with Larry Dierker.

11 Personal correspondence with Rob Andrews.

12 Personal correspondence with Mike Cosgrove.

13 Tal Smith interview.

14 Hoffmann.

15 Medich.

16 Virdon.

17 Cosgrove.

18 Siebert.

19 Hoffmann.

20 Reuss.

21 Siebert.

22 Medich.

23 Andrews.

24 Tal Smith interview.

Dierker Tosses a No-No

July 9, 1976: Houston Astros 6, Montreal Expos 0, at the Astrodome

By Gregory H. Wolf

"I KNEW I HAD A NO-HITTER AFTER the first inning," said Larry Dierker with an air of seriousness before breaking into a chuckle. "Walking back to the dugout, I wondered, 'When was the last time I got through the first inning without giving up a hit?'"[1]

Dierker had come close to a no-hitter before. As a 22-year-old in 1966, he had tossed eight hitless innings only to yield two safeties to begin the ninth and then lose to the New York Mets, 1-0. Three years later, he held the Atlanta Braves hitless for 8⅔ innings in a pitchers' duel with Phil Niekro, and ultimately hurled 12 scoreless frames, but picked up a no-decision. Dierker also had two one-hit shutouts, holding the San Diego Padres hitless for 6⅔ frames in 1971, and yielding just a single to the Mets in the third inning in 1972.

A no-hitter seemed unlikely at this point in Dierker's career. Just 29 years old, Dierker was in his 13th big-league season, all with Houston. A two-time All-Star, the 6-foot-4, 215-pound right-hander owned a 131-111 record, including a career-best 20 wins in 1969, and had logged in excess of 2,200 innings; however, he had been bothered by injuries in the previous three seasons. He missed much of the 1973 campaign with a hand injury followed by a shoulder injury, which caused him chronic pain. "Dierker was the consummate major-league pitcher," said Tal Smith, who served as Astros GM in '76. "Larry was big, strong, durable, competitive, and obviously talented. He had the complete repertoire—a good fastball, a good breaking ball and a good changeup. As such he was able to keep batters off stride and to affect their timing—the essence of getting hitters out."[2]

The Astrodome was sprinkled with a sparse crowd of just 12,511 on Friday, July 9, to see a matchup be-tween two sub-.500 clubs. Manager Bill Virdon's fourth-place Astros (39-44), a distant 12½ games behind the Cincinnati Reds in the NL West, hoped to cure their ills by playing the worst team in baseball, the Montreal Expos (25-49), who were a whopping 25½ games behind the Philadelphia Phillies.

Dierker set down the first three Expos in order. "People worried that my arm was shot that year," said Dierker, who entered the game with a dismal 4.43 ERA. "So I'd often overthrow, but I made up my mind before that game to just make good pitches and not try to throw the ball by anyone. Just mix it up and move it around. Pitch craftily, not powerfully." In the second Dierker issued a leadoff walk to Andre Thornton, who promptly stole second. In the first sequence of events that foretold a special night, Dierker first fanned Larry Parrish. Then he caught what Dick Peebles of the *Houston Chronicle* called a "sizzling liner" from Pete Mackanin and doubled Thornton off second.[3]

José Cruz put Houston on the board in the second by doubling off Montreal starter Don Stanhouse to drive in Bob Watson, who had reached first via a walk. Stanhouse, a 25-year-old right-hander who had entered the season with an abysmal 4-17 career record, was one of the surprises of the '76 season to this point (6-3, 2.18 ERA). A wild pitch and two more walks loaded the bases with one out for Dierker, who lofted a deep fly to right field to drive in Cruz for a 2-0 lead. Stanhouse's fourth walk of the frame, to Greg Gross, loaded the bases again, but Rob Andrews grounded out.

Dierker set down the Expos in order in the third and fourth, aided by two stellar defensive plays. "Enos Cabell had to charge in from third base," recalled Dierker, "and made a barehanded play but he got the runner [Pepe Mangual] easily" for the first out of the fourth. In what the *Chronicle* considered the toughest play of the game, second baseman Andrews backhanded Jim Lyttle's sharp grounder, "whirled and while in the air" made an off-balance throw to first for the second out.[4]

Ed Herrmann, Dierker's veteran batterymate, who had been acquired a month earlier from the California Angels in a trade, extended Houston's lead to 3-0 with his first NL home run to lead off the fourth. Roger Metzger followed with a single and later scored on Andrews' two-out single to end Stanhouse's night.

Dierker's bout of wildness caused a few tense moments in the fifth. After issuing consecutive one-out walks to Parrish and Mackanin, he ended the frame by retiring Larry Johnson on a fly ball and striking out Pepe Frias, stranding Parrish on third.

The bottom of Houston's lineup added two more insurance runs in the fifth off reliever Don Carrithers. Herrmann laced a one-out single to drive in Watson, who had led off with a single and had stolen second. Metzger followed with another single, plating Cliff Johnson, who was on base via third baseman Parrish's error.

"I got an adrenaline rush in the seventh inning," recalled Dierker with the same enthusiasm he had as a player. "I thought, 'Here I am in the 'Dome and my fastball is rising like it did when I was 18.'" The Astrodome crowd collectively held its breath when Mike Jorgensen led off the seventh with the Expos' first hard-hit ball of the game, but center fielder José Cruz, subbing for the injured four-time All-Star Cesar Cedeño, went to the warning track to make a routine catch.

"In the last two innings I threw nothing but high fastballs, trying to blow hitters away or get fly balls," said Dierker. "Just the opposite of my original game plan." He recalled how pitching in the cavernous Astrodome with its 406-foot center-field wall and deep power alleys helped him on this night, although he did get one more scare in the eighth. "[Pinch-hitter] José Morales hit one to deep center field that would have been out in many parks," said Dierker,

Larry Dierker earned 137 of his 139 career wins with the Astros. He is third on Houston's all-time wins list and is first in starts (320), complete games (106), innings pitched (2,294⅓), and shutouts (25). (Courtesy of Houston Astros Baseball Club).

"but José Cruz drifted back and caught it on the warning track."

The Astrodome crowd, which had been cheering loudly after every out since the seventh inning, gave Dierker a raucous round of applause when he came to the plate in the eighth inning. A longtime fan favorite, Dierker struck out against right-handed reliever Joe Kerrigan, making his first big-league appearance, but that did not matter to the Astros faithful, who gave Dierker a standing ovation.

Dierker took the mound in the ninth for a date with destiny, aiming for the fifth no-hitter in franchise history. Don Wilson, who had tragically died on January 5, 1975, under mysterious circumstances, had authored the last no-hitter, on May 1, 1969, at Crosley Field, when he turned the trick against Cincinnati one day after Reds hard thrower Jim Maloney did the same to the Astros. Wilson also fired the first no-hitter in the Astrodome, on June 18, 1967, against Atlanta. The other two no-hitters occurred in Colt

Stadium, when the team was known as the Colt .45s. Both were peculiar: A two-base error led to a run in Don Nottebart's 4-1 no-hitter versus the Philadelphia Phillies on May 17, 1963, and Ken Johnson achieved the dubious distinction of becoming the first big-league pitcher to toss a no-hitter and lose the game on April 23, 1964, against Cincinnati when two errors in the ninth led to the only run of the game.

Dierker whiffed Mangual on four pitches to lead off the ninth. He fell behind Lyttle 2-and-0, before firing three straight strikes for his eighth punchout. "[Dierker] was really throwing smoke," Ed Herrmann remarked after the game. "His fastball was hissing and he challenged every hitter."[5] With Montreal down to its final out, Jorgensen nicked Dierker's fastball meekly about 10 feet left of first base. Dierker sprinted to the bag in anticipation of a short lob from Watson for the final out, but the two-time All-Star had a different idea. "I knew Jorgensen was going to hit the ball to me," said Watson. "I grabbed the ball and raced to the bag. There was no way I was going to risk throwing the ball to Larry."[6] Watson stepped on the bag to end the game in 2 hours and 26 minutes.

Dierker jumped wildly at first base, where Watson was waiting with a hug as his teammates mobbed him. In the clubhouse after the game, Dierker soaked his sore elbow in ice while basking in the glow of one the few personal pitching achievements that had thus far eluded him. The no-hitter also inaugurated an unexpected rejuvenation from the tanned Californian.

Three starts later, he tossed his fourth and final two-hitter, and his first since 1969, by blanking San Diego at the Astrodome on July 26. In an emphatic statement that he was not washed up, Dierker posted a robust 3.03 ERA in his last 14 starts before his season was prematurely ended by arm pain. In the offseason he was traded to the St. Louis Cardinals, for whom he pitched his final 11 games in an injury-plagued 1977 season before retiring.

"I never expected to throw a no-hitter at that point in my career, especially after the injuries and arm problems," said Dierker about his special night against the Expos. "It really was a gift from God."

SOURCES

In addition to the sources cited in the Notes, the author also accessed Retrosheet.org, Baseball-Reference.com, the SABR Minor Leagues Database, accessed online at Baseball-Reference.com, SABR.org, and *The Sporting News* archive via Paper of Record.

NOTES

1   All quotations from Larry Dierker are from the author's interview with him on February 10, 2016.

2   From author's correspondence with Tal Smith on January 13, 2016.

3   Dick Peebles, "Long-Suffering Dierker Pitches No-Hitter," *Houston Chronicle*, July 10, 1976: section 3, 1.

4   Ibid.

5   Ibid.

6   Ibid.

Watson Hits for Cycle; Cruz Belts Walk-Off Double in 11th

June 24, 1977: Houston Astros 6, San Francisco Giants 5 (11 innings), at the Astrodome

By Richard Riis

BOB WATSON'S SITUATION BEFORE the Astros' game on June 24, 1977, was desperate, he told reporters crowded around his locker at the end of the game. "I've had a lot of problems lately, and, seriously, I got with my wife today and we said a prayer."[1]

Watson had been seeing a doctor weekly to correct a chemical imbalance in his blood and had been put on a salt-free diet to which Watson's body was reacting with frequent and painful leg cramps, limiting him to one at-bat over the past three games.

As if that weren't problem enough, both of Watson thumbs had been injured in recent weeks and were wrapped in tape.

But Watson wanted to play. He had told manager Bill Virdon just that in the afternoon, and the Astros skipper penciled the big first baseman into the fifth spot in the batting order for that night's game against the San Francisco Giants.

The Astros badly needed Watson in the lineup. Languishing in fifth place at 29-40, 16½ games out of first less than halfway into the season, the Astros could ill afford to be without Watson's bat for too long. Although he was fourth on the club with a batting average of .268, Watson's eight home runs were one behind catcher Joe Ferguson for the team lead and his 36 RBIs paced the light-hitting lineup.

Dan Larson (0-2, 5.96), making his first start of the season after 16 games in relief, took the mound for the Astros and retired the Giants in order on three fly balls in the top of the first.

Starting that night for the Giants was Bob Knepper, a lanky rookie left-hander called up in May after a promising four-game look-see the previous season. Virdon inserted Knepper directly into the regular rotation and his initial starts had been up and down, but a five-hit, 8-0 shutout of the Pirates his last time out had evened his record at 1-1 and lowered his ERA to 3.82.

Tonight, though, Knepper was in trouble from the outset. A single by Wilbur Howard, starting in center field in place of a slumping Cesar Cedeno (.179), and another by Enos Cabell put runners on first and second with none out in the first. With Jose Cruz at the plate, Howard took a long lead at second base, drawing a throw by Knepper that had him picked off, but in the ensuing rundown Howard advanced to third when receiver Marc Hill dropped the ball. Cruz struck out, but Ferguson walked, loading the bases. Watson followed with a triple to stake the Astros to a 3-0 lead. The Astros stranded Watson at third as groundouts by Jim Fuller and Art Howe ended the inning.

In the Houston third inning, Watson doubled with one out and made it to third on a single by Howe, but the inning ended without any scoring.

San Francisco finally got on the scoreboard in the fourth, when Darrell Evans followed a walk to Derrel Thomas with his seventh home run of the season. Gary Thomasson singled and slugging first baseman Willie McCovey, back with the Giants after a three-year exile in San Diego and Oakland, did the same. A shortstop-to-second force erased McCovey, advanced Thomas to third, and put Jack Clark on at first. After Rob Andrews went down swinging, Hill singled home Thomasson to tie the game at 3-3.

The Giants took a one-run lead in the top of the fifth inning on a leadoff home run by Bill Madlock,

On June 24, 1977, Bob Watson became only the second Astros player (after Cesar Cedeño) to hit for the cycle at the Astrodome when he accomplished the feat against the San Francisco Giants. (Courtesy of Houston Astros Baseball Club).

but Gene Pentz, taking the mound in relief of Larson after a one-out walk to Evans, set the Giants down without any further threat.

A two-out, bases-empty homer by Watson in the bottom of the fifth knotted the score again.

In the Giants' half of the seventh, a walk to Thomas, a single by Evans, and a sacrifice fly by Thomasson put San Francisco back on top, 5-4. An intentional walk to McCovey and a walk by Clark loaded the bases, but Rob Andrews flied out to right field to shut down any additional scoring.

Ferguson reached first on an error by second baseman Andrews to open the bottom of the eighth inning for Houston. San Francisco manager Joe Altobelli pulled Knepper in favor of right-handed reliever Randy Moffitt. Virdon then lifted Ferguson for pinch-runner Cedeno, who stole second. With first base open, Altobelli might have elected to walk Watson, who had three extra-base hits in three at-bats, but instead he permitted Moffitt to pitch to the

Houston slugger and Watson made him pay, smacking a single that scored Cedeno and tied the game at 5-5.

With the single, Watson had hit for the cycle, only the second Astro to accomplish this feat. (Cedeno did it twice, in 1972 and 1976.) The RBI was Watson's fifth of the game, accounting for all of Houston's runs to that point.

Virdon, taking no chances with Watson's sore legs, sent backup outfielder Art Gardner in to run for him. Watson returned to the dugout to tumultuous cheers and applause.

Fuller sacrificed Gardner to second, Howe walked, and Julio Gonzalez did likewise, loading the bases. Virdon then sent up veteran Ken Boswell, a left-handed batter, to hit for Pentz, and Altobelli countered by replacing Moffitt with his left-handed relief ace, Gary Lavelle. Lavelle, whose ERA was under 1.00 as recently as June 11and was now 1.49, would be the Giants' sole representative in the 1977 All-Star Game.

Virdon returned Boswell to the bench and sent in right-handed hitting Craig Cacek, making only his fifth appearance in a major-league game. The gambit failed to pay off. Cacek bounced to third baseman Madlock, who made a fine grab and quickly fired home to start an inning-ending 5-2-3 double play.

Still knotted at 5-5, the game proceeded to extra innings. The Giants made three quick outs in the 10th, and the Astros frustrated the 13,119 in attendance by failing to capitalize on a single by Edd Hermann (who was caught stealing), an error by shortstop Johnnie Lemaster that allowed Fuller to make it to second, and an intentional walk to Howe.

Gary Alexander, hitting for Lavelle, opened the 11th inning by striking out, Madlock grounded out to shortstop, and LeMaster flied out to right.

Right-hander Tommy Toms, making his first appearance of the season and the 15th in an 18-game career, took over the pitching duty for the Giants for the bottom of the 11th. After one out, Howard walked, advanced to second on a single by Cabell, and sprinted home with the game-winning run when.

Cruz, hitless so far, came through with a double to deep left field.

The victory went to Joe Sambito, who pitched the final three innings and allowed just one baserunner, but the star of the game—and the center of post-game attention—was Bob Watson, who had twice tied the game with clutch hits and had hit for the cycle.

"This is the first time I've hit for the cycle in my entire baseball career," said Watson. "I never even got one in the little league."[2]

The cycle, though, was of little importance, Watson said. "You don't think about things like that, you just try to hit the ball."[3] More important to the team, he stressed, was the hard-fought victory. "We've experienced a lot of bad luck this year," he said. "This is a great opportunity for us to gain some ground."[4]

The Astros did gain some ground, going 51-41 from that point, although they still finished a distant third behind the eventual world champion Los Angeles Dodgers. Watson wound up having arguably his finest season, with career highs in home runs (22), doubles (38), triples (6), runs batted in (110), stolen bases (5), and slugging percentage (.498).

It would not be the last time Watson hit for the cycle; he accomplished the feat for the Boston Red Sox on September 15, 1979, making him the first major-league player to hit for the cycle in both the National and American Leagues.

SOURCES

Galveston Daily News.

Houston Chronicle.

New York Times.

The Sporting News.

NOTES

1   "Ailing Watson Finds Cure—Giants Pitching," *San Rafael* (California) *Independent Journal,* June 25, 1977: 32.

2   Ibid.

3   Ibid.

4   "Houston Jelling? Giants Give Astros a Lift," *San Mateo* (California) *Times,* June 25, 1977: 10.

Cruz's Walk-Off Homer Preserves Niekro's Extra-Inning Complete-Game Gem

July 17, 1978: Houston Astros 2, Philadelphia Phillies 1 (11 innings), at the Astrodome

By Gordon Gattie

THE PHILADELPHIA PHILLIES WERE leading the National League East by 4½ games over the Chicago Cubs when they arrived in Houston to play the Astros for the first of a two-game series at the Astrodome. The 48-36 Phillies had their sights set on their third consecutive NL East title, led by future Hall of Famers Mike Schmidt and Steve Carlton, who were complemented by 1978 All-Stars Larry Bowa, Greg Luzinski, and Bob Boone. The Phillies' pitching staff, anchored by Carlton, Dick Ruthven, and Larry Christenson, had allowed 312 runs to date, the least in the major leagues. The Phillies were finishing their first road trip after the All-Star Game after losing two of three to the Atlanta Braves. Philadelphia sent a rested Christenson to the mound; he was only 6-8 so far and had struggled against the Astros both times he faced them. On May 9 in Philadelphia, Christenson had given up five runs in 6⅔ innings to take the loss, and nine days later in Houston, he had allowed four runs in 5⅓ innings in a no-decision.

Meanwhile, the Astros were lingering in the basement of the NL West. With a 38-49 record and 15 games behind the division-leading San Francisco Giants, the Astros struggled at the plate. Houston had scored 324 runs so far, the second lowest in the NL and the third lowest in the majors. Featuring Jose Cruz, Terry Puhl (the Astros' only All-Star that season), and Bob Watson at the plate and J.R. Richard, Ken Forsch, and Mark Lemongello on the mound, the Astros were attempting to improve upon their .500 record of the previous season.

Just before the All-Star break, the Astros had traded catcher Joe Ferguson to the Los Angeles Dodgers for two minor leaguers, shortstop Rafael Landestoy and outfielder Jeffrey Leonard, who arrived on September 11 as a player to be named later. Inserted as the starting shortstop and frequent leadoff hitter, Landestoy provided decent defense but little offensive firepower. Immediately after the All-Star break, Houston lost three of five games to the Montreal Expos. During that series, the Astros dropped into last place, where they remained for the next two weeks. Their notable lack of offense, exemplified by 8-0 and 6-1 losses in the final two games of the Montreal series, was not helping the pitching staff.

In the series opener against the Phillies, the Astros sent veteran knuckleballer Joe Niekro to the hill. Niekro, who had lost three of his last four starts, entered the game with a 5-7 record and a 5.69 ERA. In his only previous appearance against the Phillies that season, on May 18, Niekro had given up four runs on four hits without recording an out as his ERA swelled to 7.97. As a result, manager Bill Virdon dropped him from the rotation. He remained in the bullpen until late June, a stretch of five games that ended when Niekro threw 6⅔ relief innings against the Cubs, helping the Astros win a 5-4 squeaker.

Bake McBride, the Phillies' right fielder and leadoff hitter, doubled to center field to start the game, but Niekro picked him off second base for the first out. Bowa lined out and Garry Maddox flied out. For the Astros, Landestoy flied to left, Puhl grounded out to the pitcher, and Enos Cabell reached first on an error by second baseman Ted Sizemore. But Cruz grounded out to second base to end a scoreless first inning.

Both Niekro and Christenson pitched effectively during the early innings. After Luzinski reached base on catcher's interference to begin the second inning, no Phillies player reached base until the fifth inning, when Barry Foote struck out but reached first on a passed ball. Sizemore then singled to right field, but Niekro nabbed another baserunner when he picked Foote off second base to squelch the threat.

Christenson had allowed baserunners on two hits, two walks, and two errors though four innings. Niekro started the Houston fifth with a single to left field, moved to second on a bunt by Landestoy, and scored when Puhl singled to center field, giving Houston a 1-0 lead. Cabell grounded out and Cruz hit a fly ball to right field that ended the inning. In the sixth and seventh the teams traded baserunners, but no one scored and the Astros maintained their one-run lead.

Sizemore started the Phillies' eighth inning with a single to center. Bud Harrelson ran for Sizemore and Tim McCarver pinch-hit for Christenson, who had pitched a solid game by allowing only one run on five hits in seven innings while striking out three and walking three. Harrelson stole second base, but McCarver struck out. McBride followed with a single to center field, plating Harrelson and tying the game, 1-1, before Bowa grounded out into a fielder's choice and Maddox flied out to left field to end the inning.

In the bottom of the eighth, Tug McGraw replaced Christenson on the mound. Cruz opened the frame with a single to left field but was erased when Watson grounded into a 4-6-3 double play. Art Howe popped out to second for the third out. Niekro retired the Phillies in order in the top of the ninth inning, and McGraw matched Niekro by setting down the Astros in the bottom of the ninth, sending the game into extra innings tied, 1-1.

In the Phillies' 10th, Harrelson walked with one out. With Schmidt pinch-hitting for McGraw, Harrelson stole second base again, but he advanced no

Knuckleballer Joe Niekro is the Astros' career leader in wins with 144. He registered consecutive 20-win seasons in 1979 and 1980 and his 2,270 innings pitched place him second behind Larry Dierker in team history. (Courtesy of Houston Astros Baseball Club).

further as Schmidt flied out to left field and McBride struck out. Rawly Eastwick, the former Cincinnati closer acquired from the New York Yankees in exchange for Bobby Brown and Jay Johnstone about a month earlier, succeeded McGraw on the mound and responded with a 1-2-3 inning for Philadelphia.

Niekro had already faced 37 batters and was now pitching in the 11th inning. He had last pitched 10 full innings in a six-hit shutout of the San Diego Padres nearly nine years earlier, on August 21, 1969. Niekro started the 11th by inducing groundouts from Bowa and Maddox. Luzinski walked and was replaced by pinch-runner Jerry Martin, who was stranded when Rich Hebner flied out to right field.

In the bottom of the 11th inning, Cruz led off against Eastwick and belted his fifth home run of the season—his eighth game-winning hit in 1978[1] — to give the Astros an exciting 2-1 win over the first-place Phillies. Niekro gave up only one run on five hits while striking out eight hitters in his marathon complete game, his fourth of the season. Afterward, Niekro said, "I didn't get tired, I felt I could have gone two or three more innings."[2] Niekro also was happy to turn around his luck against a team that battered him two months earlier. "The last start against [the] Phillies I felt great in the bullpen but didn't have great stuff in the game. Tonight was the opposite."[3]

Eastwick suffered his first loss as a Phil, dropping to 4-2. "The pitch to Cruz was out of the strike zone," he said. "He swings at a lot of bad pitches."[4]

It was a disappointing 1978 season for the Astros but thanks to victories like this one, they at least escaped the basement, finishing fifth in the NL West, 21 games behind the Dodgers. Although they finished near the bottom of many team offensive categories that season, they did finish second in the NL with 178 stolen bases, with three players exceeding 30 steals: Cruz (37), Cabell (33), and Puhl (32). Cesar Cedeno topped the NL in stolen-base percentage, converting 23 of 25 steal attempts for a 92 percent success rate.

Niekro ended the season with a 14-14 record and a 3.86 ERA; the following two years he finished as a 20-game winner as the Astros emerged as a force in the NL West.

SOURCES

Besides the sources cited in the Notes, the author consulted the following:

AstrosDaily.com (2000-2015). astrosdaily.com/history/1978/.

Kepner, Tyler. *The Phillies Experience: A Year-by-Year Chronicle of the Philadelphia Phillies* (Minneapolis: MVP Books, 2013).

Weiss, Scott S.D. "Phillies Seasons: 1978, National League East Champions," examiner.com/article/phillies-seasons-1978-national-league-east-champions.

NOTES

1   Associated Press, "Niekro stymies Phils, 2-1," *Philadelphia Eagle*, July 18, 1978: 10.

2   Ibid.

3   Michael A. Lutz, "Cruz' Late Blast Sinks Phils, 2-1," *Gettysburg (Pennsylvania) Times*, July 18, 1978: 10.

4   Ibid.

Ken Forsch Hurls Earliest No-Hitter in History

April 7, 1979: Houston Astros 6, Atlanta Braves 0, at the Astrodome

By Chip Greene

TO RELATE EACH OF THE HISTORICAL events that converged in the Houston Astrodome the night of April 7, 1979, to the unique accomplishment that followed, a historian has to traverse the previous 65 years of baseball history.

First, one has to stop in St. Louis. There, on April 14, 1917, Chicago White Sox pitcher Eddie Cicotte threw a no-hitter against the St. Louis Browns. It was the earliest date for a no-hitter in the regular season. It would remain so for the next 62 years.

The next stop through baseball history comes in Brooklyn. It was September 21, 1934. On their way to an eventual world championship, the St. Louis Cardinals visited the Dodgers for a doubleheader. This was no ordinary season for the Cardinals pitching staff. In addition to their young superstar, Dizzy Dean, who, as the game-one starter, was in search of his 27th win of the season, St. Louis also boasted Dizzy's 22-year-old brother, Paul, a 17-game winner in this, his rookie season. Paul would start game two.

On this day, the Dodgers batters never stood a chance in either game. In the opener, Dizzy poured fastball after fastball over the plate and throttled Brooklyn, 13-0. After no-hitting Brooklyn for seven innings, Dean allowed three singles in the final two innings to finish with a complete-game three-hitter. As if that weren't enough, however, in the nightcap, Paul completed what Dizzy couldn't—he threw a no-hitter, which prompted from Dizzy the quip: "If I had known you were going to pitch a no-hitter, I'd have pitched one too."[1] No-hitters from a pair of brothers would have to wait a while.

Finally, we return to St. Louis, where, on April 16, 1978, Cardinals right-hander Bob Forsch, in his third start of the season, defeated the Philadelphia Phillies, 5-0, in what would be the first of two career no-hitters. With that, the stage was set for a very special night in Houston almost exactly one year later.

There was little to suggest that Bob Forsch's older brother, Ken, was in for a particularly effective performance that day. After winning his first major-league game as a September call-up to the Astros in 1970, Ken had spent the next three seasons as a starter, amassing an unimpressive 23-28 record, before being mostly relegated to the bullpen for the next five years. He enjoyed some good years as a late-inning specialist, including a 1976 campaign in which he tallied 19 saves and made the NL All-Star team. In 1978 Forsch made just six starts but completed four, won 10 games and produced a 2.70 ERA, and as the 1979 season dawned, Forsch once again found himself as a member of the Astros' starting rotation.

He had endured a rocky spring, however. During the exhibition season, Forsch made just two starts, worked only 10 innings, and surrendered an abysmal 27 hits. In his final spring outing, on April 3 against the Montreal Expos, he allowed 13 hits in seven innings. Sometime during that game, too, Forsch suffered an insect bite on his left elbow, and as the Astros opened their season in the Astrodome on Friday night, April 6, against the Atlanta Braves, the bite had swollen so severely that Forsch, who was scheduled to start the season's second game the following day, was questionable.

On Friday night, Houston scored two runs in the bottom of the first inning and held on to defeat the Braves, 2-1. The next day 24,325 fans were on hand as Forsch, with a career record of 55-62, overcame the bug bite and started the season's second contest. It would be the greatest game of his career.

Reflecting on his poor spring during an interview after the game, Forsch said, "After the spring I had, I figured I got it all out of my system. I said to myself, 'I've given up all the hits I'm going to give up.'"[2] And for this one night, he had.

On the mound for Atlanta was left-hander Larry McWilliams. Given his superb rookie season (9-3, 2.81) in 1978, the Braves undoubtedly felt McWilliams gave them a solid chance to even their record at 1-1. Yet after Forsch easily retired the first three batters to start the game, Houston plated two runs in the bottom of the inning, and that would be all the offense the Astros needed.

In the end, Forsch was never tested. Against the leadoff batter, Jeff Burroughs, in the top of the second inning, Forsch issued a walk on a 3-and-1 count, yet quickly retired the next three men on a foul popup, a groundout that forced Burroughs, and a strikeout. In the fourth inning, the Braves came closest to getting a hit when Glenn Hubbard stroked a sharp grounder to third baseman Enos Cabell, but Cabell fielded the ball cleanly on one hop and rifled a throw to first to beat Hubbard by two strides. With two outs in the eighth inning, Forsch issued his second walk, to Barry Bonnell, but a weak grounder to second by pinch-hitter Bob Beall snuffed out any chance Atlanta had of generating a rally. As the Braves came to the plate in the top of the ninth, trailing 6-0, Forsch stood just three outs away not only from the first no-hitter of his 10-year career, but also from joining his brother as the only siblings ever to throw one.

In the seventh inning, sensing the magnitude of what was evolving, the Astrodome crowd had begun cheering every out. Likewise, when Forsch came to bat with two outs in the bottom of the eighth, he received a 20-second standing ovation. Now, as Forsch stared in for the sign against the leadoff hitter, left-handed pinch-hitter Rowland Office, the whole stadium was abuzz with excitement. As Forsch delivered, Office watched the first pitch go by for strike one. Then he tapped a slow grounder to second and

was easily thrown out at first. That brought to the plate right-handed-hitting Jerry Royster. As the crowd held its collective breath, Royster worked the count to 2-and-1. And then, swinging away, Royster drilled a searing liner down the third-base line, but it veered foul by 10 feet. It was the hardest-hit ball of the night and proved to be the Braves' last gasp. On the next pitch, Royster grounded out to shortstop Craig Reynolds, and finally, Hubbard, too, grounded out to Reynolds. As the ball smacked into the glove of first baseman Cabell (he had changed positions in the top of the eighth), the Astros charged from their dugout and mobbed Forsch halfway between the mound and the first-base line, while the crowd stood and roared its approval. Ken Forsch had thrown the sixth no-hitter in Houston franchise history[3] and the earliest gem in the history of the major leagues.

"I realized I had the no-hitter way back in the third inning," Forsch told the press, "and in the seventh, I smelled it."[4]

"I figured that my rhythm was going so well there was no way they were going to get a hit. Now I'm gonna try to pitch another one this year."[5] He never did. Just 356 days earlier, Bob Forsch had thrown his no-hitter. Bob was at his home in St. Louis when he learned of Ken's gem. "That's just great, isn't it?" Bob said when interviewed on the phone. "I think it's fantastic. The only bad part is that it's [Ken's] first game of the season so it's all downhill from here. I'm so happy that he pitched one—I know exactly how he feels. Now that we're the first brother act, it's unbelievable … just fantastic.[6]

"Right now," Bob said, "he's getting so many phone calls. You don't realize exactly what you've done until you get home. I'm gonna try to get ahold of him in a few hours and if I can't, I'll send him a telegram in the morning."[7]

In recognition of Ken's accomplishment, four days later the Texas House of Representatives designated April 11 Ken Forsch Day in the state. That evening the Astros presented Forsch a new car in honor of his no-hitter.

NOTES

1   UPI, *Galveston* (Texas) *Daily News*, April 8, 1979.

2   UPI, *Daily Herald Suburban Chicago*, April 8, 1979.

3   The others: Don Nottebart, May 17, 1963 (Colt .45s); Ken Johnson, April 23, 1964 (Colt .45s - despite a no-hitter Johnson lost the game, 1-0); Don Wilson, June 18, 1967; Don Wilson, May 1, 1969; Larry Dierker, July 9, 1976.

4   UPI, *Daily Herald Suburban Chicago*, April 8, 1979.

5   Ibid.

6   As of October 31, 2015, the Forsches remain the only brothers to each throw a no-hitter

7   UPI, *Galveston Daily News*, April 8, 1979.

J.R. Richard Strikes Out 15 for Complete-Game Victory

August 3, 1979: Houston Astros 4, Atlanta Braves 1, at the Astrodome

By T.S. Flynn

THE HOUSTON ASTROS OWNED A 3-game lead in the National League West when they hosted the Atlanta Braves on August 3, 1979. Their starting pitcher, ace J.R. Richard, took the ball with a 9-11 record. As is often the case with pitchers' won-lost numbers, though, the sub-.500 record failed to reflect the overall strength of his performances and his value to the team. Richard began the 1979 campaign red-hot, earning four wins and one no-decision in five April starts, before losing 11 of 18 between May 1 and July 20. "I was erratic … but I also had some bad luck," Richard said by way of explaining the pile of midseason losses. "I pitched some good games, but I was paired against some of the best pitchers in baseball. If I gave up one or two runs, it seemed like I was beat."[1] In fact, he had allowed two runs in just one of his losses during that stretch. (He gave up three runs in three of the other losses, and four or more in the remaining seven.) But some of the blame for Richard's slide belonged to the Astros' weak offense, which offered Richard scant help in 1979, scoring a league-worst 583 runs for the season. (The Houston pitchers allowed 582.) Nevertheless, entering the August 3 game, Richard led the major leagues with 182 strikeouts, and he'd won his previous two starts, including an eight-strikeout complete game against the Los Angeles Dodgers on July 29. The 6-foot-8 Houston fireballer returned to the Astrodome mound on this Friday night in front of 20,716 fans, eager to add another dominant victory to his resume.

Richard wasted no time. Leadoff batter Jerry Royster struck out, Gary Matthews flied out, and Rowland Office ended the top of the first by also striking out. In the bottom of the first, Braves starter Rick Matula held the Astros to a two-out single by Terry Puhl that failed to initiate an Astros threat.

In the second Richard picked up where he'd left off, striking out Bob Horner and Dale Murphy (the third and fourth Braves strikeout victims of the night), but Murphy reached first when Richard's third strike skipped past catcher Alan Ashby. Richard's arsenal included an upper-90s fastball and a hard slider that was occasionally as impossible to catch as it was to hit. Richard threw 19 wild pitches in 1979 (12 in his first four starts, including six in one game, equaling a major-league record[2]), but his wildness, in combination with his height and pitch velocity, intimidated hitters. Richie Hebner joked that he could almost smell Richard's breath when he delivered a pitch.[3] Astros reliever Joe Sambito said, "I know a Dodger player who [said] a lot of Dodgers have come up with fake injuries rather than face J.R.—and you wouldn't believe the names. I see guys who never swing at the first pitch *always* swing at it against J.R. They take charity swings, just to keep from staying in there. That fear is such a help for a pitcher, and with Jay, it means that he has an extra half-foot of error space on his pitches that no other pitcher has; he can make more mistakes because nobody is digging in."[4] Richard anxiety even affected teammate Bob Watson, who said, "I've never taken batting practice against him and I never will. I have a family to think of."[5] On this night, control would not be a problem for the Astros starter. After Mike Lum singled to join Murphy on the bases, Richard struck out Joe Nolan and retired Pepe Frias on a fly ball to right.

With 303 strikeouts in 1978, J.R. Richard became the first NL right-hander to notch 300 in a single season in the twentieth century. In 1979 he improved upon his previous mark with 313 strikeouts. (Courtesy of Houston Astros Baseball Club).

Houston's offense gave Richard a lead in the bottom of the second when Art Howe doubled home Enos Cabell, who had led off with a single and stolen second. Ashby drove in Howe for the second Astros run. Richard's sacrifice bunt moved Ashby into scoring position, and Cesar Cedeno walked, but the inning ended when Craig Reynolds flied out to center.

Richard struck out Matula to begin the third. Then Jerry Royster walked and stole second. After walking Gary Matthews, Richard struck out Office for his seventh K of the game. Horner followed with a two-out single to center, plating the first Braves run of the night. Murphy flied out to end the inning.

In the bottom of the fourth, Richard aided his own cause with a one-out single to center. After advancing to second base on a single by Cedeno,

Richard reached third on Reynolds' fielder's choice and crossed the plate on Puhl's two-run double. The offensive outburst widened the Astros' lead to 4-1 and knocked Matula out of the game. Larry Bradford took the ball for the Braves and finished the fourth without allowing further damage. Richard then continued his domination of the Braves, retiring them in order in the fifth: Pinch-hitter Darrel Chaney struck out, Royster lofted a fly to right field, and Matthews took a third strike.

Richard was in his groove again, and the Atlanta hitters were overmatched. Astros manager Bill Virdon later insisted that Richard hadn't just regained his April form in August, he'd surpassed it. "J.R. is pitching more consistently than at any other point all year," the Houston skipper said. "His control is much better now. When J.R. gets ahead 0-and-2, he is almost unhittable. The batters just don't know what he's going to throw."[6] Richard felt the difference, too. "My rhythm is better now and I'm in a better overall groove," he said, "but I don't think I'm throwing any harder."[7]

In the sixth Richard added another Horner K to his expanding strikeout collection and continued to stymie the Braves' offense. The Atlanta bullpen held the Houston offense in check the rest of the way, but the night belonged to J.R. Richard. In the seventh, Braves pinch-hitter Jeff Burroughs swung and missed for Richard's 11th strikeout, and Matthews became number 12 when he failed to make contact leading off the eighth. The top of the ninth began with a walk to Lum. Richard retired Nolan on strikes. Frias's single to center may have given the Braves a glimmer of hope, but as had been the case throughout the game, Richard refused to buckle, as he dispatched pinch-hitter Charlie Spikes on strikes for the second out. The Houston ace told reporters after the game that it was only then that he realized how many strikeouts he'd compiled. "I wasn't aware of the strikeouts until they flashed 'King Richard' on the scoreboard and the number 14," he said. "Then I was going for the strikeout against Royster."[8] He got it.

Richard's 15 strikeouts matched his career high, which he'd set in his major-league debut nearly eight years earlier, on September 5, 1971. Of the 12 Braves batters to face Richard in this game, only Lum avoided striking out. Five of the 12 struck out twice (Royster, Matthews, Office, Horner, and Joe Nolan), including the top four in the batting order. Eight of Atlanta's nine baserunners failed to score. It was a dominant performance by a pitcher reaching the pinnacle of his career. "When J.R. is in the groove like that, there's not much anybody can do," Braves manager Bobby Cox said. "We hit about four balls hard, but somebody caught them, and that was it."[9]

The 1979 Astros were built on speed and pitching. They hit more triples (52) than home runs (49) behind a pitching staff that completed 55 games, an astounding (for its era) 34 percent of their starts. J.R. Richard led the way with a 5.6 WAR season,[10] throwing 292⅓ innings and completing 19 of his 38 starts.

He finished the season best in the National League in batting average against (.209) and strikeout/walk ratio (3.194), and he led the majors in ERA (2.71), strikeouts (313, or 90 more than second-best Nolan Ryan), strikeouts per 9 innings pitched (9.636), and fewest hits allowed per 9 innings pitched (6.773).

When asked before the 1979 season if he thought he was the best pitcher in the game, Richard said, "I don't ever say that, I let others say it for me. But to me, I'm in the game to *be* No. 1. I can't be satisfied with less. Being No. 1 is fantastic, it's the greatest thing in the world. Not being No. 1 is being an ass. I feel I'm close to that point, if not already there, because my domination instinct is greater than most people's. That's the same instinct Russia and the U.S. have in the arms race, except I don't use it to hurt anyone. I want to dominate baseball, not people. A lot of people want that, but they don't want to put in the work, to suffer, to sacrifice to do it. I do. I run more than any pitcher has ever run. I do two miles most every day in under 10 minutes. I kill myself. Being the best requires that. I've made that pact with God and myself."[11]

NOTES

1   Harry Shattuck. "J.R., Forsch Settle Down and Astros Stay Up," *The Sporting News*, August 25, 1979.

2   Mark Ribowsky. "This Pitcher Makes Hitters Tremble," *Sport*, July 1979.

3   Ibid.

4   Ibid.

5   Ibid.

6   Shattuck.

7   Ibid.

8   Tribune Wire Services. "Astros' Richard fans 15 Braves," *Chicago Tribune*, August 4, 1979.

9   Ibid.

10   WAR based on calculations from Baseball-Reference.com.

11   Ribowsky.

Acknowledgment: Brian Madigan provided research assistance for this story.

J.R. Richard's 15 K's and Bochy's Walk-Off Single Keep Pennant Hopes Alive

September 21, 1979: Houston Astros 3, Cincinnati Reds 2 (13 innings), at the Astrodome

By Mike Whiteman

SINCE ITS OPENING IN 1965, THE Houston Astrodome, known as the "Eighth Wonder of the World," had seen many epic and varied events that included sports, concerts, political conventions, and daredevil displays. It was big, like Texas, and the events were big as well. In fact, there wasn't much that couldn't be done there.

What the Dome had not seen in great quantity was pennant-race baseball. In fact, the best Astros team to date had been the 1972 squad, which won 84 games and finished 10½ games out of first place.

In 1979 things were different. The Astros were a preseason 75-to-1 longshot to win the championship,[1] and expectations were low, But the team started off fast and didn't look back. On July 4, the were playing over .600 ball and led the NL West by 10½ games. At the All-Star break, they led by 6 games. The lead dwindled and eventually evaporated, but as of September 21 it already was by far the most successful season in team history, and it wasn't over yet. The fans were on board; attendance was at its highest since 1965, the opening year of the Astrodome.

The Astros were powered primarily by a much improved pitching staff whose two aces, J.R. Richard and Joe Niekro, went about their business in totally different ways: Richard with the heat of a nearly 100-mph fastball and a hard slider; Niekro with a repertoire of pitches, including a knuckleball, that at times seemed to be floating in slow motion.[2]

Houston needed the quality pitching because its hitting was certainly not going to carry the team. The Astros had finished in the lower half of the National League in runs scored and home runs each of the previous two seasons, and were at the bottom of those categories throughout the summer of 1979. The team's most frequent cleanup hitter, Jose Cruz, had only eight home runs heading into late September. The second most frequently used cleanup hitter, rookie Jeffrey Leonard, had none. Throughout the season, manager Bill Virdon's squad needed to manufacture runs, and they were among the league leaders in both sacrifices and stolen bases.

People around baseball wondered how the Astros were faring so well. The disrespect was out in the open throughout the league. After the Phillies were shut out by left-hander Randy Niemann on July 4, manager Danny Ozark complained, "How can we lose to Randy Niemann? Our Reading farm club could beat Niemann."[3] Also count the Cincinnati ace Tom Seaver among the skeptical. "Once they stop getting all those bloop hits, the Astros are going to drop through the West Division like a lead balloon. The Astros are the luckiest team I've ever seen."[4]

While they hadn't fallen out of the race as predicted, by the morning of September 21 the Astros had fallen 2½ games behind the division-leading Reds heading into a three-game series against Cincinnati. A sweep would put the upstart Astros back on top of the standings with a week remaining in the season. A crowd of 44,975 witnessed the opening game of what appeared to be the most crucial series in the team's existence so far.

On the hill for the hosts was Richard, a 6-foot-8 right-hander who was 16-13 with a 2.92 ERA. After

Bruce Bochy, the fifth major-league player born in France, spent his career as a backup catcher. Later, as a manager, he led the San Francisco Giants to World Series titles in 2010, 2012, and 2014. (Courtesy of Houston Astros Baseball Club).

three straight seasons with 18 or more wins, he had started off slowly, and was only 7-10 at the All-Star break. He recovered well in the second half, and was 9-3 since the midsummer classic, including a 5-1, 0.67 August in which he completed all six of his starts. Richard was scary to hit against, as he mixed his fastball with a nasty slider.[5] Even teammates were loath to dig in on him, with longtime Astro Bob Watson claiming, "I've never taken batting practice against him and I never will. I have a family to think of."[6]

Toeing the rubber for the Reds was Astros antagonist Seaver, who sported a 15-6 record and a 3.27 ERA. Already an icon, Seaver came into the game with 234 career victories. While his power arsenal was slowing down a bit, requiring the use of more off-speed pitches,[7] he was still among the elite National

League pitchers. Going into the game, he had won 13 of his last 14 decisions.

This was the second matchup between the two strikeout artists this month. When they faced off on September 11 neither lasted past the sixth inning in a 9-8 Cincinnati victory that had knocked the Astros out of first place.

Richard cruised through the first inning, setting down Dave Collins, Joe Morgan, and Davey Concepcion. Seaver completed his first frame easily as well, giving up a single to shortstop Craig Reynolds, the Astros All-Star, who was erased by a double-play grounder off the bat of Cesar Cedeno.

In the top of the second, the Reds got two runs on a two-out single by Dan Driessen and a home run by Ray Knight, completing a wildly successful season in which he replaced the departed All-Star Pete Rose at third base. The Reds led 2-0, but they would score no more runs against Richard. The big right-hander allowed only one runner past second the rest of the contest, and struck out 11 batters through nine innings.

Houston got on the scoreboard in the third inning. After an error by Driessen on a grounder by Richard, Terry Puhl drove a run-scoring single to center. In the bottom of the seventh, Houston tied the game with a typical "rally"—a single (by Rafael Landestoy), a sacrifice (by Richard), and another RBI single by Puhl.

At the end of nine innings, the game was tied 2-2. A Houston loss would put them 3½ games behind the Reds with nine games left in the season, making their task of catching Cincinnati significantly more difficult.

Richard continued to be strong, striking out Collins and Morgan to complete a scoreless 10th. Seaver, meanwhile, gave way to reliever Dave Tomlin and, later, ace fireman Tom Hume.

Finally, after 11 innings, 143 pitches and 15 strikeouts, Richard left the game. It was an epic performance in the midst of the first true pennant race in the team's history. Would it be enough? In the 12th, Virdon turned to left-handed reliever Joe Sambito, who earlier in the season had a streak of 40⅔ innings without allowing an earned run. The All-Star Sambito held the Reds scoreless another two innings.

In the bottom of the 13th, Reynolds led off with a single off Hume. Cedeno, playing true Astro baseball, bunted him to second. Reds manager John McNamara had Hume intentionally walk Cruz and, after Enos Cabell grounded into a fielder's choice at second, rookie Danny Heep also walked, loading the bases.

Walking to the plate for perhaps the most important at-bat of the season was backup catcher Bruce

Bochy, a .213 hitter coming into the game. Bochy had become a semi-regular after a season-ending injury to starting catcher Alan Ashby in August. In the biggest moment of his young career, Bochy singled to left, and the opener of this series went to Houston, 3-2.

The Astros were now 1½ games in back of the Reds. With Niekro starting the next day's game, and the following week filled with road games against sub-.500 teams, the Houston faithful could be excused for dreaming about their team's first postseason appearance.[8]

SOURCES

In addition to the sources listed in the notes, the author also consulted:

Shattuck, Harry. "Astros Tighten Their Belts, Battle On, Minus Ashby," *The Sporting News*, September 22, 1979.

Shattuck, Harry. "King Richard Rules Astrodomain," *The Sporting News*, September 29, 1979.

NOTES

1   Harry Shattuck, "Astros Had a Big Year, No Matter What," *The Sporting News*, October 6, 1979.

2   Bill James and Rob Neyer, *The Neyer/James Guide to Pitchers* (New York: Fireside, 2004), 324.

3   Harry Shattuck, "Astros Shrug Off Insults, Rack Up Victories," *The Sporting News*, July 7, 1979.

4   Harry Shattuck, "Astros See Red When Cincy Takes the Field," *The Sporting News*, July 28, 1979.

5   James and Neyer, 357.

6   Mike Shatzkin, *The Ballplayers* (New York: Arbor House, 1990), 908-909.

7   James and Neyer, 379.

8   Niekro won on September 22, bringing the Astros to within a half-game of first. But they went 3-5 in their remaining games, and finished in second place behind the Reds. Emboldened by their 1979 improvement, the Astros added Nolan Ryan and Joe Morgan as free agents for 1980, and went on to win the National League West division title.

Astros Win 11-Inning Thriller to Reach Brink of World Series

October 10, 1980: Houston Astros 1, Philadelphia Phillies 0 (11 innings), NLCS Game Three, at the Astrodome

By Frederick C. Bush

THE HOUSTON ASTROS (ORIGINALLY the Colt .45s) had begun play in 1962, and the Astrodome had opened in 1965, but the team had endured a long wait for its first postseason appearance. In 1980 the Astros survived a one-game playoff with the Los Angeles Dodgers to win the NL West division with a 93-70 record. They began the NLCS against the Phillies by splitting the first two games in Philadelphia, using a four-run outburst in the 10th inning to win Game Two. Now, on October 10, 1980, the Astros were hosting the first playoff game in the Dome, which was also the first indoor playoff game in major-league history, before a rabid crowd of 44,443 Houston fans.

The Phillies were determined not to repeat their postseason failures of 1976-78, but they would have to beat an Astros team that was tailor-made for its home ballpark. The cavernous Astrodome did not lend itself to a power game—outfielder Terry Puhl led the team with 13 home runs—so the Astros used pitching, speed, and defense to overcome their opponents. In the NLCS, they also had a "tenth man" in the home crowd. As Puhl recalled years later, "One side of the Astrodome would yell 'HOUSTON.' The other side would answer 'ASTROS.' In the dugout, you couldn't talk to the player next to you because it was so loud. … I never heard the Astrodome like that."[1]

Amid the cacophony of the Dome, knuckleballer Joe Niekro, who posted a 20-12 record during the season, took the mound and proceeded to throw 10 shutout innings against the Phillies, though he received a no-decision for his effort. After Niekro retired the first two batters of the game, Mike Schmidt, who slugged 48 homers and would be voted the 1980 National League MVP, took a page out of the Astros' playbook when he singled and stole second base; however, Greg Luzinski grounded out to end the inning. The first inning was an omen for the Phillies: Though they had at least one baserunner in eight different innings (seven times against Niekro), they mounted only one real scoring threat and failed to plate a single run.

The Astros fared no better as they were held scoreless for 10 innings by Phillies starter Larry Christenson and relievers Dickie Noles and Tug McGraw. Puhl led off the bottom of the first inning with a double and advanced to third base on Enos Cabell's groundout. The rally gained momentum when Joe Morgan walked to put runners at the corners with one out, but Jose Cruz grounded into a double play that put an end to the Astros' hopes for a quick lead.

The Phillies' best scoring opportunity came in the top of the third inning when Pete Rose hit a one-out single and raced to third on Bake McBride's base hit. McBride advanced to second base on a passed ball before Schmidt hit a grounder that third baseman Cabell rifled to catcher Luis Pujols to retire Rose at home plate. Luzinski stepped up and smashed a ball to deep left field, but Cruz caught it on the warning track and the Phillies came away empty-handed.

Cruz provided the Astros with their second chance to score when he stroked a one-out triple in the bottom of the fourth inning, but his hit went for naught when Cesar Cedeño and Pujols bookended an intentional walk to Denny Walling with groundouts. A scant two innings later, the Astros had yet another

The 1980 Houston Astros team was constructed to fit the pitcher-friendly confines of the Astrodome. They went 55-26 at home en route to a 93-70 overall record and their first NL West Division title. (Courtesy of Houston Astros Baseball Club).

runner in scoring position after Cabell led off with a single and went to second base on Morgan's ground-out. Christenson then issued his second intentional walk of the game—this time to Cruz—which paid off exactly as the Phillies had hoped when Cedeño grounded into a double play.

The double play ended up being double trouble for the Astros: Cedeño dislocated his right ankle as he tripped over first base trying to beat second baseman Manny Trillo's throw. Cedeño, a speedy center fielder who had batted .309 with 32 doubles and 48 stolen bases during the season, underwent surgery immediately, and his loss was a great blow to the team. Morgan, Houston's veteran second baseman, who had been a two-time MVP and two-time World Series winner with the Cincinnati Reds, said that the Astros' rallying cry all season had been "Cesar, go score a run."[2] Nevertheless, Morgan also tried to reassure his team and its fans, saying, "This will hurt us a lot, but this team has overcome so much adversity already. I think we're strong enough to go the rest of the way without him"[3]

The Astros squandered yet another scoring opportunity in the bottom of the eighth inning. Puhl singled off Noles, who had relieved Christenson in the seventh inning, and advanced to second on Cabell's sacrifice bunt, after which McGraw took the mound for the Phillies. Morgan flied out, Cruz received the third intentional walk issued by Phillies pitchers, and Dave Bergman flied out to strand Puhl at second base.

In Niekro's 10th and final inning of work, he set down Rose, McBride, and Schmidt in order after McGraw had reached first base on an error. In light of Niekro's performance, the Phillies actually may have been happy that ace rookie reliever Dave Smith took the mound for the Astros in the top of the 11th. Smith gave the Phillies a brief glimmer of hope when he surrendered a two-out double to Garry Maddox; however, after issuing an intentional walk to Larry Bowa, Smith struck out Del Unser, who was pinch-hitting for catcher Bob Boone. The 10½ innings without a run constituted the longest scoreless tie in

NLCS history, which dated back to 1969, but the first and only run of the game would score soon.

The Phillies left McGraw in the game to pitch the bottom of the 11th inning, and Morgan lined his third pitch to right field for a leadoff triple. The usually speedy Morgan was suffering from strained ligaments in his right knee, so Astros manager Bill Virdon sent Rafael Landestoy in to pinch-run for him. Phillies manager Dallas Green turned to the evening's favored strategy and had McGraw intentionally walk both Cruz (his third of the game) and pinch-hitter Art Howe to load the bases and set up a force at any base. Virdon played a hunch by using Howe, and the intentional walk played right into his hands. As he later explained, "If I don't pinch-hit for Bergman, they may pitch to him and walk Walling. Then I'm not happy with myself. I wanted the bases loaded."[4]

Walling got into a quick 0-and-2 hole before lofting the third pitch he saw to left field for a sacrifice fly that scored Landestoy and gave the Astros a 1-0 victory. Walling was the second Astro, along with his manager, to claim that he had an idea of what the Phillies would do. He said of his at-bat against McGraw, "I kept it really simple. I knew the adversary. I watched how he was pitching to Craig Reynolds and Terry Puhl [two other left-handed hitters] and assumed he would pitch me the same way."[5]

Walling's RBI made him a hero, but it was Morgan's triple that had ignited that Astros' winning rally. Morgan had started his career with the Astros in 1963 and had been the team's starting second baseman for seven years, but he had been traded to the Reds after the 1971 season. After the 1979 season, he had signed with the Astros because, as he said, "[Originally] they were the only organization willing to sign a 5-foot, 140-pound second baseman. I always wanted to repay them for that."[6]

Though Morgan batted only .243 in 141 games that season, he was a proven winner who provided a veteran's steadiness as well as inspiration to the 1980 Astros squad. Since Morgan was the team's elder statesman, he was asked if he played the same role for the Astros that Willie Stargell had played for the Pittsburgh Pirates the previous year. After Morgan shook his head and deferred to Stargell as "special people," a reporter asked, "But do the young players here call you Pops?" Morgan smiled and said, "No, I can run faster than most of these guys. Willie can't."[7]

After their second consecutive extra-innings victory in Game Three, Morgan and the Astros hoped that they were off and running to an NL pennant.

NOTES

[1] Bill Brown and Mike Acosta, *The Houston Astros: Deep in the Heart* (Houston: Bright Sky Press, 2013), 87.

[2] Joseph Durso, "Astros Top Phils, 1-0, in 11 Innings to Lead Playoff, 2-1," *New York Times*, October 11, 1980.

[3] "Houston Astros 1980 NLCS," astrosdaily.com/history/1980/, accessed July 3, 2015.

[4] Lowell Reidenbaugh, "N.L. Playoff Gleanings," *The Sporting News*, October, 25, 1980:16.

[5] Brown and Acosta, 88.

[6] Dave Anderson, "Joe Morgan Repays a Debt," *New York Times*, October 12, 1980.

[7] Ibid.

Controversy Abounds in Wild Extra-Inning Playoff Game

October 11, 1980: Philadelphia Phillies 5, Houston Astros 3 (10 innings), NLCS Game Four, at the Astrodome

By Jim Sweetman

THE CHAMPAGNE WAS READY IN THE Astrodome. With a two-games-to-one lead in the best-of-five National League Championship Series, the Astros were one win away from their first trip to the World Series. Considering the obstacles that both they and their opponents, the Phillies, had overcome, no one was apt to be counting on an easy win. It is unlikely, though, that anyone could have foreseen the weird twists and turns that lay ahead.

Houston had started 1980 strong, surging into the division lead by the end of April. By the end of May, however, the Astros had surrendered the lead to Los Angeles. Despite losing ace starter J.R. Richard to a stroke in late July, Houston battled the Dodgers for the Western Division crown all season. When the Astros lost three straight to LA at the end of the 162-game schedule, the two teams found themselves tied for first place. Joe Niekro shut the Dodgers down in the tiebreaker game to pick up his 20th win and send the Astros into the playoffs for the first time in their 19-year history.

The Phillies had fared only slightly better. In nearly 100 years in the National League, Philadelphia had made it to just two World Series and three play-off series, but each had ended in loss. They also had a tight regular-season race in 1980, clinching the Eastern Division title over the Montreal Expos in their 161st game.

That high-pressure atmosphere continued into the first three games of the League Championship Series. Game One was close, but the Phillies earned a 3-1 win behind their ace, Steve Carlton, who would soon receive his third Cy Young Award. Things got more intense in Game Two, in Philadelphia. After

several late-inning rallies, the Astros pushed across four runs in the 10th to win the game and even the series. A pitchers' duel broke out when the action moved to the Astrodome in Game Three, with zeroes on the scoreboard through 10 innings. Houston broke through in bottom of the 11th against Philadelphia closer Tug McGraw in his fourth inning of work, plating a run on a triple by Joe Morgan and a sacrifice fly by Denny Walling.

For Game Four, Phillies manager Dallas Green sent Carlton back to the mound, while Astros skipper Bill Virdon went with Vern Ruhle, who had not pitched in nearly a week because of an injured finger.[1] The first three innings looked like a repeat of the previous game, with no runs and only three hits recorded between the two teams. In the top of the fourth, the Phillies opened with two singles. Garry Maddox then fisted a soft, low liner in front of the mound with the two runners moving. Ruhle nabbed it near the turf and threw to first for an apparent double play. Although the umpires at first and third had indicated Ruhle's catch was an out, home-plate umpire Doug Harvey, who had been partially blocked by Maddox, signaled no catch. After consulting with umpire Ed Vargo at first, Harvey signaled an out, reversing his initial call. This prompted Green and several Phillies to come out of the dugout and protest hotly.

With lead runner Bake McBride standing on third and the players and umpires uncertain what had happened, Astros first baseman Art Howe took the ball and ran to second. He and his teammates then ran off the field thinking he had recorded the third out on McBride. The umpires gathered to confer, and initially signaled the outcome as a triple play, a decision that met with more vigorous protests by Green and his players. Harvey responded by consulting with National League President Chub Feeney, who was seated near the Astros dugout. They decided to change the ruling to a double play, and allowed McBride to stay at second.

After the game, Harvey explained: "I felt that the runner at second base had gone to third base on my call. The jeopardy rule ... gives the umpire the right to correct a mistake if he feels his call has put a runner in jeopardy."[2] However, the Phillies contingent continued to believe that Ruhle had caught the ball on a bounce and that only one out was legitimate. Neither team was satisfied, but neither protested formally.[3] The inning ended when Larry Bowa grounded out.

The Astros scored first in the bottom of the inning. Enos Cabell led off with a double and moved to third on a groundout. After Gary Woods drew a walk, Howe hit a ball to deep left that Lonnie Smith

caught. Cabell tagged up and Smith, whose career was marked by slapstick hijinks in the outfield and on the basepaths, tried to throw the ball in, but it slipped from his hand and dribbled away. Seeing the misplay, Woods raced toward second and kept going to third, but Smith recovered the ball and threw to third, where Woods was tagged out.

While Ruhle held the Phillies scoreless, the Astros tacked on a run in the fifth to make it 2-0, and then loaded the bases against Carlton in the sixth. With one out, manager Green went to reliever Dickie Noles. The first batter he faced, light-hitting catcher Luis Pujols, hit a fly ball to McBride in deep right. Woods tagged at third and came home on an apparent sacrifice fly. Noles, however, threw the ball to third on an appeal play. Umpire Bob Engle granted the appeal, ruling that Woods had left early, and erasing the run. "When I saw the whole Philadelphia bench up and screaming in the dugout, I figured they

Joe Sambito pitched prior to the era in which relievers accumulated gaudy save totals, but he was a premier fireman for the Astros. In 1979 he was 8-7 with 22 saves and a 1.77 ERA, and finished fifth in Cy Young Award voting in 1980. (Courtesy of Houston Astros Baseball Club).

would appeal," Woods said. Even some on the Astros bench agreed; they did not protest the call.[4]

The Phillies chased Ruhle in the eighth with three straight singles; the last, by Pete Rose, drove in a run. Philadelphia had men at second and third and no one out when Virdon called in Dave Smith to face Mike Schmidt. With an 0-and-2 count, Schmidt fouled a ball off catcher Pujols' ankle, forcing him from the game. Bruce Bochy, who had started only two games that year, replaced him. Soon after, Schmidt beat out a grounder to second base, driving in Lonnie Smith to tie the game and sending Pete Rose, with the potential go-ahead run, to third with no outs.

Closer Joe Sambito came to the mound and struck out Bake McBride for the first out, but Manny Trillo stroked a low liner to right. Jeff Leonard, who had replaced Woods, appeared to catch the ball just above the turf. At third base, Pete Rose played it safe and waited until the out was called before coming home with the go-ahead run ahead of the throw from Leonard. Bochy, seeing Schmidt at second, where he had gone because he thought Leonard had trapped the ball, threw to first for the out on Schmidt.

The score stood at 3-2 into the bottom of the ninth. Instead of calling in McGraw, who had pitched in the three previous games, Dallas Green stuck with Warren Brusstar, who had pitched a clean eighth inning. Brusstar quickly allowed the tying run on a walk, a sacrifice, and a single by Terry Puhl. Puhl stayed at first and was doubled up on the next play when he was caught off first on a fly ball to right field.

As Green did with McGraw in the previous game, Virdon left Sambito in for his third inning to start the 10th. Like his move the day before, it didn't work. Sambito struck out leadoff batter Del Unser but gave up a single to Rose. After Schmidt lined out to left, Green called slugger Greg Luzinski off the bench. Luzinski responded with a double to the left-field corner. Jose Cruz fielded it cleanly, but Rafael Landestoy hesitated slightly before relaying it home to try to cut down Rose, who was running from first on contact. Landestoy's throw short-hopped catcher Bochy, bouncing off his chest protector just before Rose, who came in standing, checked him with a

forearm to safely reach the plate. "I knew Rose wasn't going to stop," said second baseman Morgan, who had played with him in Cincinnati. "I was yelling at Rafael all the way but with all the noise he couldn't hear me."[5] In the other clubhouse, Rose said "I had no choice but to do precisely what I did. I had to run into him because I couldn't reach home plate with my foot."[6]

The Phillies added an insurance run when Trillo doubled in Luzinski, then Bowa fanned to end the inning. In the bottom of the 10th, McGraw set the Astros down in order, quietly ending a drama- and mistake-filled game.

After the game, Morgan said, "It's just like the Dodgers series last weekend. We had it and we let it get away."[7] However, it was McGraw, who was known for his colorful quotes, who summed up the game best: "It was like a motorcycle ride through an art museum. ... You see the pictures but afterward you don't remember what you saw."[8]

SOURCES

Several details included in this article were based on a review of the original game broadcast, which can be viewed at: youtube/-2kkfWUozz4

NOTES

1 John Wilson, "'Strange' Game by Any Standard," *Houston Chronicle*, October 12, 1980.

2 "Astros Were Losers on Appeal," *New York Times*, October 12, 1980.

3 Frank Dolson, "Phillies' Emotional Roller Coaster Rolls On," *Philadelphia Inquirer*, October 12, 1980.

4 Harry Shattuck, "Phils Clip Astros in 10th to Knot Series," *Houston Chronicle*, October 12, 1980.

5 Ibid.

6 Jayson Stark, "Phils Come Up With a Surprise Ending in Wild and Crazy 5-3 Win Over Astros," *Philadelphia Inquirer*, October 12, 1980.

7 Larry Eichel, "Astro-Nots: Breakdowns Cancel Out Breaks as Houston Misses Chance," *Philadelphia Inquirer*, October 12, 1980.

8 Lowell Reidenbaugh, "Chaos or Playoff, It's Phils on Top," *The Sporting News*, October 25, 1980.

Astros Fall Short of the World Series as They Lose to the Phillies in 10 Innings

October 12, 1980: Philadelphia Phillies 9, Houston Astros 7 (10 innings), NLCS Game Five, at the Astrodome

By Frederick C. Bush

IN SPITE OF THE PREVIOUS NIGHT'S 5-3 loss in 10 innings, the Houston Astros were confident of victory as they prepared to face the Philadelphia Phillies on October 12 in the "winner-take-all" Game Five of the 1980 NLCS. In addition to being a battle-tested team that had already survived a one-game playoff with the Los Angeles Dodgers for the NL West Division title, they had won one of two games in Philadelphia and were certain that they could prevail over the Phillies in the Astrodome. The 44,802 fans in attendance shared the Astros' optimism, especially since the team's million-dollar free agent acquisition, strike-out master Nolan Ryan, was starting against rookie Marty Bystrom.

Bystrom had joined the Phillies on September 1 and had posted a 5-0 record with a 1.50 ERA that earned him the National League's Pitcher of the Month award. Ordinarily, Bystrom would not have been eligible for postseason play because he was not on the club's roster by the cutoff date of August 31; however, when the Phillies lost starter Nino Espinosa to injury, they petitioned Commissioner Bowie Kuhn and NL President Chub Feeney to allow them to add Bystrom to their postseason roster. Approval had been granted on October 7, the day of Game One of the NLCS, and now the Phillies' World Series hopes rested on the 22-year-old rookie's shoulders.

After Ryan set the Phillies down in order in the first inning, the Astros scored first for the fifth time in five games. Terry Puhl led off with a single, stole second base after Enos Cabell flied out, and advanced to third on Joe Morgan's fly ball. The Astros went out in front 1-0 when Jose Cruz doubled to bring Puhl home. The lead was short-lived, though, as the Phillies took a 2-1 advantage in the second inning on Bob Boone's single that drove in Manny Trillo and Garry Maddox.

The Astros' attempts to tie the game resulted twice in a Houston runner being thrown out at home plate. In the bottom of the second inning, Luis Pujols drew a one-out walk and attempted to lumber home on Craig Reynolds' double to right field, but he was gunned down on a perfect relay throw from the second baseman, Trillo. Reynolds advanced to third base on the throw home but was stranded there when Ryan grounded out to end the inning.

In the bottom of the fifth, Cabell notched a one-out single, advanced to second on Morgan's grounder, and attempted to score when Trillo threw Cruz's groundball wide of first base. Pete Rose, the Phillies' first baseman, who was a veteran of four World Series with Cincinnati's Big Red Machine, had the savvy to rifle the ball home to Boone, who applied the tag to Cabell and stymied another Astros scoring attempt.

Ryan continued to hold the Phillies' bats in check, and the Astros tied the game in the bottom of the sixth. Denny Walling led off with a liner to left field that Greg Luzinski dropped for a two-base error. Two batters later, Alan Ashby pinch-hit for Pujols and singled to drive in Walling, ending Bystrom's night. Warren Brusstar entered in relief and brought a quick conclusion to the inning by inducing fly balls from Reynolds and Ryan.

Larry Christenson took the mound for the Phillies in the bottom of the seventh inning and got into a predicament that threatened to blow the game open for the Astros. Puhl led off with a single, Cruz drew a two-out walk, and Walling singled home the go-ahead run. Art Howe was at bat when Christenson uncorked a wild pitch that allowed Cruz to score. Phillies manager Dallas Green had seen enough and brought reliever Ron Reed into the game, but Howe tripled off Reed to give the Astros a 5-2 lead that seemed to seal Philadelphia's fate, given that Ryan had allowed only five hits and had struck out eight batters in his first seven innings of work.

The events in the top of the eighth were best summarized by Puhl when he said after the game, "Everybody thought we were a team of destiny. They were wrong. The Phillies were a team of destiny in this series."[1] Larry Bowa led off the inning innocently enough with a looping single to center field. Boone followed with what appeared to be an easy double-play grounder. As fate would have it, the ball went behind Ryan and deflected off his glove, and both runners were safe. Astros manager Bill Virdon later said of Boone's hit, "That was the key to the whole game."[2] After Greg Gross tapped a textbook bunt down the third-base line to load the bases, Rose worked a walk from Ryan that narrowed the Astros' margin to 5-3.

Bullpen ace Joe Sambito relieved Ryan and faced Keith Moreland, who hit a fielder's choice grounder that forced Rose at second base but allowed Boone to score. Green and Virdon now engaged in a managerial chess match as Ramon Aviles ran for Moreland and Rafael Landestoy replaced Morgan as the Astros' second baseman, while Ken Forsch came in to pitch. Forsch gave up a game-tying single to Del Unser and a triple to Trillo, which scored Aviles and Unser and gave the Phillies a 7-5 lead that shocked the Astrodome crowd.

The Astros proved to be resilient and immediately reinvigorated their fans by striking back in the bottom of the eighth. In a seesaw game that was part of a seesaw series, Landestoy and Cruz drove in runs against Tug McGraw (who pitched in all five games of the series) to once again tie the game, 7-7. After Houston's Frank LaCorte and Philadelphia's Dick Ruthven each pitched a scoreless ninth, the

Canadian-born outfielder Terry Puhl notched 1,357 hits in 14 years with the Astros. He batted .281 for Houston, and is tied with Hall of Famer Craig Biggio, Enos Cabell, and Steve Finley among franchise leaders. (Courtesy of Houston Astros Baseball Club).

two teams headed into extra innings for the fourth consecutive game.

The Phillies struck in the top of the 10th behind doubles by Unser and Maddox that gave them a one-run lead. Maddox, whose hit drove in the game-winning run, recalled that LaCorte had shaken off Ashby before throwing him the first-pitch fastball that he lined to center field. He affirmed, "I was expecting a fastball, he's a fastball pitcher" and declared, "No question this is the biggest thrill I've ever had in baseball."[3]

The Astros finally had been subdued, and even Puhl—who had four hits in the game and 10 in the series to break Rose's NLCS record for hits—could do no more. Ruthven retired pinch-hitter Danny

Heep, Puhl, and Cabell in order in the bottom of the inning to preserve the Phillies' 8-7 triumph. It was a gut-wrenching end to the Astros' most successful season in their 19-year existence, and the players took it hard. Ryan, who had the game unravel on him in the eighth inning, said, "It's the biggest loss I've ever had. It was more emotional than any game I've ever been in."[4]

If there was any consolation for the Astros, it was the likelihood that the World Series would be unable to match the excitement of an NLCS about which *The Sporting News* declared, "There may never be another playoff like it!"[5] The Astros sought exactly such solace as Sambito asserted, "You can't convince me which is the better team. That's about as even a series as you'll ever find. Some guys may take it harder than others, but I'm proud to be an Astro."[6] Ashby concurred, saying, "Both teams deserve to play in the World Series. Unfortunately, only one can make it and that's the Phillies."[7]

The Phillies took time out from their champagne baths to acknowledge the Astros as a more than worthy adversary. Unser, who had scored the winning run in the decisive Game Five, waxed poetic, saying, "If you shine, it's because somebody put a light on you. We shined in this series because the Astros put

a light on us. They pushed us harder than anyone has ever pushed us."[8] Indeed, they pushed the Phillies into the World Series, where Philadelphia won its first world championship by defeating the Kansas City Royals in six games.

As for the Astros, they would have to endure two additional NLCS heartbreakers — including a 16-inning Game Six loss to the New York Mets in 1986 and a Game Seven loss to the St. Louis Cardinals in 2004 — before finally getting their first taste of World Series action in 2005.

NOTES

1   Harry Shattuck, "Astros Proud of an 'Almost' Year," *The Sporting News*, October 25, 1980: 27.

2   Joseph Durso, "Phillies Take Pennant With 8-7 Triumph," *New York Times*, October 13, 1980.

3   "Phils Were 'Just Tired of Losing,'" *New York Times*, October 13, 1980.

4   Lowell Reidenbaugh, "N.L. Playoff Gleanings," *The Sporting News*, October 25, 1980, 16.

5   Lowell Reidenbaugh, "Chaos or Playoff, It's Phils on Top," *The Sporting News*, October 25, 1980: 15.

6   "Houston Astros 1980 NLCS," astrosdaily.com/history/1980/, accessed July 3, 2015.

7   Shattuck, "Astros Proud of an 'Almost' Year."

8   Ibid.

Nolan Ryan's Fifth No-Hitter

September 26, 1981: Houston Astros 5,
Los Angeles Dodgers 0, at the Astrodome

By Frederick C. Bush

WHEN NOLAN RYAN SIGNED ON November 19, 1979, what at the time was the richest contract in baseball history with the Houston Astros, his new team went from contenders to favorites in an instant. However, though Ryan indeed had helped to lead the Astros to the 1980 NL West Division title and their first playoff appearance in 19 years of franchise history, he had not been as dominant as in the 1970s and the Astros had fallen to the Philadelphia Phillies in one of the greatest five-game playoff series of all time. Thus, both Ryan and the Astros began the 1981 season with even greater expectations.

At the onset of the players' strike on June 12, 1981, the Astros had a 28-29 record and were going nowhere. After games resumed on August 10, the Astros' fortunes reversed, and they were battling the Cincinnati Reds for the second-half division title. Entering their September 26 game against the division rival Los Angeles Dodgers, who had won the first-half title, they held a 1½-game lead on the Reds. Ryan helped maintain that lead as he pitched his fifth career no-hitter, breaking a tie with legendary Dodgers lefty Sandy Koufax, in a 5-0 shutout that lowered his league-leading ERA to 1.74.

Early in the game, neither the 32,115 fans in attendance at the Astrodome nor the national television audience watching it on NBC's "Game of the Week" broadcast, could have anticipated that they would be witnesses to a historic event. Ryan had problems with his control and needed 65 pitches to make it through the first three innings, during which he surrendered three walks and uncorked a wild pitch. If he maintained such a pace, Ryan would not even finish the game, let alone pitch a no-hitter.

The Astros got on the scoreboard against Dodgers starter Ted Power in the bottom of the third inning. Phil Garner led off with a single, but he was caught trying to steal second base. However, the next batter, Tony Scott, reached first safely on an error by shortstop Derrel Thomas and advanced to third on Jose Cruz's double. Ryan's batterymate, Alan Ashby, followed with a single that scored Scott and Cruz for a 2-0 lead.

After Ryan struck out Steve Garvey to start the fourth inning, he received a visit from his pitching coach, Mel Wright, who suggested he was overstriding.[1] Ryan corrected his mechanics, saying later, "I let up a little bit in the late innings. I didn't get as many strikeouts, but I had better control."[2] He also credited his curveball with being the key pitch of the day because it helped keep the hitters off-balance in the absence of his best fastball. The result was that he allowed no further baserunners; going back to the last batter of the third inning, he retired the final 19 Dodgers in a row.

Ryan encountered only two precarious situations. The first occurred in the second inning when he walked Garvey to start the frame, after which Garvey stole second base and advanced to third on a wild pitch. Ryan escaped that jam with two strikeouts and a fly ball that ended the inning. The second close call came in the seventh inning when Mike Scioscia hit a deep ball that right fielder Terry Puhl caught just in front of the warning track and which he said, "hung up just long enough to run under it."[3]

After the game Ryan claimed, "I really didn't think about the no-hitter. Although I knew I had one going. When the catcher [Scioscia] hit the ball in the seventh and it was caught, I thought I might have a shot at it."[4] By the top of the ninth inning,

Nolan Ryan's fifth no-hitter – against the Dodgers on September 26, 1981 – broke a tie with legendary lefty Sandy Koufax. The fact that Ryan blanked Koufax's former franchise to claim the record seemed only fitting. (Courtesy of Houston Astros Baseball Club).

everyone—including Ryan—knew that he had a shot at making history. Astros pitcher Joe Niekro declared, "I was so nervous I squeezed the cover off the baseball I was holding in our dugout."[5]

Before the last inning and its attendant drama arrived, the Astros added three more runs off Dodgers relievers Dave Stewart and Steve Howe (all three runs were charged to Stewart) in the bottom of the eighth inning. Craig Reynolds, Garner, and Cruz each drove in a run to provide a 5-0 cushion that gave Ryan plenty of breathing room when he took the mound to finish his gem.

Ryan began the ninth in style by striking out pinch-hitter Reggie Smith. He got the next hitter, Ken Landreaux, to ground out to Walling at first base. The last batter Ryan had to retire was Dusty Baker, whom he had struck out on three pitches in his previous at-bat, in the sixth inning. That strikeout had been Ryan's 10th of the game, which also made

this the 135th game of his career with double-digit strikeouts.

In spite of the pressure of the moment, Baker said, "I wasn't nervous. I was thinking that I didn't know of anybody else I'd rather have at the plate in that situation than me."[6] Ryan's first two pitches to Baker were called balls, but Baker grounded Ryan's third pitch, a curveball, to third baseman Art Howe, who threw him out to end the game. Baker conceded, "I don't like having my name on the scorecard in a game that made history for Nolan Ryan. But I am happy for him. He is a great pitcher."[7]

Ryan finished the game with 11 strikeouts, though he registered only one over the final three innings. The 34-year-old right-hander confessed, "It's hard to believe I got the no-hitter. It's the one thing I wanted. I've had a shot at it for a long time. [His fourth no-hitter had come on June 1, 1975]. At my age,

I thought I wouldn't get it. I don't have the stamina I used to have."[8]

Ryan's no-hitter was the first for the Astros since Ken Forsch spun one against the Atlanta Braves on April 7, 1979. It was also the third no-hitter of the abbreviated 1981 season after Len Barker's perfect game for the Cleveland Indians against the Toronto Blue Jays on May 15 and Charlie Lea's no-hitter for the Montreal Expos against the San Francisco Giants on May 10.

Most notably, the gem broke the record of four no-hitters that Ryan had shared with Koufax. Though Ryan had admitted that a fifth no-hitter was one of his goals, when it came to breaking the record he said, "I really don't compare myself to (Koufax). I thought it was a great honor when I broke his [single-season] strikeout record and I've got that same feeling now."[9]

Another satisfying feeling came from the knowledge that several family members — including his wife, Ruth, and his mother, Martha — had been in attendance at the Astrodome. After he was mobbed by his teammates, he was joined by family and friends as he gave an interview on the field immediately after the conclusion of the game.

Ryan also savored the fact that he had contributed to the Astros' run to the 1981 playoffs by coming through in a big-game situation in a pennant race. He went so far as to state, "This is by far the most important of my no-hitters."[10] Ryan's assessment of the significance of his feat was accurate; the Astros won only four of the final eight games that followed his no-hitter, but they maintained their lead over the Reds and finished as second-half champions of the NL West, an accomplishment that meant they would meet the Dodgers again in the first round of the playoffs.

The convergence of circumstances surrounding Ryan's fifth no-hitter led him to assert, "When it's all over, this will probably be the one I favor most, being we're in a pennant race, being on national TV, being at home and having my mother here."[11]

NOTES

1   Harry Shattuck, "Coolest in Dome? No-Hit Ryan," *The Sporting News*, October 10, 1981: 11.

2   Ibid.

3   Ibid.

4   Associated Press, "Ryan's Record Fifth No-Hitter Downs Dodgers, 5-0," *New York Times*, September 27, 1981.

5   Shattuck, "Coolest in Dome? No-Hit Ryan."

6   Ibid.

7   Ibid.

8   Astrosdaily.com, "No Hitter #5!" astrosdaily.com/history/, accessed June 8, 2015.

9   Ibid.

10   Associated Press, "Ryan's Record Fifth No-Hitter Downs Dodgers, 5-0"

11   Ibid.

Ashby's Walk-Off, Two-Run Homer With Two Outs in the Ninth Preserves Ryan's Two-Hitter

October 6, 1981: Houston Astros 3, Los Angeles Dodgers 1, NLDS

Game One, at the Astrodome

By Gregory H. Wolf

THE FIRST GAME OF THE BEST-OF-five 1981 NL West Division Series lived up to all of the pregame hype, most of which focused on the clubs' starting pitchers. The Astros' 34-year-old Nolan Ryan, not quite yet the major leagues' ageless wonder, but described by the *Houston Chronicle* as the "ace of the best pitching staff in baseball,"[1] had hurled his record-breaking fifth no-hitter in his last home start of the season, coincidentally against Los Angeles. The Dodgers' 20-year-old rookie southpaw, Fernando Valenzuela, had taken the league by storm as "Fernandomania" swept across the nation. After the "Ryan Express" and "El Toro" battled to a 1-1 stalemate through eight innings, Houston's Alan Ashby belted a dramatic walk-off home run with two outs in the ninth off rookie reliever Dave Stewart to preserve Ryan's overpowering two-hitter. "It's a daydream come true," said Ashby. "It is just like a Walter Mitty story. When you hit a home run to win it with two outs in the ninth, well, it was just the biggest moment in my career."[2]

The playoff format for the 1981 strike-shorted season provoked a heated debate. Club owners divided the season into two halves, with the division winners of each half facing off in the NLDS. Los Angeles, the first-half winner of the NL West (36-21), slumped to 27-26 in the second half. Houston improved on its losing record in the first half (28-29) to record the best record in the NL in the second half (33-20). Nationally syndicated columnist Red Smith described the entire postseason as "dishonest,"[3] as neither the NL West Cincinnati Reds (66-42) nor the NL East St. Louis Cardinals (59-43) participated despite having the best overall records in their respective divisions.

The 44,836 fans who packed the Astrodome on Tuesday, October 6, were probably not concerned as to whether Houston, with the third-best record in the division, deserved to be in the postseason or not. They came to see Ryan, lauded by the *Chronicle* as an "intense competitor who doesn't flinch,"[4] and the Astros avenge their heartbreaking defeat in the 1980 NLCS to the Philadelphia Phillies in five games. In his second season with the Astros, Ryan had posted a 11-5 record and led the majors with a 1.69 ERA in 149 innings. His postseason struggles against the Phillies (16 hits and 8 runs in 13⅓ innings) the year before seemed like a distant memory. "I might need to pitch a shutout against Valenzuela,"[5] said Ryan, recognizing that he'd need his best to defeat the Mexican-born southpaw, author of a big-league-best eight shutouts in '81.

As billed, the game shaped up as an intense pitchers' duel. Ryan yielded a one-out single to Ken Landreaux in the first inning and a one-out walk to Rick Monday in the second before retiring 16 consecutive batters. Only twice did the Dodgers hit the ball hard, both times in the fifth inning: Center fielder Tony Scott made a routine running catch on Pedro Guerrero's fly ball, and Terry Puhl camped under Mike Scioscia's deep fly on the warning track in right field.

Valenzuela, who captured both the Cy Young and Rookie of the Year awards on the strength of a 13-7 record and league-high 180 strikeouts, matched Ryan through five innings. In the second inning Cesar Cedeño slapped a one-out single and stole second but was stranded. In the fifth Art Howe rapped a one-out single, but then was caught napping by Valenzuela, who picked him off first.

Still scoreless in the bottom of the sixth, Valenzuela flinched first. Terry Puhl lined a two-out single to right. Fearing that Puhl, Houston's biggest threat on the basepaths with 22 thefts in 26 attempts, might attempt to steal and move into scoring position with Phil Garner at the plate, Dodgers skipper Tommy Lasorda called for two pitchouts. Garner, a midseason acquisition from the Pittsburgh Pirates, eventually walked. The next batter, Scott, lifted a bloop single just out of the reach of second baseman Davey Lopes. "Television replays showed that Lopes could have made the catch if he had extended his arms," wrote David Leon Moore of the *San Bernardino County Sun*.[6] Puhl scored easily while both Garner and Scott advanced to third and second respectively on Lopes' ill-advised throw to the plate. Cleanup hitter Jose Cruz grounded to first to end the frame.

With two outs in the seventh, Steve Garvey ended the Dodgers' streak of futility against Ryan by blasting the Texan's first pitch for a game-tying home run, which hit above the orange line on the wall in left-center field. It was just the third homer Ryan had surrendered all season.

The Astros threatened in the seventh when Cedeño led off with a double. According to the Associated Press, successive stellar plays in the outfield helped save a potential run. Right fielder Rick Monday made a "shoestring catch" of Howe's blooper, followed by Landreaux's "over-the-head" snare of Kiko Garcia's shot to center.[7] Valenzuela then intentionally walked Ashby to face Ryan. Cedeño stole third while Ryan batted, but the pitcher hit a weak grounder that forced Ashby at second.[8]

Puhl's leadoff single to start the eighth reignited the Astros' hopes, which were unceremoniously quashed by quick outs by Garner, Scott, and Cruz. Nonetheless, the eighth inning spelled the end for Valenzuela, who was due to lead off the ninth. He

Nolan Ryan finished his career with 324 wins, a record 5,714 strikeouts, and seven no-hitters. In his nine seasons with the Astros he was a member of the first three playoff teams in franchise history. (Courtesy of Houston Astros Baseball Club).

surrendered six hits and two walks in eight strong innings.

After Ryan set down the Dodgers in order in the ninth, Los Angeles rookie right-handed reliever Dave Stewart dispatched Cedeño and Howe. Craig Reynolds, pinch-hitting for Garcia, singled to left to bring up Ashby.

Ashby, a 29-year-old switch-hitting catcher in his ninth season, had been Houston's hottest hitter over the final five weeks of the season, batting .313 (26-for-83) and slugging all four of his home runs in that span. However, his start behind the plate was a gametime decision. According to Harry Shattuck of the *Houston Chronicle*, skipper Bill Virdon had intended to go with right-handed-hitting Luis Pujols, who might better hit Valenzuela's forkball.[9]

There also was some bad blood between Ashby and the Dodgers. In the teams' one-game playoff to determine the West Division championship the previous year, Ashby had collided violently with Dodgers catcher Joe Ferguson at home plate. According to Harry Shattuck, Ferguson slammed his knee into Ashby, in anger.[10] Though Ashby remained in the game, he suffered a separated rib that allowed him to play in only two games of the ensuing NLCS.

"It's foolish for me to say that I was thinking about hitting the ball out," said Ashby after the game, "but I was thinking about hitting something hard."[11] The good-natured Californian from metropolitan LA pulled Stewart's first pitch over the right-field wall for a dramatic, game-ending two-run homer and a 3-1 victory in the series opener. "There was no doubt when it was hit," said Puhl of the homer, which ended Houston's streak of four consecutive extra-inning games in the playoffs.[12] "I made a good pitch—a fastball, low and in," said a dejected Stewart. "He just hit it."[13]

"I ran to the plate when Alan hit the ball," said Ryan, who was on deck. "I wanted to get a good look at whether it was fair or foul. I knew he hit it far enough."[14] As the modest Ashby rounded the bases, his teammates poured out of the dugout and mobbed him at home plate. Ashby basked in the moment, jumping up and down with his hands in the air. "I don't usually do that," he said.[15] The stoic Virdon, not known for congratulatory outbursts, took Ashby's game-winning clout in stride. "He's been a big asset for us offensively," he muttered.[16]

Ashby had the heroics, but the "grandest performance," suggested the Associated Press, belonged to Ryan, who finished with a two-hitter, striking out seven and walking one. "I think he had even better stuff [tonight]," responded Ashby when asked to compare Ryan's outing to the hurler's no-hitter which Ashby also had caught less than two weeks earlier. "His curveball was even better."[17] Virdon, who had guided the Astros to their first playoff berth the previous season, agreed. "I think Nolan was capable of pitching another no-hitter tonight. He was ahead of the hitters all night."[18] The normally loquacious Lasorda, who had apparently seen enough of Ryan lately, summed up the performance in one word: "dominating."[19] Known for keeping his emotions in check throughout his 27-year Hall of Fame career, Ryan admitted, "I made a couple of mistakes they hit," but added that "overall there wasn't much difference in this game and the no-hitter."[20] It was Ryan's first victory in the postseason since he tossed seven innings of three-hit ball to defeat the Atlanta Braves in Game Three of the 1969 NLCS as a member of the "Amazin' Mets."

After winning the first two games of the NLDS in the Astrodome, Houston surprisingly lost three straight in Los Angeles. Taking the mound in that fifth and deciding game, Ryan battled Jerry Reuss for five scoreless innings before yielding three hits and a walk in the sixth, which led to three runs (two earned) in an eventual 4-0 loss.

SOURCES

In addition to the sources cited in the Notes, the author also accessed Retrosheet.org, Baseball-Reference.com, the SABR Minor Leagues Database, accessed online at Baseball-Reference.com, SABR.org, and *The Sporting News* archive via Paper of Record.

NOTES

1   Harry Shattuck, "Ashby's HR a Sweet One," *Houston Chronicle*, October 7, 1981: Section 2, 1.

2   United Press International, "Astros Win, 3-1, on Homer in Ninth," *New York Times*, October 7, 1981: B15.

3   Red Smith, "Sports of the Times. Baseball's Dishonest Season," *New York Times*, October 7, 1981: B17.

4   Shattuck.

5   Ibid.

6   David Leon Moore, "Ashby's Dream HR Is Dodgers Nightmare," *San Bernardino County* (California) *Sun*," October 7, 1981: D1.

7   Associated Press, "Astros Win on 9th Inning HR," *Detroit Free Press*, October 7, 1981: 3-F.

8   "Houston Astros 1981 Division Series," *The Astros Daily*, astrosdaily.com/history/1981NLDS/#Game1.

9   Shattuck.

10 Ibid.

11 UPI, "Astros Win, 3-1, on Homer in Ninth," *New York Times*.

12 Mark Purdy, "Ashby's Homer Tips Dodgers, 3-1," *Cincinnati Enquirer*, October 7, 1981: B1.

13 Moore.

14 Shattuck.

15 Ibid.

16 Ibid.

17 UPI, "Astros Win, 3-1, on Homer in Ninth," *New York Times*.

18 Ibid.

19 Moore.

20 Ibid.

A Second Consecutive Walk-Off Victory in the NLDS

October 7, 1981: Houston Astros 1, Los Angeles Dodgers 0 (11 innings), NLDS Game Two, at the Astrodome

By Richard Riis

WHILE MOST OF HIS ASTROS TEAM-mates in the clubhouse were celebrating the 3-1 victory secured by Alan Ashby's two-run walk-off home run in the opening game of the National League Division Series, pinch-hitter and utility player Denny Walling sought out the speed bag and weightlifting equipment.

"The speed bag is my way of releasing my frustrations," said Walling, who had struggled through the season with a .234 batting average and decided his bat felt too heavy during batting practice. "I don't like to take my problems home with me and the speed bag helps me leave them in the clubhouse."[1]

Walling, who paced the Astros with six pinch hits in 1981, understood the value of being mentally and physically prepared to hit when coming off the bench in clutch situations. His two-run pinch-hit home run in a five-run ninth inning on October 1 had helped beat Cincinnati 8-1, putting the Astros 1½ games ahead of the Reds with three games remaining in the season. Now the team was facing the Dodgers in a tightly-matched series that was apt to hinge on strong pitching and clutch hits.

With a mixture of satisfaction and resentment, 42,398 fans packed the Astrodome on the afternoon of October 7 for the second game of the series. The satisfaction came from being a game up on the rival Dodgers, while the resentment was directed against Los Angeles starter Jerry Reuss (10-4, 2.30) who, in his last start on October 2, had shattered the kneecap of Houston's number-two starter, Don Sutton, with an errant pitch, putting Sutton out of the postseason. "ASTROS, WATCH YOUR KNEECAPS," cautioned a long banner unfurled in the stands.[2]

Astros manager Bill Virdon tabbed knuckleballer Joe Niekro to start for Houston. After winning 21 games in 1979 and 20 in 1980, the 36-year-old veteran had fashioned a disappointing 9-9 record in 24 starts, but his 2.82 ERA was a career best for his 15 seasons in the major leagues.

Both the Dodgers and the Astros picked up where they had left off in the previous game, with both pitchers locked in a tense duel and both lineups squandering scoring opportunities.

The Dodgers were the first to waste an opportunity when, with two outs in the second inning, Mike Scioscia singled to center and Bill Russell walked, but Niekro struck out Reuss to end the inning.

In the third inning, Davey Lopes led off with a single to right field and advanced to second on Dusty Baker's one-out single to center. Niekro, though, got Steve Garvey to pop up to catcher Luis Pujols and Rick Monday to ground out to shortstop Dickie Thon, snuffing out the rally.

Reuss, for his part, had been untouchable, retiring 13 batters in a row before Cesar Cedeno walked with one out in the fifth inning. Cedeno broke for second on a strike to Art Howe and drew a perfect throw from Scioscia to Russell, but Russell lost his glove when Cedeno slid into the bag, and Cedeno was safe on the error. After Howe was retired on a soft fly ball to center field, Thon hit a sharp grounder between short and third and, although third-base coach Don Leppert threw up the stop sign, Cedeno rounded third for home. Russell, however, made a diving, backhanded play on the ball, and his throw home produced a head-on collision between Cedeno and Scioscia a foot in front of the plate. Scioscia held on to the ball and the game remained scoreless. "I

Phil "Scrap Iron" Garner played 6½ seasons in Houston and was a member of the 1986 division champions. In 2005, as the Astros' manager, he piloted the team to its first and only NL pennant. (Courtesy of Houston Astros Baseball Club).

assume from what happened on the play that Cedeno thought the ball went into left field," Virdon said after the game.[3]

The Dodgers again failed to score in the sixth inning. Singles by Monday and Pedro Guerrero and a walk to Russell loaded the bases, but Niekro again left the runners stranded by striking out Reuss.

Niekro was pulled for a pinch-hitter in the Astros' eighth, after surrendering seven hits and three walks but stranding all 10 baserunners. Niekro had continually found himself working out of the stretch, retiring the side in order in only two of his eight innings.

"He was close to raindrops a few times," Virdon reflected. "He did not have as good of stuff as he usually has, but he came back and that's his forte."[4]

Right-hander Dave Smith came on to pitch the ninth inning, retiring the Dodgers in order while striking out Reuss and Lopes for the second and third outs.

Phil Garner lined a leadoff single to center field to open the home half of the ninth and, one out later, advanced to second on a single by Jose Cruz. Cedeno, though, fouled out back of first base and Howe grounded to Guerrero at third for the force on Garner.

Smith made short work again of the Dodgers in the top of the 10th inning.

Reuss, fatigued after pitching nine innings of five-hit shutout ball, told Dodgers manager Tommy Lasorda he was through for the day.

"I wanted to go on," Reuss said afterward. "But the reasonable side of me said not to. If I have any doubts, that always means it's wiser to be taken out. The hard part is being honest with yourself."[5]

Steve Howe, a left-hander who had been National League Rookie of the Year in 1980 and led the Dodgers in 1981 with eight saves, took the mound for Los Angeles to open the 10th inning. Thon singled to left field to open the frame, and Pujols sacrificed him to second, but that was all the Astros were able to muster.

Houston's ace reliever, lefty Joe Sambito, took over for the Astros in the top of the 11th. After Guerrero flied out to center field, Steve Yeager, batting for Scioscia, doubled to left. Russell walked to put runners at first and second. With Howe due up, Lasorda sent in Reggie Smith to hit. Sambito struck out Smith and then fanned Mike Marshall, who was batting for Lopes, to keep the Dodgers scoreless.

Dave Stewart, who had been the losing pitcher the day before on Ashby's walk-off home run, was brought in to pitch for the Dodgers, while Yeager remained in to catch and rookie Steve Sax took Lopes' spot at second base.

Garner lined a leadoff single to center field. Conventional wisdom might have called for Tony Scott to bunt Garner to second, but Houston skipper Virdon had other ideas.

"Well, I don't pass (the bunt) up most of the time," Virdon said. "Tony has had trouble bunting of late. But the main reason was I didn't want to waste Cruz."[6]

Had Scott laid down a successful sacrifice, Virdon expected that the Dodgers would intentionally walk Cruz, the Astros' leading home run (13) and RBI (55) producer for the season. Instead, Virdon had Scott swing away. Scott, swinging at an outside fastball, slapped it into left field for a single. Garner, who had been running with the pitch, advanced to third.

Lasorda pulled Stewart and brought in lefty Terry Forster to pitch to the left-handed Cruz. Cruz popped to shallow left field for the first out. Lasorda then pulled Forster in favor of Tom Niedenfuer, who intentionally walked Cedeno before fanning Art Howe on three pitches.

With the Astros now facing a two-out, bases-loaded situation, Virdon called on Walling to bat for Dickie Thon.

Walling had been observing the Dodgers' moves from the dugout, including the insertion of Derrel Thomas as a defensive replacement in right field for Rick Monday in the eighth inning.

"I noticed that [Thomas] was playing shallow in the last few innings and remarked about it on the bench," said Walling.[7]

With Howe and Forster gone, the Dodgers had exhausted their supply of left-handed relievers, so Lasorda stayed with Niedenfuer to pitch against the left-handed-hitting Walling.

Niedenfuer delivered one fastball low, then a second for a strike. According to Niedenfuer, the next pitch was a fastball that "started way inside off the plate but faded in too much."[8]

Walling was sitting on the fastball and launched Niedenfuer's serve on a line to right, over the head of Thomas, allowing Garner to trot home with the winning run and the Astros to head to Los Angeles with a two-games-to-none lead in the best-of-five series.

"If (Thomas) had been a little deeper, he might have been able to get it," Walling mused to reporters after the game.[9]

Lasorda could only comment on the vagaries of the game: "[Coach] Danny Ozark had been placing the outfielders perfectly all game. They hit a lot of line drives right at our outfielders. That time, it just didn't work out."[10]

SOURCES

In addition to the sources cited in the notes, the author also consulted the *Los Angeles Times*, *Newsday*, and *The Sporting News*.

NOTES

1 "Astros Nip L.A., 1-0, in 11 Innings," *Paris* (Texas) *News,* October 8, 1981: 13.

2 Jeff Katz, *Split Season:1981: Fernandomania, the Bronx Zoo, and the Strike That Saved Baseball* (New York: St. Martin's Press, 2015), 242.

3 "Walling Belts in Houston's Winning Run," *Galveston* (Texas) *Daily News,* October 8, 1981: C1.

4 Ibid.

5 "Quartet Held Pitching Clinic," *Houston Chronicle*, October 8, 1981: 4B.

6 "Astros' Brains Made Right Moves," *Houston Chronicle*, October 8, 1981: 4B.

7 "Astros Win for 2-0 Series Lead," *New York Times*, October 8, 1981: B11.

8 "Walling Prepared for Chance," *Houston Chronicle*, October 8, 1981: 1B.

9 "Houston Astros 1981 Division Series," The Astros Daily, Web, July 11, 2015.

10 "Strong Suit Deserts L.A.," *Galveston Daily News*, October 9, 1981: B1.

Winning Run Scores While Heep Argues with Ump

May 9, 1983: Houston Astros 6, New York Mets 4, at the Astrodome

By Mark S. Sternman

THE HOUSTON ASTROS RALLIED from a midgame 4-0 deficit to beat the New York Mets, 6-4, on May 9, 1983, in a game featuring a controversial call that helped Houston come back.

Neither team entered the game playing well. The Astros would improve and finish third in the National League West, but entered this game in the basement. The Mets, a year away from contention, had an 8-16 record en route to a fifth last-place finish in seven seasons.

Vern Ruhle, the Houston starter, struggled against the Mets throughout his career with an ERA of 5.40, his highest against any NL opponent. True to form, New York had multiple baserunners against him in every inning. Mookie Wilson and Hubie Brooks began the game with back-to-back singles. Darryl Strawberry, playing in his fourth major-league game (and first on the road) struck out, but Ruhle hit George Foster to load the bases. Danny Heep, who had played with Houston from 1979 to 1982 before going to New York for Mike Scott, hit a sacrifice fly to put the Mets up 1-0. Brian Giles followed with an RBI single, and New York led 2-0 after half an inning.

Rick Ownbey, "the noted Frisbee champion from California who also makes doorknobs in the off-season,"[1] started for the Mets. He would finish his four-year career with a record of just 3-11. A little more than a month after this game, New York traded Ownbey and pitcher Neil Allen to St. Louis for Keith Hernandez, who starred on the 1986 World Series winners. Ownbey had opposed the Astros five days earlier at Shea Stadium, faced 11 batters, and retired just four in taking the loss. On this day, however, he started better than Ruhle, pitching around a single by Tony Scott to keep the score 2-0 after the first.

Ownbey would end his career with a 4-for-35 (.114) batting mark, but he singled off Ruhle with one out in the second and came around to score an unearned run when Dickie Thon made a throwing error on an infield single by Brooks, Hubie's second hit in two innings.

Ownbey pitched out of trouble of his own making in the bottom half of the frame. He walked Jose Cruz and balked him to second.[2] Future Met Ray Knight singled Cruz to third, but Foster threw Cruz out at the plate when he attempted to score on a fly ball by Alan Ashby to preserve New York's 3-0 lead.

Ruhle had his only scoreless inning in the third, although he gave up hits to both Heep and Giles. The pair turned a double steal with one out, but Ruhle fanned Ronn Reynolds and got a groundout from 19-year-old Jose Oquendo to keep the margin manageable.

Terry Puhl hit for Ruhle to start the third, but the Astros went down in order for the only time in the game.

Manager Bob Lillis made a double switch, keeping Puhl in the game to play right field and sending in rookie Mike Madden to relieve Ruhle. Madden, who had pitched well so far this season, retired the Mets 1-2-3 in the top of the fourth.

Cruz started another Houston threat with a two-out triple in the bottom of the inning, but Knight struck out to end the uprising.

Both teams scored in the fifth. Strawberry hit the first of his 256 career doubles, went to third on a grounder by Foster, and scored on Heep's second sacrifice fly of the game. The Mets had a seemingly comfortable 4-0 lead halfway through the game against an Astros team that had scored more than four runs only eight times in 30 games so far.

Ashby homered for Houston to lead off the bottom of the fifth, making the score 4-1. With one out, Puhl singled, went to second on an error by third baseman Brooks, and scored on a single by Omar Moreno. The Astros now trailed 4-2. Denny Walling pinch-hit for Madden. Moreno stole second, then Walling grounded to second, the last out Ownbey would get. Thon walked and the tying runs were on base. Phil Garner, who, in spite of a .238/.317/.362 slash line, hit cleanup most of the year, doubled to clear the bases and tie the game. Carlos Diaz came in to replace Ownbey, who had twice failed to retire Cruz.

Cruz hit the ball to Heep at first. According to the *New York Times*, "The umpire Terry Tata ruled that Heep failed to get to the bag on a lunge in time to make Jose Cruz the third out. As Heep was protesting the call … Garner … kept running until he scored. … Television replays appeared to show Cruz was out." After the game, Tata told Heep, "Cruz's foot was on the bag when you tagged it."[3] Cruz stole second, then Knight struck out Knight to end the inning. Houston's five-run inning gave it a 5-4 lead.

Frank LaCorte relieved Madden to begin the sixth inning. In nine years with the Atlanta Braves and the Astros, LaCorte had six times fanned at least six batters, all as a starter. On this day, against New York, he struck out six for the last time in his career and retired the side in order in the sixth, seventh, and eighth innings.

Mets pitcher Diaz did not last through the bottom of the sixth. Ashby and Bill Doran singled to put runners on the corners with none out. Puhl struck out, but Moreno stroked his second RBI single in two innings to put Houston up 6-4. Veteran Mike Torrez came on to pitch for the Mets and, like LaCorte, shut down the opposing team on just a single hit the rest of the way. Reynolds threw out Moreno trying to steal second, and LaCorte grounded out to Giles to end the sixth.

In the bottom of the seventh with two outs, the first career error by teenage Mets shortstop Oquendo put Cruz on first, but Reynolds gunned him down trying to steal to end the inning.

The eighth proceeded like the seventh. After the Mets went down meekly, a Houston batter reached with two outs when Doran beat out an infield hit, but Reynolds threw out an Astro trying to steal for the third straight inning. In 1983 baserunners against Reynolds went 27-for-38, but in this game Houston went just 2-for-5. Torrez apparently made the difference as the Astros went 2-for-2 in stolen bases before he entered the game but 0-for-3 with him on the mound. Torrez led the National League in 1983 with 19 runners caught stealing when he pitched.

Bamberger went to his bench repeatedly in the ninth inning. Pinch-hitter Ron Hodges struck out looking, but a second pinch-hitter, Mike Jorgensen, broke LaCorte's perfect streak with a single, putting the tying run at the plate. Former Astro Rusty Staub pinch-hit and struck out, leaving Mookie Wilson as the last hope for New York.

In Game Six of the 1986 World Series three-plus years later, Wilson kept the championship hopes of the Mets alive with a dramatic last plate appearance of the game, but the 1983 Mets barely resembled the team that would beat both Houston and Boston in the postseason a few years later. LaCorte completed his game-saving performance, but not before an anxious moment when Wilson sent a long drive to right field. "When I saw the ball go off the bat, I knew he hit it good," LaCorte said. "But then I saw Terry Puhl standing by the wall and I knew he had a chance to catch it."[4] Puhl made a leaping catch against the wall to end the game.

In closing out the game, LaCorte completed a five-game scoreless stretch in which he had pitched 10⅔ innings and yielded just four hits and two walks (one intentional) while striking out 10. "The key to any pitcher's success is throwing strikes," said LaCorte. His catcher, Ashby, agreed. "He's throwing the way he did in 1980, when Frank was so effective. He's getting ahead of hitters with all his pitches. And his velocity is higher (93 mph)."[5]

LaCorte earned his third save of the season in stopping New York. He finished 1983 with Houston and played for California in 1984, but he never picked up another save.

NOTES

1   Jack Lang, "Mets Rate Ownbey No. 1 Hill Prospect," *The Sporting News*, September 20, 1982: 38.

2   Ownbey had a high balk rate with New York, committing five in just 85 innings.

3   James Tuite, "Astros' Rally Beats Mets," *New York Times*, May 10, 1983.

4   Harry Shattuck, "Astros Dump Mets," *Houston Chronicle*, May 10, 1983.

5   Harry Shattuck, "A Weak Bullpen? It's Astro Pride, Joy," *The Sporting News*, May 23, 1983: 18.

Bjorkman Knocks in Five in Cup of Coffee

July 13, 1983: Houston Astros 9, Montreal Expos 4, at the Astrodome

By Greg Erion

THE HOUSTON ASTROS WERE moving up in the world. On the morning of July 2, 1983, their record of 37-40 placed them fifth in the NL West, the same position they had finished the year before. Beginning that day, they won six of seven, to close in on third place.

Montreal came to Houston for a three-game series on July 12 holding a precarious half-game lead over the Philadelphia Phillies in the NL East after losing 8 of their previous 11 contests. The trend of two teams moving in opposite directions continued that Friday night as Houston captured a 7-5 victory, thanks in part to reliever Dave Smith's four innings of scoreless pitching. Philadelphia pulled ahead of Montreal, and Houston was now one game behind the third-place Padres.

The next day Montreal faced a daunting challenge. Starting for the Astros was Nolan Ryan, winner of his last seven decisions with a 1.97 ERA to show for the season. Ryan was not only off to the best start of his career, he was in a continual duel with Steve Carlton for the all-time lead in career strikeouts. Ryan had passed Walter Johnson's long-held 3,509-strikeout record in April, only to have Carlton surge past him in June as a urinary infection and pulled hamstring limited Ryan's starts. As Ryan took the mound on July 13, his 3,573 strikeouts were right behind Carlton's 3,575 mark.

Despite the Astros' surge, their catching staff was in bad shape. Starting backstop Alan Ashby was out of the lineup with an inner-ear infection, and backup catcher Luis Pujols could not catch because of a finger injury. John Mizerock, called up from the Triple-A Tucson Toros to fill the hole, played a few games before succumbing to a sore shoulder. Pujols, despite his injury, went back into the lineup, but opposing baserunners were having a field day at his expense.[1] At this point, the serendipitous nature of baseball showed itself, shining on a minor-league catcher in his sixth professional season name George Bjorkman, who had started the season with Columbus (Georgia) in the Double-A Southern League before being called up to replace Mizerock at Tucson.

Bjorkman barely had time to adjust to Arizona's climate before getting called up by the Astros and immediately being placed in the starting lineup on July 10 against the Mets. Against vastly superior competition than he had been facing less than two weeks earlier, Bjorkman acquitted himself well. He lined out in his first major-league at-bat. "I hit a bullet to George Foster in left—it was too bad because had I gotten under it a little I have no doubt it would have gone out—I hit it right on the screws."[2] Batting in the sixth, Bjorkman singled to left as part of a three-run rally that put the Astros ahead, 5-3, in a game they ultimately lost. In the lineup again for the Friday night game, Bjorkman contributed another RBI in Houston's 7-5 victory over Montreal.

The next day, July 13, Bjorkman found himself catching Nolan Ryan before a crowd of 28,905 fans who were hoping to see the Astros continue their solid play. Facing Ryan for the Expos was 26-year-old Charlie Lea, who had a 6-5 record so far in his fourth major-league season.

Lea helped draw first blood in the third, singling in Chris Speier, who had tripled off Ryan. He would not be successful at holding the lead as the Astros scored five runs in the bottom of the inning, the big blow being a two-run triple by Jose Cruz. Bjorkman brought the fifth run of the inning home on a successful squeeze bunt off Bryn Smith, who had replaced the ineffective Lea.

Bjorkman drove in another run with a single in the fifth to make it a 6-2 lead. Ryan was holding his own but in a less than a fully effective manner, surrendering home runs to Tim Wallach in the fifth, then Andre Dawson in the sixth—that homer narrowed the deficit to 6-3. Coming to bat in the seventh inning, Bjorkman faced Smith for the third time with pinch-runner Denny Walling and Bill Doran on base. He put the game on ice with a three-run homer to left, giving him five RBIs in the game and cementing what would be a 9-4 victory for the Astros. Ryan surrendered three runs through eight innings before giving way to Bill Dawley in the ninth. In that frame the Expos scored their final run on Gary Carter's double and Speier's second hit of the game.

Ryan won his eighth straight game although he struck out only five batters. He fell further behind Carlton, who chalked up seven strikeouts in a losing effort against the Atlanta Braves. Though he was happy with the win, Ryan was less than enthusiastic about his pitching. He shrugged off the competition with Carlton and, focusing on the game, said, "It's nice to get nine runs for some breathing room. It was fortunate that I had the runs because I had good stuff but did nothing with it. I don't care about streaks, but I'm pitching better than I have since the year of the strike [1981]."[3]

Bjorkman, whose offensive outburst prevented the Expos from clawing back into a first-place tie with Philadelphia, was self-effacing. "I'm not the contributor of big hits. The everyday players have done that. I'm not making the difference."[4] Rather than savor his performance, Bjorkman shared a different perspective concerning his batterymate and future Hall of Famer: "Just catching Nolan Ryan would have been enough for me."[5]

Bjorkman was fully convinced that he would return to the minors when Ashby recovered and could play again. Astros manager Bob Lillis disagreed: "It's

a good possibility he is jumping to conclusions about being ready to go down. I might have to leave town if I did that.[6] Regardless, at that point, Bjorkman was Houston's only fully functioning catcher.

The next day Bjorkman experienced the antithesis of Ryan's fastball deliveries when he caught knuckleballer Joe Niekro. In top form, Niekro pitched a complete-game, three-hit shutout to beat Montreal 3-0 for a sweep of the series. The win, Houston's eighth in nine games, put the Astros into a tie for third with the Padres.

Niekro sang Bjorkman's praises. "George looked like he'd been catching the knuckleball for 10 years. He picked some of my best knucklers cleanly. And he called a good game. I can't say enough good things about him. He's got to be in awe just getting to the major leagues, then catching Nolan Ryan one night and the knuckleball the next. But he handled it like a veteran." Bjorkman, by this time probably in a fog, could only observe, "I had never caught a knuckleball from any pitcher before except with Joe on the sidelines. I didn't know what to expect. But Joe talked with me before the game and helped me relax." Lillis chimed in, further complimenting his new catcher, "We had to find out if he could catch the knuckleball and we got our answer."[7]

Houston continued to win, amassing 10 victories in 11 games before Ryan succumbed to the Mets 3-1 on July 17 to snap his eight-game winning streak. It was Bjorkman's third straight hitless game. After striking out once in his first five games, Bjorkman fanned eight times in his next five starts, and things got worse as major-league pitching began to catch up with him.

Hitting had never been Bjorkman's forte. He had a good eye and he clouted 28 home runs for the Triple-A Springfield Redbirds in 1981, but that was an aberration. His career minor-league average was just .244. Against a steady diet of major-league pitching, his hitting continued to deteriorate. After striking out six straight times and watching his average sink to .192, Bjorkman was sent back to Tucson.

His earlier comment about being sent back down when the regulars came back was off the mark—it was poor hitting, and 20 strikeouts in 52 at-bats, that did him in, not necessarily Ashby's return. After he was called back to the Astros in September to play in a handful of games, his major-league career was over. Lost in a surplus of catchers on the Houston roster, Bjorkman was traded to the Expos in the spring of 1984, and his professional career ended a year later.

Baseball is a fickle game. Nolan Ryan was the big story in Bjorkman's best game in the majors, continuing the strikeout duel with Carlton which lasted until September 1984, when Ryan finally pulled ahead for good. Ryan notched a record 5,714 strikeouts during his 27-year career, George Bjorkman played in the majors for two months.

NOTES

1   Harry Shattuck, "Astros Must Lasso Enemy Basestealers," *The Sporting News*, July 18, 1983: 36.

2   Juan Rosales, "George Bjorkman's First MLB Hit," Baseball Interactions," baseballinteractions.wordpress.com/.

3   "Ryan Fires and Falls Back in the Strikeout Race but Keeps on Winning, 9-4, *Los Angeles Times*, July 14, 1983: D7.

4   "Ryan, Bjorkman Modest After Victory," *Baytown* (Texas) *Sun*, July 14, 1983: 2-C.

5   Harry Shattuck, "Astros' Bjorkman in a Dream World," *The Sporting News*, August 1, 1983: 17.

6   "Ryan, Bjorkman Modest After Victory."

7   Shattuck, "Astros' Bjorkman."

Dickie Thon and the Shadow of Ray Chapman

April 8, 1984: New York Mets 3, Houston Astros 1, at the Astrodome

By Bill McCurdy

The Errant Pitch to Thon

RIGHT-HANDED HITTING DICKIE Thon of the Astros didn't move from his stance at the plate. The rising fastball from Mets pitcher Mike Torrez sailed up and in, striking him flush in the face in the left-eye region. The sickening sound of ball striking bone reverberated through the Astrodome as Thon dropped lifelessly to the ground. He fell like a sleeping pigeon falling from its roost after some alpha hunter boy with a BB gun came along and picked him out to be the next practice kill.

It happened in the Astrodome in a night game played on Sunday, April 8, 1984. It was only the fifth game of the season, but the Dickie Thon beaning in the bottom of the third inning instantly altered the mood of the 10,625 fans who had come to the Dome that night to sate their appetites for a brand-new baseball season.

No one in the media blamed Torrez, a highly respected veteran, for the pitch, which resulted in Thon being taken to the trauma unit of a hospital in the nearby Texas Medical Center. X-rays revealed a fractured orbital bone. Torrez and Thon also issued statements within 24 hours that suggested they each viewed the sad accident as simply one of those unfortunate and regrettable things that happen sometimes in the game of baseball.

"Please tell his family that I hope everything is OK," Torrez said. "The time before, I pitched him away and I struck him out. So I wanted to start him off inside. He was looking outside and he started out over the plate. My fastball took off and he didn't have time to get out of the way."[1]

"I didn't move," Thon said. "I just stood there. When I saw it, it was too late. (Torrez) called me," Thon said. "He told me he was sorry and didn't mean it. He was real nice. It was a freak accident. … I just have to keep going."[2]

Thon missed the rest of the 1984 season, but did return for 84 games in 1985. He played another nine seasons (1985-1993), but he would never again be the hard-hitting shortstop he had become in 1983. That season Thon was a National League All-Star as he batted .286 with 20 home runs for the Astros and his future was periwinkle blue in color and anticipation. It was, of course, the greatest offensive season of his 15-year career. It was also the season that set the bar for what was expected of him in the future.

Things happen. And sometimes, they don't.

In 1989 with the Phillies, Thon batted .271 with 15 home runs and 60 runs batted in. It was the only season he came close on paper to being the Dickie Thon of 1983, but those numbers for one season also possess the power of deception. A player may look better or worse, based on one season of work.

Greatness is high-level performance over time.

Greatness was not to be for Dickie Thon. Maybe it would not have happened anyway, but the injury had settled the question for all time. Within two years of the injury, the book was closed on Dickie Thon as a potential superstar; he moved on from Houston after the 1987 season.

For his 15 total seasons as a big-league shortstop, Thon still produced at a respectable level. His .264 batting mark, with 71 home runs and 435 runs batted in, were better than most middle-of-the-pack role players, especially at the shortstop position.

Ray Chapman of the 1920 Cleveland Indians as of 2016 remains the only player to have been killed by a pitch in a major-league game. Tony Conigliaro of the 1967 Boston Red Sox survived a beaning similar to the one that happened to Thon.

The Game Itself

It was only an early-season evening contest in the Dome of April 8, 1984, but it was important to both clubs. The Mets had taken the first two games of the series and were going for the sweep, sending fireballer Mike Torrez to the mound to face the mysteries of knuckleballer Joe Niekro of the Astros.[3]

The Astros were hoping that 1984 under manager Bob Lillis would be the year they turned around their slow descent to the middle of the pack in the National League West. The Mets, under manager Davey Johnson, were hoping to hang a vacancy sign on the National League East basement, where they finished in 1983.

In the bottom of the third, the Astros came close to converting Thon's beaning into runs. With two outs, Terry Puhl walked and Torrez followed by hitting Thon. Craig Reynolds replaced Thon as a pinch-runner and remained in the game at shortstop. With two now on base, Jose Cruz singled to load the bases, but Jerry Mumphrey popped out to end the threat.

With two outs in the bottom of the sixth and the game still scoreless, Ray Knight doubled off Torrez. Johnson then removed Torrez because a blister had developed on the thumb of his pitching hand. "I've had enough experience that I know if it rips, that I'm going to be out for a couple of turns," Torrez matter-of-factly stated.[4]

Tim Leary relieved for the Mets and got Phil Garner on a fly ball to right to keep the mutual goose-egg in play for the last time in the game.

After George Foster popped out to Reynolds in the top of the seventh, Darryl Strawberry doubled and went to third base on Mookie Wilson's infield single, which bounced off Niekro's leg. Hubie Brooks then singled, scoring Strawberry for a 1-0 lead, and

The future looked bright for 1983 All-Star shortstop Dickie Thon. Then, on April 8, 1984, he was hit by a pitch from the Mets' Mike Torrez that fractured his orbital bone, caused blurred vision and undermined his great potential. (Courtesy of Houston Astros Baseball Club).

sending Wilson to third base. The rally ended there, however, when Rusty Staub, batting for light-hitting catcher Junior Ortiz, hit into a 3-6-1 double play.

Right-handed reliever Vern Ruhle took over for the Astros in the top of the eighth after Niekro was lifted for a pinch-hitter. Leary singled and Wally Backman walked for the Mets, and Jose Oquendo moved the runners to second and third with a sacrifice bunt. Ruhle then intentionally walked Keith Hernandez to fill the bases for the right-handed-hitting Foster. The move backfired as Foster singled, scoring Leary and Backman for a 3-0 Mets lead. Dave Smith replaced Ruhle and struck out Strawberry and got Wilson on a pop to first to retire the side.

Doug Sisk took the mound for the Mets in the bottom of the eighth after Leary reported some discomfort in his left hamstring. Reynolds reached first on an error by Backman and moved to second base on a groundout by Cruz. Mumphrey followed with a single up the middle to bring Reynolds home with the Astros' only run of the day. After Knight fanned and Garner singled Mumphrey to second base, Alan Ashby dumped a sinking liner to center that Wilson grabbed for a questionable shoestring catch. Replay seemed to show the catch as a one-bounce trap, but first-base umpire Frank Pulli ruled Ashby out.

Was it a hit or a catch? Davey Johnson said, "When it's your guy, you always think he got it." The Astros' Bob Lillis saw it a little differently: "From where I was, it looked like it might have been in there." Wilson added, "I held it up but I didn't see the umpire make a call."[5]

The Mets took the game, 3-1, to complete the series sweep — their first in the Astrodome since July 1966.

The moral of the Mookie catch in the days prior to instant-replay umpiring assistance concluded along these lines: *Sometimes catches are all in the eye of the beholder, and, in the case of shoestring-catch situations, not all ruled hits are actually in the glove of the holder.*

Leary was the winning pitcher (1-0) and Sisk picked up his second save for the Mets. Niekro (0-2) took the loss for the Astros.

NOTES

1   Associated Press, *Galveston Daily News*, April 9, 1984: 13.

2   Gordon Edes, "Dickie Thon Is the Latest Big League Player to Attempt a Comeback After a Serious Beaning: Games' Nightmare," *Los Angeles Times*, March 18, 1985.

3   astrosdaily.com/history/1984/game19840408o.html. All facts used in the inning-by-inning narrative scoring descriptions of the April 8, 1984, game are derived from this source.

4   *Baytown* (Texas) *Sun*, August 9, 1984: 10.

5   Edes.

Ashby's Walk-Off Single Ends it in the 16th

July 15, 1984: Houston Astros 3, Philadelphia Phillies 2 (16 innings), at the Astrodome

By Alan Cohen

"My only regret is that it was not on national TV so the whole country could see it. That was a great baseball game, and I wish that more people could have been part of it. If you didn't get excited over that one, you're not a baseball fan. It had everything — great plays, strategy, everything."

—Paul Owens[1]

THE PHILADELPHIA PHILLIES, WHO were contending for the NL East lead, visited the Houston Astrodome for a four-game set in July 1984. After winning the first three games of the series, Philadelphia was in third place, 3½ games behind the New York Mets. In going for the series sweep, the Phillies sent Charles Hudson (8-6, 4.68 ERA) to the mound to face Houston's Bob Knepper (8-8, 2.78).

Neither starting pitcher would factor in the decision as the game went 16 innings. It took 4 hours and 12 minutes and 460 pitches combined for the Astros to gain a 3-2 victory and salvage the final game of the series. In spite of the game's length, few in the announced crowd of 15,276 left early as there was never any letup in excitement.

The Phillies took the lead in the second inning when Glenn Wilson walked and came around on a double by John Wockenfuss. Mike Schmidt's fourth-inning solo homer made the score 2-0. The Astros evened the score in the fifth inning when Terry Puhl singled and rookie catcher Mark Bailey homered.

Both starting pitchers went deep into the game before being lifted for pinch-hitters. Hudson left for pinch-hitter John Russell in the eighth inning.

Russell singled but was erased when Garry Maddox grounded into a double play, one of four twin killings turned by the Astros during the contest. Knepper pitched effectively until he was lifted for a pinch-hitter in the ninth inning.

Larry Andersen, the Phillies' part-time reliever and full-time philosopher (one "Larryism" being "Do they take a coffee break at the Lipton Tea Factory?"), entered the game in the eighth inning and found himself in a jam. After walking the first batter, he fielded Craig Reynolds' bunt and threw wild to first base. By the time the dust settled, there were runners on second and third with none out, but Andersen collected himself and struck out Denny Walling for the inning's first out. On orders from the dugout, he was in the process of issuing an intentional pass to Jose Cruz when he inadvertently brought his fingers to his mouth, causing home-plate umpire Joe West to call ball four. With the bases full and one out, Jerry Mumphrey hit a hard line drive directly into the glove of second baseman Juan Samuel, whose throw to first baseman Wockenfuss arrived before Cruz could get back; the double play ended the inning and the score remained tied.

Andersen gave way to Al Holland with one out in the ninth inning and once again the Phillies got out of the inning by virtue of the double-play ball. With runners on first and second and one out, manager Bob Lillis lifted Knepper for pinch-hitter Enos Cabell, who grounded into a 6-4-3 double play to send the contest into extra innings. In nine innings, Knepper allowed only three hits and struck out a career-high nine batters[2] while lowering his ERA slightly to 2.73.

In the course of his 11 years with the Astros, catcher Alan Ashby was behind home plate for three no-hitters: Ken Forsch's in 1979, Nolan Ryan's in 1981, and Mike Scott's in 1986. (Courtesy of Houston Astros Baseball Club).

First out of the pen for Houston was Bill Dawley with his 1.90 ERA. He was appearing in his 32nd game of the season, all in relief, and had a 5-4 record. In three innings, he allowed but one hit and put three more zeros onto the increasingly elongated scoreboard.

The Astros kept the Phillies off the bases and off the scoreboard with a series of fielding gems that kept the videotape guys quite busy and the crowd on its feet. Two of those plays came during Dawley's three-inning stint. Puhl victimized Philadelphia's Von Hayes with a leaping catch against the right-field fence for the third out of the 10th inning. Two innings later Puhl was at it again, racing in to make a do-or-die sliding catch on Ozzie Virgil's flare to short right field. Philadelphia third-base coach Dave

Bristol said, "If it gets by him, it's got a shot to be [an] inside the park [homer]."[3]

In extra innings the Astros mounted even more threats, only to come up empty. In the bottom of the 12th, Kevin Bass, pinch-hitting for Dawley, led off with a triple. Philadelphia manager Paul Owens decided to load the bases with intentional walks to Enos Cabell and Bill Doran. Owens again went into his bottomless basket of tricks and decided to play with five infielders, as Glenn Wilson moved from left field to right field and was positioned behind second base. Phils pitcher Bill Campbell got Reynolds on a popup to second and then third baseman Schmidt was able to turn Denny Walling's groundball into a force play at the plate. With two men down now, Wilson returned to left field and corralled a fly ball off the bat of Cruz for the inning's final out. After the game, Walling said of the odd defensive positioning, "I've never seen it used, but it didn't affect me. Seeing five guys in the infield is great. I just did a very bad job in a clutch situation."[4]

Owens told reporters, "I got that play from all the games I played in 10-man softball leagues, where they used a running shortstop or fourth outfielder you could play anywhere you wanted. The psychology of it is that you put a little more pressure on the hitter to hit the ball in the air."[5]

Joe Sambito took the mound for the Astros in the 13th inning and continued Houston's mastery of Philadelphia's batters. It was three up and three down as the Houston partisans had an opportunity to rest in their seats, awaiting the excitement of the bottom of the inning.

In the bottom of the 13th Owens, the walking strategy machine, was at it again. Mumphrey led off with a single to center field. Alan Ashby, who had entered the game after catcher Harry Spilman had injured his knee chasing a popup, bunted Mumphrey to second base and, with one out, Puhl was intentionally walked. Lillis then sent up Ray Knight to pinch-hit for Sambito. Campbell got the count to 1-and-2 before uncorking a wild pitch that threw a monkey wrench into Owens' strategy. But Owens was resourceful and once again stationed Wilson behind second base. Knight, mired in a 2-for-41 slump, looked at Campbell's next delivery for strike three. That brought up Cabell, who received an intentional walk. With the bases full of Astros, Campbell induced Bill Doran to ground out, and the game continued.

Indeed, it was as if the Astros enjoyed being on base so much that they didn't want to go home. During the course of the game, they stranded 20 runners. The Phillies meanwhile had made the most of their limited opportunities and would leave only three runners on base.

Julio Solano pitched the 14th and 15th innings for the Astros and faced the minimum of six batters, allowing only one hit, a single to Kiko Garcia. Garcia was eliminated on a ground ball double play off the bat of Virgil, the Phillies' slow-footed catcher, one of the few times the Phillies squandered a baserunner.

The snake-bitten Phils were victimized by great defense one last time in the top of the 16th inning when Hayes was once again robbed, this time by center fielder Mumphrey. Wilson had singled to reach first before Hayes sent a fly ball to short right-center field. Mumphrey raced in, made a shoestring catch, and fired to first to double off Wilson.

After close calls in virtually every inning, the Phillies ran out of luck in the bottom of the 16th. Don Carman was pitching for Philadelphia and yielded a one-out single to Cruz. After a wild pitch, Mumphrey received an intentional walk. For those who count such things, during the game's final five innings, the Philadelphia mound staff uncorked three wild pitches and yielded seven intentional walks. With runners on first and second, Ashby singled to left field to drive in Cruz with the winning run.

Credit for the win went to Houston's fifth pitcher, Frank DiPino.

During the course of the season, extra innings had not been kind to the Phillies. The loss was their seventh in as many extra-inning games. They would go on to finish in fourth place, 15½ games behind the NL East-winning Cubs, with an 81-81 record. The Astros would finish the season at 80-82, which was good enough for a tie for second place but left them 12 games behind the West Division-champion San Diego Padres.

SOURCES

In addition to the sources cited in the Notes, the author used Baseball-Reference.com.

NOTES

1   Al Morganti, "Phillies Fall in 16 Innings: Astros Prevail in Marathon, 3-2," *Philadelphia Inquirer*, July 16, 1984: E01.

2   John Nelson (Associated Press), "Astros Beat Phillies, 3-2, in 16 Innings," *Paris* (Texas) *News*, July 16, 1984: 2B.

3   Ibid.

4   Kenny Hand, "Astros Finally Solve Phils Puzzle in 16th," *Houston Post*, July 16, 1984: 7F.1.

5   Bill Conlin, "Phils, Owens Can't Dodge Doom," *Philadelphia Daily News*, July 16, 1984: 88.

Morganna Smooches Ryan

April 9, 1985: Houston Astros 2, Los Angeles Dodgers 1, at the Astrodome

By Norm King

SHE WAS THE KIM KARDASHIAN OF her day.

During the pre-Internet era, Morganna "The Kissing Bandit" Roberts was a busty stripper who gained a degree of notoriety in the 1970s and 1980s by running onto baseball diamonds, football fields, and other playing surfaces across America to kiss an athlete, and then returning to the stands whence she came.[1] She occasionally exited the field accompanied by the gendarmes of the city in question, facing trespassing charges on 19 occasions, although she was never convicted.[2]

By the mid-1980s she was famous nationwide, having kissed, among others, Pete Rose, Steve Yeager, George Brett, and Steve Garvey. Then she decided to attend the Houston Astros' season opener on April 9, 1985, against the Los Angeles Dodgers and plant a peck on Nolan Ryan.

Morganna's shenanigans aside, the Astros' first game of the season offered some intriguing scenarios. One was the matchup between two pitchers trying to rebound from mediocre 1984 seasons. Ryan was coming off an injury-plagued 12-11 campaign in which he had a 3.04 ERA and a pedestrian—for him—197 strikeouts in 183⅔ innings. Dodgers starter Fernando Valenzuela labored to a 12-17 record the previous season with a 3.03 ERA and 240 strikeouts in 261 innings.

The game also marked the return of shortstop Dickie Thon to the Astros' lineup from a horrific injury he suffered almost exactly a year earlier, on April 8, 1984, when the New York Mets' Mike Torrez hit him in the temple with a pitch, fracturing his orbital bone and ending his season.

The game also celebrated the Astrodome's 20th anniversary. Guests for the pregame ceremonies in-cluded Mickey Mantle, who hit the first-ever home run at the Dome in a 1965 exhibition game, and Olympic sprinter Carl Lewis, who threw out the ceremonial first pitch.

Morganna didn't wait long to make her appearance; she jumped out onto the field in the first inning, and ran up to Ryan on the mound with a bunch of, um, hooters and hollerers yelling their approval. Ryan, upon seeing her, went down on one knee and spread his arms as if he were going to do an impression of Al Jolson belting out *Mammy*, then reportedly said, "Hurry up, Morganna! The cops are right behind you!"[3] She bent down and kissed him, then ran over to Thon and pecked him as well. After that Morganna ran to the Dodgers' dugout, where Houston's Finest arrested her for trespassing. The game resumed after the commotion, with Ryan throwing an easy 1-2-3 inning.

Thon led off the bottom of the first for Houston and was greeted with a rousing standing ovation from the 42,876 fans before grounding out to third.

As expected, runs were hard to come by in this game, but Los Angeles managed to open the scoring in the top of the second. Mike Marshall doubled with one out and, after Mike Scioscia flied out, came home on a single by Sid Bream. Ryan shut the door after that, retiring 16 of the next 17 hitters before giving way to reliever Frank DiPino in the eighth.

Valenzuela pitched well enough to win, but was undermined by uncharacteristically poor defense by his teammates. Thon got the home crowd cheering in the third when he singled; he moved to second when Scioscia, the Dodgers catcher, threw wild trying to pick him off first. After Enos Cabell struck out, Phil Garner singled Thon home with the tying run.

Houston took the lead for good in the fourth. Number-eight batter Bill Doran hit a one-out double, bringing up Ryan. Ryan hit a grounder to second, where Mariano Duncan misplayed the ball, enabling Doran to sprint home. That made the score 2-1 and that's how the game ended.

The outcome was not a harbinger of how each team's season would unfold. Los Angeles ended up winning the National League West with a 95-67 record. They lost the NLCS to St. Louis, four games to two. Houston finished third in the division with an 83-79 record, 12 games behind the Dodgers. Aside from the intriguing pitching matchup, this was a typical National League game. The really interesting stories were Morganna's appearance and subsequent ride into judicial history, and Thon's return.

Judicial history may be overstating things a bit, but Morganna's lawyer, Richard "Racehorse" Haynes, said that she had no intention of trespassing, but that she leaned over the railing, then her boobs and gravity did the rest. As for how Newton's Law led to Morganna running to the mound to kiss a ballplayer, he explained that she "panicked and ran to pitcher Nolan Ryan as thousands of fans cheered her name."[4]

It would have been very interesting to find out what a judge thought of this explanation, but the case never went to court, as the district attorney dropped the charges at the request of the Houston Sports Association, which ran the Astrodome. This was fortunate for Morganna, as she could have been sent to jail for six months and fined $1,000.

As for Thon, his return from that horrible injury was remarkable, considering how the blow had affected his eyesight during his recovery. At one point, his vision, which was 20-20 before the accident, was at 20-150. Nevertheless he persevered, and his determination inspired his teammates. "I had a lump in my throat when he went up for the first time," said Doran. "I talked with him a lot during the spring.

He's been through so much. We just had to be patient with him and let him come through on his own."[5]

"I was anxious but not nervous," said Thon. "I'm just glad to be back and we won the game."[6]

The promising results of that first game didn't continue during the season; in fact, the injury ruined a potentially great career. In 1983, the year before the beaning, Thon hit .286 with 20 home runs and 79 runs batted in, was an All-Star, and won the Silver Slugger award at his position. It was clear early in 1985 that he was not the same. He had trouble seeing outside breaking pitches and inside fastballs. He eventually became a platoon player, and appeared in only 84 games that year, hitting .251 with six home runs and 29 RBIs. Thon ended up playing in the majors for 15 years with six different teams, and never again attained the heights he had reached in 1983.

SOURCES

In addition to the sources cited below, the author also used:

Houston.astros.mlb.com.

Galveston Daily News.

Los Angeles Times.

Miami News.

Orlando Sun-Sentinel.

Srvofficial.com.

NOTES

1   Morganna's first foray onto a field of play occurred in 1969, 1970, or 1971—sources differ—when, on a dare, she ran out to kiss Pete Rose at Crosley Field in Cincinnati.

2   ESPN *E:60* documentary, "Morganna: The Kissing Bandit."

3   Bruce Nash and Allan Zullo, *The Baseball Hall of Shame 4* (New York: Pocket Books, 1990), 132.

4   J.R. Gonzales, "30 Years Ago: Morganna the Kissing Bandit, the Dome's 20th and Stevie Ray Vaughan," *Houston Chronicle,* April 14, 2015.

5   "Ryan helps Astros start on positive note," *Baytown* (Texas) *Sun,* April 10, 1985.

6   Ibid.

José Cruz Collects His 2,000th Hit

September 15, 1985: Houston Astros 2, San Diego Padres 1, at the Astrodome

By Chip Greene

ON OPENING NIGHT 1974 IN ST. LOUIS, Arnold "Bake" McBride, a 37th-round draft pick of the hometown Cardinals in the 1970 amateur draft, started in center field for St. Louis. In the bottom of the 10th inning, the Cardinals' José Cruz, for the previous two years St. Louis's starter at that position, entered the game as a pinch-hitter. For all intents, that evening marked the beginning of the end of Cruz's tenure as a Cardinals player.

Cruz was the eldest and most talented of a trio of baseball-playing brothers from Arroyo, Puerto Rico, all of whom were signed by and played for the Cardinals. From the time he signed with the team in 1966, it was clear Cruz had major-league potential. After four minor-league seasons, he made a brief showing as a September call-up in 1970, and then he arrived for good the following summer. By all appearances, the Cardinals had found the player who would anchor their outfield for many years to come.

Alas, it was not to be. As an outfield starter the bulk of 1972 and '73, Cruz struggled mightily at the plate, failing to lift his average out of the .230s. At the conclusion of each season he went to the winter leagues to hone his stroke, and found much success there (indeed, reported the press, Cruz "burned up"[1] his league), yet back in the States he couldn't duplicate his winter performance. By the time McBride arrived in St. Louis, the Cardinals were "losing patience"[2] with Cruz, and when José was relegated to fourth-outfielder status in that 1974 season, the demotion only reinforced the perception that his days in St. Louis were numbered. That perception became reality in October 1974, when the Cardinals sold Cruz to the Houston Astros. Little could St. Louis have imagined the player José Cruz would become.

If St. Louis was willing to part ways with Cruz, Houston manager Preston Gomez was glad to have him. In November Gomez planned to tour Puerto Rico, and he wanted to personally welcome Cruz to the team.

"This boy hasn't played much the last two or three years," Gomez explained. "I will be making a trip around Puerto Rico and I will go see José play for Ponce in the Puerto Rican Winter League. I will have a chance to talk to him personally and explain our plans for him this coming season."[3]

Those plans included making Cruz the Astros' starting right fielder. In 1974 Houston had discovered an outfield gem in Greg Gross, who as the Astros' right fielder batted .314 and finished second to McBride for the National League Rookie of the Year Award. In describing his newest acquisition, though, Gomez said, "This boy Cruz is better than anybody we had on the ballclub last year. He can hit with power, has better-than-average speed, and he has a good arm.

"What I will try to do in spring training is play him in right field and move Gross over. José's arm would be stronger than Greg's, but Gross would give us a good, accurate arm in left field."[4]

Together, Gross and Cruz would flank the Astros' perennial All-Star and three-time reigning Gold Glove center fielder, Cesar Cedeño. With that alignment, Gomez envisioned an outfield that would be a significant improvement defensively from the previous year.

"We've had too many balls drop in the outfield, and too many opposition runners take the extra base," the manager said. "We'd be able to cut off a lot of balls hit into the gap with an outfield of Gross, Cedeño, and, say, Cruz."[5]

Outfielder José Cruz's 1,937 hits place him third in Astros history. Playing in the cavernous Astrodome, he led the franchise in homers with totals of 9 in 1979, 13 in 1981, and 12 in 1984. (Courtesy of Houston Astros Baseball Club).

The trio remained intact for the next two seasons. Eventually, Cedeño and Gross moved on from Houston. Other outfield personnel came and went, but Cruz remained, and finally realized the potential the Cardinals had seen in him so many years before.

All told, Cruz spent 13 seasons in Houston, and became an Astros institution. Many years after his arrival in the Astrodome, when he was in the twilight of his career, *The Sporting News* offered this preseason synopsis of Cruz's skills:

"Cruz is the all-time captain on the all-underrated team. There's no telling how much acclaim he would have received if he had ever been afforded the opportunity to play regularly in a hitter's park instead of spending the last 11 years inside the vast confines of the Astrodome.

"To his credit, the Houston outfielder adapted to what the Astrodome has to offer instead of worrying himself into premature retirement.

"Cruz drives the ball in all directions, occasionally uncorking a home run when a pitcher makes a mistake, but knowing better than to look for the long ball. At 38, Cruz seems to be as good, if not better, than ever. He's hit .300 or better each of the last three years and his 79 RBIs last year led the Astros. Cruz was fifth in the N.L. in runs produced (139) and still can run. He has 310 big league stolen bases, including 281 in 11 years with the Astros and 68 the last three seasons."[6]

That was high praise for a player who was approaching 40, and it came just seven months after one of the singular nights of Cruz's illustrious career.

On September 15, 1985, the San Diego Padres were in Houston for the final game of a three-game series. Opposing each other on the mound were veteran right-handers LaMarr Hoyt for the Padres and Nolan Ryan for the Astros. On this night, when runs would be at a premium, the Padres struck first, and quickly, scoring a run in classic fashion in the top of the first on a leadoff single, stolen base, sacrifice bunt, and sacrifice fly. That run held until the bottom of the fourth, when Cruz, who had entered the game with 1,999 career hits, made his second plate appearance of the evening. It would be a memorable at-bat.

The left-handed-hitting Cruz had always had success against Hoyt (he finished his career 8-for-16 against him, with a home run and two doubles). Leading off the bottom of the second, however, Cruz had grounded out to the second baseman. Now, with Denny Walling at second courtesy of a passed ball by Padres catcher Terry Kennedy, Cruz had a chance to tie the game. Hoyt chose fastball and Cruz swung, driving a single to straightaway center field and scoring Walling to tie the score at 1-1. It was a momentous stroke, one that gained the admiration of an opponent who knew something about big hits.

The previous week, Padres pitcher Eric Show had allowed Pete Rose's 4,192nd hit, which moved Rose past Ty Cobb as baseball's all-time hit leader. Speaking of Cruz after the game, Show offered, "He's a great hitter, and I'm someone who's given up a few famous hits.

"What makes him so great is he's unpredictable. I never know what he's going to hit."[7]

Afterward, Cruz expressed his satisfaction, saying, "It was a good feeling to get [number] 2,000, even though a hundred other guys may have that many.

That last hit is the only hit I remember."[8] It wouldn't be his last. Cruz finished his career with 2,251 hits.

For the record, rookie Glenn Davis won the game for the Astros, 2-1, in the bottom of the eighth inning when he set a Houston rookie home-run record with his 15th of the season, a solo shot that landed two rows from the top of the left-field stands and broke the Astros' rookie mark set by Joe Morgan. Yet it was Cruz's night, a great capstone to a fine Astros career.

Cruz played two more seasons in Houston, but his skills were finally eroding. In February 1988 he signed as a free agent with the New York Yankees, but he was unceremoniously released in July with a batting average of .200. Thus ended a stellar 19-year major-league career.

At the conclusion of the 2015 season Cruz remained in the top 10 of virtually all Astros offensive categories. Six times a .300 hitter, twice both an All-Star and a Silver Slugger winner, he was (as of 2016) the team's all-time leader in triples and, among other highlights, third in games played, at-bats, hits, and stolen bases.

The Astros retired José Cruz's number 25 jersey in 1992.

NOTES

1   *The Sporting News*, November 30, 1974: 49.

2   Ibid.

3   *The Sporting News*, November 16, 1974: 50.

4   Ibid.

5   *The Sporting News*, March 8, 1975: 24.

6   *The Sporting News*, April 1, 1986. 13

7   Associated Press via *Baytown* (Texas) *Sun*, September 16, 1985.

8   Ibid.

Roger Clemens Returns to Hometown Houston for All Star Game, Wins MVP

July 15, 1986: American League 3, National League 2, at the Astrodome

By Michael Huber

A CROWD OF 45,774 ATTENDED THE 57th All-Star Game, held at the Astrodome in Houston on July 15, 1986. The American League's Roger Clemens (Boston Red Sox), a hometown boy, faced off against the National League's Dwight Gooden (New York Mets). They would see each other again in Game Two of the 1986 World Series. Clemens was 23 years old; Gooden was only 21, but this was the third All-Star Game for the reigning Cy Young Award winner and former Rookie of the Year. Five starters from each All-Star squad would eventually be inducted into the Baseball Hall of Fame (National Leaguers Gary Carter, Tony Gwynn, Ryne Sandberg, Mike Schmidt, Ozzie Smith; and American Leaguers Wade Boggs, Rickey Henderson, Kirby Puckett, Cal Ripken Jr., and Dave Winfield). Three AL reserves, Eddie Murray, George Brett, and Jim Rice, also made it to Cooperstown.

There was plenty of fanfare, as this was Houston's second All-Star Game (the first was in 1968, a 1-0 win for the NL, also at the Astrodome). Vice President George H.W. Bush threw out the ceremonial first pitch. Kansas City's Dick Howser, manager of the 1985 world champion Kansas City Royals, managed the American League squad[1] and St. Louis's Whitey Herzog skippered the National League team. Honorary captains were Charlie Gehringer for the AL and Rusty Staub for the NL. Staub was the Astros' All-Star representative in the 1968 All-Star Game, which was the first to be played indoors.

Puckett led off the game with a single to center field off Gooden. He was forced at second on Henderson's grounder to Sandberg. Gooden then was charged with a balk, moving Henderson up a base. The National League starter settled down and retired Boggs and Lance Parrish to end the inning.

Clemens, making his All-Star Game debut, pitched three perfect innings. He threw 25 pitches—21 of them for strikes. "I threw strikes," Clemens told reporters after the game. "But I'm always around the plate. If I want to miss, I'll miss."[2] In retiring all nine batters he faced, the man who would strike out 4,672 hitters in his career fanned only two, Sandberg and Darryl Strawberry.

With two outs in the top of the second inning, Dave Winfield stroked a line drive to right field for a double. Lou Whitaker quickly fell behind in the count, 0-and-2, but then sent Gooden's next offering, a curveball, into the right-field grandstand, staking the American Leaguers to a 2-0 lead. Clemens struck out for the third out of the inning. Gooden was charged with two earned runs in three innings of work, which included two strikeouts.

Fernando Valenzuela came on to pitch for the National League in the top of the fourth inning. El Toro struck out the first five batters he faced (Don Mattingly, Ripken, Jesse Barfield, Lou Whitaker, and Teddy Higuera) to tie Carl Hubbell's 52-year-old All-Star Game record.[3] It was Higuera's first major-league at-bat; he had entered the game to pitch for the American League in the fourth inning. Valenzuela told reporters, "After I was removed for a pinch-hitter, I looked at the scoreboard and saw that I had tied the record. But I don't know about Carl Hubbell. I was born in 1960."[4] Valenzuela and Higuera had close-to-identical lines in the box score: Each had three innings pitched, one hit, no runs.

Valenzuela struck out five and Higuera struck out two.

In the top of the seventh inning, Valenzuela gave way to a hometown favorite, Houston Astros pitcher Mike Scott. Scott was obviously pumped, striking out Ripken and Barfield to start the inning. Frank White then entered as a pinch-hitter for Whitaker and launched a home run to deep left-center field. The American League now led 3-0, and all runs had come via the long ball from the eighth spot in the batting order.

Charlie Hough came in to pitch for the Americans and had a 1-2-3 seventh inning. In the bottom of the eighth he ran into trouble. Chris Brown led off the inning with a double. Chili Davis struck out but during his at-bat Hough uncorked a wild pitch and Brown scampered to third base. Hubie Brooks followed Davis and also struck out, but on the third strike catcher Rich Gedman was charged with a passed ball on a dropped third strike. Brown raced home and Brooks took first base. With Tim Raines batting, Hough committed a balk that advanced Brooks to second base. Raines became the third strikeout victim for Hough; then with two outs Steve Sax lined a single to left-center field, driving in Brooks. The National League team had trimmed the lead to one run, 3-2. Dave Righetti came on as the fourth pitcher for the American League. Sax stole second base but was stranded as Astros slugger Glenn Davis fouled out for the frame's final out.

The AL batters were a quick three outs in the top of the ninth, as new pitcher Mike Krukow retired Ripken, Barfield, and White. Righetti returned to the mound and retired Keith Hernandez on a groundout to start the bottom half of the inning. Jody Davis and Dave Parker then hit back-to-back singles. The call went to the bullpen and Don Aase came on to face Chris Brown. (As Aase trotted in, Detroit closer Willie Hernandez glared at him with hands on hips, in apparent disbelief at not getting the call from Howser.) The Orioles' closer, making the only All-Star appearance of his career, threw just two pitches, but he did his job. His 1-0 pitch hit Brown's bat as he tried to check his swing. The ball bounced to second baseman White, who stepped on the bag and threw to Don Mattingly at first for a rally-killing, game-ending double play.

National League pitchers struck out 12 American League batters in the game. That mark equaled a record set in 1934 by the National League pitchers and tied by the 1956 AL staff and 1959 NL staff. However, it was not enough to continue the National League dominance. National League teams had beaten the American League squad in 13 of the prior 14 games, and 21 of the last 23, but not on this evening. This victory in Houston was also the junior circuit's first win in an NL park since 1962, when the AL prevailed at Wrigley Field.[5]

Clemens was named the game's Most Valuable Player, and he enjoyed the moment. "With all of the home folks here, I was really jumping. The best part was when I walked into the dugout and saw all those great players in there with me. I thought we had made a major trade."[6] He also commented about pitching in Houston, saying, "I can say 'y'all' and not get hounded about it now. When I say it in Boston, I get hounded. In Boston, it's 'you guys.'"[7]

SOURCES

baseball-almanac.com.

baseball-reference.com.

mlb.com.

retrosheet.org.

sabr.org.

youtube.com/watch?v=TrC1BrP8Y64.

NOTES

1   The 1986 All-Star Game turned out to be Dick Howser's final game as a manager. He told reporters that he felt sick before the game. A cancerous tumor was diagnosed, and Howser stepped down as the Royals' manager. Mike Ferraro finished the season at the helm for the Royals. Howser died on June 17, 1987, at the age of 51. Robert McG. Thomas Jr., "Dick Howser Dies at 51, Ex-Manager of Royals," *New York Times*, June 18, 1987.

2   Larry Whiteside, "Clemens Wins Over NL—and Skeptics," *Boston Globe*, July 17, 1986.

3   mlb.mlb.com/mlb/history/mlb_asgrecaps_story_headline. jsp?story_page=recap_1986.

4   Michael Martinez, "American League Beats National, 3-2," *New York Times*, July 16, 1986.

5   Whiteside.

6   Martinez.

7   Dan Shaughnessy, "Hometown Cooking," *Boston Globe*, July 15, 1986.

Eight Straight Strikeouts for Jim Deshaies

September 23, 1986: Houston Astros 4, Los Angeles Dodgers 0, at the Astrodome

By Brent Heutmaker

ON SEPTEMBER 15, 1985, THE Houston Astros exchanged pitchers with the New York Yankees: Houston sent veteran Joe Niekro to New York in exchange for minor-league left-handed pitcher Jim Deshaies. The 25-year-old Deshaies pitched well for the Astros in 1986. Through August 24 he had a 9-3 record for Houston with 111 strikeouts in 125 innings. In his next three starts, though, Deshaies didn't pitch beyond the fifth inning, and allowed 20 hits and 12 runs in the games, all losses, including a 5-1 defeat by Los Angeles at Dodger Stadium on September 10. Houston manager Hal Lanier decided to have Deshaies skip a start.[1]

Deshaies made his next start on September 23, facing the Dodgers again before a crowd of 27,734 at the Houston Astrodome. Houston was closing in on the National League West Division championship, while Los Angeles had a record of 70-80 and was mired in fifth place.

Deshaies rebounded emphatically from his recent struggles. He struck out the first eight Dodgers batters. In the first inning, Steve Sax, Reggie Williams, and former Astro Enos Cabell all swung and missed at high fastballs. Cabell whiffed on a pitch that was over his head.[2] Deshaies said afterward, "If you don't get to do your job for 10 days, you want to get out there and do your best. I was pumped, no question about that."[3]

The Astros scored two runs in the first inning as they worked Dodgers left-hander Dennis Powell for two walks and a hit. Phil Garner's sacrifice fly drove in a run, and third baseman Jeff Hamilton's error led to another run.[4]

In the second inning, a classic battle occurred between Deshaies and LA cleanup hitter Pedro Guerrero. With a 3-and-2 count, Guerrero fouled off nine consecutive pitches, then struck out.[5] Alex Trevino and Hamilton went down swinging to end the inning.

The Dodgers' Dave Anderson, leading off the third, whiffed on a high fastball. Jose Gonzalez fouled two pitches back, took a ball, then swung late on the next offering to become Deshaies' eighth strikeout victim .

With that strikeout Deshaies broke the modern major-league record of seven consecutive strikeouts to start a game, set by the Chicago White Sox' Joe Cowley just four months earlier, on May 28. Deshaies also broke the National League record of six straight strikeouts to start a game.[6] (The all-time record of nine strikeouts to start a game was set by 19th-century pitcher Mickey Welch of the New York Giants on August 28, 1884.) The Astrodome crowd had been notified on the scoreboard about the record, and the fans gave standing ovations to Deshaies following both his record-tying and record-breaking strikeouts.[7]

After Gonzalez struck out, the Dodgers pinch-hit for Powell with Larry See, who popped up to second baseman Bill Doran to end the strikeout streak at eight.[8]

See had been a late-season promotion from Los Angeles' Triple-A affiliate in Albuquerque, where he had struck out 101 times before being called up. Since his call-up, he had gone down on strikes six times in 15 at-bats. In the Dodger Stadium game on September 10, Deshaies had struck out See twice.[9]

After the game Doran said, "Everybody was mad at me. They wanted me to drop it so he could get more strikeouts."[10] See, on the other hand, was proud just to make contact. "There's a lot of satisfaction in knowing he got everybody but me," the rookie told reporters.[11] I didn't want to let him get me, too. I didn't know anything was going on. I knew he'd struck out eight guys in a row, but I didn't know it was any kind of record."[12]

Anderson didn't think Deshaies was particularly overwhelming. "He threw well, but we were swinging at everything," the Dodgers shortstop said. "He was good, but we helped him by swinging. There was no trick to it. He was throwing high fastballs, and we swung."[13]

In the top of the fourth inning, the Dodgers' Steve Sax singled to left field, extending his hitting streak to 21 games. That inning ended with Deshaies striking out Guerrero again, but the gusher of K's dried up after that; Deshaies added just one more strikeout the rest of the way.

In the bottom of the fourth, Alan Ashby's home run added to Houston's lead. Deshaies went on to pitch his first complete game and had 10 strikeouts. He surrendered just two hits and one walk in the 4-0 shutout. "'I wouldn't call it a fluke, but it was a freak thing," Deshaies said of his feat. "If I'd gotten, say, just one pitch a little in or something, there might have been a hit, and no record. I didn't know about the record, but I knew I was striking everybody out. I was really pumped up, throwing almost all fastballs except the changeup to Guerrero, and once I struck out the side the first two innings, there was no way I was thinking about anything but getting strikeouts. I knew it would have to come to an end, and then I'd have to settle down. If I had pitched the whole game the way I did the first three innings, I would have blown my arm out."[14]

The radar gun showed how pumped up Deshaies was. Houston manager Hal Lanier said, "His velocity was 89 tonight, the highest it's been all season. I always ask Les [pitching coach Les Moss] before the game how the starter looks in the bullpen. Tonight,

Jim Deshaies, a rookie on the strong-armed 1986 Astros, held his own with a 12-5 record and 3.25 ERA. He set a modern record with eight consecutive strikeouts to start a game on September 23 against the Dodgers. (Courtesy of Houston Astros Baseball Club).

Mossie told me that Jimmy looked the best he had all season. (Moss) must be a genius."[15]

Deshaies normally threw about 85 miles per hour. "That's kind of a freak thing," he said of the extra hop he had to start the game. "I'd struggled my last two or three starts and had some rest. I said, 'I'm going to go out and throw fastballs and see if they can hit 'em.' They kept swinging and missing, and I kept throwing fastballs."[16]

Sax said, "He threw as hard as anybody tonight—he was up there with (Dwight) Gooden. When he throws that ball up there that's borderline, it's tough to lay off."[17]

Los Angeles manager Tommy Lasorda wasn't buying Sax's hyperbole and griped about the Dodgers swinging at the high fastball. "Not only are they balls, but even if you hit them, you hit fly balls," the Dodgers skipper said.[18]

This game was the first of three straight home shutouts by the Astros. The next night Nolan Ryan and Charlie Kerfeld combined on another two-hitter, as Ryan struck out 12. After that, Mike Scott pitched a no-hitter, striking out 13, to clinch the National League West and cap a series of amazing pitching performances by the Astros.

NOTES

1 United Press International, "Astros' Deshaies Fans First 8 for Record," *New York Times*, September 24, 1986.

2 Neil Hohlfeld, "Deshaies Pitches Astros Near Title — Lefty Fans 8 at Start to Set Major Record," *Houston Chronicle*, September 24, 1986.

3 Hohlfeld.

4 Hohlfeld.

5 Most media accounts said an inside changeup caught Guerrero looking for the third strike; UPI said he struck out swinging.

6 Hohlfeld.

7 Kevin Modesti, "Deshaies' Biggest Fans Are Dodgers — He Strikes Out First 8 For Record," *Los Angeles Daily News*, September 24, 1986.

8 Gordon Edes, "Astros' Deshaies Guns Down First 8 Dodgers, Wins," *Los Angeles Times*, September 24, 1986.

9 Hohlfeld.

10 Hohlfeld.

11 Edes.

12 Modesti.

13 Hohlfeld.

14 Edes.

15 Hohlfeld.

16 Modesti.

17 Ibid.

18 Ibid.

Mike Scott No-Hits the Giants

September 25, 1986: Houston Astros 2, San Francisco Giants 0, at the Astrodome

By Frederick C. Bush

MOST PRESEASON PROGNOSTI-cators had predicted that Houston would finish in third place or lower in 1986, but as the Astros prepared to face the San Francisco Giants on September 25, they knew that a victory would clinch their first National League West title since 1980. The Astros featured a powerhouse pitching staff whose 3.15 team ERA that season was second in the NL only to the 3.11 posted by the New York Mets. The fact that staff ace Mike Scott was the starter on this day gave the Astros favorable odds to clinch the division before 32,808 hometown fans in the Astrodome.

The prowess of the Astros' pitching staff already had been on prominent display the previous two nights. On September 23 Jim Deshaies tied a major-league record by striking out the first eight Los Angeles Dodgers batters he faced on his way to a two-hit shutout in which he totaled 10 strikeouts. The next night, Nolan Ryan held the Giants hitless into the seventh inning, registered 12 strikeouts in eight innings, and combined with Charlie Kerfeld on a two-hit shutout. On this day, Scott's performance would make his fellow moundsmen almost appear to be slackers.

The game began on an inauspicious note as Scott hit Giants leadoff batter Dan Gladden with his first pitch. He later confessed, "I was out of control. The crowd was into it, and I was pumped up."[1] Gladden stole second base and, after Robby Thompson flied out, advanced to third on Will Clark's groundout. Scott retired the next hitter, Candy Maldonado, to end what would be the Giants' only scoring threat that day.

In the bottom of the first inning, Giants starter Juan Berenguer retaliated against the Astros by hit-ting their leadoff man, Billy Hatcher, with his first pitch. Hatcher turned the tables by stealing second base, just as Gladden had done for the Giants, but he was erased from the basepaths when Giants catcher Phil Ouellette gunned him down as he tried to steal third. Berenguer allowed back-to-back singles to Denny Walling and Glenn Davis but pitched out of trouble to keep the game scoreless.

In the top of the second inning, Scott walked Chili Davis, who also proceeded to steal second base. But at this point Scott settled down. He struck out Bob Brenly and Ouellette and retired Jose Uribe on a pop fly to second baseman Bill Doran to begin a string of innings in which he retired 19 consecutive batters. By the end of the game, he had thrown 69 of his 102 pitches for strikes and had struck out 13 Giants.

Scott held the Giants spellbound throughout the game with his split-fingered fastball. Giants manager Roger Craig had to be struck by the irony that he was the man who had taught Scott the pitch after the 1984 season. Scott had finished that campaign 5-11 with a 4.68 ERA and had sought help from Craig, who at the time was out of baseball. Craig recalled, "The first three times I worked with him he didn't pick it up, then he just got it. Right then I knew the guy was going to have a good one, but I didn't know he'd be that good."[2] Scott threw the split-finger so well now that many opponents, including Craig, had accused of him of scuffing the ball. No such accusations were forthcoming on this day, though, and Craig claimed to be so impressed by Scott that sometime in the fourth or fifth inning he told one of his coaches that the Giants would not get a hit off him.[3]

Though Berenguer's performance did not match Scott's, he did keep the Astros off the scoreboard for four innings. In the top of the fifth, however, Walling

1986 Cy Young Award winner Mike Scott became the first pitcher to clinch a division title with a no-hitter when he spun a gem against the San Francisco Giants on September 25 of that year. (Courtesy of Houston Astros Baseball Club).

grounder, but Doran scooped up the ball on the run and fired it to shortstop Craig Reynolds to get the force out on Ouellette at second base. The only other time the Astrodome crowd gasped at the thought that Scott might lose his shot at a no-hitter occurred in the very next at-bat. Mike Aldrete, who had spoiled Nolan Ryan's no-hit bid in the previous game, hit a long fly ball that Hatcher caught "in full stride 10 feet from the fence" in center field.[5] Ryan, who had pitched five no-hitters but had never seen a teammate pitch one, said, "I was nervous. ... Any little thing can end it. Now I know what I've put everybody else through."[6]

From that point on, the spotlight was solely on Scott, who would get to bask in its full glow. He struck out Gladden and Thompson to start the ninth inning and then got Clark to hit a weak grounder to the first baseman, Davis, who retired Clark himself and started the victory celebration. Scott had made a slow trot to cover first base and admitted, "I told (Davis) to take it himself because I didn't want to bobble it."[7]

When it was over, Scott had accomplished the dual feat of pitching a no-hitter and clinching a division title, which was a first in major-league history. The New York Yankees' Allie Reynolds had come closest to the achievement when he had clinched a tie for the American League pennant with a no-hitter against the Boston Red Sox on September 28, 1951. As for Scott's team, the Astros, they won the right to face the New York Mets, their 1962 NL expansion brethren, in what was now being called the "Silver Anniversary Series."[8]

Scott's no-hitter was the most dominant performance of the Astros' three consecutive shutouts, prompting Deshaies to quip, "It sure is hard to sustain any kind of fame around this place."[9] The Astrodome crowd was so excited that they did not want to leave the stadium. So many fans stayed to celebrate that Scott was carried back onto the field to a new round of cheers a full 30 minutes after the last pitch. Kerfeld, the Astros' popular reliever, was elated for both his team and its fans and declared, "Shakespeare couldn't have written this any better.

gave Scott all the run support he would need in this game when he hit a one-out solo home run over the wall in right-center field to give the Astros a 1-0 lead.

Scott was well aware of the game situation, saying, "About the fifth inning, I knew they didn't have a hit, but I didn't think about going for (the no-hitter) until the seventh. At that point, I decided to go for it."[4] Scott had struck out the side in the bottom of the sixth inning and, after he decided "to go for it," he struck out the first two batters in the seventh inning as well. In the bottom of the seventh, Walling scored his second run of the game on Jose Cruz's two-out single to give the Astros their final margin of 2-0.

Scott allowed one final baserunner in the eighth inning on a one-out walk to Ouellette. The next batter, Harry Spilman, who was pinch-hitting for Uribe, almost broke up the no-hitter with a sharp

We wanted to get this one for the city of Houston and we got it."[10]

After the celebration was over, the Astros made it clear that there was one additional accolade they believed Scott had earned. Catcher Alan Ashby said, "I personally felt he had the Cy Young Award wrapped up already, but if this doesn't win it for him, then something is really fouled up in the system."[11] In spite of the superlative season that Scott already had been enjoying, the Dodgers' Fernando Valenzuela was mentioned most often as the likely recipient of that award and, as coincidence would have it, Valenzuela had won his 20th game of the season with a two-hit victory over the Astros just three days earlier. Scott finished the season with an 18-10 record and led the league with 306 strikeouts, a 2.22 ERA, and 275⅓ innings pitched, but it was most likely his no-hitter that vaulted him past Valenzuela and garnered him the 1986 NL Cy Young Award.

NOTES

1 Neil Hohlfeld, "Great Scott! Astros clinch, Pitcher saves best for last," *Houston Chronicle*, September 26, 1986.

2 Roy S. Johnson, "Astros Clinch With Pizzazz On No-Hitter By Scott," *New York Times*, September 26, 1986.

3 Neil Hohlfeld, "'Great Scott' Clincher," *The Sporting News*, October 6, 1986: 12.

4 Hohlfeld, "Great Scott! Astros clinch, Pitcher saves best for last."

5 Johnson, "Astros Clinch With Pizzazz."

6 Hohlfeld, "'Great Scott' Clincher."

7 Johnson, "Astros Clinch With Pizzazz."

8 Ivy McLemore, "Great Scott! Astros clinch NL West with no-hitter," *Houston Post*, September 26, 1986, astrosdaily.com/history/19860925/, accessed June 10, 2015.

9 Hohlfeld, "'Great Scott' Clincher."

10 McLemore, "Great Scott! Astros clinch NL West with no-hitter."

11 Eddie Sefko, "Astros agree: Cy Young Award should go to Scott," *Houston Chronicle*, September 26, 1986.

Staving Off Scott

October 15, 1986: New York Mets 7, Houston Astros 6 (16 innings), NLCS

Game Six, at the Astrodome

By Rory Costello

TIME AND AGAIN DURING THEIR RUN to the world championship in 1986, the Mets clawed back in desperate situations. Later this October, they were all but eliminated in Game Six of the World Series, when the Red Sox were one strike away from winning it all for the first time since 1918. Yet in Game Six of the NLCS that year—an excruciating 16-inning battle—the Mets also climbed out of a deep hole. The incredibly suspenseful game had sportswriters from around the nation at their best. Mike Downey of the *Los Angeles Times* wrote, "They [the Astros] made the Mets sweat and suffer, made them charge from behind and gasp to stay in front. . .They were enervated, drained, battle-fatigued."[1] In his chronicle of the '86 Mets, *The Bad Guys Won*, author Jeff Pearlman also vividly portrayed the mental and physical exhaustion that the players felt. *Newark Star-Ledger* columnist Jerry Izenberg devoted an entire book to this single contest entitled *The Greatest Game Ever Played*.

Unlike Game Six of the '86 World Series, New York's season would not have ended with a loss to Houston. The Mets had won three of the first five games, including a 12-inning 2-1 victory the day before at now-demolished Shea Stadium. Had the Astros won Game Six, though, they would have sent Mike Scott to the mound the next day. Scott had thrown a five-hit shutout in Game One, making a single second-inning run stand up. He went all the way again to win Game Four, 3-1. He was on a lethal roll with his split-fingered fastball.

The Mets continued to believe that something else was helping Scott's splitter to "drop off the table." Davey Johnson showed a group of reporters eight balls that were scuffed in exactly the same spot—a mark about the size of a 50-cent piece. Johnson said, "It [sandpaper] is in his palm. He doesn't rotate the ball, he just makes a grinding motion. It's blatant to me." However, NL president Chub Feeney called Scott "innocent until proven guilty"—though he added, "We will be watching closely the next time he pitches."[2]

Had the series gone to Game Seven, Scott would have faced Ron Darling. Darling had pitched well during the regular season (15-6, 2.81) but had given up four runs in five innings pitched in Game Three, which the Mets came back to win on Len Dykstra's two-run homer in the bottom of the ninth. In 2006, Darling said, "I felt I couldn't give up any runs because Mike Scott wasn't going to."[3]

The adverb "desperately" has often been used to depict how much the Mets wanted to win Game Six. In their own words, this supremely confident team—viewed as arrogant in many quarters—didn't go quite that far. It is fair to say, however, that there were strong psychological undercurrents as the series shifted back to the Astrodome.

A note on that venue is in order, too. The Astrodome—once known as the Eighth Wonder of the World—hosted its last big-league game in 1999. It then fell into disuse and disrepair, and parts were demolished in late 2013, though most of it was still standing as of 2015. In 1986, however, the dome was also home to the Houston Oilers of the NFL. The Oilers had hosted the Chicago Bears just three days before Game Six—yard lines were still visible on the Astroturf.

The starters in Game Six were both lefties: Bob Knepper for Houston and Bob Ojeda for the Mets. The reliable Ojeda had gone the route as the Mets won Game Two, 5-1. But the Astros got to him for three runs in the first inning, and it might have been more except that Kevin Bass was tagged at home on a missed suicide squeeze attempt. Ojeda settled down after that and did not allow another run before coming out for Rick Aguilera in the sixth inning. Aguilera pitched three shutout innings, giving up just one hit.

Meanwhile, Knepper—17-12, 3.14 in the regular season, with a no-decision in Game Three—was cruising. He'd given up just two hits and a walk as he took a shutout into the ninth inning. Yet the Mets broke through for the tying runs; pinch-hitter Dykstra ignited the rally with a leadoff triple. Again Johnson made the unorthodox choice to send the lefty swinger up against Knepper. Also, whereas Bass in right field and José Cruz in left were playing deep, center-fielder Billy Hatcher remained shallow, and he could not get back to make the play.

Mookie Wilson singled off the tip of Bill Doran's glove to score Dykstra. One out later, Keith Hernandez doubled, Wilson scored, and Houston closer Dave Smith entered. Smith, who'd given up Dykstra's homer in Game Three, was ineffective again. He walked the first two men he faced, which enabled the third run to score on Ray Knight's sacrifice fly. With the count 1-2 to Knight, home plate umpire Fred Brocklander—whose controversial call at first base took a vital run away from Houston in Game Five—had the Astros screaming again when he called a ball.

Roger McDowell entered in the bottom of the ninth for the Mets and went on to pitch five superb innings. He faced the minimum 15 batters; the only baserunner he allowed, Bass, was caught stealing second base. It was McDowell's longest relief stint ever in the majors; his only longer outing came in one of his two big-league starts as a rookie in 1985. Smith pitched a scoreless 10th for Houston, and Larry Andersen blanked the Mets from the 11th through the 13th.

Glenn Davis was only the second power hitter in Astros history. He hit 30-plus homers three times and when he departed Houston after the 1990 season, his 166 HRs were second only to Jimmy Wynn's 223. (Courtesy of Houston Astros Baseball Club).

In the 14th, the Mets got a run against veteran reliever Aurelio López. The portly Mexican was no longer "Señor Smoke" at this stage of his career, but he contained the damage with runners on second and third. Jesse Orosco came on to try to get the save for the Mets, but with one out, Hatcher pulled a drive high and deep. Would it stay fair? It hit the screen on the left-field foul pole, and the game was tied again.

After a scoreless 15th, New York put up three runs in the top of the 16th against López and Jeff Calhoun. One question about this game is why Hal Lanier chose not to use lefty Jim Deshaies—twice passed over for starting assignments—at any point. Lanier said that Deshaies had not faced that kind of pressure before. But bullpen coach Gene Tenace apparently told Lanier that Deshaies didn't have good stuff while warming up.[4]

Yet the tension was far from over—the Astros chipped away for two. They had the tying run on second base and the winning run on first with Bass at the plate. Hernandez warned the weary Orosco (accounts vary as to the choice of words) not to throw a single fastball. The count ran full, and Mets announcer Bob Murphy said, "Pulsating baseball…Nobody has sat down for the last four or five innings…Incredible." Finally—on the sixth straight breaking ball—Bass fanned.[5] The Mets had won the NL pennant, and Orosco leaped in exultation. It had been the longest game in terms of innings in postseason history.[6]

Even if Houston had extended the series, at least some of the combative Mets still liked their chances against Scott. After Game Four, Ray Knight said, "You have to get that [the talk of scuffing] out of your mind and start thinking, 'What approach is best suited to hit this pitch?' and then you have to make adjustments at the plate."[7] Scrappy Wally Backman said, "We're ticked and we're not going to take this lying down. I don't care if he scuffs 400 balls. I don't care if they're scuffed before the game. I don't think any pitcher can beat us three times in a row."[8]

On the flip side, however, Backman admitted, "If we had lost and had to face Scott tomorrow, I wouldn't have slept at all." Gary Carter also said, "Mike Scott was our incentive to win."[9] Davey Johnson added, "Amen. I feel like I'm on parole, like I've just been given a pardon."[10] Perhaps a better choice of words would have been "reprieve"—the 1986 Mets just went from one grueling drama to the next.

SOURCES

Internet resources

Baseball-reference.com

Retrosheet.org

NOTES

1 Mike Downey, "All That Houston Has Ahead of It Now Is a Winter of Wondering," *Los Angeles Times*, October 16, 1986.

2 Harig, "Mets accuse Houston's Mike Scott of scuffing baseball" and "Feeney clears Scott—for now," Associated Press, October 15, 1986.

3 Richard Sandomir, "Mets' Announcers Slide into New Roles," *New York Times*, October 14, 2006.

4 Gordon Edes, "Mets Admit They're Glad to Get Off Scott-Free," *Los Angeles Times*, October 16, 1986.

5 Mike Downey described Bass as "overanxious" and Bass later confirmed this in a December 2010 meeting with SABR's Larry Dierker (Houston) chapter. See Bill McCurdy, "1986 NLCS Game 6: A Sacher Masoch Revisitation" (http://bill37mccurdy.wordpress.com/2010/12/15/1986-nlcs-game-6-a-sacher-masoch-revisitation/)

6 On October 9, 2005, the Astros and Atlanta Braves played 18 innings in Game Four of the National League Division Series.

7 Harig, "Mets accuse Houston's Mike Scott of scuffing baseball"

8 Terry Taylor, "Mets complain Mike Scott is 'scuffing' their attack," Associated Press, October 14, 1986.

9 Wire service reports, October 17, 1986.

10 Associated Press, October 16, 1986.

You Gotta Like these Kids

July 16, 1987: Houston Astros 2, Philadelphia Phillies 1, at the Astrodome

By Joe Thompson

RAIN, THUNDERSTORMS, AND A blistering heat index of 102.9 degrees did not diminish the anticipation of Astros fans longing for the second half of the 1987 baseball campaign to get under way. On July 16, 1987, a hot and muggy night in Houston,[1] an eager crowd of 19,614 made its way into the cool, climate-controlled environment of the Astrodome to watch the Astros face off against the Philadelphia Phillies. The series was important for both clubs because each had failed to play up to its potential during the first half of the season. Both teams hoped to jump out to a fast start after the All-Star break in order to gain momentum that might lead to a chance to play in the postseason.

The Philadelphia Phillies, who were 42-44, came to Houston looking for any type of boost to help salvage a disappointing season. Picked by some to overtake the New York Mets in the National League East, the Phillies had struggled to put wins together in the early part of the season[2] and entered the All-Star break having lost three out of their last four games against the struggling Atlanta Braves. They entered the second half of the season in fifth place, 14 games behind the division-leading St. Louis Cardinals.

The Astros, with a record of 44-43, were 2½ games behind the division-leading Cincinnati Reds in the National League West. They sputtered into the series with the Phillies as losers of five of their previous six games, but they now hoped to repeat what they had done in the second half of the 1986 season when they went 49-25 won the division going away.[3] Catcher Alan Ashby described the team's problem for the first half of the 1987 season: "For some reason, we haven't been doing the little things it takes to win a division. … Maybe it's going to take something like [shortstop] Craig Reynolds going out on the mound

and getting bombed [in the first game after the break in 1986]. … That game really seemed to get us going last year."[4]

The Astros, looking for anything that might change their bad fortunes on the field, made some changes before the Phillies series even started. Slugger Glenn Davis and relief pitcher Charlie Kerfeld showed up with new hairstyles. Both players, according to *Houston Chronicle* writer Eddie Sefko, looked like members of a rock band.[5]

On June 19 the Astros had traded veteran third baseman Phil Garner to the Los Angeles Dodgers.[6] Garner's departure left a hole at third that the club filled by promoting Ken Caminiti, a powerful switch-hitting youngster, from its Double-A team at Columbus (Southern League). Caminiti led Columbus with 15 home runs and 69 RBIs at the time of his call-up but was surprised to make it to the big-league squad: "I thought I was going to Tucson. Then they asked me if I could get to Houston today and I told them I could leave right then."[7] The Astros inserted Caminiti into the starting lineup immediately in the hope that he could provide a spark. Caminiti did not let the club down.

The Astros' hopes of getting the series off to a hot start took a slight hit on the day of the first game when scheduled starter Nolan Ryan injured his foot. "I was walking along the property when I stepped in a hole," said Ryan, whose 4-10 record was misleading. (His ERA was 3.17 and he had struck out 143 in 110⅔ innings.) The veteran flamethrower made light of the injury: "I guess it goes right along with the type of year I'm having."[8]

With the "Ryan Express" unavailable to start, the Astros turned to the "Bonham Bullet," right-hander Danny Darwin, to face off against Kevin Gross for

Rifle-armed Ken Caminiti was one of Houston's many rising stars in the early 1990s. Only Doug Rader played more games at third base for the Astros than Caminiti did in his 10 seasons in Houston. (Courtesy of Houston Astros Baseball Club).

the Phillies. Darwin had come to the Astros in 1986 primarily as a starter. During the first half of the 1987 season, the Astros used him as a starter and occasional reliever. In 20 games he had amassed116 innings, a 5-6 record, and a 3.71 ERA.

Gross had spent his entire career with the Phillies since being drafted by the club in 1981 and made his major-league debut on June 25, 1983. Heading into the series with the Astros, Gross had a 6-8 record with a 4.41 ERA in 104 innings (17 starts). Although the numbers for both pitchers were unspectacular, each proved highly effective on this night.

Darwin and Gross made it through the first few innings unscathed. The Phillies' first shot at getting on the scoreboard came in the top of the second when Darwin hit Chris James and walked Luis Aguayo. The rally quickly ended when Gross grounded to third. The Astros did not fare much better off Gross during the first few innings. They loaded the bases with two outs in the first but came up empty. Their other serious threat came in the bottom of the fifth when Caminiti barely missed a home run in his second major-league at-bat. The ball bounced off the right-field wall and by the time Phillies right fielder Glenn Wilson got the ball back into the infield, Caminiti stood at third with his first major-league hit. The Astros failed to capitalize, though, as Craig Reynolds grounded out to first and, after a walk to Darwin, rookie Gerald Young lined into a double play.

The first run of the game came off Darwin in the top of the sixth when Juan Samuel singled and scored from third on a double-play ball hit by Von Hayes. After Samuel's hit, Darwin dominated the Phillies hitters the rest of the night, allowing only a single by Lance Parrish and a walk to Hayes.[9]

Though Darwin pitched nine innings and gave up just one run on four hits, the night belonged to the two Astros rookies, Young and Caminiti. Caminiti quickly won the crowd over with his defensive prowess when he made an off-balance throw to retire Hayes in the first, and an acrobatic catch on a line drive off the bat of Parrish in the second. "He saved a couple of runs right there," Astros manager Hal Lanier said.[10] By the time Caminiti came to the plate in the seventh inning, he was already a fan favorite. The rookie responded to the crowd by launching a long home run to center off Gross to tie the game, 1-1. The Astros faithful demanded a curtain call from the young slugger after he circled the bases, and his teammates forced him to comply. "They pushed me out of the dugout," said Caminiti. "They don't give curtain calls in Columbus. There's usually only about 100 to 150 people there."[11]

The coup de grâce for the two rookies came in the ninth inning. Young made two game-saving catches in center field in the top of the inning to keep the game tied. Caminiti walked with one out, went to third on a single by Craig Reynolds, and scored the game-winning run when Young delivered a single off Phillies reliever Michael Jackson. "You Gotta Like These Kids," proclaimed the Astrodome scoreboard throughout the night.[12] Certainly Young and Caminiti gave Astros fans reason to feel optimistic about the future.

NOTES

1 wunderground.com/history/airport/KHOU/1987/7/16/ DailyHistory.html?req_city=&req_state=&req_ statename=&reqdb.zip=&reqdb.magic=&reqdb.wmo=.

2 Sam McManis, "Major League Baseball: Sam McManis' National League Preview," *Los Angeles Times*, April 5, 1987.

3 Eddie Sefko, "Astros Search for Second-Half Spark," *Houston Chronicle*, July 16, 1987.

4 Ibid.

5 Ibid.

6 "Astros Trade Garner to Dodgers," *Los Angeles Times*, June 19, 1987.

7 Sefko.

8 "Ryan Misses Start Due to Foot Injury," *Washington Post*, July 17, 1987.

9 Nehl Hohlfeld, "Astros' Future Haunts Phillies," *Houston Chronicle*, July 17, 1987.

10 Hohlfeld.

11 Ibid.

12 Ibid.

The "Ryan Express" Whiffs 16, including Number 4,500, in Command Performance

September 9, 1987: Houston Astros 4, San Francisco Giants 2, at the Astrodome

By Gregory H. Wolf

AGELESS WONDER NOLAN RYAN was in the midst of one of the strangest seasons a big-league pitcher had ever experienced. Neil Hohlfeld of the *Houston Chronicle* considered it "unreal in the negative sense."[1] From June 17 to July 29 Ryan had lost eight consecutive starts as the Astros provided him only eight runs of support while he was on the mound. In the days before the sabermetric revolution helped change the way a pitcher's victories were viewed, the 40-year-old "Ryan Express" was just 6-14 heading into his start against the San Francisco Giants on September 9; however, the fireballer's ERA (2.79) trailed only that of Los Angeles's Orel Hershiser (2.71), his 210 strikeouts were second only to those of teammate Mike Scott, and he easily led all major-league hurlers by holding opposition to a .193 batting average.

In a performance described by Terry Blount of the *Houston Post* as "masterful" and by Hohlfeld as "mindboggling," Ryan continued his season-long re-emergence as one of the game's most dominant hurlers by striking out 10 of the last 12 batters he faced to set an Astrodome record with 16 strikeouts, including his 4,500th victim, over eight innings against San Francisco.[2] "He's amazing," said Giants pilot Roger Craig. "Nobody's ever lived who can throw like that for as long as he has."[3]

The reigning NL West champion Astros had played lackluster ball to that point in 1987. Following a dismal seven-game losing streak, second-year manager Hal Lanier's squad had won four of its previous six and was in second place (69-69), 5½ games behind

Giants. The hottest team in baseball, San Francisco (75-64) was on a roll, having won 22 of its last 31 games.

Ryan began the game by whiffing Eddie Milner swinging, prompting a hearty round of applause from the 25,620 spectators in the Astrodome on a Wednesday evening. He racked up two more punchouts in the second (both swinging) before reminding everyone that he also swung a bat. Kevin Bass led off the frame with a single off Giants starter Atlee Hammaker, and Glenn Davis followed with a walk. Ryan, who had managed just two hits in 48 at-bats, hit what Ray Ratto of the *San Francisco Chronicle* called a "slow, well-placed and highly improbable, but true" two-out grounder to center field, driving in Bass for the game's first run.[4] Gerald Young's double drove in Davis and made it 2-0. For Ryan, driving in a run was almost as likely as striking out 15 or more in a game; in 773 starts he punched out at least 15 batters 26 times; in 852 at-bats he knocked in 36 runs.

San Francisco threatened in the third when Milner lined a one-out single to center field, stole second, and moved to third on Chris Speier's groundout. After issuing a walk to Mike Aldrete, Ryan got out of the jam by inducing Candy Maldonado to ground out to third baseman Ken Caminiti.

The Astros broke the game open in the third when, with Alan Ashby aboard, Bass launched his 17th round-tripper of the season to make it 4-0. Kelly Downs relieved Hammaker and shut down the Astros for the remainder of the third and fourth to keep the Giants in the game.

In 1987 Nolan Ryan became the first pitcher to lead his league in ERA (2.76) and strikeouts (270) and not win the Cy Young Award, thanks to his shocking, hard-luck 8-16 won-lost record. (Courtesy of Houston Astros Baseball Club).

Ryan issued his second and final walk of the game, to Jose Uribe, to lead off the fifth. Uribe stole second and scored on Milner's one-out single to short right field, ending Ryan's streak of 22⅔ scoreless innings in the Dome. The Giants seemed to have Ryan on the ropes. Speier followed with a single, then Aldrete singled to drive in Milner and slice the lead to 4-2. With runners on first and second, Ryan was laboring, but then he turned it up a notch. "At that point, you could see him really get after it," said teammate Bill Doran. "It was like he wasn't going to give them anything."[5] Ryan struck out both Maldonado and Will Clark to end the threat.

From the fifth through the eighth, the Astros managed only two hits, both in the sixth inning with one out. One of those was a single by Ryan, who collected a career-best two hits in a game for the 11th and last time. Craig Lefferts, the Giants' fourth reliever, got out of that jam by retiring Doran and Jose Cruz.

Ryan continued his pitching clinic in the sixth inning by striking out the side. He also yielded his sixth and final hit, Uribe's liner to center. In the seventh he retired the side in order, whiffing two more to bring his total to 13. The frame ended when Aldrete hacked and missed on Ryan's 117th pitch of the game to become the Express's 4,500th strikeout victim. The partisan crowd gave Ryan, who was born and raised in Texas, a standing ovation. The stoic Ryan, who rarely acknowledged his own feats, expressed his thanks by coming out for a curtain call between innings.

It appeared as though Ryan's night was over. The 21-year veteran, who entered the season with 253 career wins, had been suffering from elbow tenderness throughout the 1987 season. He had pitched as many as eight innings just once, and was on a 110-pitch limit, but to the crowd's delight, the Texas institution was back on the mound to start the eighth. With his fastball topping out at 98 miles per hour, Ryan fanned the side on 14 pitches, sending the Astros faithful into another raucous standing ovation. And once again Ryan made a curtain call between innings. "There's nothing more rewarding than hearing the cheers of the home crowd," said Ryan, whose evening was over.[6] Reliever Dave Smith tossed a 1-2-3 ninth to pick up his 23rd save and preserve Ryan's victory in 2 hours and 43 minutes.

"Anytime you get a strikeout total like that, you've got to have a good curve ball going," said Ryan. "My rhythm was so good I could have thrown my curve ball even harder."[7] In addition to setting an Astros record for strikeouts in the Astrodome and chalking up his 4,500th punchout, Ryan tied his personal-best strikeout total in the NL, matching the 16 whiffs he had as a member of the New York Mets in a complete-game 2-1 victory over San Diego on May 29, 1971. It was also the most strikeouts he had in a game since fanning 16 as a California Angel in a complete-game victory over the Detroit Tigers on June 9, 1979. "The pitch count has been expanded to 125 the last two or three starts," explained a genuinely pleased Ryan. "I think tonight is definitive proof that I'm over my elbow problems."[8] Ryan threw 89 of his 131 pitches for strikes, including 26 swinging strikes. The Giants struck out swinging 12 times.

Ryan's performance drew raves from players, coaches, and the press. "It's unbelievable that he's still throwing with that kind of velocity at his age," raved Lanier.[9] "I'm not going to belabor it," said batterymate Alan Ashby, who caught Ryan's record-breaking fifth no-hitter (and his only one as an Astro) on September 26, 1981. "All I'm going to say is that I've seen him eight years now and I've never seen him better."[10] Said Speier, who tagged Ryan for two hits, "It's tough on a hitter when he's getting the

curve ball over. … Plus he has the change-up now."[11] Ray Ratto considered Ryan's outing "hardly shocking," and noted that he systematically tortured the Giants.[12] Dating back to September 24, 1986, it was Ryan's sixth consecutive start with at least 10 strikeouts against San Francisco, during which he totaled 73 punchouts in 41⅓ innings.

Notwithstanding Ryan's victory and strikeout milestones, the Astros took a nosedive, winning just six of their final 23 games to finish in third place with a disappointing 76-86 record. Ryan was one of the team's few bright spots in spite of finishing with an 8-16 record. He paced the NL in ERA (2.76), and led the major leagues in strikeouts (270), strikeouts per nine innings (11.5, to set a new career best), fewest hits per nine innings (6.5) and lowest opponents' batting average (.200).

SOURCES

In addition to the sources cited in the Notes, the author also accessed Retrosheet.org, Baseball-Reference.com, the SABR Minor Leagues Database, accessed online at Baseball-Reference.com, SABR.org, and *The Sporting News* archive via Paper of Record.

NOTES

1 Neil Hohlfeld, "Ryan Fans 16; Astros Win 4-2," *Houston Chronicle*, September 10, 1987: Section 3, page 1.

2 Terry Blount, "Giants Admire Ryan's 16, but Their Lead Is Even Prettier," *Houston Post*, September 10, 1987: 10; and Hohlfeld.

3 Ray Ratto, "Ryan Mows Down Giants; A's Win. Astros Win, 4-2, Behind His 16 K's," *San Francisco Chronicle*, September 10, 1987: 67.

4 Ibid.

5 Hohlfeld.

6 Ivy McLemore, "Ryan One-Man Show Against Giants," *Houston Post*, September 10, 1987: 1D.

7 Ratto.

8 Hohlfeld.

9 McLemore.

10 C.W. Nevius, "Ryan Heats Up and Chars the Giants," *San Francisco Chronicle*, September 10, 1987: 76.

11 Blount.

12 Ratto.

"The Game that Would Never End"

June 3, 1989: Houston Astros 5, Los Angeles Dodgers 4 (22 innings), at the Astrodome

By Joe Thompson

THE ASTROS PREPARED FOR A FOUR-game series at the Astrodome against the Los Angeles Dodgers starting on June 1 having just completed their best road trip of the season. On May 24, after losing four in a row, the Astros left for a six-game road trip against the Pittsburgh Pirates and St. Louis Cardinals. Perhaps in fear of falling to last place in the National League West, Houston caught fire, sweeping three games from both teams. Back in Houston, the Astros won the first two games of the series against the Los Angeles Dodgers to run their winning streak to eight games. They entered their June 3 game against the Dodgers in third place, two games behind the division-leading San Francisco Giants.

On Saturday, June 3, a rambunctious crowd of 34,425 made their way out of the muggy Houston heat into the cool, air-conditioned Astrodome to cheer on their local nine, the hottest team in the majors. Confidence around the clubhouse and in the stands was the highest it had been all season. The Astros sent Bob Knepper to the mound to face Dodgers starter Tim Leary. Right from the start, the game turned out to be something different than anyone expected.

The Astros' winning streak appeared to be in jeopardy even before some fans took their seats. In the top of the first inning with one out, the Dodgers' Jeff Hamilton (who would play a prominent role in the game's outcome), singled off Knepper to drive in Mike Davis and Kirk Gibson for a 2-0 lead. In the top of the third inning, Eddie Murray scored the Dodgers' third run on a wild pitch by Knepper.

The Astros got on the board in the bottom of the fourth when Glenn Davis homered off Leary,[1] but the Dodgers went back up by three runs in the top of the fifth on Kirk Gibson's solo home run. Leary

kept the Astros' bats relatively quiet until the sixth inning. With two outs, he surrendered back-to-back walks to Bill Doran and Glenn Davis. Dodgers manager Tommy Lasorda brought in left-hander Ricky Horton, who walked Terry Puhl to load the bases. On came Tim Crews, who allowed a two-run single to Ken Caminiti to make it 4-3, and a run-scoring single to Rafael Ramirez, to tie the game.[2]

Neither team managed another run for the rest of Saturday night. The game remained deadlocked, 4-4, after nine innings. The Astros nearly won the game in the bottom of the 11th inning off Dodgers reliever Alejandro Pena. With Craig Reynolds on third and Billy Hatcher on second, Gerald Young flied out to center field. Center fielder John Shelby made a solid throw to catcher Mike Scioscia who tagged Reynolds to complete the double play and keep the game going. In the bottom of the 15th, the Astros threatened again to end the game against Orel Hershiser, who was making a rare relief appearance. Hershiser, the defending NL Cy Young Award winner, had other plans. "I knew when Hershiser came in, (the game) was going to last a while," said Glenn Davis.[3] With the bases loaded and one out, Alex Trevino flied out to left field. Chris Gwynn caught the ball and fired to home to cut down the speedy Puhl and keep the game going.[4]

Jerry Crowe of the *Los Angeles Times* wrote that as the game continued, both teams "pulled [out] all of the stops in the late innings." In the bottom of the 21st, the Dodgers put pitcher Fernando Valenzuela at first base, moved first baseman Eddie Murray to third (where he hadn't played in 11 years), and let third baseman Hamilton pitch. "It felt to me that we were conceding the game," said Hershiser.

At first, the move worked well for the Dodgers. Hamilton, throwing in the low 90s, breezed through the 21st without allowing a baserunner. But fortunes changed in the bottom of the 22nd. Doran led off the inning with a single to right. Davis grounded out to the pitcher. Hamilton intentionally walked Puhl and struck out Caminiti. Ramirez took advantage of the makeshift defensive alignment and lined a shot that caromed off Valenzuela's glove at first and into right field. Mike Davis threw home but the throw sailed up the third-base line, allowing Doran to score the winning run.[5] At 2:50 A.M. on Sunday, after more than seven hours of baseball, the longest night game ever in the National League up to that point was over.

Dodgers announcer Vin Scully expressed the exhausted emotions of both sides in his usual genteel manner as he called the end of the game for fans who stayed up to watch all 22 innings: "Once again we can look at the reaction of the managers and this time it's the scene you can take to bed. The joy of [Astros manager Art] Howe and the shocked look on Lasorda and Hamilton is still steaming. What a finish. What a game."[6] Scully was right about Hamilton. The Dodgers third baseman became only the second nonpitcher in 26 years to get a decision. "I was excited about getting to pitch but that doesn't mean much when you lose," Hamilton said. "I'm mad about losing but I still can't believe I was out there. I've always wanted to pitch."[7]

The game ranked high in baseball history both for how long it took and the number of innings played. The 7 hour 14 minute, 22-inning game was the longest night game in major-league history. The game eclipsed the previous record previously held by Milwaukee Brewers and Chicago White Sox on May 8 and 9, 1984. (The game was interrupted by an American League-imposed curfew. The National League had no such curfew restrictions. The longest game by innings in the major leagues was a 1-1, 26-inning tie between Boston and Brooklyn on May 1, 1920.[8]

Some other notable performances: Hershiser recorded a no-decision despite pitching seven innings of three-hit ball on just two days' rest. Astros hurler Jim Clancy pitched five scoreless innings on two days' rest to get the win. Dodgers third baseman/losing pitcher Jeff Hamilton led LA with three hits. Dodgers center fielder John Shelby went 0-for-10. Three Astros, Glenn Davis, Ken Caminiti, and Rafael Ramirez, each got three hits.

The *Wall Street Journal* picked the marathon as the most remarkable game of the 1989 season.[9] And 15,000 viewers across the Southwest missed the end of the game. Home Sports Entertainment, which carried most Astros games during the season, was not a 24-hour operation. Viewers in the Houston area continued to see the game on a local channel after HSE went dark at 4 A.M. The 15,000 fans outside the local area saw the game disappear from their screens at 2 A.M. After several viewers complained, a representative said that the network would look into preventing this from happening again.[10]

NOTES

1   ESPN Classic, "June 3, 1989 – *4th inning – Glenn Davis hits a solo shot against LA's Tim Leary. (1:17, Porter - Dodgers),*" astrosdaily.com/media/; Jerry Crowe, "Dodger Defeat Takes 22 Innings," *Los Angeles Times*, June 4, 1989: B1.

2   Ibid.

3   Alex Truex, "For Astros, 22 + 13 = 10 in a Row," *Houston Chronicle*, June 5, 1989.

4   Ibid.

5   Crowe.

6   ESPN Classic, "June 3, 1989 – *22nd inning — Rafael Ramirez plates Bill Doran to end the marathon contest. (2:01, Scully — Dodgers),*" astrosdaily.com/media/.

7   "A Long Night in Houston," *New York Times*, June 5, 1989.

8   Ibid.

9   Frederick C. Klein, "On Sports: The Baseball Plays of 1989," *Wall Street Journal*, October 5, 1989.

10 Jeff Frank, "Plug Yanked on Many Astro-Game Viewers," *Houston Chronicle*, June 5, 1989.

"Don't You Ever Play Nine-Inning Games?"

June 4, 1989: Houston Astros 7, Los Angeles Dodgers 6 (13 innings), at the Astrodome

By Joe Thompson

THE MARATHON 22-INNING GAME OF the preceding night left the Astros and Dodgers players mentally and physically exhausted. Nevertheless, the teams had one more game to the series left. The Astros trudged their way into the Astrodome around noon to prepare for Sunday's game, but their pregame agenda on the wall noted only one item: "Flex, 1pm." No batting practice. No infield. Flex. The pre-game note for the players surprised Astros manager Art Howe: "I don't think I've ever seen a game where two teams just came to the park, put on their uniforms and went at it."[1]

After the previous game had ended at 2:50 A.M, players scrambled to get a few hours of sleep before Sunday's 1 P.M. scheduled start. Astros first baseman Glenn Davis spent the night on a bunk in the team lounge behind the Astros weight room. "I've slept in worse," Davis said of his makeshift accommodations. "Being an outdoors guy, I've learned to rough it."[2] At 12:30pm, less than an hour before the national anthem, Davis got the wakeup call. "I'll be up in about 30 minutes," Davis said as he shuffled into the clubhouse. Sunday's starting pitcher for the Astros, Bob Forsch (1-1, 3.90 ERA), told Davis. "I give your wife a lot of credit having to wake up next to that every morning."[3]

The win against the Dodgers the night before meant that the Astros winning streak had reached nine games and put them only 1½ games behind the first place San Francisco Giants in the National League West Division. The Dodgers, on the other hand, sent Tim Belcher (4-4, 2.95 ERA) to the mound for Sunday's game as the team tried to salvage a game in the series.

The Dodgers appeared refreshed from the previous night as Chris Gwynn, Dave Anderson, and Kirk Gibson hit consecutive singles in the top of the first. Gwynn scored from third when Eddie Murray flied out to center. Kirk Gibson then stole second, Forsch intentionally walked Mike Davis to load the bases, and then Mike Scioscia cleared the bases with a grand slam. Indeed, before most Astros fans had taken their seats, the Dodgers led 5-0. Jeff Hamilton, the everyday third baseman and losing Dodgers pitcher from the previous night, got a little revenge for the loss by doubling Scioscia home in the third to increase the lead to 6-0. Any momentum Houston might have had coming into Sunday's game from the previous night seemed long gone by the third inning.

In the bottom of the second, Greg Gross got Astros first hit, but the team failed to score against Belcher. Over the first four innings, Belcher struck out five Astros while allowing only two hits. Belcher cruised along until the bottom of the fifth when the Dodger's momentum turned on a disputed call.

After Gross flied out to center field, Rafael Ramirez, the hero from the previous night's game, beat out a roller to second for an infield hit. Craig Reynolds singled and the Astros' young catcher, Craig Biggio, drew a walk to load the bases. Billy Hatcher, pinch-hitting for Forsch, stepped up to the plate. The speedy Hatcher hit a groundball to first baseman Murray, who threw to Belcher, covering at first base. "I didn't have to see the replay," Belcher said, "In my opinion, it wasn't even close."[4] First base umpire Paul Runge disagreed and called Hatcher safe. Although TV replay clearly showed that Hatcher was out, the umpire's call stood. Ramirez scored from third to give the Astros their first run. The controversial play changed the entire complexion of the game when the next batter, Louie Meadows, who started the game in left for Hatcher, launched a grand slam—his first home run of the season—over the right-field wall to make the score Dodgers 6, Astros 5.

"I'd be the first one in line to congratulate Louis Meadows for hitting the … out of the ball," Belcher said after the game, "but, in my opinion, the whole inning was set up by a bad call at first base. If we get the correct call there, it's a different inning."5 Meadows' slam marked the first time in the 24-year history of the Astrodome in which one game featured two grand slams.

Despite giving up five runs to the Astros in the fifth inning and perhaps because the Dodgers' bullpen needed rest from the night before, Belcher remained in the game. Manager Tom Lasorda's decision to keep him in paid off as he gave up only two more hits over the sixth, seventh, and eighth innings. Houston relievers Dan Schatzeder and Danny Darwin also kept the Dodgers' bats quiet from the sixth inning through the top of the ninth.

Jay Howell replaced Belcher in the bottom of the ninth and retired the first two batters. Craig Biggio then stepped up to the plate, with both his nine-game hitting streak and the Astros' nine-game winning streak on the line. Bill Brown, Astros announcer, said it best on the call: "To left field, and … it's … gonna … go, home run! Biggio has tied it!"6 Biggio's blast landed 390 feet from home plate. "I threw it and he hit it. … That's about the size of it," Howell said.

For the second straight game, the Astros and Dodgers headed to extra innings. The Dodgers, who had managed only four hits off Astros pitching since the fourth inning, threatened in the top of the 12th against the Astros' closer, Dave Smith. Willie Randolph led off the inning with a single, but was caught stealing on a laser from Biggio to second baseman Bill Doran. Chris Gwynn then hit a triple that would have scored Randolph had he not been thrown out at second. On the next play, Anderson hit a fly ball to left on which Gwynn tagged up and

attempted to score. Reynolds, who normally played shortstop and was playing the outfield for just the fourth time in his 15-year career, made a shoestring catch and threw a one-bounce strike to Biggio, who blocked the plate and tagged out Gwynn to preserve the tie. Brown exulted, "What a play by Reynolds in left! That is one of the great plays of this season! He is not an outfielder by trade and [Reynolds] just gambled all the way."7

An inning later, former Cy Young Award winner Mike Scott, who had pitched a four-hit shutout against Dodgers ace Fernando Valenzuela two nights earlier, made his first relief appearance for the Astros since 1985. After Scott retired the first two batters, Jose Gonzales tripled and Scioscia walked. But Scott struck out pinch-hitter Rick Dempsey to end the threat and send the game to the bottom of the 13th.

The Dodgers' Alejandro Pena faced Doran to begin the bottom of the inning and walked him. With Ramirez at the plate, Doran lit off for second. When Dempsey's throw to Randolph sailed over his head and into center field, Doran made his way to third. Pena then intentionally walked both Ramirez and Reynolds to set up a force play at every base. Biggio came up to bat and hit a sharp grounder to second. Randolph gloved it and fired an unbelievable throw to home to force Doran. With one out and no more pinch-hitters available, Howe decided to let Scott, a bad hitter,(3-for-29, .103), hit for himself. Scott hit the first pitch to center field. Ramirez tagged at third and scampered home with the game-winning run. "And instead of winning it with his arm," Bill Worrell said on the broadcast, "the Cy Young Award winner from two years ago wins it with his bat."8

The Dodgers left Houston after the game with their bullpen spent. Belcher, who had gone eight innings and given up five runs while walking one and striking out six, could not wait to leave the Astrodome. "I'm just glad to be getting the hell out of here," he told reporters. "These guys could beat the '27 Yankees, the way they're playing."9

NOTES

1   Al Carter, "No-Doze Astros Lead LA lullaby," *Houston Chronicle*, June 5, 1989.

2   Ibid.

3   Ibid.

4   Jerry Crowe, "In 13 Innings, Astros Finish 4-Game Sweep," *Los Angeles Times*, June 5, 1989.

5   Ibid.

6   Ibid.; astrosdaily.com/audio/89biggio.mp3.

7   astrosdaily.com/audio/89scott.mp3.

8   Ibid.

9   Crowe.

Mike Scott Strikes Out 15 in 10-Inning Complete Game Walk-Off Win for Astros

June 8, 1990: Houston Astros 3, Cincinnati Reds 1 (10 innings), at the Astrodome

By Michael Huber

THE 1990 SEASON WAS TWO MONTHS old, and two teams heading in opposite directions began a three-game series on a Friday night at the Astrodome. The Cincinnati Reds had the best record in all of baseball at 34-15. The Houston Astros dwelled in the cellar with the worst record in the National League (20-34), 16½ games behind the Reds. They had lost seven games in a row. But before a crowd of 23,453, the hometown Astros began a significant turnaround. In the bottom of the 10th inning, pinch-hitter Glenn Wilson crushed a three-run home run to preserve a victory for Houston's Mike Scott, who pitched all 10 innings and struck out 15 Cincinnati batters, earning the victory.

As he took the mound, Scott had a surprisingly poor 2-6 record. He had won 20 games the season before, and the Astros knew he had the tools to be successful. In this game, his command and control of pitches was evident early on. He struck out the side in the first inning (all swinging), and then struck out two batters in each of the second and third innings (again, all swinging), setting down the entire Cincinnati lineup in order through three frames. Of Scott's first 30 pitches, 26 were strikes. Opposing Scott was lefty Tom Browning, who entered the game with an unremarkable 5-4 record but an impressive 2.30 ERA. He also struck out the side in the bottom of the first, but allowed a one-out single to Bill Doran. Houston touched Browning for a walk and a single in the bottom of the second, but he struck out two Houston batters. He retired the Astros in order in the bottom of the third, collecting another

strikeout. At the end of the third inning, there was no score and fans had already seen 13 strikeouts.

Scott was on auto-pilot. He struck out Chris Sabo looking to lead off the fourth. Billy Hatcher beat out a groundball to third. Hatcher moved to second on a balk but Scott struck out Barry Larkin and got Eric Davis to foul out down the right field line to end any hopes of a threat. For the next several innings, Browning and Scott faced the minimum number of batters. Scott struck out Todd Benzinger swinging in the fifth and again struck out the side, all swinging, in the Reds' sixth. Browning allowed a single to Eric Yelding to lead off the Houston sixth, but picked him off.

Three up and three down went the Reds in the seventh, but Scott did not collect a K, a small moral victory on this night when the 1986 Cy Young Award winner was at his best. Houston mounted a rally in its half with one-out singles by Ken Caminiti and Eric Anthony, but Rafael Ramirez grounded into a 6-4-3 double play to end the inning. Scott chalked up one more strikeout in the top of the ninth, and the game entered extra innings in a scoreless tie. Scott had faced 28 batters through nine innings and allowed one hit, walked none, and struck out 14 Cincinnati batters. Browning had also pitched nine innings, facing 31 batters, allowing five hits and two walks, but no runs.

That set up an exciting 10th inning. Scott returned to the mound. Hatcher grounded out, then Larkin laced a line-drive single to right field. Davis grounded out with Larkin advancing a base. With Paul O'Neill

Glenn Wilson, a native of the Houston area, was a strong-armed right fielder who led the NL in outfield assists with the Phillies from 1985-87. He was traded home to Houston by the Pirates in 1989. (Courtesy of Houston Astros Baseball Club).

batting, Larkin stole third base. O'Neill walked and Benzinger delivered an RBI single to right field. Scott struck out Mariano Duncan for the third out, but the Reds had taken a 1-0 lead.

Cincinnati manager Lou Piniella pulled a double switch, bringing in Ken Griffey to play first for Benzinger and calling on Randy Myers to relieve Browning. Myers was looking for his 12th save of the season. He struck out Caminiti leading off. Anthony walked and Louie Meadows ran for him. Ramirez hit a groundball single through the left side, and Alex Trevino lifted a fly ball to left-center field, advancing Meadows to third with two outs. This would have brought Scott to the plate, but skipper Art Howe opted instead for pinch-hitter Glenn Wilson, who was batting .226 with just 15 runs batted so far. Myers missed the strike zone on the first two offerings and then Wilson sent the 2-and-0 pitch out of the ball-park for a walk-off win, 3-1.

The 15 strikeouts were a career best for Scott. Fourteen were swinging strikeouts. After the game, he told reporters, "When people are not scoring, the pitching's got to hold the other team down. And when we're struggling, you've got to get some runs. That's just all part of being a team. You've got to pick each other up."[1] Scott threw 116 pitches, 90 of them for strikes.

In addition to snapping the losing streak, the walk-off victory started a six-game winning streak. (Houston swept its three-game series with Cincinnati and its next series, with the Los Angeles Dodgers.) Before this stretch of games, Houston had not won more than three in a row all season.[2] Before the game, Mike Scott had had only three outings of seven or more innings, with only one win to show for it. The Astros were not scoring runs and Scott wasn't getting people out. After this game, Scott had 12 starts of at least seven innings, winning six and losing three. His earned-run average fell from 5.53 coming into the

June 8 game to 3.81 at the end of the season. The last Houston starter to pitch into the 10th inning had been Nolan Ryan, on July 1, 1985, against the San Diego Padres.[3]

Despite this burst of confidence, Houston went 54-53 over the rest of the season and finished in fourth place in the National League East, but that was better than dead last.

SOURCES

In addition to the sources mentioned in the Notes, the author consulted baseball-almanac.com, baseball-reference.com, mlb.com, retrosheet.org, and sabr.org.

"Astros 3, Reds 1," *New York Times*, June 9, 1990.

NOTES

1 Jayne Custred, "Clancy, Scott turn in back-to-back gems," *Houston Chronicle*, June 10, 1990.

2 The Astros put together another six-game winning streak, in August, but they also suffered two more seven-game losing streaks (one in June, as they were swept by the Reds and Dodgers, and one in July).

3 Jayne Custred, "Scott, Wilson power Astros to 3-1 victory," *Houston Chronicle*, June 9, 1990.

Close, but No No-No; Astros Squeeze Past Reds 1-0 in 13 Innings

April 24, 1991: Houston Astros 1, Cincinnati Reds 0 (13 innings), at the Astrodome

By Matt Henshon

"I CAN'T BE CONCERNED WITH THE fans," Astros manager Art Howe said after a 1-0 victory in extra innings over the Cincinnati Reds. "I have to worry about [Darryl] Kile's arm."[1] Howe had received an earful from the 10,869 in the Astrodome when public-address announcer J. Fred Duckett told them Kile had been lifted for a reliever. The issue was the circumstances under which Howe decided to remove Kile—in the seventh inning of a potential no-hitter, a game that the Astros eventually won, 1-0, in extra innings.

To top it off, April 24, 1991, was the 22-year-old Kile's first major-league start. A year earlier he had been seen as a can't-miss prospect in the Astros' system, lumped together with Steve Avery and Andy Benes "as the best pitching prospects in the minors in 1989."[2] But after a season at Triple-A Tucson, where he went 5-10 with a 6.64 ERA,[3] Kile's future was somewhat suspect.

The Reds entered the game as defending World Series champions with a 91-71 regular-season record in 1990, but were off to a modest 7-6 start in the early days of the 1991 season. The Astros, in contrast, were coming off a 75-87 season in 1990, and were off to a similarly uninspiring 6-8 start.

Kile cruised through the first three innings with the only blemish on his pitching line a leadoff walk in the second inning to Paul O'Neill. He opened the fourth with a walk as well, to the number-two hitter Herm Winningham, but stranded Winningham on base. Kile went through the fifth and the sixth innings setting down Cincinnati in order, striking out Winningham to end the sixth with his 65th pitch of the game.

Meanwhile, Reds hurler Jack Armstrong, who was 1-1 with an 8.00 ERA going into the game, matched Kile almost pitch for pitch, leaving two on in the first and then cruising through the second, third, and fourth in order. In the fifth the Astros' Tuffy Rhodes reached on a one-out single, but Armstrong escaped the inning on a fielder's choice and a strikeout.

As the seventh inning approached, Howe was faced with his decision. While Kile had thrown just 65 pitches through six innings, he had his longest outing of his rookie season (three innings) just four days earlier, on April 20. (He had, however, thrown 41 pitches, while giving seven earned runs in 1⅓ innings a week earlier.) After the game Howe acknowledged that he faced a tough choice: "It was a no-hitter! I thought and thought about it. But my No. 1 concern was that young man's arm. He was so pumped up, he could have gone out there and had something bad happen, because he hasn't pitched this long before."[4]

For his part, Kile didn't complain. "I probably could have thrown just one more inning, anyway," he said. "I would have liked to try, but the main thing was to win the game."[5]

Howe did concede that Kile "still looked strong when I took him out. But I didn't want to wait until he didn't look strong."[6]

Howe elected to go with lefty Al Osuna to start the seventh against the heart of the Reds' lineup, which consisted of Barry Larkin (a 1990 All-Star with splits of .301/.358/.396), O'Neill (.270/.339/.421 in 1990), and Hal Morris (.340/.381/.498 in 1990). While Larkin was a right-handed batter, the other two were lefties. Osuna, making his eighth appearance of the young season and entering the game with a 1.69 ERA, set the Reds down in order.

Armstrong came out to pitch the bottom of the seventh, and after one-out singles by Luis Gonzalez and Jeff Bagwell, he snuffed out the rally with a 6-4-3 double play pitch. Osuna returned to the mound for the eighth and continued his early-season mastery by again retiring Cincinnati in order.

Mark McLemore led off the bottom of the eighth with a walk but Reds manager Lou Piniella continued to stand by Armstrong. Switch-hitter Dave Rohde hit for Osuna and advanced McLemore to scoring position with a bunt, but Armstrong justified Piniella's confidence by striking out Eric Yielding looking and getting Steve Finley to fly out to center.

Art Howe sent Curt Schilling out to start the ninth. Like Kile, Schilling was considered a top young right-handed prospect. Houston had acquired him in the offseason in a trade that sent first baseman Glenn Davis to Baltimore. Davis, a former first-round pick, had been a cornerstone of the franchise in the 1980s, hitting 30 or more home runs three times from 1986 to 1989, but in 1990 he was injured and played in only 93 games. In exchange for Davis, the Astros had received a package of Schilling, right-handed starter Pete Harnisch, and center fielder Finley.

With the pitcher's spot due to lead off the top of the ninth, Piniella sent former Astro Bill Doran to the plate to pinch-hit for pitcher Armstrong. On a 2-and-1 count, Schilling gave up the Reds' first hit, ending the possibility of the first NL multiple-pitcher no-hitter since 1956.[7] Doran advanced to third on a wild pitch with two outs, but Schilling got Larkin swinging to end the threat.

In the bottom of the 11th Casey Candaele walked. Eric Yelding bunted and the throw to first by Reds pitcher Don Carman hit Yelding in the foot and bounded into right field. Even as Candaele scampered around the bases, home-plate umpire Terry

Tata called Yelding out for interference — he had been running inside the baseline. That sent Candaele back to first base. Yelding was still furious after the game ended, telling his teammates, "Have a good year. I'm out of here."[8] In the top of the 12th, Winningham led off with a bunt single. Larkin, who was described as "the best offensive shortstop" in the NL,[9] sacrificed the Winningham to second, but the threat was extinguished when, after an intentional walk, the Astros' Dwayne Henry induced successive fly balls to end the inning.

Finally, in the bottom of the 13th, the Astros broke through against Reds reliever Scott Scudder. Rafael Ramirez singled to left with one out. After a walk to catcher Craig Biggio, Ken Caminiti hit a grounder to short but the Reds could get only the out at second. Ken Oberkfell batted for pitcher Henry and looped a ball that caromed off the outstretched glove of second baseman Mariano Duncan, allowing Ramirez to score and ending the evening with a 1-0 Astros victory.[10]

NOTES

1 Terry Blount, "Astros Disarm Reds in 13 Innings; No-Hit Bid Ends in Ninth," *Houston Chronicle*, April 25, 1991.

2 Bill James, *The Baseball Book 1990* (New York: Villard Books, 1990), 299. (Kile's name was surrounded by stars, indicating a highly-touted prospect.)

3 Bill James, *The Baseball Book 1991* (New York: Villard Books, 1991), 91.

4 Blount.

5 Blount.

6 Blount.

7 Reds pitchers John Klippstein, Hershell Freeman, and Joe Black combined for a no-hitter against the Milwaukee Braves in 1956. Mark Langston and Mike Witt of California had the most recent (as of 2016) combined AL no-hitter, against the Seattle Mariners in 1990.

8 Blount.

9 James (1990), 301.

10 Blount.

Incaviglia Wallops Two HRs and Drives in Franchise-Tying Seven Runs

June 14, 1992: Houston Astros 15, San Francisco Giants 7, at the Astrodome

By Chip Greene

FOR FANS OF THE HOUSTON ASTROS, the month of June 1992 hadn't yet delivered much excitement. In what had been so far a poor season, the Astros began their campaign with a promising 9-6 start, but after that had achieved a dismal record of just 17-29. For a team that hadn't finished higher than third place in the past five years, it was shaping up to be yet another forgettable season.

On this Sunday afternoon at the Astrodome, though, the fans were about to be treated to a spectacular, record-tying individual performance. The Astros' opponent was the San Francisco Giants. So far in the season, they had fared better than Houston had. Despite their loss to the Astros the previous night, the Giants stood three games over .500 and were lodged in a three-way tie for second place in the National League's Western division, six games ahead of last-place Houston. Five days earlier, San Francisco's left-handed relief pitcher Dave Righetti had come out of the bullpen to make his first start since 1983, when he was with the New York Yankees. Tonight, Righetti made his second start for San Francisco. It didn't last very long.

For that matter, neither would the game last long for the Astros' starter, Jimmy Jones. From their opening at-bat, the Giants had no trouble solving the offerings of the Houston right-hander. Behind a single, a sacrifice bunt, a walk, and a double, San Francisco put two runs on the board in the first inning, then added another in the second. Meanwhile, Righetti got off to an effective start, shutting out the Astros over the first two innings while limiting them to two walks and no hits. When the Astros came to the plate in the bottom of the third, they trailed 3-0.

Now Houston quickly solved Righetti and set the stage for what was one of the Astrodome's most impressive batting performances. Rafael Ramirez's leadoff double to left began the inning and commenced Righetti's unraveling. After pinch-hitter Juan Guerrero, batting for Jones, flied out, Houston produced in succession a walk, another fly out, a two-run double (by Ken Caminiti), an intentional walk, and another double (by Eric Anthony), which drove home the tying run. That brought to the plate 28-year-old slugger Pete Incaviglia. He was about to have one of the best offensive showings of his major-league career.

For a former first-round draft pick, Peter Joseph Incaviglia's career undoubtedly hadn't gone the way he had once envisioned. At Monterey (California) High School, Incaviglia had three times been named the state's high-school baseball player of the year. A corner infielder with immense power, the right-handed slugger drew enough notice from major-league scouts that he was drafted by the San Francisco Giants in the 10th round of the June 1982 amateur draft, the 247th player selected. (With the 39th pick of that draft, the Giants also chose another high-school player from California, Barry Bonds.) Despite being selected, Incaviglia opted to play college baseball. "I thought school was more important at that time," he remembered years later.[1]

As it turned out, if Incaviglia was going to play college baseball, it wasn't going to be at a California university. Despite his schoolboy success and subsequent interest from the major leagues, he was overlooked in his home state. "We were a small town," he later related, "so most of the colleges just didn't know

Pete Incavigilia spent only two seasons as an Astro, in which he hit 11 of his 206 career home runs. A prototypical all-or-nothing slugger, Incaviglia struck out 1,277 times in 4,233 career at-bats. (National Baseball Hall of Fame, Cooperstown, New York).

much about me or our team. The only in-state offer I got was to play option quarterback for [the University of] California and Coach Joe Kapp."[2] Fortunately for Pete, one out-of-state school had heard of Incaviglia, and it made him an offer.

One day, as Incaviglia took his swings during high-school batting practice, a former member of the Oklahoma State University Cowboys baseball team, who was playing minor-league ball in the area, saw him and was duly impressed. OSU offered Incaviglia a scholarship, so he packed his bags and headed for Stillwater, Oklahoma. What happened over the next three years was nothing short of sensational, and it earned Incaviglia a first-round ticket to the major leagues.

In 1999, the year after his final major-league season, Incaviglia was enshrined in the OSU Athletics Hall of Honor. His biography on the Hall's website is a testimony to the greatness of the slugger's college career: "Pete Incaviglia," it reads, "is the most recognized power hitter in Oklahoma State and NCAA baseball history."[3] Indeed, consider these accomplishments:

- In the most impressive season in NCAA history, as a junior in 1985, Incaviglia set season records for home runs (48), RBIs (143), total bases (285), and slugging percentage (1.140).
- He set the NCAA career record for home runs (100) and slugging percentage (.915) and as of 2016 held the Big Eight career records for RBIs (324) and total bases (635).
- Incaviglia was named first-team All-America in 1984 and 1985 by the American Baseball Coaches Association, *The Sporting News*, and *Baseball America*

It took eight picks before Incaviglia, who many teams felt had no natural defensive position, was selected in the June 1985 amateur draft; he was chosen by the Montreal Expos. Incaviglia had no desire to play in Montreal, refused to play for the Expos, and was traded to the Texas Rangers in November. "I really didn't have any negative feelings toward Montreal," Incaviglia explained. "I just really didn't want to play in Canada. I'm tickled to death to be playing baseball close to where I played college ball. I'm glad to be in the Southwest, because I wanted to play in warm weather."[4] By the following spring, without any minor-league seasoning, Incaviglia was the Rangers' starting left fielder; however, the relationship soon soured.

Over the next five years, Incaviglia slugged 124 home runs for the Rangers. Yet he also struck out 788 times, twice leading the league. Moreover, he proved to be "less than a one-dimensional player … a home-run threat [who didn't hit for average] … who struck out," but "was [also] a liability in the outfield [and didn't] run well."[5] For two years the Rangers tried to trade him but found no takers. Finally, feeling Incaviglia wasn't worth his $1.675 million salary,

Texas released him during spring training in 1991. In April Incaviglia signed with the Detroit Tigers, but that season he spent two months on the disabled list, batted just .214, and hit only 11 home runs in 97 games. Additionally, by the fall, his weight ballooned to 250 pounds. In October, the Tigers allowed Incaviglia to become a free agent.

Enter the Astros. Needing an outfielder, Houston took a flyer on Incaviglia, signing the "relatively cheap"[6] veteran in January 1992 to an incentive-laden $1.1 million contract. Incaviglia was thankful for a shot to redeem himself and salvage his career.

Now, with the score 3-3 and two men on, Incaviglia, who had entered the game with just two home runs and had struck out in his first at-bat this day, blasted Dave Righetti's offering for a three-run homer, making it 6-3 in favor of the Astros. After the Giants failed to score in the fourth against reliever and eventual winner Rob Murphy, Houston added three more in its half of that inning on a two-run triple by Steve Finley and a sacrifice fly by Caminiti.

Dave Burba, who had relieved Righetti with one out in the fourth inning, issued a leadoff walk to Eric Anthony in the fifth, bringing up Incaviglia, who drove Burba's offering deep over the wall in left field, his second homer of the game as well as fourth and fifth RBIs, giving the Astros an 11-3 lead.

After Jones's departure in the third inning, the Astros bullpen shut down the Giants over the next three innings. So in the Houston sixth, with two outs and a runner at third, Incaviglia came up again with the score still 11-3. This time he struck out.

In the eighth, with the score 12-3, the Astros came up for what would be their final at-bats. With one out, Houston produced a single by Benny Distefano and a double by Anthony. Again, Incaviglia strode to the plate. With Burba still on the mound, Incaviglia lined the ball deep to center, it dropped for a hit, and both runners scored as Incaviglia stopped at second with a double. Two batters later, a single by Rafael Ramirez scored Incaviglia, who trotted home with the Astros 15th run. In the top of the ninth, the Giants scored four runs, highlighted by Kevin Bass's three-run homer, to make the final score 15-7.

In the slugfest, Incaviglia had amassed 10 total bases and had driven home seven runs to tie an Astros record. It was the eighth time in his career that the slugger had hit two home runs in one game.

NOTES

1   ncaa.com/news/baseball/article/2012-04-20/incaviglia-sets-single-season-standard.

2   Ibid.

3   okstate.com/sports/2015/3/17/GEN_2014010114.aspx.

4   *The Sporting News*, November 18, 1985: 49.

5   *The Sporting News*, April 15, 1991: 18.

6   *The Sporting News*, February 3, 1992: 30.

Darryl Kile Tosses No-Hitter

September 8, 1993: Houston Astros 7, New York Mets 1, at the Astrodome

By Chip Greene

IN 1992 THE HOUSTON ASTROS finished fourth in the National League Western Division, with an 81-81 record. Determined to upgrade its starting pitching, the team made two major free-agent signings within a three-day span in December. First, on December 1, the Astros landed a former Cy Young award winner, right-hander Doug Drabek, for $4.25 million; then, on the 4th, for $3.75 million, left-hander Greg Swindell, who had won 72 games in his seven major-league seasons. Right away, the two were penciled in atop the Astros' starting rotation.

Joining the two newcomers as the third and fourth starters in the rotation were two holdovers, right-handers Mark Portugal, entering his fifth season with Houston, and Pete Harnisch, a 1991 All-Star who had contributed 21 wins in his two seasons with the Astros.

As for his fifth starter, Houston manager Art Howe anticipated a battle in the spring between two young right-handers, Brian Williams, a former first-round draft pick; and 24-year-old Darryl Kile who, in 44 starts over the past two seasons, had won just 12 of 34 decisions, yet had shown flashes of brilliance. The Astros liked the potential of their starting rotation.

In baseball, as in life, the best-laid plans often go awry, particularly when free agency is concerned. Certainly no one involved with shelling out $8 million for two top-of-the-line starters could have imagined that they would in 1993 produce a combined record of 21-31, and that the other three journeymen starters would pick up the slack in dramatic fashion, by combining for an impressive record of 49-21, to help lead the Astros to an 85-77, third-place season. Such, though, is why they play the games.

Rarely in baseball history has a team reaped the performances that the Astros' third, fourth, and fifth starters produced in 1993. Portugal, who finished 18-4, and Harnisch, 16-9, each with sub-3.00 ERAs, fashioned what became the finest seasons of his career. But it was Kile (15-8, 3.51), a future 20-game winner, who that season enjoyed the trio's finest hour. It would have been hard to see it coming, as during the spring he wasn't even assured a spot in the starting rotation. Yet that season, Kile had perhaps a little extra motivation.

Throughout the year, Kile pitched with a heavy heart. His sorrow began on the first day of spring training. As camp got under way and he prepared to battle Brian Williams for a rotation spot, he learned that his father, David, had developed a blood clot in the brain. Kile left camp to be with his father. Then, on February 24 David Kile died of a heart attack.[1]

During his time away from the team, Kile played catch with his brother. When he returned to camp a week later, however, Kile understandably pitched poorly, and his chances to claim the fifth starter's spot seemed precarious. Psychologically, though, Kile maintained a strong frame of mind.

"I got to say goodbye to him," Kile reasoned during a training-camp interview. "That was the important thing. Now, I have to go back to work and try to win a job. I worked hard all winter, and it's time to make it pay off."[2]

Yet his father would never be far from his thoughts. "I don't think I'll ever get over it," Kile said, "because my father was my best friend. But in order to be a man, you've got to separate your personal life from your work life."[3]

After several shaky outings, Kile improved; during one spring performance, he threw five shutout innings and struck out nine. "It was the best I've ever seen him throw," manager Howe raved. "He didn't throw one pitch above the belt. I wish he could bottle the way he threw today."[4]

As training camp ended, Kile won a spot in the rotation. But with the Astros' limited need for a fifth starter over the first month, he began the year in the bullpen. Through his first 11 appearances, Kile made five starts and won four games (one in relief). Then, from the first of week of June through the remainder of the season, he pitched exclusively as a starter. He was on top of his game.

Although the Astros stood 20-13 by mid-June in games started by the bottom third of the rotation, their record in starts made by Drabek and Swindell was just 12-15. Told of the comparison and asked specifically about Kile's performance, Howe said, "That's interesting because you know the big guys are going to start winning some more games. Darryl's pitched very well in what probably is the toughest role [fifth starter] for a pitcher. He's got good stuff, period. When he throws strikes, he can be very tough."[5]

As the season progressed, Kile kept getting tougher, never more so than on the evening of July 3 at home versus the Cardinals. That night, as he ran his season's record to 9-1, Kile not only tossed his first major-league shutout, but he also hit his first career home run. By game's end, his consecutive scoreless innings streak had reached 23⅔ innings and his ERA dropped to 1.99. Kile endured a few bumpy starts after that but by early September his ledger stood at 14-6 with a 3.33 ERA. The stage was set for Wednesday night, September 8, at the Astrodome against the New York Mets.

Playing out the string toward an eventual 103-loss season, the Mets were an abysmal team. The previous night, in the second of this three-game series in Houston, New York had dropped its fifth consecutive game. This night, opposing Kile, the Mets sent to the mound 39-year-old left-hander Frank Tanana, whose record stood at 6-14 in what would be the final season of a 21-year career. The game proved to be no contest. In the second inning, the Astros' Ken Caminiti blasted his 12th home run of the season to

Darryl Kile pitched the Astros' sixth no-hitter in the Astrodome – and ninth in franchise history – against the New York Mets on September 8, 1993. In 1997 he posted a 19-7 record with a 2.57 ERA. (Courtesy of Houston Astros Baseball Club).

put Houston on the board, 1-0; in the third inning, the Astros got two more runs on three hits off Tanana, including two doubles; in the fifth inning, Tanana's last, Houston's Andujar Cedeño connected for his seventh home run; and in the bottom of the eighth, the Astros capped their scoring when two errors by the Mets led to three unearned runs. In all, Houston scored seven runs in the game.

While his teammates generated plenty of offense, Kile mowed down the Mets, with the exception of one bizarre play. After he retired the first 10 Mets batters in order, Kile walked Jeff McKnight in the fourth inning. He retired Eddie Murray for the second out. On a pitch to the next batter, Joe Orsulak, the ball got away from catcher Scott Servais, and McKnight took off from first base. Servais, thinking the pitch had hit Orsulak, failed to chase the ball, so first baseman Jeff Bagwell charged, grabbed the ball, and attempted to throw out McKnight at third. Bagwell's throw sailed wide and McKnight, who never stopped running, scored. Kile was charged with a wild pitch and Bagwell's error made the run unearned.

That was it for the Mets. In each of the final five innings Kile retired New York in order, with the help of two outstanding defensive plays in the seventh by third baseman Caminiti and shortstop Cedeno. As Kile took the mound in the top of the ninth, the crowd of 15,684 stood as he retired Todd Hundley on a grounder, struck out pinch-hitter Tito Navarro, and then, with a 1-and-2 count, got pinch-hitter Chico Walker to swing and miss on a breaking ball. With his strikeout of Walker, his ninth of the game, Kile pumped his right fist and was mobbed on the mound by his teammates amid an embrace from Servais. Kile had thrown the ninth no-hitter in the Astros' history.

Afterward in the locker room, his hair matted from a postgame dousing, Kile reflected on his accomplishment. "The only thing I can think of that would be more exciting would be to win the seventh game of the World Series," he said. "I thought I'd be nervous in the ninth but I just wanted to make certain I kept doing the things that got me that far."[6]

There was, too, from reporters the obligatory question about Kile's father.

"It's something I wish he could have been here to see and be a part of, and who knows, maybe he did."[7]

Of that, there could be no doubt.

NOTES

1   Darryl Kile himself died at the age of 33 of a heart attack, caused by 90 percent blockage of two coronary arteries, on June 22, 2002, while pitching for the St. Louis Cardinals.

2   *The Sporting News*, March 8, 1993.

3   *The Sporting News*, March 29, 1993.

4   *The Sporting News*, March 8, 1993.

5   *The Sporting News*, June 21, 1993.

6   Associated Press, *Sandusky* (Ohio) *Register*, September 9, 1993.

7   Ibid.

Harnisch's Loses No-Hitter on Controversial Call, Settles for One-Hitter

September 17, 1993: Houston Astros 3, San Diego Padres 0, at the Astrodome

By Alan Cohen

"It was a tough play I needed to make, and I didn't make it" —Pete Harnisch[1]

SOMEWHERE AROUND THE FIFTH inning of a potential no-hitter, the whispers begin in the stands. Nobody uses the dreaded "no-hitter" term for fear of jinxing the pitcher. All anyone might say is that things are starting to get interesting. People aren't as quick to leave their seats for the refreshment stands in case they miss something.

On September 17, 1993, the San Diego Padres visited the Astrodome to play the opening game of their series with the homestanding Astros. Twenty-six-year-old Pete Harnisch (14-8, 3.23 ERA, including three shutouts) toed the rubber for Houston and was opposed by Andy Benes (15-12, 3.57 ERA). San Diego's none-too-potent offense was even further diminished as star hitter Tony Gwynn was on the shelf for the season. He had suffered a knee injury against Atlanta on September 5, and went to the disabled list with a .358 batting average, which placed him second in the league for the season.

The Astrodome was known as a pitchers' park and this Houston team boasted some outstanding arms. During the previous homestand, Darryl Kile had thrown a no-hitter, the ninth in franchise history, against the Mets on September 8. Over the course of the season, each starter in the Astros' rotation had recorded at least one shutout.

Each pitcher was on his game and the scoreboard had nothing but zeros through five innings. By that point Benes had yielded two hits while Harnisch had yielded none, with only two runners having reached base against him. He had walked Dave Staton in the second inning and had hit Phil Plantier with a pitch in the fourth. In the field, only two defensive plays were the least bit out of the ordinary. Second baseman Craig Biggio neatly pocketed a groundball by Jarvis Brown to end the third inning, and one inning later shortstop Andujar Cedeno moved swiftly to his left to grab Ricky Gutierrez's groundball, after it had been deflected by Harnisch, and nail him at first with an off-balance throw.

In the top half of the sixth inning, Benes led off for San Diego and struck out swinging. The next batter was the speedy leadoff hitter Jarvis Brown, who had flied out and grounded out his first two at-bats. He laid down a bunt that rolled slowly and came to a stop midway between the mound and home plate. In fielding the bunt, Harnisch lost his footing and his low, wide throw skipped under the glove of first baseman Chris Donnels. Donnels said, "I saw the throw go behind [Brown] and I tried [unsuccessfully] to reach through him and pick it up."[2] Official scorer John Wilson, after deliberating for 30 seemingly endless seconds and viewing the videotape, ruled it a hit, much to the dismay of the 29,595 amateur scorekeepers in the stands.

Wilson felt it was a pretty cut-and-dried decision. "He had to pick it up with his bare hand and throw off-balance. It's a play that's called a hit 99 percent or more of the time in normal circumstances."[3] After the game, Wilson said, "I'm giving no consideration to changing the call. All scorers hope that the first

Astros right-hander Pete Harnisch was 16-9 with a 2.98 ERA in 1993. That year, on September 17, he lost a no-hitter on a controversial call and settled for a one-hit, 3-0 shutout against San Diego. (Courtesy of Houston Astros Baseball Club).

hit is a clean one. But in the world we live in, that's not the way it is."[4]

Brown added, "I didn't think they'd give me a hit. But I thought it was. I just laid it down. I didn't bunt it as far as I wanted to, but in a place where the pitcher and catcher had to go for it."[5]

Benes pitched a 1-2-3 bottom of the sixth inning. When Harnisch matched him in the top of the seventh there was a growing tide of grumbling that Wilson had erred in awarding Brown a hit in the prior inning. The angriest of the grumbles came from Astros pitcher Mark Portugal who groused, "Our official scorer needs to take a tour of major-league stadiums and see how it's done."[6]

Benes returned to the mound for the seventh inning and things got really messy really quickly.

Singles by Steve Finley and Luis Gonzalez set the table for Ken Caminiti, and the Astros third baseman doubled to drive in the first run of the game. With runners on second and third, Benes gave an intentional pass to Kevin Bass, loading the bases. They weren't loaded for long. A two-run double by Donnels plated two runs and made the score 3-0. Benes was finished. Mark Davis entered the game for the Padres and there was no further scoring. The last outs of the inning came when Harnisch hit into a double play, but he would not need any more runs anyway.

Harnisch kept rolling along, retiring the side in order in each of the last two innings to record his fifth consecutive win and improve his season's record to 15-8. He made fast work of the Padres, needing only 107 pitches, 67 of which were strikes, and the fans were sent into the night air after only 2 hours and 6 minutes in the air-conditioned dome. The whitewash lowered Harnisch's ERA to 3.09, and it was his fourth and final shutout of the season, enough to lead the National League. His final 2.98 ERA was sixth-best in the league. He became the third Astros pitcher to reach the 15-win plateau in 1993—Mark Portugal (15-4) and Darryl Kile (15-6) were the others—the first time in the 32-year history of the Houston franchise that had happened.[7] Harnisch finished with a 16-9 record.

Houston manager Art Howe summed it up. "It was all Harnisch tonight."[8] Harnisch, for his part, felt strong all night. "My fastball was maybe as good as it has been—not velocity-wise, but I spotted it really well." His catcher, Eddie Taubensee, concurred. "He was remarkable. He pitched inside tremendously."[9]

It was Harnisch's second one-hitter of the season, and the 21st in the history of the Houston franchise. He had hurled a 4-0, one-hit shutout against the Cubs on July 10 at Chicago. Harnisch would never get that elusive no-hitter. The closest he would come after that Friday night in Houston was six seasons later, on August 19, 1999. He was with Cincinnati then and took a no-hitter into the seventh inning against the Pirates, only to have it broken up by Pittsburgh's Mike Benjamin. It was the only hit he allowed before leaving the game after eight innings. As with the game in Houston, runs were tough to come by. It wasn't until the bottom of the eighth inning that the Reds got their only run of the game, via a Sean Casey homer. Reds reliever Scott Williamson made the run stand up and Harnisch was credited with the 1-0 win. That was also the last season in which he reached double-digits in wins, tying the career high of 16 that he had established in 1993.

Despite Harnisch's victory the Astros were in third place, 17½ games out of the division lead. It wasn't a bad team, but they had the misfortune of being in the same division as Atlanta and San Francisco, two teams that would win more than 100 games that season. The Astros' third-place finish spelled the end of Howe's five years as manager of the Astros.

The Padres were a much worse picture of futility. It was the second time they had been victimized by a one-hitter in two weeks. Three Braves pitchers had held them to one hit, which came with two outs in the eighth inning, in a 1-0, 10-inning Atlanta win on September 9. San Diego switched general managers in June, and no fewer than 46 players were on the roster at one time or another. After the loss on September 17, they were in last place in the seven-team NL West, 38 games out of first place. A greater embarrassment was that they trailed the expansion Colorado Rockies in the standings. They finished the season 61-101, six games behind the Rockies.

Tony Gwynn returned the next season and reeled off the first of four consecutive batting championships. He helped lead Padres from the ashes as they won division titles in 1996 and 1998.

Pete Harnisch remained in the majors through 2001 and posted a career record of 111-103, but there were few experiences that came close to matching that evening in 1993.

SOURCES

In addition to the sources included in the end notes, the author used Baseball-Reference.com.

NOTES

1 Alan Truex, "Bunt Hit Denies Harnisch: Scorer's Ruling of 'No Error' Costs Astros' Right Hander," *Houston Chronicle*, September 18, 1993: S1.

2 Chris Haft, "Harnisch Halts S.D. on 1-hitter," *Houston Post*, September 18, 1993: C-13.

3 Truex.

4 Truex.

5 Jody Goldstein, "Brown's Bunting for Single Just What the Lead Hitter Does," *Houston Chronicle*, September 18, 1993: S5.

6 Haft.

7 Truex.

8 Haft.

9 Ibid.

Jeff Bagwell Homers Three Times, Twice in One Inning

June 24, 1994: Houston Astros 16, Los Angeles Dodgers 4, at the Astrodome

By Frederick C. Bush

THE 1994 MAJOR-LEAGUE BASEBALL season remains infamous for the players' strike that began on August 12 and resulted in the cancellation of the remainder of the regular season and the postseason. At the time of the strike, Matt Williams of the San Francisco Giants was on a pace to match Roger Maris' single-season home run record of 61; Tony Gwynn of the San Diego Padres was hitting .394 and had a chance to become the first player to bat .400 for a full season since Ted Williams in 1941; and the Montreal Expos, who had made the playoffs only once in their 35-year history—ironically in the strike-shortened 1981 season—had the best record in baseball at 74-40. The Houston Astros, who had won their last National League West title in 1986, were another team that lost an opportunity to try to end a playoff drought. Their 66-49 record had them only a half-game behind the Cincinnati Reds in the new NL Central Division at the time the strike began.

The Astros' offensive leader in 1994 was first baseman Jeff Bagwell, who, in spite of winning the 1991 NL Rookie of the Year Award and posting three solid seasons to begin his career, was still largely unknown outside of Houston. Bagwell was among the NL leaders in several offensive categories that season, which led Astros left fielder Luis Gonzalez to assert, "We consider him a superstar. He should get more notoriety, with the numbers he's putting up day after day."[1] On June 24, 1994, Bagwell had a game that catapulted him into the nation's consciousness as he hit three home runs—including two in one inning—in a 16-4 rout of the Los Angeles Dodgers.

The Astros sent right-hander Shane Reynolds to the mound that day to oppose former 20-game winner Ramon Martinez, the brother of future Hall-of-Famer Pedro Martinez. Both pitchers were unsteady in the first two innings, with Reynolds balking once and hitting a batter and Martinez uncorking a wild pitch, but nothing hinted at the Astros' offensive explosion to come.

Ken Caminiti led off the bottom of the second inning with a double, advanced to third on Luis Gonzalez's groundout, and scored when Martinez unleashed a wild pitch with Andujar Cedeno at the plate. The Astros added to their lead in the third when James Mouton tapped a bunt single and Craig Biggio followed with a double to send him home. Bagwell then recorded his first RBI of the game with a single that scored Biggio for a 3-0 Astros lead, after which Martinez settled in for a time and set the Astros down in order in the fourth and fifth innings.

Reynolds allowed the Dodgers' first run in the top of the sixth and was relieved with two outs and two runners on by Dave Veres, who retired Raul Mondesi for the final out of the inning. In the bottom of the frame, the Astros went to work on Martinez and the Dodgers bullpen. First, Bagwell hit a one-out solo home run to increase the lead to 4-1. After Caminiti walked and scored on singles by Gonzalez and Cedeno, Martinez was replaced by Roger McDowell, who fared no better. Mike Felder greeted him with a single that scored Gonzalez, and then he and Cedeno moved up when McDowell threw a wild pitch. Scott Servais reached first on a squeeze bunt that scored Cedeno, advanced to second on Veres' sacrifice, and he and Felder scored on Mouton's single that put a quick end to McDowell's mound stint.

When Rudy Seanez, the Dodgers' third pitcher of the inning, entered the game, the Astros were leading 9-1. Seanez ended up being a relief pitcher in name only as he surrendered a single to Biggio and completed a Dodger-pitchers trifecta with a wild pitch that allowed Mouton and Biggio to advance a base. The wild pitch became irrelevant when Bagwell worked a 3-and-2 count and sent the sixth pitch he saw over the right-field fence for his second homer of the inning. Seanez struck out Caminiti to end the inning, but the damage was done as the Dodgers now trailed the Astros, 12-1.

Bagwell had tied a major-league record by hitting two home runs in one inning and was only the 28th player to accomplish the feat. He joined Lee May as the second Astros hitter to homer twice in an inning; May had done so 20 years earlier, on April 29, 1974. Bagwell was not yet finished, though, and before this game was over he would tie another Astros single-game home-run record.

In the top of the seventh inning, Veres walked two of the first three Dodgers batters he faced and allowed an RBI single to Delino DeShields that made the score 12-2. The Astros got that run back in the bottom of the frame when Felder hit a two-out triple off the latest Dodgers reliever, Brian Barnes, and scored on Servais' single. The closest the Dodgers would get to the Astros came in the top of the eighth when Chris Gwynn and Mondesi hit back-to-back solo homers off Veres. The big lead allowed Astros manager Terry Collins to let Veres finish the inning without concern and, at the end of the eighth, the Astros still held a 13-4 lead.

Los Angeles scored no more runs, but the Astros were about to pummel the Dodgers' pitching staff some more. After Barnes retired Biggio to begin the bottom of the eighth, Bagwell hit his third homer of the game to join Jimmy Wynn, Lee May, and Glenn Davis as the only Astros to do so. Barnes came unraveled as Caminiti walked, Gonzalez singled, and Cedeno doubled them both in for a 16-4 lead that was the final score. Though Barnes allowed no ad-

ditional runs, he did become the fourth Dodgers pitcher to unleash a wild pitch, and he walked pinch-hitter Andy Stankiewicz before Omar Daal relieved him and ended the inning on a fly ball by Mouton.

Once Tom Edens had set the Dodgers down in order in the ninth to seal the victory, the focus turned to Bagwell's performance. The Astros had pounded out 17 hits to score a season-high 16 runs, and Bagwell had been at the forefront of the attack. This scenario was nothing new. Bagwell "has been carrying us the whole year," Gonzalez said. "We've got a good offensive club, and he's our horse."[2] After his four-hit, six-RBI game, Bagwell led the NL in four offensive categories: RBIs (74), extra-base hits (44), slugging percentage (.713), and total bases (185). He was second in batting average (.357) and home runs (23).

Bagwell's teammates were frustrated that, in spite of his stellar numbers, he was still only fifth in the voting for the NL's All-Star Game starter at first base. "If you put up All-Star numbers, you should be a starter on the All-Star team," Caminiti argued, and he lamented that most fans and media members still asked, "Jeff who?"[3]

Bagwell did not share his teammates' concern about his recognition, or lack thereof. "It's not what the media says about you that's important. It's what your peers say."[4] His attitude about his All-Star status was the same: "It's not about what a player does; it's how a team does. We haven't won anything yet. We need to do that first. Then, the votes will come."[5] Bagwell's teammates need not have worried about his receiving his due. NL All-Star manager Jim Fregosi selected him as a reserve first baseman, which showed what Bagwell's peers thought about him.

Bagwell's season ended when he suffered a broken wrist after being hit by a pitch from the San Diego Padres' Andy Benes on August 10, just two days before the players' strike began. He finished the season with a .368 batting average, 39 home runs, and an NL-leading 116 RBIs and 104 runs scored, and he won the Gold Glove Award for his work at first base. The national media had noticed Bagwell, too, and he became the first Astros player to receive the NL Most Valuable Player Award. In the lost season of 1994, the award was Bagwell's and the Astros' gain; had it not been for the strike, he would have missed the remainder of the season and would have been far less likely to have won the MVP award.

SOURCES

In addition to the sources cited in the Notes, the author also consulted the following:

Astrosdaily.com.

Houston.astros.mlb.com.

New York Times.

NOTES

1   Alan Truex, "Bagwell Nails Dodgers With HR hammer," *Houston Chronicle*, June 25, 1994.

2   Ibid.

3   Jayne Custred, "Bagwell Anonymous to All-Star Voters," *Houston Chronicle*, June 26, 1994.

4   Truex.

5   Custred.

Astros Erase 11-Run Deficit in Biggest Comeback in Astrodome History

July 18, 1994: Houston Astros 15, St. Louis Cardinals 12, at the Astrodome

By Bob LeMoine

THE 1994 SEASON HAD NOT BEEN A piece of cake for St. Louis Cardinals manager Joe Torre, and as he took a bite of his birthday cake on July 18, he felt much older than his birth certificate indicated. "I'm 94," Torre joked. "Before the weekend, I was 53." It had been a grueling weekend in Colorado for Torre and the Cardinals as the Rockies trounced them in a four-game sweep, outscoring the Cards 43-17 and outhitting them 53-33. St. Louis was now 42-46, 10½ games behind division-leading Cincinnati in the National League Central. Perhaps Torre was glancing at some frosting when he remarked, "But right now, it's a matter of confidence. We need a pitcher to get us back on track."[1] Torre probably felt even older by the end of this night.

The Cardinals were in Houston to begin a three-game series against the Astros, who stood at 52-40 and were only 2½ games behind Cincinnati. They were sending to the mound Brian Williams, whose record stood at 5-5 with a 5.55 ERA. He was opposed by the Cardinals' Allen Watson, who was 6-4 with a 5.10 ERA. The crowd of 24,012 at the Astrodome had no idea they were about to witness one of the most remarkable comebacks in baseball history.

Bernard Gilkey led off the first for the Cardinals, was hit by a pitch, and moved to second base on a wild pitch. Ozzie Smith reached on an infield single, and a passed ball put runners at second and third. Gilkey scored on a single by Gregg Jefferies single, and Smith scored when Craig Biggio made an error on a grounder hit by Ray Lankford. With two out, Mark Whiten doubled to score Lankford, and the Cardinals led 3-0 after one inning. In the second inning, Tom Pagnozzi doubled to left and scored on Gilkey's single. Then Jefferies homered to deep right field, driving Williams from the mound to a chorus of boos as the Cardinals built a 6-0 lead.[2] Astros manager Terry Collins brought in Tom Edens to relieve Williams, but he fared just as poorly. Lankford singled, stole second, and scored on a double by Todd Zeile to give the Cardinals a 7-0 lead after two innings.

The Cardinals' Geronimo Pena led off the third inning with a double and scored as pitcher Watson, a good hitter, tripled to left field. A single by Gilkey scored Watson. Ozzie Smith singled and scored along with Gilkey on Lankford's single. The score at the end of three innings was St. Louis 11, Houston 0.

The Astros started to get to Watson in the bottom of the fourth. Luis Gonzalez doubled and scored on Tony Eusebio's single. Andujar Cedeño doubled Eusebio to third and he scored on Mike Felder's infield hit to cut the deficit to 11-2. Mike Hampton, a 21-year-old rookie working exclusively out of the bullpen, pitched a 1-2-3 inning in the fifth, and the Astros again chipped away at the Cardinals' lead in the bottom of the inning. Jeff Bagwell led off with a home run. James Mouton singled scored on another double by Cedeno, to deep left-center. Houston had cut the St. Louis lead to 11-4. Hampton again held the fort and pitched his second 1-2-3 inning in the top of the sixth.

The historical timing of this game was appropriate as two days later NASA commemorated the 25th anniversary of the Apollo 11 moon landing. The Astros decided to celebrate early by going into their own orbit and scoring 11 runs on seven hits in the bottom of the sixth.

Kevin Bass, a fan favorite during two stops in Houston that totaled 10 seasons, had his finest year in 1986 when he batted .311 in 157 games for the Astros' NL West Division championship squad. (Courtesy of Houston Astros Baseball Club).

Craig Biggio led off with a walk and scored on pinch-hitter Kevin Bass's double to left. Torre replaced Watson on the mound with Frank Cimorelli. The rookie, in what would be his final major-league appearance, retired Bagwell but walked Ken Caminiti. Gonzalez singled to score Bass and make the score 11-6. Cimorelli hit Mouton with a pitch to load the bases and Eusebio walked, scoring Caminiti. Torre made another pitching change, bringing in Bryan Eversgerd, who gave up a single to center by Cedeño that scored Gonzalez and Mouton as Eusebio advanced to third on an error by center fielder Lankford. After trailing 11-0, the Astros suddenly had the tying run on base. "As we kept getting closer we started smelling it," Bass said, "After we made it 11-7, we felt pretty good because we had three innings left and

were within a grand slam. It just snowballed from there."[3]

Mike Felder followed Cedeño with a triple to center, tying the game, 11-11. Felder said he was so excited by the hit that "I almost fell at first base."[4] Standing on third, Felder waved his arms in celebration, and the crowd followed suit with a deafening roar.[5] Felder had entered the game in the third inning, pinch-hitting for the pitcher Edens, and had remained in the game to play center field in place of Steve Finley. "I didn't anticipate getting five at-bats," he said after the game. "I pinch-hit for the pitcher in that situation, and I thought I was going to have a short night. But it turned out to be a full night and a productive one. The best thing that came out of it was that it helped us win a game tonight."[6]

The Astros' sixth inning wasn't done. Biggio reached on an infield single to third, but Felder had to hold at third. Bass then singled to right, scoring Felder and giving the Astros the lead, 12-11. "I think that's the first time in my career that I've had two hits in one inning," Bass said. "That was a tremendous comeback. ... That just shows that anything can happen in this game."[7] Torre, his birthday cake now a distant memory, made his third pitching change in the inning, bringing in Steve Dixon—also making what would be his final big-league appearance. After Biggio stole third and Bagwell walked to load the bases, Caminiti singled to left, scoring Biggio and Bass and extending the Astros' lead to 14-11. A walk to Gonzalez loaded the bases again, and Mouton's sacrifice fly scored Bagwell. Finally, after 11 consecutive Astros batters had reached base, the Cardinals had at last recorded the second out. Eusebio grounded to third to end the inning, but the Astros were now in command, 15-11.

After pitching scoreless seventh and eighth innings, Todd Jones began his third inning of relief in the ninth. With two outs, Tom Pagnozzi singled home Mark Whiten to make the score 15-12, but pinch-hitter Gerald Perry struck out to end the game and cap off the greatest comeback in Astros history. The 11-run rally tied the National League record set by two clubs. The Cardinals rallied from a 11-0 deficit to win 14-12 on June 15, 1952, and Philadelphia Phillies overcame a 12-1 deficit to win 18-16 on April 17, 1976.

"Easily the Cardinals reached the nadir of what is fast becoming a ghastly season," wrote Rick Hummel in the *St. Louis Post-Dispatch*.[8] Torre took much of the blame for the loss. "I just pitched the wrong pitchers," he said. "It was my fault we lost."[9]

Torre remembered the game years later in his book *Chasing the Dream*. "July 18 has become a dreaded date for me. I can hardly remember ever getting a hit as a player or a win as a manager. ... The game in Houston was a catastrophe. ... On top of that, I got up in the middle of the night to go to the bathroom and broke my toe on the end of the bed."[10]

Terry Collins had a much different memory. "That was unbelievable. I've never been behind 11-0 and come back to win, not even in the Pacific Coast League where the ball flies around and you get crazy scores," he said. "We were down 11-0 and our guys didn't stop playing. They just kept pecking away and kept getting base hits. I can't believe what I saw."[11]

NOTES

1 Rick Hummel, "Cardinals' Rocky Mountain Low Closed the Curtain at Mile High," *St. Louis Post-Dispatch*, July 19, 1994: 5C.

2 Jim Moloney, "Down 11, Astros Triumph," *Houston Post*, July 19, 1994. Accessed May 18, 2015 astrosdaily.com/history/19940718/.

3 Ibid.

4 "Down 11-0? No Problem, Stros Houston's Amazing," *Austin (Texas) American-Statesman*, July 19, 1994.

5 Alan Truex, "Astros Rally One for the Books," *Houston Chronicle*, July 19, 1994: 1.

6 W.H. Stickney Jr., "Felder Caps Night to Remember," *Houston Chronicle*, July 19, 1994.

7 Ibid.

8 Rick Hummel, "New Low: Cards Blow 11-0 Lead; Astros' 15-12 Comeback Ties Mark," *St. Louis Post-Dispatch*, July 19, 1994: 1C.

9 Associated Press, "Astros Rally From 11-0 Hole," *Lexington (North Carolina) Dispatch*, July 19, 1994: 1B.

10 Joe Torre and Tom Verducci, *Chasing the Dream: My Lifelong Journey to the World Series: an Autobiography* (New York: Bantam, 1997), 163.

11 "Astros Rally From 11-0 Hole."

Larry Dierker Wins Managerial Debut

April 1, 1997: Houston Astros 2, Atlanta Braves 1, at the Astrodome

By Frederick C. Bush

AFTER THE HOUSTON ASTROS FIN-
ished in second place in the NL Central Division
for a third consecutive season in 1996, they hired
Larry Dierker, the former Astros pitcher-turned-
broadcaster, to replace hyper-intense Terry Collins
as their new manager. Dierker's hire was met with
laughter and derision throughout the media and
by a number of baseball insiders, since he had
never managed or coached at any level. However,
the Astros' brain trust—owner Drayton McLane,
president Tal Smith, and general manager Gerry
Hunsicker—believed that the insights Dierker had
provided as the team's radio commentator over the
past 18 years could translate into strategic success on
the field. Dierker quickly gained the support of his
players, something Collins had lost. As first baseman Jeff Bagwell put it, "Dierker's a good baseball
man, and he's going to be fine."[1]

Most outsiders doubted Bagwell's words, and
they deemed it appropriate that Dierker's managerial debut would fall on April Fools' Day. Dierker
put his situation in perspective when he asserted that
the worst thing that could happen is that "I won't
be very good at it and I'll get fired … [then] I'm
back in the (broadcast) booth somewhere or I take
my pension."[2] Dierker had made sure to surround
himself with knowledgeable coaches, most notably
former Astros manager Bill Virdon, to reduce the
likelihood of making too many rookie managerial
mistakes. Though it was uncertain how he would
fare over the course of a full season, his immediate
prospects were not helped by the fact that the Astros
were facing 1996 NL Cy Young Award winner John
Smoltz and the defending NL champion Atlanta
Braves on Opening Day, April 1, 1997.

In an attempt to make Dierker feel at ease, his
former broadcasting crew—with the exception of
the ever-professional Milo Hamilton—all donned
Hawaiian shirts for a pregame photo they took with
the new skipper. Dierker had worn Hawaiian shirts
for years because, as he said, "You never see a guy in a
Hawaiian shirt having a bad time."[3] Though he could
no longer wear his former attire-of-choice during
games, Dierker still appeared to be having a good
time as he ran down the line and slapped hands with
all of his players and coaches when his name was announced during the pregame introductions.

Once the game got under way, the 44,618 fans,
the largest Opening Day crowd in Astros history,
watched Shane Reynolds begin the season in style
by striking out the first two Braves hitters, Kenny
Lofton and Mark Lemke. He then got in a jam by
allowing a base hit to Chipper Jones and a double to
Fred McGriff, a situation that resulted in Dierker's
first managerial decision that counted. As Dierker
later recalled, "[Catcher] Brad Ausmus looked over to
see if I wanted to walk Ryan Klesko. I shook my head
no, and Shane retired him on a soft groundball."[4] It
was a case of "so far, so good" for both Dierker and
Reynolds.

The Astros jumped on Smoltz immediately with
back-to-back singles by leadoff batter Craig Biggio
and Pat Listach, and both runners advanced an extra
base when left fielder Klesko booted Listach's hit.
Bagwell came to bat and hit a sharp grounder to third
base that left Jones with no play anywhere other than
at first base. Biggio came home on the play to give
the Astros a 1-0 lead, but that was all Smoltz would
allow for the time.

Jones tied the game with a two-out, line-drive
home run to center field in the top of the third

inning. A fan threw the home-run ball back onto the field, which sparked some overzealous and ill-advised behavior. The first 30,000 people who had entered the Astrodome had received souvenir baseballs that contained printed information about Dierker's four Opening-Day starts as an Astros pitcher. Now, 50 or so fans threw their baseballs onto the field, endangering the players and resulting in a delay of several minutes as groundskeepers retrieved the balls.

After order was restored and Reynolds retired McGriff for the Braves' third out, the Astros set to work to recapture the lead in the bottom of the third inning. Ausmus led off with a single, and pitcher Reynolds put down a sacrifice bunt that advanced Ausmus to second base. After Biggio singled, Listach's sacrifice fly scored Ausmus to give the Astros a 2-1 lead that held up as the final score.

Sean Berry tried to add to the Astros' run total in the fourth when he swung for the fences and hit a hard drive to center field, but Kenny Lofton caught up to it for a long out. Later, Lofton robbed Luis Gonzalez of extra bases in the seventh inning with a spectacular catch against the wall. On that occasion, for the second time in the game, play had to be stopped after a fan threw his souvenir baseball onto the field and hit Lofton in the back with it. Lofton was okay, but the Astros' promotional department likely regretted that it had passed out the baseballs before the game rather than afterward.

In spite of the interruptions, the focus remained on the duel between Reynolds and Smoltz. Reynolds proved to be a worthy adversary for the Cy Young Award winner as he held the Braves to one run, and he ended his day by striking out two of the final three batters he faced—Jones and Klesko—in the eighth inning. Reynolds pitched so well that the only other major decision Dierker had to make was to take him out of the game after the eighth, and that was not a difficult choice since Reynolds had thrown 122 pitches.

Billy Wagner, who had earned the closer's role after an impressive rookie season in 1996, put an exclamation point on the game in the ninth inning by striking out the final two Braves batters, Jeff Blauser

and pinch-hitter Mike Mordecai. When it was over, Dierker's managerial record stood at 1-0. He kept the ball that was the last out of the game and the scorecards from both dugouts as mementos of his successful Opening Day debut.

Everyone who was associated with the Astros in any way raved about both the team and its new manager. "Nobody's talking about Bud Selig and Don Fehr," McLane declared, referring to Major League Baseball's recently signed labor pact that finally ended the strife from the 1994 players' strike. "They're excited about the Astros. People are excited about Larry Dierker, too."[5] McLane's enthusiasm was echoed by an Astros season-ticket holder who said, "Larry Dierker is one of us. ... I know he makes me feel like a kid again."[6]

More important to the Astros' prospects for the 1997 season was the fact that Dierker had elicited the same emotions from his players. Center fielder Derek Bell said, "When he went down the line shaking everyone's hand, that was awesome. That set the tone. That was just another example of how he's not just our manager, he's one of the guys."[7]

Dierker himself downplayed the significance of his first victory. Even in retrospect, after his managing days had ended, he said merely, "This made me 5-0 in openers, but I had no delusions of grandeur. We never won the pennant when I won on Opening Day as a pitcher and this win didn't assure us of anything."[8]

He also recalled that he had been surrounded by reporters after the game and seemed satisfied to note that "except for a few national correspondents who were there to cover the debut of the freak show manager, the media seemed happy, almost festive."[9] The reactions of the media, fans, and players demonstrated that Dierker had gone from joke to genius in the stroke of a single victory, a transformation that would be confirmed when the Astros finished the 1997 season as NL Central Division champions.

NOTES

1   Carlton Thompson, "Dierker Feels First-Game Jitters," *Houston Chronicle*, April 2, 1997.

2   Bob Nightengale, "Astros Respond to Laid-Back Larry," *The Sporting News*, May 5, 1997, 20.

3   Ed Fowler, "If the Hawaiian Shirt Fits, Wear It," *Houston Chronicle*, April 2, 1997.

4   Larry Dierker, *This Ain't Brain Surgery* (Lincoln: University of Nebraska Press, 2003), 64.

5   David Barron, "Giving the Team a Hand," *Houston Chronicle*, April 2, 1997.

6   Ibid.

7   Thompson.

8   Dierker, 66.

9   Ibid.

First Interleague Game in the Astrodome

June 13, 1997: Minnesota Twins 8, Houston Astros 1, at the Astrodome

By Steve West

AFTER DECADES OF ATTEMPTS TO get the American and National Leagues to play interleague games during the regular season, the idea finally came to fruition during the 1997 season, as baseball tried whatever it could to bring back fans after the 1994 strike. The initial plan was for each division to play its counterpart, so the AL East would play the NL East, and so on. The schedule in 1997 had each team playing one three-game series against each team in the other division; for the Houston Astros that meant they would get a slight advantage by playing three of those series at home and two away. On the other hand, adjusting the schedule to accommodate interleague play meant teams had a lot of two-game series to play. "I think baseball should change. But it needs some work. The two-game series aren't good," said Minnesota Twins pitcher Bob Tewksbury.[1]

For their first series, the Astros were scheduled to play at home against the Twins. Although they had played American League teams in the Astrodome before, all those had been exhibitions, so this would be the Astros' first game played for keeps against an AL team.

Even though one of the primary reasons for interleague play was the expected attendance boost, the first interleague game in the Astrodome did not fulfill the hype. While the attendance of 30,956 was the fifth largest crowd in 29 home games to that point in the season, it was about average for Friday night crowds the Astros drew all season long.

Still, the idea that interleague play would be a big draw was there. Astros president Tal Smith said, "Fans in a one-team city like Houston should have the opportunity to see star players from American League teams. If fans like it, that's what we have to do."[2] Astros infielder Bill Spiers wasn't so sure. "Maybe we'll see added fans because of it. We'll see what happens," he said.[3]

There may have been a different reason for the big crowd for this game, though. "If the Twins didn't have Chuck Knoblauch, nobody would really care," said Kenny Hand, former *Houston Post* columnist.[4] Knoblauch, the Twins second baseman and a three-time All-Star, grew up in Bellaire, a Houston suburb 15 minutes from the Astrodome. "It's a place where I saw my first major-league game and went to many, many Astro games as a kid," said Knoblauch.[5]

Like other players, Knoblauch was a little confused by interleague play. "You had to fight through telling yourself it was a real game," he said.[6] His teammate Paul Molitor agreed. "You had to keep reminding yourself that this was a real game. … You have to say, 'We're playing in Houston.' But as hard as it was to realize, you have to understand it's going to show up in the standings."[7]

Meanwhile, the Twins had to make some adjustments, coming into a National League park. With no designated hitter available, Molitor started at first base, playing in the field for just the second time all season. Pitchers had to bat, which made Brad Radke the first Twins starting pitcher to bat since 1972, the year before the DH came into effect. "I haven't hit since high school," he said.[8]

The two teams were headed in different directions in the standings. The Astros came into the game in a virtual tie with Pittsburgh for first place in the NL Central, albeit with a record of 32-33; the Twins' 28-35 record put them in fifth place in the AL Central, six games off the lead. Houston started Donne Wall, 2-2 with a 5.27 ERA in five starts, and Minnesota countered with Radke, who was 5-5 with a 4.60 ERA in 14 starts.

Leading off the game for the Twins, Knoblauch hit the first pitch for a single. That was just the start of an exciting day for Knoblauch, who was the star of the game in more ways than one. With the next batter, Rich Becker, at the plate, Knoblauch was out on a strike-him-out-throw-him-out double play. Knoblauch singled in the third, and was again caught stealing, but he also hit a two-run triple in the fourth and an RBI double in the eighth to complete a four-hit day in front of a hometown crowd.

In the top of the second Ron Coomer reached on an error and scored on a triple by Roberto Kelly, who scored himself when Pat Meares singled, giving the Twins a 2-0 lead. Jeff Bagwell hit his 20th home run of the season to cut it to 2-1 in the bottom of the third, but after Knoblauch's fourth-inning triple made it 4-1, Molitor extended the lead with a two-run homer off reliever Jose Lima in the seventh. After Knoblauch's RBI double in the eighth,

Molitor reached on an error by Spiers, bringing home Knoblauch for the final run in the 8-1 Twins victory.

The final word on the potential of interleague play went to Tal Smith. He looked at the large and early-arriving crowd as a good thing, but cautioned that "as far as the long-range picture, we've got to give it some time."[9]

NOTES

1 "Twins' Knoblauch Eager for Trip Home to Houston," *Galveston Daily News*, June 13, 1997.

2 Adam King, "Interleague Play Gets Mixed Reviews," *Brazosport* (Texas) *Facts*, June 14, 1997.

3 Ibid.

4 Ibid.

5 "Twins' Knoblauch."

6 "Cubs Still Can't Beat AL Team," *Syracuse Herald-Journal*, June 14, 1997.

7 Ibid.

8 "Twins' Knoblauch."

9 King.

Astros Clinch First National League Central Division Title

September 25, 1997: Houston Astros 9, Chicago Cubs 1, at the Astrodome

By Frederick C. Bush

AFTER PLAYING SECOND FIDDLE during each of their first three seasons in the National League Central Division, the Houston Astros clinched their first title exactly 11 years to the day after Mike Scott's no-hitter won the NL West in 1986. The Astros had blown a chance to win the division in 1996, but general manager Gerry Hunsicker believed the team had learned from its experience. "There were enough people talking about it, and I think it might have inspired the club," Hunsicker said, "Guys were saying, 'It's just not going to happen this year.'"[1] The fact that the NL Central had been derided as the "Comedy Central" all season — the Astros were the only team to finish above .500 — gave the team additional motivation to clinch the division with a victory rather than to back into the playoffs. On September 25, lefty Mike Hampton pitched a dominant four-hitter to lead the Astros to a 9-1 win over the Chicago Cubs that set up a postseason matchup against the Atlanta Braves.

The Astrodome crowd of 35,623 witnessed a pitchers' duel between Hampton and Cubs starter Geremi Gonzalez for much of the game until the Astros broke things open in the bottom of the seventh inning.

Houston struck first when Ricky Gutierrez walked to lead off the bottom of the third and scored on Craig Biggio's two-out double. The Astros increased their lead to 2-0 in the fourth when Jeff Bagwell led off with a double, advanced to third base on right fielder Sammy Sosa's throwing error, and scored on a sacrifice fly by Luis Gonzalez.

The Astros got a scare in the fifth inning when Cubs hurler Gonzalez hit Biggio with a pitch that knocked off his batting helmet. Trainer Dave Labossiere rushed to home plate to attend to the team's All-Star second baseman, who was lying motionless on the ground. Biggio later recalled, "I wasn't knocked out, but I was dazed and scared. … When I got up I knew I was OK."[2] It was Biggio's 34th hit-by-pitch of the season, which led Bagwell to declare, "I'm getting tired of seeing Bidge get hit. That was scary."[3] The Astros and their fans breathed a collective sigh of relief as a wobbly Biggio stayed in the game.

The Cubs scored their lone run in the top of the seventh inning when Jose Hernandez slugged a two-out triple and scored on Mike Hubbard's single. The run cut the Astros' lead in half, but Houston would soon put the game out of the Cubs' reach.

Gonzalez walked Bill Spiers and Gutierrez to start the Astros' half of the seventh inning, and then Brad Ausmus blasted a three-run homer that made it 5-1. Gonzalez retired Hampton, and then was replaced by Dave Stevens, who walked Biggio on five pitches. With Derek Bell at bat, Biggio stole second and third before he scored on Bell's double. After Stevens hit Bagwell with a pitch, Cubs manager Jim Riggleman replaced him with Ramon Tatis, who lasted only one batter. Tatis was relieved by Ramon Morel after he surrendered an infield single to Luis Gonzalez that loaded the bases. Morel walked Richard Hidalgo to force Bell home, and Spiers followed with a single that drove in Bagwell. Morel retired the final two Astros hitters, but the Cubs now trailed 8-1.

Hampton set the Cubs down in order in the top of the eighth before the Astros added one more run to their tally in the bottom of the inning. Biggio drew a one-out walk and scored on Bagwell's triple to make

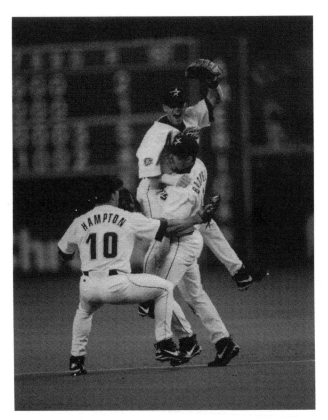

Jeff Bagwell, Craig Biggio, and Mike Hampton celebrate the final out of the Astros' 9-1 victory over the Chicago Cubs on September 25, 1997, that clinched the franchise's first NL Central Division title. (Courtesy of Houston Astros Baseball Club).

the final score 9-1. It seemed fitting that the two franchise cornerstones had put an exclamation point on the division-clinching victory. Biggio, who was headed to the playoffs for the first time in his 10-year career, could barely contain himself. He recounted that, as the Astros took the field in the top of the ninth, "I was hyperventilating, I was just so excited. I knew we had it won. I couldn't calm down."[4] After Hampton retired Sosa for the final out of the game, Biggio leaped into Bagwell's arms to start the Astros' celebration.

As fireworks went off, confetti rained down, and Kool and the Gang's song "Celebration" blared from the speakers, Astros fans overwhelmed the security guards who were supposed to maintain order and poured onto the field. The fans' celebration was peaceful, so the Astros returned from their clubhouse to join the party that was taking place on Astrodome floor. Luis Gonzalez declared, "Our fans were tre-

mendous tonight. ... It was like we had a 10th person on the field. It was a great feeling, especially late in the game when we got that lead."[5] After a three-game finale against the Pittsburgh Pirates, the Astros and their fans would be able to look back at all the team had accomplished.

Hampton's complete-game win over the Cubs gave him a 15-10 record for the season, an amazing turnaround from the 2-6 mark he had in mid-June. Manager Larry Dierker had asked Hampton to make the transition from a power pitcher into a sinkerball pitcher, and he knew that Hampton would likely experience some rough spots at first. Dierker said, "I told him he might have to take a step backward before taking two forward, but that if he did take two steps forward, he could be a number-one pitcher in the rotation. ... I was talking about being an ace-of-the-staff type pitcher."[6] While Daryl Kile paced the Astros in wins with 19, Hampton's 15 were second on the staff and both he and Kile finished among the NL's top 10 in wins, innings pitched, and complete games.

Bagwell and Biggio played in all 162 of the team's games and both posted MVP-worthy numbers. Bagwell batted .286 with 40 doubles and 43 home runs, stole 31 bases, and scored 109 runs while amassing a team-record 135 RBIs. Biggio batted .309 with 37 doubles and 22 homers, stole 47 bases, scored a team-record 146 runs and had 81 RBIs as the Astros' leadoff hitter. Colorado's Larry Walker was voted the 1997 NL MVP, as Bagwell and Biggio finished third and fourth respectively behind Walker and Los Angeles Dodgers catcher Mike Piazza.

While individual accolades would have been a nice reward, the division title was far more satisfying, especially since the iron-man performances of Bagwell and Biggio were not the team norm. Over the course of the season, several starting players had missed games with injuries, including Opening Day starter Shane Reynolds, right fielder Derek Bell, and shortstop Tim Bogar. The Astros' injuries made it appropriate that, in an odd twist of fate, their division-clinching game was featured on the hit television show *ER*, which was set in a fictional Chicago hospital. *ER* was broadcasting a live episode on September 25, and the Astros-Cubs game was shown periodically in the background. Ausmus's seventh-inning homer that blew the game open was captured in the episode, a serendipitous event that pleased the Astros catcher, who said *ER* "was his favorite series and he was taping the program to watch later, not knowing he would be on the show."[7]

The person with the right to be the most pleased, however, was Dierker. From the moment he had been lured out of the Astros' broadcast booth to become the skipper, Dierker had been subjected to everything from doubt about his managerial capabilities to outright ridicule from some corners of the baseball world. Now, 159 games into his first season, he was the manager of a division champion. Though he had sometimes been tentative in his new position, he had confirmed the Astros' faith in his abilities. "I haven't tried as hard as I will next year," he vowed. "I'll have a foundation with some success where I can be a little more insistent [with his players]."[8]

Dierker, who had a 33-year history with the Astros—a time that included, most notably, 13 sea-

sons as a pitcher and 18 as a broadcaster—savored the moment, saying, "I played on teams that didn't come close to winning a title. It means something to win, and to be wearing this uniform."[9]

NOTES

1 Alan Truex, "Bring on the Braves/Hampton, Ausmus Lead Rout as Astros Claim Central Crown," *Houston Chronicle*, September 26, 1997.

2 Mickey Herskowitz, "Special Moments From a Coronation," *Houston Chronicle*, September 26, 1997.

3 Ibid.

4 Ibid.

5 Michael Murphy, "Astros Clinch Championship With Authority," *Houston Chronicle*, September 26, 1997.

6 Neil Hohlfeld, "1997 National League Central Champions/StrongerRrotation Was Starting Point to Run at Title, *Houston Chronicle*, September 26, 1997.

7 "1997—Season Recap," astrosdaily.com/history/1997/, accessed June 27, 2015.

8 Joe Drape, "A Company Man Succeeds as Astros' Manager," *New York Times*, September 27, 1997.

9 Herskowitz.

The Big Unit Fans 16 in Third Straight Shutout in the Dome

August 28, 1998: Houston Astros 2, Pittsburgh Pirates 0, at the Astrodome

By Gregory H. Wolf

THE REIGNING NL CENTRAL CHAM-pion Houston Astros made a bold move at the July 31 trading deadline in 1998 by acquiring left-hander Randy Johnson from the Seattle Mariners in a trade the club hoped would propel them to their first World Series appearance. The trade, however, was risky. The 34-year-old, 6-foot-10 hurler with his signature mullet haircut had won the AL Cy Young Award the previous season with a 20-4 record, but had unexpectedly struggled prior to the deadline, winning just nine of 19 decisions and posting a 4.33 ERA. Furthermore, the impending free agent, whose market value probably exceeded what the Astros could pay, essentially made him a two-month rent-a-pitcher. Houston also had to part with two highly touted prospects, pitcher Freddy Garcia and infielder Carlos Guillen, both of whom eventually developed into All-Stars. Nonetheless Astros GM Gerry Hunsicker decided to go for broke and pulled the switch on one of the biggest in-season trades in franchise history.

Those concerns were probably forgotten when the Big Unit whiffed 12 Pittsburgh Pirates in seven innings to win his first start with the Astros, and then fashioned consecutive five-hit shutouts in his first two starts in the Astrodome. Johnson was a physical marvel, to say the least. "[His] arm is 38 inches long, which means that he is actually delivering the ball three feet behind a left-handed hitter's back," wrote umpire Durwood Merrill. "The amazing part is that the ball winds up on the outside of the plate, causing the left-handed hitter to lean so far forward that he's almost falling on his nose."[1]

As the Astros prepared to play the first game of a three-game set with the Pirates on August 28, second-year skipper Larry Dierker's squad was hot. Houston had won 18 of 25 games since acquiring Johnson and held a comfortable 10-game lead in the NL Central (83-51). A victory would match its win total from the previous season. Though manager Gene Lamont's Pirates harbored no postseason hopes, the club was playing its best ball of the season. They had scored four or more runs in 15 consecutive games and were riding a nine-game winning streak that pushed their record to 64-68, good for third place in the Central Division.

The game was scoreless through the first five innings. The Pirates tallied five singles and had men in scoring position in the first, third, and fourth innings, but came up empty each time. Johnson struck out 10, six of them swinging. The Pirates' talented 26-year-old Mexican-born right-hander Francisco Cordova pitched just as well, though not as overpoweringly, yielding just two hits.

Brad Ausmus, Houston's hardscrabble catcher, led off the bottom of the sixth with a double down the left-field line. He went to third when Cordova balked while facing his mound opponent, who later whiffed. Craig Biggio, who entered the game batting a team-high .328, hit a slow bouncer back to Cordova, whose throw to catcher Jason Kendall "seemed in time to get [Ausmus]," in the opinion of Paul Meyer of the *Pittsburgh Post-Gazette*. However, home-plate umpire Bill Hohn saw it differently, ruling Ausmus safe and sending the crowd of 40,709 in the Astrodome into a loud cheer.[2] "I thought he was out," said Kendall, the Bucs' All-Star backstop. "It was a bang-bang play."[3]

Ausmus was unequivocal in his perception of the play that gave Houston a 1-0 lead: "No question I was safe. My foot went right between his legs and touched the plate."[4] Biggio, who had earned his fifth consecutive and last of seven All-Star berths a month earlier, stole second, but was stranded when Cordova retired the next two batters.

After racking up his 12th punchout in the seventh inning, Johnson yielded a one-out single to Adrian Brown in the eighth. It was the third hit of the game for Brown, a mid-August call-up who had entered the game batting .414 (12-for-29) in his last eight contests. Shortstop Kevin Polcovich fanned for the third time, and then Kendall lined a single to short right field. An error by flychaser Richard Hidalgo enabled Brown to advance to third, but Johnson defused the threat by inducing Kevin Young to pop up.

Ausmus led off the eighth by placing a bunt perfectly between right-hander Mike Williams, who had just entered the game in relief of Cordova, and first base. Williams was charged with an error on his wild throw to first, enabling Ausmus to reach safely. Williams fanned Johnson, but the ball got away from Kendall, permitting Ausmus to advance to third. It was déjà vu all over again as Biggio hit a slow chopper with the infield drawn in. Shortstop Lou Collier fielded the ball cleanly but his throw to the plate was high, allowing Ausmus to slide home safely and giving the Astros a 2-0 lead.

"I don't know if it's [Ausmus] being so fast or me hitting the balls slow enough for him to score," joked Biggio after the game.[5] Not only was Ausmus deceptively fast for a catcher, he was hot, too. He had entered the game having collected hits in his last seven consecutive at-bats. "My legs actually feel very strong," he said after the game, and credited his backup, Tony Eusebio, whose sturdy play in 38 starts thus far had given him a chance to rest.[6] Ausmus drew praise, even wonder, from his skipper, who spent 13 of his 14 years pitching in the big leagues with the Astros. "You think about how many games he's caught, and he's still running like that," said Dierker.[7]

"Johnson had the Pirates guessing as he seemingly got stronger as the game progressed," wrote the

Randy Johnson went 10-1 with a 1.28 ERA, 116 strikeouts, and 4 shutouts in 11 starts for the 1998 Astros. He finished his career with 303 wins and stands second all-time with 4,875 strikeouts. (Courtesy of Houston Astros Baseball Club).

Houston Chronicle's Joseph Duarte.[8] With his fastball reaching speeds of 96 to 98 miles per hour, coupled with a deadly slider, the Big Unit struck out the side in the ninth; Freddie Garcia swung and missed on Johnson's 133rd pitch to end the game in 2 hours and 23 minutes.

"He overpowered us—plain and simple," said Lamont of Johnson's superlative performance, in which he did not walk a batter.[9] Johnson's 16 strikeouts set an Astros record for left-handers, and were the most since Nolan Ryan fanned 16 on September 9, 1987. (Don Wilson set the club mark with 18 on July 14, 1968, at Cincinnati's Crosley Field.) "It's not as though we had chance after chance," continued Lamont. "With him striking so many guys out, it's tough when you can't put the ball in play."[10] It was Johnson's 98th game with at least 10 strikeouts, breaking the tie he had with another dominant southpaw, Sandy Koufax; Ryan's record of 215 such games seemed out of reach. Biggio summed up Johnson's outing in four words: "He was totally dominant."[11]

A humble player despite his pitching prowess, Johnson was quick to give the Pirates credit. "Pittsburgh is a very disciplined and scrappy team," he said. "Those are the teams that make me work hard [because they] don't give me any room for error."[12] Unflappable on the mound, Johnson's concentration and ability to tune out all distractions on or off the field contributed to his success. "I realize that I have to be focused the entire game," he said. "With a one-run game, the tying run is up every inning."[13]

"At this rate, Randy Johnson may never lose a start at the Astrodome," wrote Duarte jokingly, but he was right—at least for the regular season.[14] Johnson's third straight shutout at home improved his overall record to 5-1. He pitched only two more times in the Astrodome in '98. He blanked the Reds 1-0 on September 7 and beat the St. Louis Cardinals five days later, though his scoreless-inning streak at the Dome ended at 36 innings when the Redbirds scored in the first. In two months with the Astros, Johnson enjoyed one of the best stretches any Houston pitcher had ever had. He went 10-1, carved out a 1.28 ERA, and struck out 116 in 84⅓ innings. Remarkably, he finished seventh in the NL Cy Young Award voting despite making just 11 starts.

Houston's acquisition of Johnson helped transform the team from a dark-horse challenger for the NL pennant to one of the favorites. Houston finished with a team-record (as of 2016) 102 victories. Against the surprising San Diego Padres in the NLCS, Johnson's winning streak in the Astrodome ended in Game One when he succumbed in a pitching duel with Kevin Brown, who fanned 16 and surrendered just two hits in eight scoreless innings to win the game, 2-1, in the Padres' eventual 3-games-to-1 upset of the Astros.

After the season Johnson, who resided in Phoenix in the offseason, surprised the baseball world by signing a four-year free-agent deal with the Arizona Diamondbacks for a reported $52 million, making him the second-highest-paid player in baseball. The Big Unit's tenure in Houston was brief, and some may even consider it a bad move in light of what the club surrendered to get him, but for just over two months Johnson rocked the Dome like few pitchers had before or since.

SOURCES

In addition to the sources cited in the Notes, the author also accessed Retrosheet.org, Baseball-Reference.com, the SABR Minor Leagues Database, accessed online at Baseball-Reference.com, SABR.org, and *The Sporting News* archive via Paper of Record.

NOTES

1   Durwood Merrill, *You're Out and You're Ugly* (Ashland, Oregon: Blackstone Publishing, 1998), quoted in Bill James and Rob Neyer, *The Neyer/James Gide to Pitchers* (New York: Fireside, 2004), 258.

2   Paul Meyer, "Pirates' Streak Ends. Johnson Fans 16, Allows 7 Singles; Astros Win, 2-0," *Pittsburgh Post-Gazette*, August 29, 1998: C1. According to both Baseball-Reference.com and Retrosheet.org, Ausmus scored on a fielder's choice enabling Biggio to reach first safely.

3   Neil Hohlfeld, "Ausmus Defies Conventions," *Houston Chronicle*, August 29, 1998: 8B.

4   Ibid.

5   Ibid.

6   Ibid.

7   Ibid.

8   Joseph Duarte, "Bucs Amount to Nothing vs. Johnson," *Houston Chronicle*, August 29, 1998: B1

9   Meyer.

10 Ibid.

11 Duarte.

12 Ibid.

13 Ibid.

14 Ibid.

Kevin Brown Outduels The Big Unit In the Postseason

September 29, 1998: San Diego Padres 2, Houston Astros 1, NLDS Game One, at the Astrodome

By Paul Geisler

THE 1998 HOUSTON ASTROS STRODE into the postseason with the confidence due the franchise's best team ever. They had won 102 games in the regular season, the only time as of 2016 that the Astros produced more than 100 wins in a season, and most prognosticators and pundits favored them to make the World Series and play the New York Yankees (who had won 114 games).

Powered by the Killer Bees of Craig Biggio, Jeff Bagwell, and Derek Bell, the strong Astros offense led the National League in runs scored (874), runs batted in (818), runs per game (5.40), and on-base-percentage (.356), and carried the lowest payroll ($41 million) of any team in the playoffs. "We're a great club," boasted Bagwell. "Anything less than getting to the World Series is going to be a disappointment for us."[1]

They had also acquired pitching ace Randy Johnson from the Seattle Mariners at the July 31 trade deadline, when they led the NL Central Division by 3½ games. Johnson won 10 games for Houston and lost only one, with a 1.28 earned-run average. Houston won nearly 70 percent (37 of 53) of its remaining games, finishing with a 12½-game lead over the second-place Chicago Cubs in the NL Central Division. Average home attendance increased by nearly 10,000 fans.[2]

The Astros opened the playoffs at home against the San Diego Padres in a best-of-five series. The two teams shared several common threads. "Actually, they're a lot like us," observed Astros pitcher Mike Hampton. Each team carried a dominant pitching staff and a strong lineup. Padres Ken Caminiti, Steve Finley, and Donne Wall had formerly played for the

Astros, while Astros Bell, Ricky Gutierrez, Brad Ausmus, and Sean Bergman were former Padres.[3]

Moreover, Padres owner John Moores lived in Houston before he bought the team in 1995. A graduate and supporter of the University of Houston, Moores followed the Astros as a youngster, rooting for his favorite players, Nolan Ryan and Terry Puhl.[4]

The mayors of the two cities offered the traditional wager on the outcome of the series. Houston Mayor Lee Brown put up 10 pounds of Texas barbecue to match San Diego Mayor Susan Golding's offer of a crate of avocados, five pounds of chips, and a gallon of salsa.[5]

Houston called on "guardian angel" Randy Johnson, the "ace up their sleeve,"[6] to start against the Padres' Kevin Brown. San Diego general manager Kevin Towers said he would "take Kevin Brown head-to-head with Randy Johnson in any game on AstroTurf, cement, asphalt, grass, you name it. ... I don't care where it is."[7] The hard-throwing right-hander had finished second in earned-run average in the National League (2.38), second in strikeouts (257), and fourth in wins (18). But Astros outfielder Carl Everett was still not convinced: "I don't give anybody credit until after they do something. He has to pitch [today], so right now, who is Kevin Brown?"[8]

A crowd of over 50,000 filled the Astrodome on the afternoon of Tuesday, September 29. Both pitchers proved themselves worthy, as neither team scored through the first five innings. To that point Johnson allowed just four hits while striking out five and walking only one. Brown came in a notch better, giving up only one hit and one walk with nine strikeouts in the first five frames.

The Astros posed the only real early scoring threat, in the bottom of the third inning, when Brad Ausmus' one-out single was followed by two consecutive passed balls by Padres catcher Carlos Hernandez. But with Ausmus perched on third base, Brown answered with strikeouts of Johnson and leadoff hitter Biggio.

Tony Gwynn led off the sixth inning for San Diego with a double on a shot down the left-field line, the first of three consecutive hits off Johnson. Gwynn stayed at second base on Greg Vaughn's infield single to third, then Ken Caminiti loaded the bases with a broken-bat bloop single to right.

Jim Leyritz immediately broke the deadlock with a fly ball to deep center field that allowed Gwynn to score the game's first run. The other runners advanced as well, but Johnson halted any further action with a strikeout and a groundout to end the inning with the Padres in front 1-0.

Ausmus reached third base again in the bottom of the sixth inning. After the catcher's leadoff single, Johnson fouled out on a bunt attempt. Brown hit the next batter, Biggio, and then Billy Spiers' groundout advanced the runners to second and third. However, third-place hitter Bell struck out swinging, stranding the two runners in scoring position.

Though Johnson allowed the lead runner to reach base in four straight innings (the fourth through the seventh), he managed to keep the score 1-0 until Greg Vaughn led off the top of the eighth by clobbering a 2-and-0 pitch far down the left-field line and over the wall for a home run. Vaughn, who terrorized NL pitchers during the regular season with an impressive 50 home runs and 119 runs batted in, had given the Padres a 2-0 lead. Johnson, the Astros' ace, closed out the inning with no further damage. He had pitched well, though not his best, giving up just two runs on nine hits and a walk in eight innings while striking out nine.

Brown responded in the bottom of the eighth with three strikeouts, though he did issue a walk to Dave Clark, pinch-hitting for Johnson. In his eight innings on the mound, Kevin Brown had outdueled Johnson and had shut down the mighty Houston attack, allowing no runs and only two singles, both to eighth-place hitter Ausmus, while throwing 119 pitches. He walked two and hit a batter but struck out 16 Astros, a Division Series record, and fell only one strikeout short of Bob Gibson's postseason record of 17 set in Game One of the 1968 World Series.

"This is the best I've seen him," said Houston manager Larry Dierker of Brown. "He wasn't throwing a lot of slow stuff. It was tough to get a good pitch."[9]

"He kept them honest by throwing one pitch that was moving in and one that was moving away," said former Astro turned ESPN announcer Joe Morgan. "He was in complete control."[10]

Houston reporters offered some colorful interpretations of the pitching masterpiece. One scribe opined that Brown mowed down the Astros "like he was wielding a buzz saw. Those closest to the field must have gagged on the sawdust."[11] A second writer put a Texas spin on the game, stating, "It was as if he rode into town and stole the sheriff's horse. He showed up at Johnson's big playoff dance and did a soft-shoe on the head of a pin."[12]

Everett, who was 0-for-4 with two strikeouts in three trips against the Padre ace, now knew who Brown was and praised his work, saying, "I give Brown his credit. He kept hitting those spots, and that's what good pitchers do."[13]

Houston reliever Jay Powell struggled in the top of the ninth. He walked Carlos Gomez with one out before striking out John Vander Wal, pinch-hitting for Brown. Powell then uncorked a wild pitch that enabled Gomez to reach second with two outs, and hit Quilvio Veras with a pitch to put runners at first and second. Doug Henry replaced Powell on the mound and struck out Ruben Rivera to end the Padres threat.

Still down 2-0, Houston managed a semblance of a rally in the bottom of the ninth against shutdown closer Trevor Hoffman. Spiers hit a groundball past third for a double to open the inning. After Hoffman set down Bell on a fly out and Bagwell on strikes, Moises Alou grounded a ball to third baseman Caminiti, whose wild throw allowed Spiers to score from second. Alou was credited with an infield hit but no RBI. But with the tying run aboard, Everett flied out to center to end the game with the final score Padres 2, Astros 1.

The "Killer Bees" had gone 0-for-10 with seven strikeouts. Combined with the previous year's playoff performance, they were now 2-for-47 with 15 strikeouts in the postseason, prompting the *Houston Chronicle*'s Joseph Duarte to rename them the "Killer Freeze."[14]

"It was just one of those days," said Biggio. "This year we're confident. And we still are."[15]

Houston evened the series with a 5-4 victory in Game Two, but lost the next two games in San Diego, 2-1 and 6-1. No previous 100-win team had dropped a Division Series, and *The Sporting News'* Jay Greenberg had argued in late September that all three rounds of the playoffs should be best-of-seven series. His prediction: "Certainly one of these years, somebody good is going to get it in the back." The 1998 Houston Astros fulfilled that prophecy.[16]

NOTES

1 Carlton Thompson, "Playoff Experience No Longer New," *Houston Chronicle,* September 29, 1998.

2 Carlton Thompson, "Johnson's Efforts Make New Teammates Better," *The Sporting News,* September 28, 1998: 76.

3 Thompson, "Astros Note Similarities with Padres," *Houston Chronicle,* September 28, 1998.

4 Mickey Herskowitz, "Astros Like Family to Padres' Moores," *Houston Chronicle,* September 29, 1998.

5 "Mayors Make Wager on Astros-Padres," *Houston Chronicle,* September 30, 1998.

6 Thompson, "A Tall Order—Randy Johnson," *Houston Chronicle,* September 29, 1998.

7 Thompson and Joseph Duarte, "Astros Padres Summary," *Houston Chronicle,* September 29, 1998.

8 Duarte, "A Pair of Aces," *Houston Chronicle,* September 29, 1998.

9 W.H. Stickney Jr., "Brown Gets Drop on Johnson," *Houston Chronicle,* September 30, 1998.

10 David Barron, "ESPN's Morgan Heaps Praise on Brown," *Houston Chronicle,* September 30, 1998.

11 Dale Robertson, "B's Flail Away, Hope This Year Isn't Last Year," *Houston Chronicle,* September 30, 1998.

12 Fran Blinebury, "Familiar Scene as Padres Ace Slams the Door," *Houston Chronicle,* September 30, 1998.

13 "Astros Summary."

14 Duarte, "Press-Box View Astros Padres," *Houston Chronicle,* September 30, 1998.

15 Jayne Custred, "Offensive Problems Don't Deflate Astros," *Houston Chronicle,* September 30, 1998.

16 Jay Greenberg, "Postseason Preview," *The Sporting News,* September 26, 1998: 59.

Spiers' Walk-Off Single Ties the NLDS

October 1, 1998: Houston Astros 5, San Diego Padres 4, NLDS Game Two, at the Astrodome

By Paul Geisler

THE HOUSTON ASTROS WERE brimming with confidence when the postseason got underway in 1998. They won 102 games in the regular season, the only time the Astros have produced more than 100 wins in a season. Most prognosticators and pundits favored them to make the World Series and play the New York Yankees (who won 114 games to set a new American League record).

The Astros were a well-balanced team. Their offense, led by the Killer Bees—Biggio, Bagwell and Bell—paced the National League in runs per game (5.40) and on-base-percentage (.356). They also acquired pitching ace Randy Johnson from the Seattle Mariners at the trade deadline, July 31, when they led the NL Central Division by 3½ games. As an Astro, Johnson won 10 games and lost only one, with a 1.28 earned-run average. Houston won nearly 70 percent (37 of 53) of its games in August and September, finishing 13 games ahead of second-place Chicago. Home attendance increased by nearly 10,000 fans per game after the trade.[1]

The Astros began the playoffs against the San Diego Padres in a best-of-five series, opening September 29 at the Astrodome. Johnson pitched well, allowing two runs in eight innings and striking out nine. He received no support, however, as Astros batters struck out 16 times in eight innings against Padres ace Kevin Brown. They managed an unearned run off closer Trevor Hoffman in the ninth but left the tying run on base as they lost, 2-1.

A quirky television schedule inserted an odd day off before the next game. So on Thursday, October 1, 45,550 fans gathered in the Astrodome, hoping their team could even the series before heading to San Diego. The Astros started 19-game winner Shane Reynolds against Andy Ashby (17-9) of the Padres. "I was nervous; everybody was nervous," said Reynolds. "A dome full of people yelling, it's a no-lose situation."[2]

The Astros offense regained its regular-season form early against Ashby, producing three runs in the first three innings. Jeff Bagwell had all three RBIs with a run-scoring groundout and a two-run single. Reynolds held the Padres scoreless until the sixth inning, when three consecutive hits produced two runs. He completed seven full frames, allowing only those two runs on four hits and one walk on just 74 pitches, including 55 strikes. He had no quarrel with the decision to go to the bullpen in the eighth despite the low pitch count: "There's no sense in me having to go out there and pitch every inning with as good a bullpen as we've got."[3]

Jay Powell took over for Reynolds and turned in a perfect top of the eighth. Derek Bell increased the Astros' lead to 4-2 in the bottom of the inning with a home run off former Astros pitcher Donne Wall, setting up one of the most famous ninth innings in Astros history.

Leading by two runs, Houston skipper Larry Dierker called on hard-throwing closer Billy Wagner, while Brad Ausmus replaced Tony Eusebio at catcher. Although Wagner had missed about three weeks in the middle of the season after being hit by a line drive, he had managed 30 saves in 35 chances.

Tony Gwynn grounded to first baseman Bagwell for the first out. Next, Ken Caminiti beat out an infield single. Greg Vaughn flied out to center for the second out.

With one out left, Padres manager Bruce Bochy chose to pinch-hit for left-handed hitting Wally Joyner and sent righty Jim Leyritz to the plate.

A versatile infielder who played second, short, and third, Bill Spiers was a member of the Astros' three consecutive championship squads in 1997-99. His best year was 1997, when he batted .320 in 132 games. (Courtesy of Houston Astros Baseball Club).

Leyritz had already made a name for himself with his late-inning heroics in the postseason. In 1995, his 15th-inning home run had given the Yankees a 7-5 win and a two-games-to-none lead over Seattle in the division series. The next year, his three-run homer off Atlanta closer Mark Wohlers had tied Game Four of the World Series, enabling the Yankees to eventually win that game, even the Series, and then to go on to win it.

Facing Wagner for the first time, Leyritz got advice from his teammates: He throws hard and rarely uses his slider. "If he's going to get beat, he's going to get beat with a fastball."[4]

Bagwell did not hold Caminiti on first, with two outs and a two-run lead in the ninth. Caminiti slipped easily to second base uncontested on a 1-and-2 pitch,

which Leyritz took for a ball. Wagner and Leyritz battled to a full count, leaving the Padres down to what was potentially their last strike of the game. Dierker hoped for a changeup or a slider, anything to change the pace, but the fastballs kept coming. "I called all fastballs," catcher Ausmus admitted. "If he's going to get beat, it's going to be on his best pitch."[5]

Still facing fastballs, Leyritz drilled a 98-mph fastball from Wagner just over the wall, inches inside the right-field foul pole, to tie the game, 4-4. Wagner stood on the mound and smiled. "I just laughed because I pretty much know I supplied all the power for that home run."[6] "It shocked me," he added. "I can't believe that ball stayed fair. ... I made the pitch where I wanted it. He just hit it out."[7]

Wagner then gave up a single to Carlos Hernandez, followed by another to Chris Gomez. George Arias came on to pinch-hit for pitcher Donne Wall, and Andy Sheets ran for Hernandez at second base. Arias struck out swinging to end the 28-pitch inning, but the Padres had tied the game, and Wagner had blown the save.

"They didn't hang their head or show any signs of sinking," Dierker said, describing his team's spirit when they came into the dugout after the top of the ninth. "They were all moving around, bouncing, alive. No sense of fear. You could read it on their faces that they knew they were going to get a run."[8]

With Dan Miceli pitching for San Diego in the bottom of the ninth, leadoff batter Ricky Gutierrez reached safely on a slow roller to shortstop. Attempting to bunt Gutierrez to second, Ausmus fell backward yet still managed to accomplish the sacrifice. With the winning run in scoring position, Bochy called for Hoffman, his ace reliever, who had tied a National League record with 53 saves that season.

With Hoffman straight out of the bullpen, Gutierrez took off for third base on the first pitch to the next batter, Craig Biggio. Hoffman never looked at Gutierrez on second. "I didn't really think he'd go in that situation," Hoffman admitted. "But with that high leg kick, maybe I should have gone to the slide step."[9]

"Stealing that base was the first thing that went through my head," said Gutierrez, who never had a steal sign from the Astros' dugout. "They really didn't pay any attention to me. …When I saw his leg kick, I took off."[10]

"It really changed the inning," reflected Padres outfielder Tony Gwynn. "Now, we've got to bring the outfielders in, and you've got to decide whether you're going to pitch to Biggio or not."[11]

The Padres walked Biggio intentionally, hoping for a double play from the next batter, Billy Spiers. "I sort of thought they might walk me, too," Spiers said, but Bochy went against the percentages and chose to have the right-handed Hoffman pitch to left-handed Spiers rather than walk him and pitch to right-handed Derek Bell, who had just homered in the bottom of the eighth.[12] With a runner on third and only one out, and a tie score in the bottom of the ninth, Spiers faced Hoffman.

Unlike Wagner and his fastballs, Hoffman relied heavily on his changeup, which looked "like a (badminton) shuttlecock," according to Dierker.[13] Hoffman fed Spiers a steady dose of the pitch, and worked him into a one-ball, two-strike hole. Still, Spiers managed to loop Hoffman's next pitch just over second baseman Quilvio Veras, and in front of right fielder Gwynn. Gutierrez "sprinted down the line and took a flying leap onto home plate to end it."[14]

"That wasn't just the biggest hit of my career—that was the biggest hit of my life," said Spiers.[15] "It was backyard stuff, what you dream about as a kid."[16]

"This was just typical of the games we've played against them all year," mused Biggio after the game. "This was a lot of fun. This is what you play for."[17]

Houston had evened the series at one game apiece. Next, they traveled to San Diego, where they lost 2-1 and 6-1, dropping the series to the Padres, three games to one. The Killer B's and the potent Astros' offense managed only one run in each of the three defeats. Despite a 1.93 earned-run average for the series, Randy Johnson was tagged with two of the three losses.

No 100-win team had ever dropped a division series. Many debated, even in 1998, the wisdom of determining winners in the postseason with a best-of-five series. In late September Jay Greenberg argued in *The Sporting News* that all three rounds of the playoffs should involve best-of-seven series. He predicted, "Certainly one of these years, somebody good is going to get it in the back."[18]

NOTES

1   Carlton Thompson, "Johnson's Efforts Make New Teammates Better," *The Sporting News*, September 28, 1998: 76.

2   "Astros Padres Summary," *Houston Chronicle*, October 2, 1998.

3   Ibid.

4   Joseph Duarte, "Fantastic Finish—Wagner Sees Visions of Wohlers after Leyritz's Tying Homer," *Houston Chronicle*, October 2, 1998.

5   Carlton Thompson, "Hitting Back—Spiers' Single in Ninth Pushes Astros Past Padres 5-4, Evens Series," *Houston Chronicle*, October 2, 1998.

6   Michael Murphy, "Inspired Victory—Quiet Steal, Spiers' Hit Lift Astros," *Houston Chronicle*, October 2, 1998.

7   Thompson.

8   Fran Blinebury, "What Good Is an Easy Victory?" *Houston Chronicle*, October 2, 1998.

9   W.H. Stickney Jr., "Hoffman Falls Asleep at the Switch, Fails to Stall Winning Rally," *Houston Chronicle*, October 2, 1998.

10   Thompson.

11   Ibid.

12   Dale Robertson, "The Other Billy Deserves a Save," *Houston Chronicle*, October 2, 1998.

13   Ibid.

14   Blinebury.

15   Thompson.

16   Robertson.

17   Thompson.

18   Jay Greenberg, "Postseason Preview," *The Sporting News*, September 26, 1998: 59.

A "Perfect Launch" to the Final Season in the Astrodome

April 6, 1999: Houston Astros 4,
Chicago Cubs 2, at the Astrodome

By Mike Huber

AN OPENING DAY RECORD CROWD of 51,668 saw the Houston Astros take on the visiting Chicago Cubs in the 35th and final home opener to be played in the Astrodome.[1] This was the Cubs' first season opener in Houston since April 10, 1962, when they played at Colt Stadium, losing 11-2 to the Astros.[2] Chicago would not be victorious this day, either.

Former astronaut Neil Armstrong was on hand to throw out the ceremonial first pitch. This was a treat for the fans. Astros owner Drayton McLane Jr. said, "I called him, and he said, 'I don't do public events.'" However, the famous astronaut "relented after McLane explained the historical significance of the game."[3] Flanked on both sides of the infield by 70 current NASA astronauts, the first man on the moon "delivered a one-hop pitch"[4] to second baseman Craig Biggio. Armstrong had been present with 23 astronauts on April 12, 1965, to celebrate the first National League game played at the Astrodome. During the pregame ceremonies and introductions of players, the NL Central Division championship banner was raised, to the roar of the crowd.

Houston manager Larry Dierker sent Shane Reynolds to the mound to face Chicago's Steve Trachsel. It was Reynolds' fourth straight Opening Day start for the Astros. "Opening night is always special," he said. "This one was even more special because it's the last one in the Dome. I think a lot of guys were a little nervous in the beginning. We went through some Pepto-Bismol."[5]

Mark Grace silenced the buzz in the crowd with a second-inning home run to right field, giving Chicago a 1-0 lead. The fan who caught the ball was coerced by others in his section to take a page out of the Cubs fans' playbook, as if this were Wrigley Field: He threw the ball back.[6] Tony Eusebio doubled to start the bottom of the third and scored on a one-out single by Reynolds. The Astros loaded the bases with two outs, but Ken Caminiti grounded out to first on a 3-and-2 pitch, and the inning ended with the score tied.

The top of the fourth inning saw a controversial call by home-plate umpire Frank Pulli. Mickey Morandini led off for Chicago with a double to right field. Sammy Sosa topped an offering by Reynolds in front of home plate. Reynolds pounced on the ball and threw to first baseman Jeff Bagwell, but the ball hit Sosa in the back. Morandini raced home with what appeared to be the Cubs' second run, but Pulli ruled that Sosa was inside the baseline, called him out for interference, and sent Morandini back to second. Mark Grace then singled, advancing Morandini to third, and when Henry Rodriguez followed with a single to center, Morandini scored the Cubs' second run of the game after all. Regarding the rule on base-path interference, Grace said, "We only got one run, but we easily could've gotten more. Last year we got the call and it really saved our bacon."[7] Manager Jim Riggleman complained, "It's almost impossible to run where the rulebook says you have to run."[8]

In a three-pitch span in the bottom of the fourth inning, Trachsel allowed home runs to the first two batters, Carl Everett and Richard Hidalgo, as the Astros went on top, 3-2. Trachsel appeared to settle down after that, but it was too late, as Chicago couldn't muster any more offense. Houston added a fourth run in the fifth. Bagwell singled to left with

Neil Armstrong, the first man to walk on the moon under the auspices of Space Center Houston in July 1969, threw out the first pitch in the space-age Astrodome's final home opener in April 1999. (Courtesy of Houston Astros Baseball Club).

two down, went to second on a walk to Caminiti, and scored when Everett lined a single past first base. The clubs posted zeros the rest of the way, and Houston emerged with a 4-2 victory.

Sosa, the 1998 National League Most Valuable Player, went 0-for-4 with three strikeouts (two by Reynolds). After the game Sosa told reporters, "I'm not Superman. I'm going to have a lot of games like this. You have to give a lot of credit to Reynolds and their bullpen."[9] Sosa had hit 66 home runs for the Cubs in 1998. Two bright spots for the Cubs were the performance of Grace, who was 3-for-3, including a home run in his first at-bat of the season, and a 2-for-3 outing by Rodriguez (two singles, but he was erased when caught stealing on a hit-and-run attempt in the top of the second).

Reynolds needed only 75 pitches to get through six innings, and struck out seven Chicago batters. He was relieved by Scott Elarton, who pitched scoreless

seventh and eighth innings. In the ninth, Houston closer Billy Wagner wasted no time in striking out Benito Santiago and Jose Hernandez, then fired a 98-mph fastball to Gary Gaetti.[10] The ball shattered the bat of Gaetti, who lifted a weak pop fly to short, ending the game.

For the Cubs, Trachsel labored through six innings (108 pitches) and was charged with four runs on seven hits. Matt Karchner and Brad Woodall each pitched an inning.

Everett and Hidalgo combined to go 3-for-7 at the plate, with two homers, three runs scored, and three driven in. Everett said after the game, "I never look at how far my home runs go. But the ball Richard (Hidalgo) hit would have broken the glass (behind the left-field seats) at the new ballpark."[11] Eusebio had a single and a double in four at-bats.

The *Chicago Tribune's* Paul Sullivan wrote, "The Cubs would be more than happy to volunteer to take a wrecking ball to the place called the 'eighth wonder of the world,' considering it has been their personal dome of doom for 35 years."[12] The Opening Day loss gave the Cubs a record of 81-134 in the Astrodome, a woeful .377 percentage.[13]

The Astros split the first homestand of the 1999 season with three wins and three losses, but they finished April with a 13-9 mark and were never below .500 after April 17. Houston finished every month in 1999 with a winning record, on the way to the

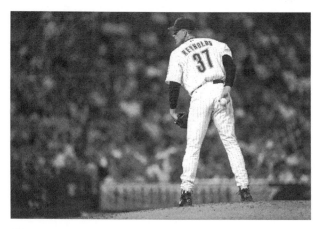

Shane Reynolds won 103 games with the Astros from 1992 to 2002, placing him eighth on the franchise's all-time victories list. He made five consecutive Opening Day starts from 1996 to 2000. (Courtesy of Houston Astros Baseball Club).

National League Central Division flag.[14] And it all began with this victory on Opening Day.

SOURCES

In addition to the sources cited in the Notes, the author consulted baseball-reference.com and retrosheet.org. The author thanks Gregory Wolf, Darrell Pittman, and Bill McCurdy for their assistance in obtaining sources.

NOTES

1   The Astros were 17-18 in Opening Day games in the Astrodome.

2   Paul Sullivan, "Dome Is Doom for Cubs: 2 Homers Lift Astros in Opener," *Chicago Tribune*, April 7, 1999. The record crowd surpassed the previous high of 44,618 for the 1997 opener against the Atlanta Braves.

3   "One Giant Throw: Neil Armstrong Opens Last Season at Astrodome," *Lubbock* (Texas) *Avalanche-Journal*, April 7, 1999.

4   Ibid.

5   Carlton Thompson, "Astros 4, Cubs 2 — Perfect Launch for All Systems — Astros Display Power, Pitching for Record Opening-Day Crowd," *Houston Chronicle*, April 7, 1999. Hereafter referred to as "Perfect Launch."

6   Joseph Duarte, Raising the Roof: Farewell Season in Dome Is Off to a Record Start," *Houston Chronicle*, April 7, 1999.

7   Sullivan.

8   Ibid.

9   "Perfect Launch."

10   Carlton Thompson, "All Systems Go for This Launch," *Houston Chronicle*, April 7, 1999.

11   "Perfect Launch."

12   Sullivan.

13   For the 1999 season, the Cubs won only two of six games against the Astros in the Astrodome. Chicago also lost five of six to Houston at Wrigley Field.

14   Houston spent 138 games in first place.

Beat-Down at the Dome: Astros Spank Bucs While Setting Team-Record For Runs and Doubles

May 11, 1999: Houston Astros 19, Pittsburgh Pirates 8, at the Astrodome

By Matthew Henshon

RUNS HAD HISTORICALLY BEEN HARD to come by in the Astrodome, but on May 11, 1999 — in the building's last season — the Astros proved an exception to the rule, blasting the Pirates 19-8 in front of 18,450. The Dome had opened as the modernistic "eighth wonder of the world,"[1] but its design made the games played there seem to be part of the Deadball Era, when runs were at a premium, extra-base hits were infrequent, and "it [took] three players to make a run."[2] With their new $250 million downtown park (built by Halliburton Corporation, under the leadership of former Defense Secretary Dick Cheney) nearing completion, the Astros gave their fans a night to remember in the old Dome.[3]

The Astros, coming off a 102-win season, entered the game with a 19-12 record, good for first place in the NL Central under manager Larry Dierker. The Pirates, meanwhile, were a surprising 16-15 after finishing last in the NL Central in 1998 with just 69 wins under manager Gene Lamont. Sean Bergman took the mound for Houston, while Lamont countered with Todd Ritchie, an offseason scrap-heap signing who entered the game at 2-1 with a 2.53 ERA on his way to a career year. He would end up with 15 victories and the sixth best ERA in the NL.

The game itself was relatively uneventful through the top of the third, with the score tied 1-1. Ritchie was touched up for a run in the first when Ken Caminiti singled to score Jeff Bagwell. The Pirates starter then helped himself at the plate in the top of the second by singling to extend the inning, after which Al Martin drove in Warren Morris.

The Astros scored three in the bottom of third. Craig Biggio was hit by a pitch, Derek Bell reached on an error by shortstop Pat Meares on what might have been a double-play ball, and Bagwell drilled a two-run double. One out later, Carl Everett's ground-out scored Bagwell to make it 4-1. Richard Hidalgo doubled with two out but the Pirates avoided more damage when right fielder Brian Giles threw out Hidalgo at the plate as he tried to score on Tim Bogar's base hit.

Houston blew open the game in the fourth and fifth innings. The Astros sent nine men to the plate and scored five runs in each inning. In the fourth, Biggio doubled with one out, Bell reached on an error by third baseman Ed Sprague, Bagwell walked, and Caminiti banged out a two-run double. After Chris Peters replaced Ritchie for the Pirates, csingles by Everett and Hidalgo knocked in three more runs as Houston increased its lead to 9-1.

Pittsburgh got two runs back in the top of the fifth on Martin's second home run of the season but that had no effect on the Astros. In the fifth another error by Sprague allowed leadoff batter Bergman to reach base. Then came consecutive hits by Biggio, Bell, and Bagwell (a double), a sacrifice fly by Caminiti, another base hit by Everett (who had a career-high five RBIs on this night), and a two-out RBI double by Paul Bako.

With a 14-3 lead after five innings, the Astros tried to put the game on cruise control, but the Pirates got three back in the top of the sixth. A single by Brant Brown, a double by Sprague, and a three-run homer

Jeff Bagwell was Houston's first Rookie of the Year, in 1991, and first National League MVP, in 1994. He amassed 2,314 hits and holds franchise career records of 449 home runs and 1,529 RBIs. (Courtesy of Houston Astros Baseball Club).

by Morris chased Bergman, who wound up with the win despite a messy pitching line that included 11 hits and six runs in five-plus innings. He was apologetic after the game, saying, "The offense was definitely the story. The way I pitched was unacceptable. We scored runs, and I should have been able to get guys out. I didn't do my job."[4]

Dierker went with lefty Trever Miller to replace Bergman, and he got out of the sixth without allowing any more scoring. The Pirates picked up two runs in the seventh off Jeff McCurry, who had—somewhat curiously—replaced Miller after Giles lined out to start the inning. Jason Kendall singled, Brown doubled, and Sprague knocked them both in with a double. Brian Williams finished the seventh and pitched a clean eighth inning as well.

With the Pirates trailing 15-8, manager Lamont inserted catcher Keith Osik to make his first major-league pitching appearance in the bottom of the eighth. Osik was the first position player to pitch for Pittsburgh since outfielder John Cangelosi did so on May 3, 1988.[5] After getting Derek Bell to foul out, Osik walked Jack Howell (pinch-hitting for Bagwell) and Billy Spiers. Everett doubled to score Howell, Hidalgo was hit by a pitch and, after Bako struck out, Bogar doubled down the third-base line to clear the bases and give the Astros a 19-8 lead.

In the ninth, fireballing Astros closer Billy Wagner, who had not pitched in six days, came on to get some work and close out the game. He did it with ease, on two strikeouts and a fly ball.

Asked about Osik's pitching after the game, Everett said, "I treated it like BP. A guy used to throwing from a flat surface isn't normally going to throw as hard as a guy used to throwing off a mound."[6] For his part, Osik said, "I was just trying to help the bullpen. Those guys have been pitching their butts off and someone needed to suck up an inning for them."[7]

The Astros' starting pitcher, Bergman, was unable to finish the sixth inning despite an 11-run lead. "It was kind of an ugly game from both teams' standpoint," manager Dierker said. (The Pirates made five errors.) "This is not the type of game I would have preferred, but you certainly want to be on the winning end of it."[8]

The Astros' 19 runs tied a club record and their 10 doubles set a new team mark.[9] Everett, for one, was not surprised: "If we put our heads together like this, there's no telling how many times we can do it. It's a great club, and everyone can hit."[10]

The game was long enough, at 3 hours and 22 minutes, to be described in the *Houston Chronicle* as a "marathon."[11] (By 2014 a major-league game lasted an average of 3 hours and 8 minutes.[12]) Everett said after the game, "I think we were more anxious to try and get this game over with. Your feet start hurting."[13]

NOTES

1 James Gast, *The Astrodome: Building an American Spectacle* (Boston: Aspinwall Press, 2014), 130.

2 Bill James, *The Baseball Abstract 1983* (New York: Ballantine Books, 1983), 66-67. James credits Craig Wright; see also, John Thorn and Pete Palmer, *The Hidden Game of Baseball: A Revolutionary Approach to Baseball and Its Statistics* (Garden City, New York: Doubleday Dolphin, 1985), 82.

3 Gary Gillette and Eric Enders (with Stuart Shea and Matthew Silverman), *Big League Ballparks: The Complete Illustrated History* (New York: Metro, 2009), 462.

4 Joseph Duarte, "Astros Break Out Their Whipping Sticks; Runs Record Matched in 19-8 Rout of Pirates," *Houston Chronicle*, May 12, 1999): Sports, 1.

5 Ibid.

6 Associated Press, "Astros Prevail With an Unusual Onslaught," available at articles.latimes.com/1999/may/12/sports/sp-36552.

7 Ibid.

8 Duarte.

9 Ibid.

10 Ibid.

11 Ibid.

12 Ted Berg, "Why Are Baseball Games Getting So Much Longer?" *USA Today*, September 30, 2014. ftw.usatoday.com/2014/09/mlb-games-length-three-hours-pace-of-play.

13 Ibid.

A Scary Situation for the Houston Astros

June 13, 1999 / July 23, 1999: Houston Astros 4, San Diego Padres 3, at the Astrodome

By Brent Heutmaker

IN JUNE 1999 THE HOUSTON ASTROS were starting a 10-game homestand against the San Diego Padres. This was the Padres' first trip to the Astrodome since they had eliminated Houston from the playoffs the previous October. Houston's record was 36-23 while San Diego stood at 24-36. After the teams split the first two games, 39,773 fans were on hand for the Sunday afternoon rubber match, which featured Houston's Shane Reynolds on the mound against San Diego's Heath Murray. But this game would not be remembered for anything that happened between the lines.

San Diego broke on top with a run in the third inning. In the fourth, Murray got out of a jam. Craig Biggio and Ricky Gutierrez had singled to put Astros at first and second with no outs. Murray struck out Jeff Bagwell and Derek Bell before Richard Hidalgo flied out to end the inning. In the sixth inning, Murray allowed a single to Reynolds. Biggio singled and Gutierrez sacrificed the runners to second and third. After an intentional walk to Bagwell, Bell, who up to that point had hit into a team-worst nine double plays,[1] hit an opposite-field grand slam home run into a picnic area inside the right-field foul line.[2] Suddenly, the Astros had a 4-1 lead

San Diego manager Bruce Bochy said, "I don't know how that ball stayed fair. And I don't know how it reached the fence. It just kept going. Tony (Gwynn) was there and just ran out of room."[3]

Murray said, "I don't know what to do. The pitch Bell hit was three inches off the ground. It was the hitters leading up to Bell that hurt me. If I get Biggio, Gutierrez doesn't bunt. It's sad, because that is the best I've been all year. I felt awesome. Mechanically, I was right there. It seems like I can't get through the

sixth. If I expect to pitch up here, I have to go longer. But I know I can do it. I know I have the stuff."[4]

Not long after was when things got weird and scary. In the eighth inning, with Houston still leading 4-1, San Diego reliever Trevor Hoffman had thrown one pitch to Jeff Bagwell when Houston manager Larry Dierker suffered a grand mal seizure in the dugout. Medical personnel treated Dierker for more than 20 minutes before he was taken to Methodist Hospital. The seizure was caused by a tangle of blood vessels in his brain that had ruptured. Dierker had brain surgery and missed the next 27 games.

Bagwell described what happened: "I was getting ready to step in, and the umpire said, 'Hold on,' I looked around, and everybody was running to the dugout. Larry had collapsed. He couldn't talk. He was shaking violently. He was shaking the whole time. It was shocking. We're all stunned."[5]

Astros owner Drayton McLane Jr. talked with San Diego owner John Moores about how to resolve the unfinished game. They agreed to suspend the game until San Diego's next trip to Houston. McLane said, "For the San Diego players as well as our players, their heart just wasn't into finishing this game, and the umpires felt the same way."[6]

Medical problems had already affected the Houston coaching staff. Hitting coach Tom McCraw was on medical leave while undergoing treatment for prostate cancer, and first-base coach Jose Cruz was on leave undergoing treatment for an irregular heartbeat. Harry Spilman was filling in for McCraw. The Astros would be two coaches short until Cruz's return about a week later.

Houston general manager Gerry Hunsicker promoted bench coach Matt Galante to interim manager. Galante had been a coach in the Houston organization since 1980 and had been the bench coach for a year. Galante said, "You never want to take over under these circumstances. I really don't feel like I'm taking over, because this is Larry's team and things are going to be done the same way. We're going to play the game the way we've always played it. Hopefully, Larry will be back shortly; until then, we're just going to try to win them one by one for Larry"[7]

Galante talked about being two coaches short, "I think we'll be OK there. I think I can handle my bench job as well as run the team until Larry gets back. Cheo (Cruz) will be back (Friday), so that will help us."[8]

The completion of the suspended game was scheduled for Friday, July 23. The Padres and Astros were to play a regularly scheduled game that night. While Dierker was out, Galante's managerial record was 13-14. Galante never managed again in the major leagues.

Since returning from the surgery, Dierker's Astros had a 5-3 record. Dierker said of the rescheduled game, "We don't want to miss the opportunity to close out that win. We have placed a great deal of importance on this one inning."[9]

Dierker hadn't thought much about how it would feel to be back in the dugout to finish the game. "I've had people ask me what is it going to be like to sit in that chair. Are you going to have anxiety over what happened? I don't even remember if I was sitting in that chair or standing at the rail. I don't know where I was when it happened. Whenever it happened I was immediately unconscious. From what I've heard, everybody was suffering a lot more than I was. I was the one that looked like I was in agony. In reality I was unconscious and wasn't feeling any pain. I never had experienced any pain, whether pre-surgery, the day before or the day after. Other than the fact I lost about a week there where I don't have a good memory, I'm not going to worry about having a flashback."[10]

The managers had to make lineup changes for the rescheduled game. Shane Reynolds had pitched recently and was unavailable to continue the suspended game. Dierker would have his closer, Billy Wagner, ready to pitch the ninth inning and would have an-

Larry Dierker compiled a managerial record of 448-362 (.553 winning percentage). His win total is second to Bill Virdon's 544 in Astros history, and he guided Houston to four NL Central titles (1997-99 and 2001). (National Baseball Hall of Fame, Cooperstown, New York).

other reliever warming up. If Houston extended its lead, Dierker planned to have Wagner not pitch the ninth inning.[11]

The day before the rescheduled game, the National League had ruled that Trevor Hoffman didn't have to return to the game, even though the rules specified that a new pitcher had to complete at least one at-bat. Tony Gwynn had already been taken out of the game. San Diego catcher Greg Myers and outfielder Gary Mathews Jr. had to be replaced—Myers was on the disabled list and Matthews had been sent to San Diego's Triple-A affiliate in Las Vegas. Bochy conceded, "We know the odds are against us winning that one."[12]

Houston failed to score in the bottom of the eighth inning. In the top of the ninth, Wagner allowed solo home runs to Phil Nevin and Rubin Rivera but escaped with the save as the Astros held on to win the game, 4-3. "I think if anything else would have happened I would have had another seizure," Dierker joked. I think Shane (Reynolds, the starter, who got the victory) would have had one right along with me."[13]

Wagner said, "It was very odd. There was a lack of the adrenaline rush. Usually you have the eight innings to build up to that and get into it. But nonetheless, you have to be prepared to go out there and make pitches, and you know, those are the games you've just got to battle through and just take it and go home."[14]

Speaking of Wagner's difficulties, Dierker said, "I think it was tough. In a sense, it seemed like a free save. But in another sense, to go out in the beginning when we're just starting to play is not something he's used to. I'm not going to say he doesn't pitch as well as he usually does; he was still pitching the same velocity. I don't know if he had the same kind of control or not, but he certainly made it interesting."[15]

Heath Murray, the losing pitcher for San Diego, had actually pitched that same night for Las Vegas. Murray could have lost games on the same night for two different teams in two different leagues. Fortunately for him, Las Vegas rallied from a 4-1 deficit to defeat Nashville 5-4.[16]

Houston also won the regularly scheduled game, 7-4. The Astros' Mike Hampton picked up his 13th victory against 3 defeats. Bell hit a home run in that game, too.

Dierker guided Houston to its third consecutive NL Central title and managed the Astros through 2001, winning one more division title in his final season.

NOTES

1 Carlton Thompson, "Umpires Suspend Game After Dierker's Collapse—Bell's Grand Slam Provides 4-1 Lead Over Padres," *Houston Chronicle*, June 14, 1999.

2 Bill Center, "Well-Placed Slam Gets Bell Hot Again," *San Diego Union-Tribune*, June 14, 1999.

3 Ibid.

4 Ibid.

5 Associated Press, "Dierker Has Seizure; Astro Game Suspended," *Los Angeles Times*, June 14, 1999.

6 David Barron, John P. Lopez, Jerry Wizig, and Carlton Thompson, "Circle of Support—Seizures Overcome Astros Manager—Dierker's Condition 'Stabilized' After Convulsions at Dome Game," *Houston Chronicle*, June 14, 1999.

7 Thompson.

8 Ibid.

9 Joseph Duarte, "Dierker Won't Have Any Flashbacks to June 13 Seizure," *Houston Chronicle*, July 23, 1999.

10 Ibid.

11 Ibid.

12 Bill Center, "Hoping for Another Split Tonight," *San Diego Union-Tribune*, July 23, 1999.

13 Megan Dickson, "Astros Hold On in Suspended Game," *Houston Chronicle*, July 24, 1999.

14 Ibid.

15 Ibid.

16 Bill Center, "Rehabbed Gomez Returns to Majors but Not to the Lineup," *San Diego Union-Tribune*, July 24, 1999.

"It's Lima time, baby"

September 11, 1999: Houston Astros 5, Chicago Cubs 3, at the Astrodome

By Chad Osborne

JOSÉ LIMA MADE A BOLD PREDIC-tion during spring training in 1999.

The 26-year-old Houston Astros hurler claimed he would win 20 games in the coming season.

That prediction may have left some people scratching their heads. A year earlier he had predicted a 15-win season for himself and won 16. However, from 1995 through 1997, Lima had managed only nine wins against 21 defeats. And he was just one year removed from a particular spring-training game in '98 in which the Kansas City Royals belted the right-hander. There were "whispers" that the Astros might consider releasing Lima after that awful outing.[1]

Lima, however, proved doubters wrong on Saturday, September 11, 1999, when, from the Astrodome mound, he pitched his team to a 5-3 win over the Chicago Cubs.

The Dominican righty proved himself as not only a fantastic young major-league pitcher, but, for the second consecutive year, an extraordinary prognosticator, particularly when it came making self-assured predictions.

"I told you it was going to be Lima time, and it's Lima time, baby," he said after the win. "The reason I said that back in spring training was that I believe in myself."[2]

Lima, who improved to 20-7 with the victory, pitched effectively through seven innings, but gave up consecutive singles to Cubs pinch-hitters Lance Johnson, Roosevelt Brown, and Mickey Morandini to load the bases in the eighth. With no one out, Mark Grace lifted a sacrifice fly to center field that scored Johnson and cut the Astros' lead to 5-3.

With slugger Sammy Sosa strolling to the plate, already with 59 home runs on his stat sheet for the season, Astros manager Larry Dierker had seen enough from his starting pitcher. Dierker pulled Lima, who walked off the mound angry[3] before a crowd of 52,010, the largest home crowd for an Astros game to that point in the '99 season.[4]

Lima wanted to finish what he had started. He had allowed seven hits, including a single by Sosa in the fourth, struck out seven Cubs and allowed no walks.

Jay Powell replaced Lima. The righty got Sosa to strike out swinging on a 2-and-2 count, then walked Henry Rodriguez, but induced Glenallen Hill to line out to second, stymying the Cubs' rally.

Houston threatened with a couple of baserunners in the bottom of the eighth, but failed to add to its lead. Billy Wagner slammed the door on Chicago's chances in the ninth. The lefty closer needed only nine pitches to retire the side. It was his 36th save of the season, tying the franchise record set by Doug Jones in 1992.[5]

As the Cubs' Lance Johnson grounded out to short to end the game, Lima "bolted from the dugout to retrieve the ball" from Wagner.[6]

"This one was for the fans," Lima said in the next day's *Houston Chronicle*. "The fans have been so great to me. I'm just thankful that I was traded from Detroit to Houston. That changed my whole career."

Lima, whom Detroit sent to the Astros in a nine-player swap before the 1997 season, began this game as well as he could have hoped. He struck out the side—Bo Porter, Chad Meyers, and Grace—all swinging.

By the time Lima had given up his first hit of the contest, his teammates had already given him a quasi-comfortable 3-0 lead. The Astros got on the scoreboard in the second when Tony Eusebio singled home Carl Everett from second with two

Flamboyant pitcher Jose Lima found the Astrodome perfectly suited to his pitching style. After notching 16 wins in 1998, he predicted he would win 20 in 1999; he finished the season with 21 victories. (Courtesy of Houston Astros Baseball Club).

outs. Everett had led off the inning and reached base after being hit by a pitch from Chicago starter Micah Bowie. The left-hander struck out Lima next to end the inning with runners stranded on first and second.

Bowie wasn't so lucky in the third. He began by walking Craig Biggio, who scampered to second on a wild pitch to Ricky Gutierrez. Five pitches later, Gutierrez singled to center, and Biggio raced home with the Astros' second run. After walking Jeff Bagwell to put Astros at first and second, Bowie caught a break. He struck out Everett swinging and Cubs catcher Jose Molina gunned down Gutierrez trying to steal third.

Now with two outs, Ken Caminiti strolled to the plate and slapped a groundball single to left, scoring Bagwell. The Astros led 3-0.

The Cubs tried to bounce back in the fourth, getting a run off Lima, who had been stellar to that point. Grace slapped a grounder between first and second for a one-out single, Chicago's first hit of the

game. Sosa moved Grace to third with a bloop single to short right field. Rodriguez grounded into a force at second, scoring Grace to cut the home team's advantage to 3-1.

Houston got the run back in the bottom half of the frame when Eusebio hit a solo home run deep to right-center field. It was his fourth homer of the season, and it gave Houston a 4-1 advantage. The Astros picked up another run in the fifth when Ryan Thompson singled to center, scoring Gutierrez from second.

The run spelled the end for Bowie, who finished the game giving up six hits and five runs, all earned, in 4⅔ innings. Bowie took the loss, which dropped his record to 1-6.

Houston's win was its ninth in a row, a season high, and 19th in 27 games.[7] (The Astros won the next day to sweep the Cubs, and eventually extended their winning streak to 12 games before losing 8-6 to Philadelphia in 10 innings on September 15 in the Astrodome.) The win improved Houston to 88-56, as the first-place Astros maintained a three-game lead over Cincinnati in the National League Central.

The Cubs, losers of five in a row, dropped to 56-86 and 31 games behind Houston.

One of the few bright spots for the Cubs during the '99 season was Sosa's pursuit of a second consecutive year of 60 home runs. Sosa led St. Louis slugger Mark McGwire 59 homers to 55. During the thrilling 1998 home run chase, McGwire had totaled 70 and Sosa 66. In '99 McGwire would again eclipse Sosa, 65-63.

Sosa failed to reach 60 the next day in the Astrodome, which he revealed was not his favorite place to swing a bat.

"I never liked this place," Sosa said. "I mean the Astrodome, not the city. I like Houston fine. But I've never had any luck here. I'm so happy knowing that tomorrow is my last game here. When I come back next year, no more Astrodome."[8]

The ballpark closed at the end of the '99 season, perhaps to the delight of many hitters. "The Dome walls seem to pulse, a haunting place, as if the product of the pen of Edgar Allen Poe," wrote Mickey Herskowitz in the *Houston Chronicle*.

Sosa was 1-for-10 in the series in Houston and was hitting just .125 with one home run off Lima that season.[9]

However, the slugger insisted he was not pressing at the plate. "I never press," Sosa said. "They're just pitching me great. Good pitching is going to beat good hitting. I don't want it (hitting 60th) to get to me. I just want to be relaxed and do my job. I'm going out there and keep hacking and looking for my pitch."[10]

Lima's win made him the sixth Astros pitcher at that point to win 20 or more in a season, the first since Mike Scott hit the milestone in 1989. Dierker was the first, with exactly 20 in 1969. Others included J.R. Richard (20) in 1976, and Joe Niekro in both 1979 (21) and 1980 (20). Mike Hampton won also 22 for the Astros in '99. Subsequently, Roy Oswalt won 20 games in both 2004 and 2005, and Dallas Keuchel won 20 in 2015.

On this Saturday, taking Lima out of the game in the eighth was a tough decision for Dierker, who "described himself as ambivalent even as he strolled to the mound" to remove the pitcher.[11]

"When you're going for 20," Dierker said, "you'd like to get a complete game. My heart is with the starting pitcher. He wants to go on. You saw how late I went out. I had really mixed feelings. I believe he probably could have gotten Sosa out. But Sammy has four home runs off him in the last couple of seasons. If he hits one here, it puts them ahead."[12]

After the game, Lima said, "I'm the kind of guy who wants to finish what he started."[13]

After "seeming irritated"[14] while walking off the mound, Lima was dancing near the dugout once Wagner recorded the final out, celebrating 20 wins and an uncanny ability to predict his fortune.

"I know people think bad when José Lima does his dance, but that is just José Lima, that's not going to change," the flamboyant pitcher said. "This (game ball) is for my mother and for the fans of the Astros. They stayed for the whole game."[15]

NOTES

1   Mickey Herskowitz, "Lima Delivers on His Promise; José Proving His Act Belongs in The Show," *Houston Chronicle*, September 12, 1999.

2   Ibid.

3   Michael A. Lutz, "Lima First in NL With 20 Wins," Associated Press, September 12, 1999.

4   Herskowitz.

5   Ibid.

6   Ibid.

7   Carlton Thompson, "Lima Delivers on His Promise; Righthander Downs Cubs for 20th Win," *Houston Chronicle*, September 12, 1999.

8   Herskowitz.

9   Ibid.

10 Lutz.

11 Herskowitz.

12 Ibid.

13 Ibid.

14 Lutz.

15 Ibid.

Astros Clinch Third Consecutive NL Central Title in the Last Regular-Season Game at the Astrodome

October 3, 1999: Houston Astros 9, Los Angeles Dodgers 4, at the Astrodome

By Frederick C. Bush

A SELLOUT CROWD OF 52,033 FANS turned out for the Houston Astros' October 3, 1999, season finale against the Los Angeles Dodgers to commemorate the 35-year history of the Astrodome. The Astros had prepared a grand celebration to bid farewell to the venerable stadium, and many luminaries from the franchise's past were in attendance. Craig Cullinan, the "last survivor"[1] of the club's founders, was present, as was Fred Hofheinz whose father, Roy Hofheinz, another of the team's founders, had been the driving force behind the construction of the Dome. Players who had been selected to the All-Astros team—which included Nolan Ryan, Cesar Cedeno, and Jimmy Wynn, among others—were on hand to join the festivities, and Texas music icon Willie Nelson was slated to bring down the final curtain with a short concert.

Because of its historical significance as the end of an era, the game had been sold out months in advance; no one could have anticipated that it would also be of great importance to the Astros' hopes for a third consecutive NL Central Division title. As fate would have it, the Astros began the day with a one-game lead over the Cincinnati Reds, which meant that they could clinch the division with a victory over the Dodgers and set off a dual celebration of both past and present in the Astrodome.

After manager Larry Dierker had thrown out the first pitch and country-music legend Charlie Pride had sung the national anthem, Mike Hampton—a 21-game winner starting on three days' rest—took the mound for the Astros against Dodgers rookie Robinson Checo. The Dodgers were out of contention, but their failure to field their best lineup no doubt caused the Reds and their fans considerable chagrin. Los Angeles' refusal to risk injury to staff ace Kevin Brown by starting him on three days' rest could be justified, but there was no such defense for not starting their best hitter, Gary Sheffield. Many observers concluded that the Dodgers were giving Houston a present for the Dome's "going away" party, but the Astros still had to accept the gift by winning the game.

The outcome of the contest became a foregone conclusion after the first inning. Checo struck out leadoff hitter Craig Biggio but then walked four consecutive batters, pushing across Stan Javier for the first run of the game. Daryle Ward, a rookie who had been named the MVP of the Triple-A New Orleans Zephyrs, followed with a double that cleared the bases and gave the Astros a 4-0 lead. Ward, the son of former major-league outfielder Gary Ward, had been productive in his limited time with the Astros and said of his penchant for clutch hits, "I think that just making sure you're breathing every day is a lot more pressure than coming out here and playing a baseball game. Little kids play it, so I might as well play it like they do."[2]

Hampton was grateful for the early lead and echoed Ward's demeanor when he said, "I was able to relax. I wasn't tired. I was pumped up. It was a lot of fun to be out there."[3] The Dodgers scored one run in the third inning when Hampton walked Eric Young, who advanced to second on a wild pitch and scored on Raul Mondesi's single. It was the only run surrendered by Hampton in seven innings of work. The Astros regained their four-run margin on Ken Caminiti's solo home run off reliever Matt Herges in the bottom of the third.

The Astros increased their lead to 6-1 in the bottom of the fifth when Jeff Bagwell scored his second run of the game, trotting home on Tony Eusebio's groundout. Then they broke the game open with three more runs in the sixth inning for a 9-1 lead. Bagwell also scored in that inning to finish with an NL-leading 143 runs for the season. He walked twice in the game for a total of 149 to lead the NL and break Jimmy Wynn's single-season Astros record.

The only bump in the road came when reliever Jay Powell allowed the Dodgers three runs in the ninth inning. Powell, who was rusty from eight days of inaction, gathered himself by feeding off the frenzied fans. Afterward, he recalled, "The crowd really had me pumped up. ... The last time I heard anything like that was when I pitched in the World Series [for the Florida Marlins in 1997]."[4] Powell struck out Mondesi to end the game and sent his teammates and the fans into complete delirium.

The Astros' 97th victory of the season, second only to the 1998 squad's 102 wins, had earned them their third consecutive division title. The triumph gave Hampton his NL-leading 22nd win of the season, which set a team record, breaking a tie with teammate Jose Lima (who won 21 games in 1999) and All-Astros team member Joe Niekro.

In spite of the Astros' victory total and all of their individual accomplishments (in addition to Bagwell's and Hampton's league-leading totals, Biggio led the NL with 56 doubles), the 1999 campaign had been a difficult one as a rash of injuries that had plagued the team. The setbacks began with the loss of slugging left fielder Moises Alou to a freak treadmill accident in the offseason and included Dierker's seizure in the dugout on June 13 that required brain surgery (Dierker came back after missing 27 games). The fact that they had persevered and had emerged triumphant led Dierker to assert, "I think this will be probably the most satisfying season that any of us

Lefty Mike Hampton won 22 games in 1999, one more than teammate Jose Lima, to set a Houston franchise record. He was the winning pitcher in the Astros' division title-clinching games in 1997 and 1999. (Courtesy of Houston Astros Baseball Club).

will ever have, because we have had to overcome so many obstacles."[5]

Throughout the game, the stadium's video screens had shown notable Dome moments, among them Nolan Ryan's record-setting fifth no-hitter and Mike Scott's 1986 NL West-clinching no-hitter. The crowd recognized the significance of this day and, though the team had guaranteed itself at least one home playoff game, fans emptied the Dome's gift shops of 5,000 T-shirts, 6,000 commemorative baseballs, 2,000 pins, and 15,000 programs.[6]

The initial on-field celebration involving fireworks and confetti had become commonplace, but the ceremonies that followed were unique. After the Astros had engaged in the obligatory champagne shower in the clubhouse, they returned to the field for a victory lap and then watched as the members of the All-Astros team were introduced to the crowd. The heroes of Astrodome seasons past relished the

In the final regular-season game in the Astrodome, on October 3, 1999, the Astros routed the Dodgers 9-4 to finish the season with a 50-32 home record and a third consecutive NL Central Division championship. (Courtesy of Houston Astros Baseball Club).

moment as "Wynn blew kisses to the crowd, and [Jose] Cruz ran laps around home plate to show he was still in shape."[7] Dierker, another member of the All-Astros team, who had made his first start for the then Houston Colt .45s on his 18th birthday in 1964, remembered his first impression of the Astrodome: "It looked like a giant flying saucer. When I walked inside for the first time, I felt like I was walking into the future."[8]

The future was precisely what Roy Hofheinz had in mind in 1965 when he had declared, before the first game in the Astrodome, "Nobody can ever see this and go back to Kalamazoo, Chicago, New York, you name it, and still think this town is bush league, that this town is Indian Territory."[9] The Dome and the NASA Space Center had helped transform Houston from "big city backwater" into a corporate metropolis with the nation's fourth largest population. Astros

President Tal Smith said of the Dome's contribution to that change, "This was truly a revolutionary venture. It wasn't just a new ballpark. There were people who would line up to tour the building even without an event. They would marvel at it."[10]

The once futuristic Astrodome was outdated now, and the Astros were set to move into their new downtown ballpark in 2000. After Willie Nelson ended his show with the appropriately-titled song "The Party's Over,"[11] the video screens showed an image of the Dome's original scoreboard—the largest of its time in 1965—that had fallen victim to the desire for more seats in the 1980s, and then the overhead lights were turned off.

NOTES

1   Mickey Herskowitz, "Baseball in the Dome Grand Finale, '99 Clincher, Nostalgia Mix Magnificently," *Houston Chronicle*, October 4, 1999.

2   Michael Murphy, "Ward's Early Spark Ignites a Wildfire," *Houston Chronicle*, October 4, 1999.

3   Carlton Thompson, "What a Ride! Astros Capture 3rd Consecutive NL Central Title," *Houston Chronicle*, October 4, 1999.

4   Ibid.

5   David Barron, "Astros Pile on Titles: 3-Time Division Champs Win Dome's Last Regular-Season Game," *Houston Chronicle*, October 4, 1999.

6   Ibid.

7   Ibid.

8   Herskowitz, "Baseball in the Dome Grand Finale, '99 Clincher, Nostalgia Mix Magnificently."

9   Jim Yardley, "Last Innings at a Can-Do Cathedral," *New York Times*, October 3, 1999.

10 Ibid.

11 Nelson's song was even more appropriate than the title indicates: It begins with the lines "Turn out the lights, the party's over/ They say that all good things must end."

Astrodome Goes Out With a Whimper Not a Bang

October 9, 1999: Atlanta Braves 7, Houston Astros 5, NLDS Game Four, at the Astrodome

By Greg Erion

ELEMENTS AND MOSQUITOES could not defeat the Houston Astrodome. If only the Astros might have been able to say the same of their experiences in playoffs. In 1999 Houston achieved its third straight division championship. The Astros were hoping to do better in the playoffs than in the previous two seasons when the Atlanta Braves and then the San Diego Padres eliminated them in divisional play.

Postseason play would involve a milestone for the Astros. The Houston Astrodome, described at its creation as "Eighth Wonder of the World," was in its last season of use as a venue for major-league baseball. Starting in 2000, Enron Field would host Astros games.[1] Houston's clinching its division over the Cincinnati Reds on the last day of the season, as well as the impending playoffs, overshadowed the Astrodome's last days as a baseball stadium. Most fans in "Space City" were looking to avenge Atlanta's sweep of Houston in 1997; saying farewell to the Astrodome was a side issue.

As the initial round of the playoffs began, Houston seemed well suited to break its run of disappointing performances. An axiom of the game is that in a short series quality pitching will prevail. Houston had a brilliant pitching staff led by starters Mike Hampton (22-4), Jose Lima (21-10), and Shane Reynolds (16-14), with Billy Wagner (4-1, 39 saves, 1.57 ERA) anchoring the bullpen. There was reasonable hope that they would hold their own.

But the Astros were going up against a superlative group of Atlanta Braves pitchers including future Hall of Famers Tom Glavine, Greg Maddux, and John Smoltz, backed by reliever John Rocker. Their individual won-lost statistics in 1999 might not have matched those of the Astros, but the Braves led the majors in ERA at 3.63, a significant factor in their 103-59 regular-season record. Moreover, Glavine, Maddux, and Smoltz had a combined 9-0 record in the previous four years of NLDS play.

The Braves had won all four divisional series and were riding a 10-game NLDS winning streak, which began in 1995 and included the sweep of Houston in 1997. In that series, Atlanta's staff generated a 1.67 ERA, holding Houston to a team batting average of .167. Highlighting Houston's haplessness, Jeff Bagwell and Craig Biggio, the Astros' vaunted "Killer Bee" sluggers, hit a combined .083 with no extra-base hits or RBIs.

The series began on October 5, in Atlanta, when the Astros snapped the Braves' winning streak with a 6-1 victory over Maddux. Houston lost the second game 5-1 and the third, a 5-3 heartbreaker in 12 innings, after the Astros had the bases loaded with no outs in the 10th but failed to score.

On October 9, facing elimination in Game Four of the best-of-five series, Houston called on Reynolds, who had won the first game, to stave off elimination. He faced Smoltz, who was making his first appearance in the series. Previously, he had appeared in four previous divisional series, fashioning a 3-0 record.

Atlanta drew first blood when Gerald Williams led off the game with a double, went to third on a fly ball, and scored on a sacrifice fly by Chipper Jones. Reminiscent of the previous game, Houston loaded the bases in the bottom of the inning on a single and two walks but could not score. In the second, the Astros put two more men on base but again failed to

A part-time shortstop on the Astros' three consecutive NL Central Division title-winning teams in 1997-99, Tim Bogar went a combined 3-for-4 at the plate in two games against the Atlanta Braves in the 1999 NLDS. His RBI double in Game Four was the last hit in the 'Dome. (Courtesy of Houston Astros Baseball Club).

advance anyone home. The Braves scored a second time in the third on Smoltz's leadoff double and Bret Boone's single.

Going into the top of the sixth, the score remained at 2-0. Brian Jordan (who would hit .471 in the series) led off with an infield single. Four consecutive singles followed as the Braves erupted for five runs. Houston manager Larry Dierker removed Reynolds after the second hit of the inning and called in Chris Holt, but he was ineffective as well. Scott Elarton finally ended the deluge after giving up a two-run single to Williams.

Smoltz pitched scoreless ball until Tony Eusebio led off the seventh with a home run. In the eighth, after allowing a single and hitting a batter, Smoltz

served up a three-run homer to Ken Caminiti to make the score 7-4. Caminiti was the only bright spot in Houston's offense in the series. He hit .471 with three home runs and eight RBIs (more than half the team's 15). As a team, Houston hit just .220.

Terry Mulholland relieved Smoltz but after a single and a double led to another run, Kevin McGlinchy replaced Mulholland. Finally, with Craig Biggio due up and representing the tying run John Rocker came in to quell the rally. Biggio came to the plate with a .111 average and struck out, ending the threat.

Rocker held the Astros scoreless in the ninth as the Braves took their fifth straight divisional series.

They eventually reached the World Series only to be swept by the Yankees.

Astros manager Larry Dierker was downcast by the loss to Atlanta. "The hard thing is having to spend six more months trying to get in again. We've been in this position three years in a row and haven't gotten past the first step. It has been very frustrating." Accounts of the game noted only in passing that it was the final game played at the Astrodome.[2]

Houston had hopes that the 35-year-old ballpark might finally host a World Series but it was not to be. Bagwell echoed Dierker in summing up the disappointment: "What a way to close the Dome. Losing a third straight postseason."[3]

Usually a ballpark's final game is marked with a ceremony of some kind. Nine days before, another stadium had bowed out as a site for major-league baseball. On September 30 the Los Angeles Dodgers defeated the San Francisco Giants in the final baseball game played at Candlestick Park. (The NFL's San Francisco 49ers continued to play there through 2013.) The Giants' farewell before 61,389 spectators included appearances by such luminaries as Willie Mays and Juan Marichal.[4] The Giants were not in the playoffs, however. Houston was.

No such ceremony took place for the last game played at the Astrodome.

Only when Caminiti flied out to center fielder Andruw Jones in the bottom of the ninth to end Houston's playoff hopes did the Dome's tenure as a major-league park come to an end. That finish could have extended through the League Championship Series to the World Series had the Astros advanced.

Because of this uncertainty, closing ceremonies were held on October 3 when the last regular-season game was played at the Astrodome. That contest saw Mike Hampton not only capture his 22nd victory of the year but also clinch the division championship for Houston. Prior to the game Charley Pride sang the National Anthem. Gene Elston introduced numerous former Astros to the 52,033 fans who were showered with red, white, and blue confetti in a 90-minute ceremony that took place after the game to give the ballpark a proper sendoff.[5]

As the Astrodome passed from the major-league scene there were any number of memories that could have been conjured up about what was originally called Harris County Domed Stadium.

As a 1964 press release noted, the Astrodome was "the world's first air-conditioned, domed, all-purpose stadium."[6] While the facility was innovative, it did challenge normal play on the field. Glare off the roof during day games interfered with fielders tracking fly balls. Judge Roy Hofheinz, owner of the Astros and a visionary who spearheaded the development of the park, resolved the problem by coating the roof with a blue acrylic substance. The glare disappeared — but then, with sunlight blocked, the grass, a Bermuda hybrid created to flourish indoors, died.[7]

To replace it, Hofheinz had Monsanto create AstroTurf, an artificial grass. While balls bounced true on the flat surface something was lost from the essence of the game. Richie Allen summed it up: "I don't want to play on no place my horse can't eat off of."[8]

Another distinctive characteristic of the Astrodome was the first animated scoreboard, a structure that cost $2 million and was programmed to "explode" when Astros hit home runs, ridicule opposing pitchers being taken out of games, and overwhelm the game on the field in general. In short, with a pyrotechnical scoreboard, the Dome, and AstroTurf, baseball became a sideshow, one that generated a distinctive style of play at one of the most pitcher-friendly ballparks in the game.[9]

The ballpark was as unique as it was innovative. Its features changed how fans came to experience a game. By the time the Astrodome hosted its last game in October 1999, most ballparks had animated scoreboards and explosive devices signaling home runs, and domed fields (often featuring retractable roofs) were no longer exceptional. The game had almost become secondary to spectacle.

NOTES

1   The facility was renamed Minute Maid Park in 2002 after Enron went bankrupt.

2   Clifton Brown, "As Usual, Astros Fail and Braves Advance," *New York Times*, October 10, 1999: SP6.

3 Curt Smith, *Storied Stadiums: Baseball's History Through Its Ballparks*, (New York: Carroll & Graf Publishers, 2001), 425.

4 "Candlestick Winds Down," *Washington Post*, October 1, 1999: D7.

5 Richard Justice, "Astros Take NL Central, Mets, Reds to Do Battle," *Washington Post*, October 4, 1999: D1; Melanie Hauser, "Victory Ends Nail-Biting Time for Houston," *New York Times*, October 4, 1999: D2.

6 Smith, 311.

7 Lowell Reidenbaugh, *The Sporting News: Take Me Out to The Ball Park* (St. Louis: The Sporting News Publishing Co., 1983), 126.

8 Smith, 314.

9 Data based on Retrosheet for the years 1965-1996 prior to the introduction of interleague play reflected 8 percent fewer runs scored at the Astrodome than at its National League counterparts. The Astrodome generated 79 home runs per year for the same period. All other parks averaged 121 home runs per year.

Astrodome as the Home to Sports Other Than Baseball

By Alan Reifman

LIKE OTHER CIRCULAR-SHAPED, MUL-tipurpose stadiums of the so-called Cookie-Cutter Era (1961-1971),[1] the Astrodome hosted both major-league baseball and National Football League teams. However, having earned the nickname "Eighth Wonder of the World" as the first domed stadium of its time, the Astrodome also attracted headliner events in many other sports. These include the UCLA-University of Houston college basketball "Game of the Century" (1968), the tennis "Battle of the Sexes" between Billie Jean King and Bobby Riggs (1973), a gymnastics exhibition by 1972 Olympic triple Gold Medalist Olga Korbut of the Soviet Union (1973), and championship fights involving legendary boxers Muhammad Ali (1966, 1967, two in 1971) and Sugar Ray Leonard (1981). According to Brock Bordelon's article "Ode to the Astrodome," that's not all: "It ... hosted polo matches, soccer and ice hockey games, bullfights, auto races, rodeos, conventions, [and] boat shows," along with an Evel Knievel motorcycle jump.[2]

Following is a detailed review of the nonbaseball athletic history of the Astrodome, focusing on the more mainstream sports played under the roof.

Football

As a home for football, the Astrodome and other fixed-roof, multipurpose stadiums generally had two major advantages and two major disadvantages. The advantages were protection from harsh weather and, specifically for the home team, amplification of crowd noise. For players a disadvantage was the absence of natural sunlight. This required artificial turf, which could be punishingly hard in addition to presenting other injury hazards, such as players' cleats getting caught and nasty rug burns. Of Astroturf, "The former trainer for the Houston Oilers claims the stuff was 'a definite factor' in the team's losing four of its best players to knee injuries last season."[3] For fans the disadvantage involved sight lines and viewing angles. With most of the action in a baseball game taking place in a diamond-shaped area, and football being played on a rectangle, seat locations that were good for viewing one of the sports usually were not good for viewing the other. The Astrodome sought to mitigate this problem somewhat through the use of movable seating sections in the lower deck.[4]

Houston Oilers

The NFL's Houston Oilers were a 29-year tenant of the Astrodome (1968-1996). The Oilers originally played in the 1960s American Football League, which eventually merged with the older NFL. Although the Astrodome was available for the Oilers in 1965, the team did not actually move in for another three years. Contract disputes delayed the Oilers' debut at the Dome: "Originally scheduled to play at the brand new Harris County Domed Stadium, the Oilers at the last minute decide[d] to play at Rice Stadium,[5] when they reject[ed] terms of the lease. Without the Oilers using the new stadium it would be renamed the Astrodome."[6]

A November 20, 1978, contest at the Dome between the Miami Dolphins and Oilers was voted in a 2002 fan survey as one of the all-time greatest NFL *Monday Night Football* games. Bum Phillips, the Oilers' coach in the latter half of the 1970s, recalled, "No one had ever taken the pro game to [the same enthusiasm of] the college level, where [all the fans] had pompoms and stuff like that."[7] In this game (and many others), Oilers running back Earl Campbell amazed observers by bowling over opposing players, his jersey often in tatters from defenders grabbing at him in unsuccessful attempts to tackle him. During

Another packed house at the Astrodome. (Courtesy of Houston Astros Baseball Club).

the Oilers' Astrodome years, their best playoff finishes were trips to the American Football Conference championship game (the qualifying game to get to the Super Bowl) after the 1978 and 1979 regular seasons. Both games were played in Pittsburgh, with the host Steelers winning each time.

Toward the end of the Oilers' time in Houston, owner Bud Adams vigorously lobbied for improvements to the Astrodome's football facilities and threatened to move the team to other cities. In September 1988 the Dome's large animation scoreboard in the outfield was decommissioned and removed to increase football seating capacity by roughly 12,000 (from 50,594 to 62,439). According to the Astrodome's application form for the National Register of Historic Places (2013), the removed scoreboard area "stretched 474 feet across the centerfield wall behind pavilion seats, and measured more than four stories high. Weighing 300 tons and requiring 1,200 miles of wiring, the sign encompassed more than half an acre."[8]

The increased capacity did little to stabilize the Oilers' status in Houston. A variety of developments led to fan discontentment to Adams's decision to move the team to Nashville, Tennessee. On January 3, 1993, Houston blew a 35-3 lead in a playoff game at Buffalo, demoralizing much of the Oilers' fan base.[9] Further, as a sign of how poor the Dome's football playing conditions had become, a 1995 preseason exhibition game between the Oilers and San Diego Chargers was canceled when the Astroturf field was ruled unfit for play.[10]

In 1993 Adams had begun campaigning for a new stadium to be built mostly with taxpayer dollars. Houston Mayor Bob Lanier refused to support the use of city tax funds for that purpose, nor did Adams find much support among the media, other sports owners, or other major players in the city.

As a result, Adams looked to Nashville, which along with the state of Tennessee was wooing him.[11] His eventual deal with Nashville, reached in November 1995, involved construction of a new stadium at a total cost of nearly $300 million—none borne by Adams—and a 30-year commitment[12] by the Oilers (later renamed the Tennessee Titans) to play in it. When it opened in 1999, the stadium seated 67,000 and included 120 luxury boxes. Adams also received a $28 million relocation fee and 100 percent of stadium revenue. (A few years after the Oilers left, Houston got a new football stadium built with extensive public funds.)

Other Professional Football Leagues

American sports have always featured upstart professional leagues attempting to compete (or at least coexist) with their more established counterparts. The American Football League was just one example. The 1970s and early 1980s were very active times for new leagues. Two had franchises in Houston: the World Football League (1974 and part of '75) and the United States Football League (1983-1985). With the WFL, finances were so bad that franchises were locating to new cities literally on a week-to-week basis. The USFL also had financial difficulties. It won an antitrust lawsuit against the NFL in 1986, but the $1 damage award (tripled to $3 under antitrust law)[13] obviously could not sustain the league.

The Astrodome hosted a team in each of these leagues. The Houston Texans of the WFL skipped town after only 11 games of the 20-game 1974 season, moving in midseason to become the Shreveport Steamer. The Houston Gamblers played during the USFL's final two seasons. Despite the Gamblers' brief existence, several big names were associated with the franchise. Quarterback Jim Kelly began his professional career with the team before going on to a Hall of Fame career with the Buffalo Bills of the NFL. Jack Pardee, a longtime NFL player and coach, was a head coach of the Gamblers; he later became a Houston coaching mainstay, leading the University of Houston from 1987 to 1989 and the Oilers from 1990 to 1994. Two assistant coaches for the Gamblers were Darrel "Mouse" Davis, known for the "Run and Shoot" offense, and John Jenkins, later a University of Houston head coach.

University of Houston

The University of Houston Cougars had a long run in the Astrodome (1965-1997), moving there from Rice Stadium. One highlight of the Cougars' Dome tenure was a nationally televised Monday night game on September 12, 1977, in which the Cougars defeated UCLA, 17-13. From 1995 to 1997 the Cougars gradually increased the number of games played on-campus at Robertson Stadium, then moved there full time in 1998. The university's new athletic director wanted its football games to have a campus atmosphere.[14]

In addition, Houston had not drawn well at the Dome. In 1989, despite a 9-2 record and an offense that averaged over 50 points per game—earning quarterback Andre Ware the Heisman Trophy—the Cougars' average home attendance was only around 28,000. In their final year at the Astrodome, it was below 20,000.[15]

The phasing out of the University of Houston's Astrodome tenure coincided with the demise of the Southwest Conference, of which the school was a member from 1976 to 1995. Well before officially disbanding, many of its schools, including the University of Houston, got in trouble with the NCAA, which may well have been a major factor in the Cougars' failure to build more of a following.

After the Southwest Conference folded, Houston landed in Conference USA, so instead of getting to play annual games against prominent in-state rivals Texas and Texas A&M, the Cougars instead played a conference schedule against distant schools like Memphis. Cincinnati, and Tulane. These new opponents presumably carried relatively little interest to football fans in the Houston area.

A college football bowl game, the Astro-Bluebonnet Bowl was played in the Astrodome from 1968 to 1984, and in 1987.

Basketball

College basketball's "Game of the Century," a 71-69 win for the University of Houston Cougars over the UCLA Bruins, was played in the Astrodome on January 20, 1968. Houston and UCLA had played in the previous year's Final Four (a 73-58 Bruins win) and Cougars coach Guy V. Lewis dreamed up the idea of a rematch in the Astrodome. The floor for the game was shipped from the Los Angeles Sports Arena and placed in the middle of the vast Astrodome floor. The list of superlatives associated with the game is extensive: a record basketball crowd at the time (52,693), first nighttime national telecast of a regular-season college basketball game, a battle of two legendary coaches (Lewis and UCLA's John Wooden) and two legendary big men (UCLA's Lew Alcindor, later known as Kareem Abdul-Jabbar, and the University of Houston's Elvin Hayes), both teams undefeated coming in, and play-by-play of the national telecast being done by an up-and-coming broadcasting star, 33-year-old Dick Enberg.[16]

UCLA had a more successful experience in the Astrodome in 1971. The NCAA Final Four was held there, with the Bruins capturing the national championship. The 1971 Final Four presaged a later trend of the Final Four regularly being held in football/baseball-sized domed stadiums. The small size of a basketball court (94 x 50 feet), compared with a 100-yard-long football field, makes a game very difficult to view from the upper decks of a stadium. However, the novelty of basketball in a dome and the ability to sell more tickets than in a conventional arena kept domed stadiums viable as hoop hosts.

The Astrodome also played a limited hosting role for NBA basketball. In the Rockets' first season in Houston (1971-72) after they moved from San Diego, the team played eight home games at the Astrodome (along with six at the adjoining Astrohall exhibition center, 21 at Hofheinz Pavilion on the University of Houston campus, and the remaining six games spread between El Paso, San Antonio, and Waco).[17]

The NBA held its annual All-Star Game at the Astrodome on February 12, 1989, with a crowd of 44,735 attending. On this day, Kareem Abdul-Jabbar came full circle, playing in his final All-Star Game near the end of his illustrious 20-year NBA career in the same building in which he had played for UCLA in the 1968 Game of the Century.

One additional piece of US pro basketball history, fascinating though obscure, is tied to the Astrodome.

The American Basketball Association, which lasted from the 1967-68 season to 1975-76, was a rival to the NBA before folding and having four of its teams absorbed into the older league.[18] On May 28, 1971, a so-called "Supergame" was held at the Astrodome, pitting all-star teams from the NBA and ABA against each other. Attendance was 16,364. According to blogger David Friedman:

> The game used NBA rules in the first half (24-second shot clock, no three-point shot[19]) and ABA rules in the second half (30-second shot clock, three-point shot). Walt Frazier came off the bench to make seven of his eight field-goal attempts in the first half and the NBA led 66-64 after Elvin Hayes' first half-buzzer beater. The game went back and forth until the NBA took a 108-98 lead in the fourth quarter. [Rick] Barry and Charlie Scott rallied the ABA to within a point with 47 seconds left, but Oscar Robertson drained two free throws to put the NBA up 123-120 with 32 seconds left. Frazier closed out the scoring with two more free throws at the 11-second mark. Frazier finished with a game-high 26 points and won a car as the game MVP.[20]

Tennis

Situated historically within the Women's Rights Movement of the 1960s and '70s, the September 20, 1973, Billie Jean King-Bobby Riggs tennis match at the Dome drew great international attention. A crowd of 30,472 attended; estimates of the television audience have ranged from 50 million viewers worldwide to 50 million in the United States and 90 million worldwide. The 55-year-old Riggs, who won the Wimbledon and US Open singles titles in 1939 and won again at the US Open in 1941, created a classic male-chauvinist persona (whatever his private attitudes actually were). If a male player as far removed from his prime as Riggs could defeat a top female player in her prime (King was 29), the implication would be that women's tennis just wasn't very good.

Prior to playing King, Riggs had defeated another leading women's player, Margaret Court, 6-2, 6-1, on May 13, 1973, in a much more low-key setting.

King later described the high stakes of the match: "I thought it would set us back 50 years if I didn't win that match. ... It would ruin the women's tour and affect all women's self esteem."[21] King and Riggs opted to play a three-out-of-five-sets match, presumably so that each could showcase his/her endurance. This decision is noteworthy because even today, more than 40 years after the King-Riggs match, major women's championships still use a two-out-of-three format. King showed considerably greater fitness than Riggs, garnering a straight-sets victory, 6-4, 6-3, 6-3.

Soccer

Two soccer teams, the Houston Stars of the United Soccer Association (1967-1968) and Houston Hurricane of the NASL (1978-1980) called the Astrodome home during their brief runs. A recent history of soccer in Houston said the Stars led the league in attendance with an average attendance of over 19,000.[22]

"The Superstars"

A made-for-television sports franchise in the 1970s was ABC's *The Superstars*. Superstar competitions pitted athletes from different sports against one another in several events, including swimming, running, tennis, and weightlifting. Athletes received points based on their performance in each event (10 for first place, 7 for second, etc.). Contestants could not compete in their own sport. Most of the Superstar programs featured competitions between men, but women also competed. There were also "Superteam" and "Celebrity Superteam" battles.

In 1975, the first year women competed, the Astrodome hosted the two semifinal competitions (covered by *Sports Illustrated*[23]). The final round was held at the main Superstars complex in Florida. Events contested in Houston included tennis, softball throwing, basketball shooting, swimming, rowing (held at Lake Conroe), bicycling, bowling, obstacle course, 60-yard dash, and one-fifth-mile run (because there wasn't enough space in the Dome for a traditional quarter-mile oval).

Top finishers at the Astrodome included diver Micki King, speed skater Dianne Holum, and softball player Joan Joyce (first semifinal); and volleyball player Mary Jo Peppler, basketball player Karen Logan, and former Olympic sprinter Wyomia Tyus (second semifinal). Peppler went on to win the overall title in Florida. Billie Jean King took fifth in the second semifinal group and qualified for the finals, but she did not compete.[24]

Rodeo

The Houston Livestock Show and Rodeo, which was founded in 1931 and as of 2016 was held at NRG (formerly Reliant) Stadium, took place in the Astrodome from 1966 to 2002.[25] Rodeo competitions are sanctioned by the Professional Rodeo Cowboys Association. Contested events include bull riding, saddle bronc riding, calf roping, steer wrestling, and an all-around title.[26] The annual event also features other festivities such as popular musical performers and a barbecue contest.

Conclusion

During its first decade (1965-1975), the Astrodome hosted an array of sporting events whose breadth and importance arguably have not been equaled by any other US sports venue within a 10-year period. The Astrodome was the only football-and-baseball-sized domed stadium during this decade. Novelty and uniqueness were probably the main reasons for the Astrodome attracting the events it did, rather than the quality of the viewing experience (especially from the upper decks).

Once the Superdome opened in 1975 for the NFL's New Orleans Saints, it too began to attract major sporting events outside of its primary sport, including the basketball Final Four and prizefighting. At this point, the Astrodome's uniqueness was lost.

The Astrodome's precedent of hosting a major basketball game in a baseball/football-sized stadium has stood the test of time in some ways, but not others. The men's basketball Final Four has consistently been held in domed stadiums rather than conventional arenas since the 1990s. However, every NBA team that once used a dome as a full-time home (e.g., the Detroit Pistons in the Pontiac Silverdome from 1978-1988) has abandoned the concept.

Some seemingly good news for the Astrodome's legacy is that its application to the National Register of Historic Places was approved in 2014. Such a designation may be less important than it seems, however. National Register status does not prevent the demolition of a building.[27] Further, there are 1.5 million structures in the Register, hardly making it an exclusive club.

One can find positive and negative aspects of the Astrodome's nonbaseball activities. The college basketball Game of the Century and the King-Riggs tennis match were glamorous, exciting, and historic events that enhanced the Dome's reputation. However, the physical facilities left much to be desired for athletes and spectators alike.

NOTES

1 These stadiums include Atlanta-Fulton County (opened in 1965), Busch II (St. Louis, 1966), Oakland-Alameda County (1966), RFK (Washington, 1961), Riverfront/Cinergy (Cincinnati, 1970), Shea (New York, 1964), Three Rivers (Pittsburgh, 1970), and Veterans (Philadelphia, 1971). Years are from ballparks.com.

2 Brock Bordelon, "Ode to the Astrodome," *Astros Daily*. astrosdaily.com/history/odetodome/.

3 Kenneth Denlinger, "Artificial Turf Brings Cheers—And Groans," *St. Petersburg Times*, September 28, 1971.

4 Louis O. Bass, "Unusual Dome Awaits Baseball Season in Houston," *Civil Engineering: The Magazine of the American Society of Civil Engineers* (January 1965). columbia.edu/cu/gsapp/BT/DOMES/HOUSTON/h-unusua.html.

5 The history of football in Houston during the Astrodome years cannot fully be understood without reference to Rice Stadium (on the Rice University campus), three miles away. Even though the annual enrollment at Rice, an academically elite institution, has typically been only a few thousand, the school erected a 70,000-seat stadium in 1950. Designed specifically for football, the stadium has a number of positive features, including a high percentage of seats between the goal lines. In fact, when Houston was awarded Super Bowl VIII (1974), it was held at Rice Stadium, rather than the city's regular NFL home, the Astrodome. In the author's view (developed while living in Houston from 1989 to 1991), Rice's location in a residential neighborhood precluded greater use of the stadium for high-attendance (e.g., NFL) games, due to concerns over noise, traffic, and other disturbances. The university's own team does not draw well. According to one recent estimate, Rice University's home games draw between 13,000 and 20,000 fans (*The Pecan Park Eagle*, Rice Stadium Dreams, http://bill37mccurdy.com/2011/08/26/rice-stadium-dreams/).

6 Sports E-cyclopedia. Houston Oilers. sportsecyclopedia.com/nfl/tenhou/houoilers.html.

7 Mike Diegnan, "MNF's Greatest Games: Miami-Houston 1978," ESPN.com, December 4, 2002. espn.go.com/abcsports/mnf/s/greatestgames/miamihouston1978.html.

8 National Register of Historic Places, Registration form for Houston Astrodome (2013). nps.gov/nr/feature/places/pdfs/13001099.pdf.

9 One of the author's friends who lived in Houston at the time told him that, after the loss to Buffalo, some of her neighbors went out into the street and publicly burned their Oilers' paraphernalia!

10 Associated Press, "Astrodome Game Off Because of Rug," *Los Angeles Times*, August 20, 1995. articles.latimes.com/1995-08-20/sports/sp-37194_1_exhibition-game.

11 Raymond J. Keating, "The NFL Oilers: A Case Study in Corporate Welfare: How Houston's Struggle Against Stadium Subsidies Failed," *The Freeman*, Foundation for Economic Education (April 1, 1998). fee.org/freeman/the-nfl-oilers-a-case-study-in-corporate-welfare/.

12 John Glennon, "Former Mayor Recalls Bud Adams' Decision to Move Team to Nashville," *The Tennessean*, October 21, 2013. archive.tennessean.com/article/DN/20131021/SPORTS01/310210071/Former-mayor-recalls-Bud-Adams-decision-move-team-Nashville.

13 Paul Domowitch, "USFL Dealt Crippling Blow[;] Jury Awards $3 In Antitrust Suit," *Philadelphia Daily News*. July 30, 1986. articles.philly.com/1986-07-30/sports/26099171_1_usfl-attorney-harvey-myerson-damage-award-nfl-attorney.

14 James Beltran, "Next Season's Home Games to Be Played at Robertson," *Daily Cougar*. archive.thedailycougar.com/vol63/86/News1/862698/862698.html.

15 *University of Houston 2015 Football Media Guide*. grfx.cstv.com/photos/schools/hou/sports/m-footbl/auto_pdf/2015-16/misc_non_event/15mediaguide.pdf.

16 Eddie Einhorn (with Ron Rapoport), *How March Became Madness: How the NCAA Tournament Became the Greatest Sporting Event in America* (Chicago: Triumph, 2006). Einhorn produced the television broadcast of the UCLA-Houston "Game of the Century," and his book provides extensive interviews with many of the principals from the game. The book also comes with a DVD of the second half of the UCLA-Houston basketball game (the only footage that exists of the original broadcast).

17 *Houston Rockets 2008–09 Media Guide*. nba.com/media/rockets/MediaGuide0809_page173.212.pdf.

18 These teams were the Denver Nuggets, Indiana Pacers, San Antonio Spurs, and the then-New York Nets.

19 The NBA adopted the three-point shot in 1979-80.

20 David Friedman, "Supergames I & II: The 1971 and 1972 NBA-ABA All-Star Games," *20-Second Time-Out Blog* (February 23, 2009). 20secondtimeout.blogspot.com/2009/02/abas-unsung-heroes.html. One more Supergame was played the next year at Nassau Coliseum on Long Island, New York.

21 Larry Schwartz, "Billie Jean Won for All Women." espn.go.com/sportscentury/features/00016060.html.

22 "A Soccer History of Houston." *U.S. National Soccer Players.* ussoccerplayers.com/a-soccer-history-of-houst.

23 Curry Kirkpatrick, "There Is Nothing Like a Dame," *Sports Illustrated,* January 6, 1975. si.com/vault/1975/01/06/616978/there-is-nothing-like-a-dame.

24 An excellent historical website on the competition exists, known as "The Superstars.org." Within the larger website, pages detailing the Astrodome event are thesuperstars.org/comp/75wpr1.html and thesuperstars.org/comp/75wpr2.html.

25 "Looking Back at the History of the Rodeo," *Houston Chronicle,* February 13, 2015. chron.com/entertainment/rodeo/article/Looking-back-at-the-history-of-the-rodeo-6070965.php.

26 "Several World Titlists Win Big Bucks at Houston Rodeo," *Livestock Weekly,* March 19, 1998.

27 Associated Press, "Astrodome Named Historic Place," ESPN.com, January 31, 2014. espn.go.com/mlb/story/_/id/10385397/houston-astrodome-added-national-register-historic-places.

50 Years and Counting: What Does the Future Hold for the Astrodome?

By Justin Krueger

IT HAS BEEN 50 YEARS SINCE THE Astrodome first opened to worldwide acclaim as the world's first domed, air-conditioned, multipurpose facility. From the beginning it was more than just a building; it was an experience of awe and a demonstration of civic swagger.[1] As the brainchild of enigmatic former Houston mayor and political stalwart Judge Roy Hofheinz, the Astrodome opened to much fanfare, including a visit from President Lyndon B. Johnson and first lady Lady Bird Johnson at an exhibition game between the Houston Astros and New York Yankees.[2]

By 2015, on the 50th anniversary of its opening, the Astrodome had not aged gracefully. Since it had been vacated by its longtime tenants the Houston Oilers (who became the Tennessee Titans) in 1996 and the Houston Astros in 1999, the Astrodome had outlived its usefulness as a sports facility.

Since the Houston Astros played their last game in the Astrodome on October 9, 1999, the stadium's most notable use was as an emergency refuge for some 25,000 evacuees from New Orleans who had been displaced by Hurricane Katrina in 2005.[3]

On its half-century anniversary, the structure that once captured the public's imagination for its innovation presented itself as a dingy, outdated, and unused structure. Placed in the shadow of the much newer, larger, and boxier NRG Stadium (home of the Houston Texans), the Astrodome sat much like an abandoned puppy that is desperately looking, praying, and hoping for someone to care for it before it is too late.

As regional officials discussed plans for its future, or its lack thereof, the Astrodome was still very much in the public consciousness. For many Houstonians it served as a cultural icon of a bygone era, as was evidenced by the sale of Astrodome seats and other surviving memorabilia in 2013, 2014, and 2015 that netted around $1 million each time. There have also been successful sales of patches of Astroturf and furniture from the stadium's luxury suites.[4]

In an attempt to continue to raise awareness and support for the preservation of the Astrodome, Houston Arts & Media in January 2016 announced the "Our Astrodome Art Contest," through which children and adults could submit their best "artistic and imaginative representations of the 8th Wonder of the World." The contest was part of a growing movement to garner support to save and repurpose the Astrodome. Positioning the Astrodome alongside the Alamo as the two defining architectural icons of Texas, Houston Arts & Media hoped to turn the conversation about the Astrodome away from its state of abandonment and toward both the significance of its past and the possibilities for its future.[5]

To many citizens who arrived in Houston—whether by birth or by choice—after the novelty of the Astrodome had worn off, the dilapidated arena was an eyesore to which they had no attachment. Those who opposed the Dome's preservation believed it should be razed to make room for additional parking for fans who attend Houston Texans games and the Houston Livestock Show and Rodeo.

The potential destruction of the Astrodome loomed as a sad fate for the first sports venue that rendered the outdoor elements completely inconsequential. Mosquitos, rainouts, and heat exhaustion were rendered moot[6] and made attending a baseball game much more enjoyable than it had been at its predecessor, Colt Stadium, which had been the home

Bill Virdon became the Astros' manager in 1975 and guided the team to its first two playoff appearances in 1980 and 1981. As of 2016, he still led the franchise in managerial victories with 544. (Courtesy of Houston Astros Baseball Club).

of the Colt 45s (later renamed the Astros) from 1962 to 1964. Former Astros great Jimmy Wynn emphasized the importance of the Astrodome when he said, "If it wasn't for Judge Hofheinz getting this built, baseball wouldn't have survived in Houston, the heat and the humidity was just too much."[7]

Beyond its significance to baseball in the subtropical climate of the Gulf of Mexico, *Los Angeles Times* architecture critic Christopher Hawthorne has noted that the Astrodome is a monument to the "American confidence and Texas swagger of the 1960s" as it perfectly captured this place in time.[8] Such a statement about the impact and value of the Astrodome raises the question of what the future of the Astrodome is to be.

Except for the Texas-sized rats that called it home, the Astrodome has sat vacant since 2008, when it was closed to the public due to a litany of code violations.[9] Since that time various proposals to repurpose the Dome—from a shopping mall to an amusement park and everything in between—have been debated and rejected. All the while, the stadium continued to

deteriorate to the point that demolition seemed imminent, so much so that proponents of its preservation got it added to the National Register of Historic Places in 2014, for its architectural and cultural significance, in an attempt to eliminate destruction as a viable option; however, while such designation allowed Harris County to gain state and federal tax credits, it did not automatically save the Astrodome from demolition.[10]

Many observers believe that the Astrodome's demolition would be "a failure of civic imagination"[11] and a counterintuitive move for the largest major city without any zoning restrictions, one that thrives on reimagining itself through innovation. As of 2016 the Astrodome existed as a ward of Harris County, which owned the structure, and its fate rested largely with four Harris County commissioners and Harris County Judge Ed Emmett,[12] who said he saw the stadium as a sound structure that has already been paid for by the county and that he believed a solid and mutually advantageous plan should be developed for all parties that had an interest in the Dome's fate. As of 2016, however, Emmett was unable to garner unanimous support for any proposal from Harris County's commissioners, the public, or the major tenants of the NRG Complex (the Houston Texans, the Houston Livestock Show and Rodeo, and the Offshore Technology Conference).

If the Astrodome was to survive, officials had to imagine new possibilities for it to keep it in touch with the newer, younger population of Houston. The value of repurposing the city's icon would be not only to breathe life into the Dome but also to once again put Houston at the forefront of architectural innovation.[13] The primary roadblock to accomplishing this feat was that Houston has a "history problem."[14] The city's diverse population has a tendency to look forward, without an appreciation for a past in which it had no part; it considered the building to be too old to be useful but too new to be worthy of historic preservation.

Another roadblock was the lack of a shared vision for the future of the Astrodome. After a failed 2013 referendum to repurpose the Astrodome, the

Houston Texans and the Houston Livestock Show and Rodeo commissioned a study to find another option for a resolution of what could be done with it.[15]

The resulting NRG Astrodome proposal, which had an estimated total project cost of $66 million, called for the removal of the entire Astrodome structure except for the giant drive-through concrete pillars encapsulating the outdoor perimeter of the Astrodome. The proposal would have freed up approximately 8.8 acres of open space and created 385,000 square feet of usable green space within the concrete pillars. The proposal followed the precedent of Houston's Discovery Green, an enormously popular and successful repurposing of urban green space located downtown near Minute Maid Park, the successor to the Astrodome as the home of the Houston Astros. The proposal would have also opened up the flow of traffic around the Astrodome and would have created a pedestrian thoroughfare to an open area that could have been used for outdoor activities and programmable space. A 25,000-square-foot Astrodome replica, an Astrodome Hall of Fame, and a restaurant would have been located at the center of the area.[16] In the end, the removal of the Astrodome as central to the plan left the proposal as nothing more than another interesting idea that was rejected.

The latest idea as of this writing was to repurpose the structure into an indoor multi-use park and to continue to make the Astrodome a place for traditional outdoor activities in a climate-controlled arena, a plan for its future similar to Judge Roy Hofheinz's initial vision of bringing baseball indoors.[17] Though the new proposal was certainly plausible, Emmett readily admitted that "the worst thing you can [do] is repurpose and then have the repurposing fail."[18] To this end, due diligence was paid to determine the feasibility and benefit of such a project, including a study from the Urban Land Institute and a visit to Tropical Islands resort in Krausnick, Germany.

In March 2015 the Urban Land Institute, an advisory panel of experts in real estate, land-use planning, and development, released its recommendations for the Astrodome at the behest of the Harris County Commissioners Court.[19] First and foremost, the group reached the unanimous decision that the Astrodome should be conserved and repurposed for civic use.[20] In very general terms, the institute's proposal planned to keep about 100,000 square feet of green space in the center of the Astrodome, with areas for events around the sides of the structure. The plan also called for about 1,500 parking spaces on the dome's lower level.[21]

What the actual park might look like if that plan was followed was anyone's guess, but it could include observation decks, trails, exercise facilities, and space for festivals. According to Todd Mead, a panel member and senior associate at PWP Landscape Architecture in Berkeley, California, the proposal is "built upon the idea of a park that's indoors that makes an outdoor connection and a civic contribution as well."[22] Another possibility could be to add adventure elements which could "include zip lines—allowing adventuresome folks to speed down the equivalent of an 18-story building from the upper levels inside the Dome."[23]

In addition to soliciting the Urban Land Institute's ideas, Houston city and county officials visited the Tropical Islands, a domed facility near Berlin, to explore an alternative proposal for the Astrodome.[24] Built in 2000 on an old Luftwaffe airfield, the dome was to serve as an airship hangar for the German company CargoLifter AG; however, in 2002, the company went insolvent and the dome closed. The facility was turned into an indoor rainforest with more than 50,000 plants, water, and beach, accommodations for 6,000 visitors, a hot-air balloon and an adventure park.

The final obstacle to the preservation of the Astrodome was funding, a major sticking point as evidenced by a failed bond referendum in 2013 in which 53.5 percent of voters said no to the $200 million initiative to repurpose the Astrodome with public monies.[25] Emmett then presented the idea of developing a public-private partnership that would be overseen by a conservancy, which would allow for the collection of funds from a variety of sources and would thus negate the need for taxpayer funds.[26]

Historic tax credits, philanthropic donations, and the creation of tax-increment reinvestment zones would likely alleviate the need to call for a bond referendum on the Astrodome,[27] which it was thought might give this idea the traction it needed to finally put the Astrodome toward the path of revitalization.

Houston preservationist James Glassman has called the Astrodome "the physical manifestation of Houston's soul."[28] It is *the* architectural landmark of Houston, but it is currently relegated to a purgatory of neglect and limbo in which its glorious past has been lost.

The biggest question facing the future of the Astrodome was solved on January 27, 2017. On that date the Texas Historical Commission voted to make the first domed stadium in the world a State Antiquities Landmark. The Astrodome now joins other sites, such as the Alamo in San Antonio and the State Capitol in Austin, with such a lofty designation.

NOTES

1   Richard Justice, "Astrodome Remembered as Baseball Innovation,"MLB.com, April 18, 2015.

2   Nate Berg, "Houston's Astrodome: 'the Eighth Wonder of the World'—a History of Cities in 50 Buildings, Day 12," *The Guardian*, April 9, 2015.

3   Wayne Chandler, "Astrodome," *Texas State Historical Association*, June 9, 2010.

4   Mike Acosta, "Astroturf: Then, Now and Possibly Again." *Our Astrodome*, 2015.

5   Craig Hlavaty, "Astrodome Art Contest Announced for Artistic Houstonians," Chron.com, *Houston Chronicle*.

6   Jeré Longman, "Dirty and Dated, but Irreplaceable," *New York Times*, May 26, 2013.

7   Justice.

8   Christopher Hawthorne, "Why the Astrodome Is Worth Saving," *Los Angeles Times*, November 5, 2013.

9   Ibid.

10 "Astrodome Named Historic Place," Associated Press, January 31, 2014.

11 Longman.

12 "About Our Astrodome," *Our Astrodome*, 2015.

13 "About Our Astrodome."

14 Berg.

15 "Statement Regarding NRG Astrodome Proposal," *Houston Livestock Show and Rodeo*, July 10, 2014.

16 "Astrodome Site Study," *NRG*, February 2014.

17 Emmett.

18 Marcelino Benito, "Could a German Tropical Paradise Help Save the Astrodome?" KHOU, May 3, 2015.

19 Houston Astrodome, Urban Land Institute.

20 Pat Hernandez, "Urban Land Institute Proposes Astrodome Plan," *Houston Public Media*, December 19, 2014.

21 Craig Hlavaty, "New Urban Land Institute Plan for Astrodome Calls for Multi-Usage, Parking Below," Chron.com, *Houston Chronicle*, March 23, 2015.

22 Ralph Bivins, "Visions of a New Life for Houston's Historic Astrodome," *Urban Land*, January 29, 2015.

23 Ibid.

24 Benito.

25 Berg.

26 Gabrielle Banks, "A New Plan Emerges to Save the Astrodome," *Houston Chronicle*, July 28, 2015.

27 Hlavaty, "New Urban."

28 Longman.

The Astrodome by the Numbers

By Dan Fields

0

Pitches thrown by winning pitcher Frank Carpin of the Astros on May 5, 1966, against the Cubs at the Astrodome. As he entered the game with two outs in the top of the 13th, the score was tied 3-3 with runners on first and second. The runners advanced on a double steal before he threw a pitch. When the runner on third broke for home, Carpin stepped off the rubber and threw him out at the plate. The Astros scored in the bottom of the 13th to give him the victory.

1st

Regular-season game played indoors, between the Astros and the Phillies on April 12, 1965, at the Astrodome. The Astros were held to four hits and lost 2-0. More than 20 US astronauts threw out ceremonial first pitches from behind the Houston dugout.

1st

Major-league game played entirely on artificial turf, between the Astros and the Phillies on July 19, 1966, at the Astrodome. Houston won 8-2; Turk Farrell pitched a complete game and hit a three-run homer. During the first half of the 1966 season, the field featured Astroturf only on the infield, with painted dirt in the outfield.

1

"Rainout" at the Astrodome, on June 15, 1976. Local flooding from heavy rains prevented the umpires and all but about 20 fans from reaching the stadium for the scheduled game between the Astros and the Pirates.

2

Consecutive one-hitters by Houston pitchers at the Astrodome, by Jerry Reuss on June 18, 1972, against the Phillies and Larry Dierker on June 19 against the Mets.

2

Home runs by Lee May of the Astros in the sixth inning on April 29, 1974, off Burt Hooton and Jim Kremmel of the Cubs, and by Jeff Bagwell of the Astros in the sixth inning on June 24, 1994, off Ramon Martinez and Rudy Seanez of the Dodgers.

2

All-Star Games played at the Astrodome. On July 9, 1968, NL pitchers (including future Hall of Famers Don Drysdale, Juan Marichal, Steve Carlton, and Tom Seaver) limited the AL to three hits, and the NL won 1-0. On July 15, 1986, Roger Clemens of the Red Sox pitched three perfect innings and was named the game's MVP; the AL won 3-2. Fernando Valenzuela of the Dodgers struck out five consecutive batters during the fourth and fifth innings to match Carl Hubbell's 1934 record for an All-Star Game.

3

Players who hit a home run at the Astrodome in their first major-league at-bat: pitcher Jose Sosa of the Astros on July 30, 1975 (his only career home run); Will Clark of the Giants on April 8, 1986 (284 career home runs); and pitcher Dustin Hermanson of the Expos on April 16, 1997 (two career home runs).

4

Wild pitches by Phil Niekro of the Braves in the fifth inning on August 4, 1979 (second game of doubleheader), against the Astros at the Astrodome. He threw six wild pitches during the game.

4

Shutouts pitched by Randy Johnson in his first four starts with the Astros at the Astrodome, from August 7 to September 7, 1996. In those four games, he struck out 51 batters and walked four.

4

Players who hit for the cycle at the Astrodome: Dave Kingman, Giants, on April 16, 1972; Cesar Cedeño, Astros, on August 2, 1972; Bob Watson, Astros, on June 24, 1977 (11-inning game); and Andujar Cedeño, Astros, on August 25, 1992 (13-inning game).

6

No-hitters at the Astrodome. All were thrown by Houston pitchers: Don Wilson on June 18, 1967, against the Braves; Larry Dierker on July 9, 1976, against the Expos; Ken Forsch on April 7, 1979, against the Braves; Nolan Ryan on September 26, 1981, against Dodgers; Mike Scott on September 25, 1986, against the Giants; and Darryl Kile on September 8, 1993, against the Mets. Ryan's no-no made him first pitcher with five no-hitters, and Scott became the first pitcher to clinch a playoff berth with a no-hitter.

7

Double plays turned by the Astros on May 4, 1969, against the Giants at the Astrodome. This was a new NL record and tied the major-league record set in 1942. First baseman Curt Blefary participated in all seven double plays.

8

Consecutive hits by the Astros in the 12th inning on June 2, 1966, against the Reds at the Astrodome. The Astros scored eight runs during the inning and won 11-3.

8

Consecutive batters struck out to begin the game by Jim Deshaies of the Astros on September 23, 1986, against the Dodgers at the Astrodome—a 20th-century record.

9

Home runs allowed by Houston pitchers in 51 games at the Astrodome in 1981 (strike-shortened season).

J.R. Richard intimidated hitters with a combination of his 6-foot-8 frame and explosive pitches. His career ended prematurely after he suffered a stroke on July 30, 1980, during a workout at the Astrodome. (Courtesy of Houston Astros Baseball Club).

10

Hits allowed by Joaquin Andujar of the Astros in a shutout of the Reds on June 26, 1976, at the Astrodome.

10

Walks allowed by J.R. Richard of the Astros in a shutout of the Mets on July 6, 1976, at the Astrodome.

11

Consecutive home losses by the Astros from July 23 to August 17, 1966. During the streak, they had a record of 4-11 on the road.

11-0

Score by which the Astros trailed the Cardinals after three innings on July 18, 1994, at the Astrodome,

Being interviewed after his record-setting fifth no-hitter in 1981, Nolan Ryan posted a 106-94 record with a 3.13 ERA and 1,866 strikeouts in nine seasons with the Astros, He was a two-time NL ERA leader (1981, 1987) and two-time strikeout leader (1987, 1988). (Courtesy of Houston Astros Baseball Club).

before scoring two runs each in the fourth and fifth innings and 11 runs in the sixth inning. They held on to win 15-12.

12 and 30

Home runs at the Astrodome and on the road, respectively, by Jeff Bagwell of the Astros in 1999.

15

Home runs by the Astros at the Astrodome in 1979, the fewest in any season at the ballpark.

16

Innings in Game Six of the NLCS on October 15, 1986, at the Astrodome. The Mets beat the Astros 7-6 to clinch their third NL crown. It was the longest postseason game up to that point: 4 hours, 42 minutes.

19

Home runs by Tony Perez at the Astrodome, the most by any player who was never on the Astros. He hit 17 with the Reds and two with the Expos.

20th

Win of the 1986 season by Fernando Valenzuela of the Dodgers, on September 22 against the Astros at the Astrodome. He became the first Mexican-born pitcher to win 20 games in a season.

22

Innings in a June 3, 1989, game between the Astros and the Dodgers at the Astrodome. The game, which the Astros won 5-4, lasted 7 hours and 14 minutes and set a major-league record for the longest night game. LA center fielder John Shelby went hitless in 10 at-bats.

24

Innings in a game on April 15, 1968, in which the Astros beat the Mets 1-0 at the Astrodome. Three players had at least nine at-bats without a hit.

25

Consecutive games with a base hit at the Astrodome by Rusty Staub of the Astros, from May 31 to July 25, 1967.

36-45

Home record of the Astros in 1965, the worst single-season record at the Astrodome.

55-26

Home record of the Astros in 1980 and 1998, the best single-season record at the Astrodome.

66th

Home run of the season by Sammy Sosa of the Cubs on September 25, 1998, off Jose Lima of the Astros at the Astrodome.

71

Home runs allowed by Houston pitchers at the Astrodome in 1998, the most in any season in the ballpark.

82

Home runs by the Astros at the Astrodome in 1998, the most in any season in the ballpark.

106th

Appearance of the 1974 season by reliever Mike Marshall of the Dodgers, on October 1 against the Astros at the Astrodome.

113-103-2

Regular-season record of the Houston Oilers at the Astrodome from 1968 through 1996. The team had a 3-2 record in playoff games at the stadium.

208

Feet above second base of the gondola in which Mets play-by-play announcer Lindsey Nelson broadcast a game between the Astros and the Mets on April 28, 1965, at the Astrodome.

Craig Biggio's 20-year Astros career included 3,060 hits, 1,844 runs scored, 668 doubles, 291 home runs, 1,175 RBIs, and 414 stolen bases. (Courtesy of Houston Astros Baseball Club).

.228

Batting average of the Astros at the Astrodome in 1981, the lowest single-season average at the ballpark. The Astros hit .257 on the road that year.

.268

Batting average of the Astros at the Astrodome in 1994, the highest single-season average at the stadium. The Astros hit .275 on the road that year.

326-229

Regular-season record of Bill Virdon as a manager at the Astrodome, the most wins and most losses by any manager there. He had a record of 7-5 with the Pirates (1972 and 1973), 316-215 with the Astros (1975 to 1982), and 3-9 with the Expos (1983 and 1984).

500th

Career home run by Willie Mays of the Giants, on September 13, 1965, off Don Nottebart of the Astros at the Astrodome. He became the fifth player to reach the milestone.

1,564-1,210

Regular-season record of the Astros at Astrodome from 1965 through 1999. They had a record of 5-8 in the playoffs.

1,776th

Career walk by Nolan Ryan of the Astros on June 5, 1981, to Lee Mazzilli of the Mets at the Astrodome. Ryan passed Early Wynn to become baseball's all-time walk leader.

4,000th

Career strikeout by Nolan Ryan on July 11, 1985, against Danny Heep of the Mets at the Astrodome. Ryan became the first player to accomplish this feat.

54,037

Attendance at a September 28, 1999, game between the Astros and the Reds, the most for a major-league game at the Astrodome.

858,002

Home attendance of the Astros in 1975, lowest in a single season at the Astrodome.

2,706,017

Home attendance of the Astros in 1999, highest in a single season at the Astrodome.

ASTRODOME CAREER LEADERS

Batting

Games

931	Jose Cruz
857	Craig Biggio
791	Cesar Cedeño
765	Terry Puhl
700	Bob Watson

Plate appearances

3686	Craig Biggio
3639	Jose Cruz
3233	Cesar Cedeño
2843	Jim Wynn
2832	Jeff Bagwell

At-bats

3197	Jose Cruz
3141	Craig Biggio
2872	Cesar Cedeño
2383	Terry Puhl
2369	Bob Watson

Runs

535	Craig Biggio
465	Jeff Bagwell
426	Cesar Cedeño
416	Jim Wynn
412	Jose Cruz

Hits

949	Jose Cruz
913	Craig Biggio
810	Cesar Cedeño
704	Jeff Bagwell
683	Bob Watson

Doubles

201	Craig Biggio
174	Cesar Cedeño
165	Jose Cruz
164	Jeff Bagwell
132	Jim Wynn

Triples

50	Jose Cruz
44	Joe Morgan
37	Roger Metzger
35	Terry Puhl
33	Craig Reynolds

Home runs

126	Jeff Bagwell
97	Jim Wynn
72	Glenn Davis
66	Cesar Cedeño
64	Craig Biggio

RBIs

469	Jeff Bagwell
460	Jose Cruz
389	Cesar Cedeño
356	Bob Watson
341	Jim Wynn

Walks

458	Jim Wynn
444	Jeff Bagwell
444	Joe Morgan
398	Jose Cruz
395	Craig Biggio

Intentional walks

79	Jose Cruz
64	Jeff Bagwell
44	Bob Watson
43	Glenn Davis
42	Cesar Cedeño
42	Jim Wynn

Strikeouts

489	Jim Wynn
485	Craig Biggio
441	Jeff Bagwell
401	Jose Cruz
400	Doug Rader

Hit by pitch

92	Craig Biggio
43	Jeff Bagwell
25	Cesar Cedeño
22	Glenn Davis
22	Bob Watson

Batting average (min. 1,400 at-bats)

.303	Jeff Bagwell
.297	Jose Cruz
.291	Craig Biggio
.288	Bob Watson
.284	Kevin Bass

On-base percentage (min. 1,400 at-bats)

.421	Jeff Bagwell
.404	Joe Morgan
.383	Craig Biggio
.382	Jim Wynn
.371	Jose Cruz

Slugging percentage (min. 1,400 at-bats)

.546	Jeff Bagwell
.488	Glenn Davis
.457	Jim Wynn
.432	Cesar Cedeño
.430	Craig Biggio

OPS (min. 1,400 at-bats)

.966	Jeff Bagwell
.843	Glenn Davis
.840	Jim Wynn
.815	Joe Morgan
.813	Craig Biggio

Stolen bases

263	Cesar Cedeño
194	Craig Biggio
151	Jose Cruz
138	Joe Morgan
113	Terry Puhl

Pitching

ERA (min. 500 innings)

2.58	J.R. Richard
2.66	Ken Forsch
2.70	Mike Scott
2.71	Larry Dierker
2.77	Nolan Ryan

Wins

87	Larry Dierker
73	Joe Niekro
65	Mike Scott
59	Nolan Ryan
57	Don Wilson

Losses

52	Joe Niekro
49	Larry Dierker
47	Bob Knepper
45	Don Wilson
44	Nolan Ryan

Winning percentage (min. 50 decisions)

.704	Mike Hampton
.646	Shane Reynolds
.640	Larry Dierker
.619	Mike Scott
.618	Jim Deshaies

Games pitched

299	Dave Smith
206	Ken Forsch
203	Joe Niekro
176	Larry Dierker
171	Joe Sambito

Games started

169	Larry Dierker
155	Joe Niekro
147	Nolan Ryan
144	Bob Knepper
136	Mike Scott

Complete games

67	Larry Dierker
43	Joe Niekro
43	J.R. Richard
42	Don Wilson
27	Bob Knepper

Shutouts

17	Larry Dierker
15	Bob Knepper
15	Joe Niekro
15	Mike Scott
11	J.R. Richard

Saves

107	Dave Smith
49	Billy Wagner
39	Joe Sambito
33	Fred Gladding
27	Ken Forsch
27	Doug Jones

Innings pitched

1272	Larry Dierker
1189	Joe Niekro
995	Bob Knepper
989⅔	Nolan Ryan
951	Don Wilson

Walks

413	Nolan Ryan
412	Joe Niekro
370	J.R. Richard
361	Larry Dierker
320	Don Wilson

Intentional walks

28	Ken Forsch
28	Dave Smith
24	Larry Dierker
23	Larry Andersen
21	Bob Knepper

Strikeouts

1004	Nolan Ryan
882	Larry Dierker
754	J.R. Richard
729	Mike Scott
671	Don Wilson

Home runs allowed

69	Larry Dierker
68	Don Wilson
67	Bob Knepper
60	Mike Scott
54	Shane Reynolds

Hit by pitch

37	Darryl Kile
26	Jack Billingham
24	Nolan Ryan
23	Larry Dierker
23	Don Wilson

Wild pitches

67	Joe Niekro
61	J.R. Richard
52	Larry Dierker
48	Nolan Ryan
47	Don Wilson

ASTRODOME SINGLE-SEASON LEADERS

Batting

Games: 82 by Ken Caminiti, 1989; Jeff Bagwell, 1999

Plate appearances: 371 by Craig Biggio, 1999

At-bats: 328 by Enos Cabell, 1978

Runs: 75 by Craig Biggio, 1997

Hits: 104 by Derek Bell, 1998

Doubles: 27 by Craig Biggio, 1999

Triples: 8 by Joe Morgan, 1965; Joe Morgan, 1967; Bill Doran, 1984; Craig Reynolds, 1984; Steve Finley, 1991; Craig Biggio, 1997

Home runs: 23 by Jeff Bagwell, 1994

RBIs: 68 by Jeff Bagwell, 1998

Walks: 83 to Jim Wynn, 1969

Intentional walks: 14 to Rusty Staub, 1968

Strikeouts: 72 by Jim Wynn, 1969; Lee May, 1972

Hit by pitch: 18 by Craig Biggio, 1997

Batting average: .373 by Jeff Bagwell, 1994 (strike-shortened season); the highest average in a full-length season was .353 by Jose Cruz, 1978

On-base percentage: .477 by Jim Wynn, 1969

Slugging average: .816 by Jeff Bagwell, 1994 (strike-shortened season); the highest average in a full-length season was .673 by Jeff Bagwell, 1998

OPS: 1.275 by Jeff Bagwell, 1994 (strike-shortened season); the highest OPS in a full-length season was 1.132 by Jeff Bagwell, 1998

Stolen bases: 41 by Eric Yelding, 1990

Pitching

ERA: 1.11 by Nolan Ryan, 1981 (strike-shortened season); the lowest ERA in a full-length season was 1.57 by Mike Cuellar, 1968

Wins: 13 by Larry Dierker, 1969; Mike Hampton, 1999

Losses: 10 by Don Wilson, 1973

Games pitched: 44 by Joe Boever, 1992; Doug Jones, 1992

Games started: 21 by Jerry Reuss, 1973; J.R. Richard, 1976; Joe Niekro, 1984; Pete Harnisch, 1992

Complete games: 13 by Larry Dierker, 1969; J.R. Richard, 1978

Shutouts: 4 by Larry Dierker, 1976; Bob Knepper, 1981; Bob Knepper, 1986; Mike Scott, 1986; Mike Scott, 1988; Randy Johnson, 1998

Saves: 20 by Billy Wagner, 1999

Innings pitched: 170 by Larry Dierker, 1969

Walks: 86 by J.R. Richard, 1976

Intentional walks: 9 by Juan Agosto, 1988; Doug Drabek, 1993

Strikeouts: 175 by J.R. Richard, 1978

Home runs allowed: 17 by Jose Lima, 1998

Hit by pitch: 9 by Jack Billingham, 1971

Wild pitches: 16 by J.R. Richard, 1979

ASTRODOME SINGLE-GAME LEADERS

denotes extra-inning game

Batting

Runs: 6 by Edgardo Alfonzo, Mets, 8/30/1999

Hits: 6 by Edgardo Alfonzo, Mets, 8/30/1999

Doubles: 3 by more than 20 players; Doug Rader is the only player to do it twice—on 8/10/1968 (first game of doubleheader) and 5/25/1975*, both with the Astros

Triples: 3 by Ernie Banks, Cubs, 6/11/1966; Craig Reynolds, Astros, 5/16/1981

Home runs: 3 by Jim Wynn, Astros, 6/15/1967; Jeff Bagwell, Astros, 6/24/1994; Edgardo Alfonzo, Mets, 8/30/1999

RBIs: 7 by Pete Incaviglia, Astros, 6/14/1992

Walks: 4 by more than 20 players; Joe Morgan is the only player to do it three times—on 5/19/1967 with the Astros, 5/19/1974 with the Reds, and 8/20/1980 with the Astros

Intentional walks: 3 by Jim Wynn, Astros, 7/11/1970*; Jose Cruz, Astros, 8/23/1980*; Jose Cruz, Astros, 10/10/1980* (League Championship Series); Bill Doran, Astros, 7/2/1983; Terry Puhl, Astros, 8/8/1984*; Jeff Treadway, Braves, 9/11/1992; Jeff Bagwell, Astros, 5/21/1997*

Strikeouts: 5 by Adolfo Phillips, Cubs, 6/10/1966*; Ron Swoboda, Mets, 4/15/1968*; Eric Davis, Reds, 4/25/1987*; Andujar Cedeño, Padres, 7/6/1995*

Hit by pitch: 3 by Glenn Davis, Astros, 4/9/1990*

Stolen bases: 5 by Tony Gwynn, Padres, 9/20/1986

Pitching

Innings pitched: 12 by Turk Farrell, Astros, 6/16/1965*; Bob Gibson, Cardinals, 5/1/1968*

Runs allowed: 10 by Darryl Kile, Astros, 4/10/1996; Carlos Crawford, Phillies, 6/7/1996; Ismael Valdez, Dodgers, 5/26/1998

Hits allowed: 16 by Don Wilson, Astros, 8/15/1970

Walks: 10 by J.R. Richard, Astros, 8/10/1975; J.R. Richard, Astros, 7/6/1976*

Intentional walks: 4 by Bill Campbell, Phillies, 7/15/1984*

Strikeouts: 16 by Nolan Ryan, Astros, 9/9/1987; Randy Johnson, Astros, 8/28/1998; Kevin Brown, Padres 9/29/1998 (Division Series)

Home runs allowed: 4 by Phil Niekro, Braves, 4/12/1970; Bob Knepper, Astros, 5/17/1987

Hit by pitch: 4 by Tom Candiotti, Dodgers, 9/13/1997

Wild pitches: 6 by J.R. Richard, Astros, 4/10/1979; Phil Niekro, Braves, 8/4/1979 (second game of doubleheader)

Balks: 3 by Dave Smith, Astros, 6/25/1982

SOURCES

Society for American Baseball Research. *The SABR Baseball List and Record Book* (New York: Scribner, 2007).

baseball-reference.com

houston.astros.mlb.com/hou/history/index.jsp

nationalpastime.com

retrosheet.org/boxesetc/H/PK_HOU2.htm

The Astrodome:
Back to the Future, Part 4

By Bill McCurdy

The Abandoned Astrodome in 2005, 40 Years Beyond Its Glorious Start. (Photo courtesy of Bill McCurdy).

RISING FROM THE PRAIRIE GRASS, A few miles south of downtown Houston, from the grazing land that only recently, in half-century terms, had been the longtime home to large herds of beef cattle, the brand-new Astrodome now stood boldly on those same plains as a spot-on caricature of every large incoming spaceship depicted in all of those Grade-B sci-fi drive-in movie theater films of the 1950s and early 1960s.

They didn't call the new climate-controlled covered venue the Astrodome when construction started. They simply called it "the dome"—the short version of its full legal name, the Harris County Domed Stadium.

No matter. It still looked like a landing of the galaxy's largest alien flying saucer or some architect's Salvador Dali-like view of the future by the time of its early 1965 completion.

It also is notable, whether it is attributed to destiny or coincidence that the sci-fi alien space invader films and the new Houston Astrodome both came into being as the separate market products of promoters with similar but different objectives.

Those old space invader movies for the summer night drive-ins always bore two goals: (1) to be as convincing as possible that earthlings needed to live in fear of alien invaders who may come here sometime soon to either enslave or exterminate us; and (2) to make the threat of an alien invasion sufficiently credible as to promote bodily closeness between all the teenage couples who came there in cars to watch these fairly predictable plots unfold.

The Astrodome, on the other hand, came into being to promote something else—something straight out of tomorrow's science fiction imagery—and that was the idea that it would soon be possible to play baseball indoors and in air-conditioned comfort. This discovery would also bring customers together under one roof, but not out of fear and trepidation.

The reward of the Astrodome's presence, at a site near two of Houston's oldest (but then fading) drive-in theater glories, the South Main and Trail, would be everyone's easy, but abruptly dramatic, entry into the world of tomorrow—one where shared comfort would be as much the major attraction as the game or featured event itself. Whereas the drive-in movie theater once offered people the chance to view a usually indoor event presented outdoors, the Astrodome inversely now trumpeted a tomorrow in which panoramic sporting events, and all other major presentations on that colossal scale, could be watched in the comfort of a climate-controlled enclosure.

For Houstonians in the spring of 1965, much of the "tomorrow land" marketing aspects of this neo-sacred architectural coming all seemed to arrive almost at the last minute. By this time, we locals had traveled at least 10 years from the earliest whispers of an indoor baseball park as the answer to hot and humid Houston's desire for big-league status.

Now, as Houston waited through the last offseason prior to the grand opening of tomorrow, there came upon us an abrupt nickname change in the marketing plan for the team's identity. It was a surprising change, but it also made perfect sense, given the great notion of the future that already had been sold to us about watching baseball indoors.

Our new Houston National League club had spent the first three seasons (1962-64) of its new big-league life celebrating a wild, but predictably Western mode shoot-'em-up identity as the Colt .45s, playing in a temporary uncovered venue called Colt Stadium—a place that had been conveniently thrown together on the same new parking-lot area where the fabulous Harris County Domed Stadium arose slowly before

our coveting eyes and sweaty faces—from the world's biggest hole-in-the-ground.

What's in a name?

Sometimes nothing. Sometimes everything. In either case, the new Houston landmark really didn't have a stadium name with any panache, whether it mattered a hill of beans or not.

Perhaps Judge Roy Hofheinz, president of the Houston Sports Association, owner of the MLB franchise, first thought that his Colt .45s could keep on losing those big-league shootouts with all of the Gary Cooper and John Wayne-level clubs of the National League and still draw more fans once the action moved into his enclosed and completely comfortable new mega-arena.

Who really knows the true complete story on the name change, but something happened—and it apparently had nothing to do with the sudden appearance of a John Hamm-like character and the crew from cable television's recent *Mad Men* series showing up to "rethink" and "rebrand" the campaign.

It simply is pure rascally fun to speculate.

Judge Hofheinz enjoyed dining at Alfred's, a great kosher deli fairly near the new stadium on Stella Link Drive. That's a fact we may state from some personal observation over time, even if we were never so elevated in stature as to be on speaking terms with Houston's "wizard of awes." Perhaps it is less romantic to consider that the Judge's awakening to the need for a new, zippier stadium name and Houston club identity may have hatched in the wake of a lunch fare that built its muses into a fully loaded pastrami on rye.

Whimsy aside, we don't really know that much about Judge Hofheinz's deli habits, but the possibility of gastric influence on the team name change is simply too amusing a possibility to ignore. We saw him downing what appeared to be Alfred's pastrami once, but it could have been something else. Alfred served a lot of good stuff that could alter one's view of the future, particularly the near future.

All we know for fairly sure is that, sometime after the gates closed on Colt Stadium (i.e., "the skillet") in 1964 and before Christmas of that same year, Judge Hofheinz apparently went through an auspicious change of heart, mind, and vision about the identity of the club, its new indoor home, and its shared use with other sporting and entertainment enterprises.

The new domed stadium belonged to Harris County, Texas, but the Houston MLB franchise had been the driving force behind its creation as the soon-to-be principal tenant.

Getting that special brand name, "The Astrodome," proved itself to be a move that preceded an incredible roll of time and events into history.

Christmas 1964: What's an Astro? And what's an Astrodome?

Very few presumed that the new "Astros" had been named for "Astro," the family dog on the then-popular *Jetsons* cartoon TV series about future family life in the space age.[1] And most of us presumed it to be pretty much of a marketing homage to NASA, the astronauts who now lived among us, and the growing local reputation of Houston as "Space City, USA!"

The domed stadium's new public face as the "Astrodome" itself soon found an eloquent explanation in its official name-change introduction in a speech in behalf of all the other new tenants by University of Houston President Phillip Hoffman.

"The dictionary describes an astrodome as — 'a transparent domed-shaped projection above an airplane from which navigators view the stars,'" Hoffman said. "The Astrodome here will be a domed-shape projection above the ground from within which the spectators can view the stars or rodeos, football teams, and baseball teams."[2]

That same news article notes that the official name remains the "Harris County Domed Stadium," even as all new business reference to the place now shifted totally to its brilliantly fresh identity as the Astrodome.[3]

If there were ever a time to establish major-league baseball as the predominant domed-stadium tenant, this was it, the time from Christmas 1964 to Opening Day in April 1965.

There is no question in hindsight. Many factors converged into the two big tethered name changes:

(1) It was time for the Houston club to do a 180-degree turn from its Western past and to capitalize upon its growing identity as the headquarters of NASA and the dynamic face of tomorrow.

(2) A change at this time, in these special ways, gave Judge Hofheinz and his ballclub the ability to market their "Astros" as the team of tomorrow, now playing in baseball's home of tomorrow.

(3) For Hofheinz, the swift change to "Astros" eliminated the nettlesome ongoing threat from the Colt Manufacturing Company that they might choose to sue him and the ballclub for copyright violations for never having obtained a working agreement to brand the team the Colt .45s.

It is interesting to note, too, that after the news broke about the change of the Houston baseball team's name from Colt .45s to Astros, an unidentified "young student from Chicago's Teachers College" included this quote among several other remarks that he or she wrote to the club in conjunction with a ticket order:

"The new home of the Astros must stand with architectural structures as one of the wonders of the world."[4]

Thanks to this anonymous soul, an unforgettable greeting to the entire planet was about to rainbow its way into the skies over Houston:

"Welcome to the Astrodome, the Eighth Wonder of the World."

It became a greeting that comforted people with the idea that their initially awestruck sightings of the place were normal. How could they not be? A first sighting of the Astrodome was "amazing" back in a time in which that once rarefied adjective was not simply handed out to every mild stimulation people encountered daily, starting with their first sip of coffee in the morning.

Frame the moment in your minds, disbelievers, and welcome back to the future! — "Behold the Astrodome, The Eighth Wonder of the World."

Amazing? Yes. Yes, it is!

"Wonder of the World" or not, the practical question lingered: Could this new wonderland handle a high fly ball most of the time without evoking some kind of ground rule governing balls that hit the interior exposed underside of the roof?

The suspicion was helped along by the fact that the entirety of the mighty Astrodome was not totally evident from any of our first-time sightings from the parking area. Half of the beast laid buried underground.

Without information about the enormously deep underground base of the playing field, the still-imposing structure that new visitors saw from their exterior ground-level approach did not appear tall enough to handle fly balls from what appeared to be its ground-level base.

Of course, it wasn't tall enough, if that first uninformed look was the whole of it. We had to know the "hole of it" to understand that any home run hit in this shimmering structure from the future was going to have to start its ascent from 30 feet deeper in this hallowed Texas area of Mother Earth.

Hardly any of us knew that singularly important fact at first sighting. As the result, we got stuck on the question that haunted us from the very first time we heard of the plan to build the world's first enclosed, air-conditioned venue.

If a ball is headed to the moon, how could they possibly build a ballpark with a roof on the top?

As kids who grew up on baseball as played by the Double-A Texas League Houston Buffs in traditional old Buff Stadium, we knew too much about the game of baseball to be sucked in by that kind of ballyhoo. Why, some of those of high fly balls in Buff Stadium seemed to have traveled halfway to the moon before they began their stratospheric descents to earth. That's why they called them moon shots.

The Visual Problem for Outfielders

As things turned out, it wasn't batted balls hitting the roof that was the problem in the first year of Astrodome baseball. It was the fact that during day games fly balls were hiding from bewildered outfielders in the clear pane grid panel. They just couldn't pick up the flight of the ball in the gridded gray girders and clear pane mix of light that was the new mother ship's way-up-there background.

The solution produced a chain of natural events that would alter how all future team sport games soon would be played, indoors or outdoors, pretty much forever.

They painted the Astrodome roof to improve the ball-in-flight sightlines of the fielders. Painting the clear light panes killed the playing field grass, of course; so the Astros spent the rest of the first season painting the grass green while they looked hard for a permanent solution.

When the highly rated San Antonio high-school running back Warren McVea signed to play football for the University of Houston in 1965 as the first black to integrate NCAA-level college football in the state of Texas, the kid known as Wondrous Warren was a natural marketing complement to the "Eighth Wonder" stadium that planned to house the UH Cougars home games, starting in the fall of that same first season of 1965.

Sadly, the baseball problems with the dying grass turf flowed directly into the football season and they became a big reason for Warren McVea's poor footage start at UH in September 1965. The decline in the field's playing surface into a slippery sandlot of dirt and dead grass hurt all the players, but especially the running backs. The problem had to be solved before it made a farce of the whole Astrodome concept as the playing field venue of the future.

The permanent solution turned out to be the 1966 installation of an artificial turf manufactured by Monsanto. Christened into the market as Astroturf, it soon was being installed in professional and amateur fields as the economic solution to natural grass maintenance.

Astroturf was installed in the Astrodome in strips that zipped together. As workers installed the new Astroturf infield prior to the start of he 1966 season, Houston writing sage and icon Mickey Herskowitz suddenly remarked, as he watched, "This is wonderful. Now Houston has the only field in the big leagues with its own built-in infield fly."[5]

There has never been any doubt in my mind that Mickey Herskowitz is the author of one of baseball's wittiest quips of all time. It's been with me since my recollections of first reading it in his *Houston Post* column—and it's been reinforced over the years by hearing Mickey flip into his oral storytelling mode to describe how it happened:

"I was sitting there—just watching the turf crew zip in the new infield sections when, all of a sudden, there it was, rattling out of my brain and falling off my tongue," Herskowitz has said, fast on his way to expressing the killer punch line: "Now Houston has the only field in the big leagues with its own built-in infield fly."

Word gets around—especially the expression of brilliantly funny thought.

In a column he wrote for the *Amarillo Daily News* on March 29, 1966, Frank A. Godsoe attributed the quote to Vin Scully of the Los Angeles Dodgers. According to Godsoe, Vin Scully shared the following clever line about the Astroturf and the Astroturf installation: "*This is the only ballpark in the world,*" he crooned, "*that has a built-in infield fly.*" [6]

Sometimes great minds do independently drink from the same rivers of imagination, and sometimes too, people do innocently use free-floating ideas without attribution to source because these thoughts seem to be orphans of some unidentified person's brainstorm. In September 2015, I decided to contact Vin Scully directly and ask him about the Godsoe attribution he received for the long ago "built in infield fly." [7]

On the same day, Vin Scully emailed his brief but firm answer back to me through his Los Angeles Dodgers staff. Scully said that he didn't even remember his usage of the famous quote in the cited instance, adding his clearly expressed wishes that we should "please credit Mickey (Herskowitz)" with its origin.

Thank you, Vin Scully, for your legendary forthrightness. And so we shall, right here and now, but as we always have, but now with even greater legitimacy, credit writer Mickey Herskowitz with one of the best lines in baseball history.

Texas fiction author Larry McMurtry, of *Lonesome Dove* and *The Last Picture Show* fame, enjoyed playfully bantering in the *Texas Observer* about his cynicism regarding the Astrodome's expensive comfort aims. His description of the place was nothing less than a caricature of his view that this striking new face of the future was little more than a costly war against perspiration.

McMurtry's 1965 critique of the covered stadium as a waste of public funds, relative to other community needs, wasted no words or time on subtlety. McMurtry wrote, "The huge white dome poked soothingly above the summer heat-haze like the working end of a gigantic end of a rub-on deodorant." [8]

Ironically, the Astrodome would survive over time to personify one of McMurtry's favorite themes, the abandonment of that which was once deemed valuable. The Dome would make it to 2015 as its own poignant version of the *The Last Picture Show.*

About the later rival construction in Irving, Texas (near Dallas), of Texas Stadium, a venue that included a roof with an open sunroof, Mickey Herskowitz again waxed philosophically: "Now Dallas has tried to follow Houston, but they have ended up building a Half-Astrodome for themselves." [9]

That being said, we weren't worried about anything that Dallas or New Orleans might do in the short time that followed the opening of our Houston Astrodome. We were first—and the Astrodome stood strong as the symbol of all our tomorrow's dreams coming true.

Simply put, the Astrodome sprang to life at just the right time for those of us who made up Houston's ambitious young adult population. The Dome became our tangible template for that elusive but attractive future we visualized as ours in the land of opportunity in a growing, bigger, better world that Houston was now on its way to becoming, big league and all.

Moreover, those of us original Astrodome fans who have made it this far into the 21st century with our young-adult-to-senior bond with the Astrodome would also live to see how time, age, and change in the 21st century culture would come to ambivalently view the value of the aging architectural dark star from yesterday's Houston future.

For some of us, the Astrodome had become a valued historic Houston architectural landmark on a level with the Eiffel Tower in Paris.

For others, many of whom were now taxpayers who had moved to Houston after the Dome's last season as home to the Houston Astros in 1999, this world-class contribution to architectural history had become nothing more than a financial burden that needed to be demolished.

Deep in the Heart of Houston

Following quickly on the heels of the new Astros/Astrodome name evolutions, the big times in the new music hall of sports and special events took off with all the speed of a shooting star hurtling through space.

The stars at night were big and bright, right from the start in Texas. Baseball, of course, led off the stellar new indoor-world lineup of firsts on April 9, 1965, with a 2-1 preseason win by the brand-newly named Houston Astros over Mickey Mantle and the New York Yankees before a packed house crowd that included President Lyndon B. Johnson. Mantle claimed the Dome's first home run with a mighty center-field blow that would also stand as the Astrodome's first hit, run, and RBI—and the Yankees' only tally of the night. With the score tied at 1-1 in the ninth, Astros pinch-hitter Nellie Fox singled over short, scoring Jimmy Wynn from second base with the first exhibition-game-winning run in Astrodome history.[8] A few days later, Dick Allen of Philadelphia would get the first official home run in the Astrodome on Opening Day, April 12, 1965, in a 2-0 win by the Phillies over the Astros.[10]

On September 11, 1965, the Houston Cougars hosted the first football game ever played in the Dome against the Tulsa Golden Hurricanes.[11] The game also drew notice as the first appearance by UH's Warren McVea, the first black running back to ever play for a major college football team from the South. The Cougars lost 14-0 that day on a field of dead grass and swirling dirt that was far more conducive to slipping and sliding than it was to quick cuts and gliding. McVea went on to a landmark career as the most elusive runner in Cougar history. His running sleight-of-hand-foot-and-eye work against third-ranked Michigan State in East Lansing, Michigan, in 1967 led the Cougars to a 37-7 win that vaulted UH into the college football big time. In the process, it obliquely elevated Coach Bill Yeoman into light as a civil-rights leader on the major-college football level. And that would become a reputation that Yeoman may have tried to shed because of his apparent-to-everyone-around-him belief that he was more of an accidental tourist on the right side of this rocky civil-rights road to profound change. Those of us who got to know him, even slightly from the fringe as UH alumni who only saw him at games or UH luncheons, felt an earnest truth about the man. Bill Yeoman was, and is, a man without a racially or ethnically biased bone in his body or soul. In fact, Yeoman eloquently once stated his position when the subject of prejudice arose. He said that his only prejudice in life was against bad football players.

On December 17, 1965, Judy Garland became the first really big star to perform in a show at the Astrodome.[12]—How appropriate!—Who else but Judy Garland, little Dorothy Gale from Kansas herself, could possibly have been the first person to have found the Astrodome at the end of this magical rainbow from a somewhere place called tomorrow? Almost prophetically, "Over the Rainbow" was one of Judy's songs that long-ago night.

The Houston Livestock Show and Rodeo, an annual two-week Western cultural roots event in Houston, one with a history going deep into the early years of the 20th century, got its first start in the Astrodome in February 1966. Over the years, the biggest stars in music from a variety of our American musical genres provided the musical entertainment at each daily performance. Elvis Presley later performed six times at the rodeo in February-March of 1970, returning for a one-night-sellout seventh performance on March 3, 1974, that broke all previous attendance records.[13]

On November 14, 1966, Muhammad Ali defended his heavyweight boxing championship of the world by knocking out Houstonian Cleveland Williams in the third round of a scheduled 15-rounder.[14] Although it was not so named, it could have been called the original "rope-a-dope" match, but, in this case, so designated in honor of those who paid good money to watch an event that didn't last nine minutes.

On January 20, 1968, the college basketball "Game of the Century" between the two top college teams in the land, UCLA and UH, drew an amazing record crowd of 52,693 to the Astrodome.[15] It was a titanic encounter of future Hall of Fame coaches and players as UH's coach Guy Lewis and star center Elvin Hayes squared off against coach John Wooden and star center Lew Alcindor (later better known as Kareem Abdul-Jabbar) and their powerful companions from UCLA. The UH Cougars won the game, 71-69, behind the energy and power of Elvin Hayes' 39 points, but the real winner was college basketball as a new money game in televised sports. Moreover, it was another contribution to the momentum of an age in which networks like ESPN would later help the fans use 24/7 sports programming to feed a growing obsessive-compulsive use of sports as the cure for tedium and boredom in everyday life.

By 1970, movie producer/director Robert Altman used the Astrodome as the setting for *Brewster McCloud*, a film about an eccentric young man who made his home in the almost endless supply of nooks and crannies and other easy hiding places of the Dome.[15] What the movie lacked in depth found compensation in its theatrical contribution to the idea that the Astrodome personified the model for a kind of magical setting in which greater things beyond the ordinary were expected.

Speaking of such, after Elvis left the building on the heels of his first six rocking performances in 1970, but before he could return as a crowd energizer in 1974, the much ballyhooed "Battle of the Sexes" took place on September 20, 1973, in a tennis match that pitted prominent female star Billie Jean King against over-the-hill male star and consummate gate hustler Bobby Riggs. King defeated Riggs handily in three straight sets. Although it was more of a publicity stunt than a competitive match, the event is credited with drawing attention to the abilities of female athletes and as a booster to all kinds of women's sports.[16]

On September 9, 1968, after three years of stalled lease negotiations, the Houston Oilers lost to the Kansas City Chiefs, 26-21, in the technically second regular-season NFL game ever played in an indoor venue. The 1932 NFL championship game was played indoors at Chicago Stadium due to bad weather.

The Oilers called the Astrodome home through 1996, their last year in Houston before their move to Tennessee.[17]

Everything … bloodless bullfights, the 1989 NBA All-Star Game, the 1968 and 1986 MLB All-Star Games, the 1980 and 1986 National League Championship Series and a few MLB Divisional Series Games … these all took place in the Astrodome.[18]

On June 15, 1976, the only "rainout" in Astrodome history even canceled a game between the Astros and the Pittsburgh Pirates due to heavy flooding that made it impossible for fans to reach the ballpark.[19]

In the end, and after her splendid day in the sun had long ago disappeared into darkness, the Astrodome achieved a service to humanity that elevated her importance to another level of merit. As you may well remember, in September 2005, the Astrodome became the survival shelter for thousands of New Orleanians who had been forced from their homes by Hurricane Katrina.[20]

God Bless you for being there, old girl! And if that statement of gender partiality strikes you as this writer's personal anthropomorphic projection of bias, perhaps you are correct. I do tend to perceive the appearance of strong character, patient loyalty, and dedication to service beyond personal gain as primarily a feminine spiritual profile—and one that may not be as obvious, or as frequently present, in most of us males.

Foamer Homers.[21] On a minor and far more frivolous historical note, it took nine years, but the Astros also came up with a way to mix beer sales into the joy of Astrodome baseball. Starting Tuesday,

June 4, 1974, in a series played against the Montreal Expos, the Astros decided it was time to give the legal-aged world "foamers" as part of their baseball-fan experience. They installed a digital clock on the outfield wall that turned orange whenever the clock reached an even number of minutes in time, such as 7:48 or 8:12.

Any time an Astros batter happened to hit a home run while the *clockwork orange* rule was in effect, everyone of legal age (18 years or older) was entitled to a "foamer," the club's cute word for one free beer per customer. The foamer deal closed after eight innings, but that proved to be only a minor ceiling on a promotional program that proved quite popular with beer-drinking fans for about three seasons.

Like all things promotional, it ran its course as an assumed or measurable boost to attendance as the Astros grew from free beer to winning baseball as their best hope for long-range success.

Foamer homers were Astrodome history lite, but they were history with a categorical head of its own, all the same.

The Long Road Trip of 1992. Overt politics finally played the big house when the 1992 Republican Convention was held at the Astrodome and nominated George H.W. Bush as their candidate for president of the United States. The convention imposed an unusual unconditional hardship upon the Astros' schedule.

To free the Republicans for an extended use of the Astrodome, the Astros were forced to go on a 26-game road trip from July 27 through August 23. It was the longest road trip for any big-league club since the notoriously bad 1899 Cleveland Spiders had to play out a 50-game road trip to defend themselves from the angry fan mobs and empty seats at home.[22]

In Houston, the search for new events and new records never stopped over the 35 years of the Astros' residential leadership (1965-1999), but after baseball moved to a new house downtown in 2000, the grand old 1965 girl of tomorrow seemed to be totally ignored as a future Houston issue in the stampede to move on without a real plan for the old venue beyond that then unmentionable word—demolition.

Mad Dogs and After-Midnight Field Goals

Here's where all the participatory history of the Astrodome gets downright personal, if only on a humble but limited plane.

In the summer of 1979, and as a ferociously loyal UH alumnus, the muses and I convinced the Athletic Department at the University of Houston of two unmet football-marketing needs:

(1) UH needed a ferocious canine mascot to help our live Cougar Shasta mascot on the home-game sidelines as the symbol of our then famous "Mad Dog Defense."

(2) UH needed to build some traditions. We suggested they retire the No. 1 from player jerseys after 1979, but also start selling the actual No. 1 game jerseys to fans posthaste. This was still in the monogrammed T-shirt time when no one could buy the actual jerseys of any team in any sport.

UH officials bought both ideas at our first meeting. The "Mad Dog Defense" idea sold itself. I showed up at the UH proposal meeting with my English bulldog, Babe McCurdy. Babe's face and her two underbite-driven fangs did the rest.

The No. 1 UH red jersey was a big seller at UH. The bug in the brew was that UH never clinched the part of the plan that called for the retirement of No. 1 to honor the fans because of the program's need to

Babe McCurdy, Mascot, "Mad Dog Defense" at all 1979-80 UH Cougar Astrodome Games, plus 1980 Cotton Bowl. (Photo courtesy of Bill McCurdy).

seemingly always give that number to a new hotshot recruit who simply couldn't commit without it.

Mad Dog Babe, however, was a big success, even getting her name and picture placed in the school's 1980 yearbook, *The Houstonian*, where she also encountered the error of editorial gender bias that any canine of ferocity most certainly had to be male. The UH year book referred to her as "he."[23]

What did Mad Dog Babe do at the Astrodome?

We know what you're thinking. Yes, she did that too, but her planned performances were worth it to her loyal handler, her team, and to all who saw her perform, or became radical enough as fans to wear her "Mad Dog Defense" red tee shirts, shirts that included an artistic impression of Babe's face in the middle of the lettering, to Cougar games at the Astrodome.

Oh, yes, it was a team effort. Babe and her trainer/handler could not have done it as easily without the help of her two separate year high school age "Astrodome Showtime" sideline assistants. Mike Hoyt served as the Mad Dog's helper in 1979; Ryan Kirtley performed the same faithful sideline duty in 1980. They were both great kids who loved and took good care of Babe during our Astrodome adventure. UH working student Mark Hunter also was a big member of our Mad Dog Helper team during the 1979 season. In the end, it may have been the two most magical years in all our lives. It had to be. Our little world stage was the Astrodome.

Our main act? Mad Dog Babe sometimes led the actual UH Mad Dog Defense team out of the tunnel and onto the field at the start of a game. She also could growl or attack any object on command. This part of her great thespian ability really defied her true nature as a canine pussycat that actually loved people, especially kids. The piece de resistance of her Mad Dog caricature, of course, was her ability to attack and destroy an image of the game's foe whenever she heard the "Cougar Fight Song." Sad to say, she had no "off" button. When Babe heard a recording of the Cougar fight song at home, she wanted to do the same thing there.

And all we had at home were couches, chairs, table legs, and rugs.

Mad Dog Babe's big night in the Astrodome came long after midnight on Sunday morning, October 12, 1980, due to a sports weekend in Houston of most unusual circumstance.

An evening UH Cougars home game against the Texas A&M Aggies had been pushed back to a start of 11:33 P.M. on Saturday, October 11, due to an unexpected conflict with the earlier, but slow-to-finish NLCS game played in Houston earlier that same day by the Houston Astros and Philadelphia Phillies. As a result, the Cougars' 17-13 win over Texas A&M would be concluded deep into the wee hours of Sunday morning, October 12. The pigskin contest turned out to be the only college football game of the 20th century requiring time from two contiguous calendar days for completion. [24]

As a minor lost-to-history-until-now result, a halftime skit that that we had planned for the Mad Dog at our normal game-time start on Saturday was now set to unfold in the wee small hours of the following Sunday morning.

A Field Goal Attempt by a Mad Dog?

Mad Dog Babe made it too—with the proxy support of her beloved handler and staff.

Babe did the barking. Yours truly kicked the ball off a tee for her at halftime. Setting up on the 25-yard line, "Babe's growl-triggered proxy kick" sailed through the uprights for a 35-yard, good-as-gold, first and only ~~ever~~ unofficial field goal ever kicked in the Astrodome between midnight and dawn.

The mention of dawn is important to the time frame in which this "record" stands forever. There may have been other field goals kicked in the Dome prior to noon in some other year by high-school teams playing early games there during their playoff seasons. We are 100 percent certain, however, that no other mad-dog souls have ever done the same deed, unofficial, or otherwise, in the wee small hours of the morning. And it was all in fun—in the name of love.

Our problem that night, beyond the solitary cheer of "Sign him up!" was the fact that the ball carried all the way into the end zone and was retrieved by a fan. We had a hard time getting the ball back for Babe's showcase, but we finally pled our case successfully for the game ball's surrender. Babe's growl helped.

Thank you, ghost of Babe McCurdy, for giving both you and your now ancient handler our Andy Warhol time as minor performers in the history of the grand old Astrodome.

Our participatory roles were minor, but the Mad Dog Defense era simply deepened the writer's bond with the Astrodome.

When in the spring of 2015 we attended the 50th anniversary party of the April 9, 1965, opening of the Astrodome, we were among the legions that lined up for the long walk and short visit inside the now-gutted bowels of the still-strong structure we once celebrated. It was all I could do hold together a groundswell of powerful emotion once we descended into the belly of the wondrous old whale.

There was nothing remote about these powerful feelings.

I was not meditating on our soulful losses by the Astros in either the 1980 or 1986 NLCS appearances, or any other painful times at the Astrodome.

Nope. I was suddenly again missing the joy of an old friend, and for an almost eternal moment. This writer was looking around for the wonderful presence of Mad Dog Babe.

"Where are you, Babe? Your soul still seems to be here!"

The Larger Realization

It took a few moments, but it came to me with a luminosity that seemed to push back the gathering darkness of dusk. It wasn't the soul of sweet old Babe that I sensed in the belly of the now-aging Astrodome back on April 9, 2015, although I could hardly keep from wishing that to be true. I even played with the idea of echoing her name with a loud call for "BABE" into the darker shadows of day's end. The dimming darkness cluster of night was starting to surround us in that ancient sacred place.

I just knew. If the canine soul of Babe McCurdy were present, and recoverable at all, she would have

come bounding to me by now, like the brindle and white bowling ball from Heaven's Lanes she always used to be.

But it wasn't Babe's spirit I truly sensed in that moment. It was my own soul that I found, reawakening to the gift of a brief but sweet moment with an age-contemporary friend of my entire adult lifetime, the Houston Astrodome.

April 9, 2015: On the field inside the Astrodome for only the second time since the last Mad Dog Babe season of 1980. (Photo courtesy of Bill McCurdy).

It was a friendship the old girl shared with every other person among the 30,000 people who came to her birthday party that afternoon, even with the couples who brought their small children to visit with the Astrodome, as if they were taking their kids to visit one of the family elders that the children never had met prior to this special day.

Separation and reunion, involving some special person, place or aspect of our lives, can hit us like a brick sometimes. And this was one of those times.

In separation, we most often dull our feelings to escape the pain of physical, emotional and spiritual separation and loss. In reunion, and maybe even more so when the reunion is unexpected, we sometimes are flooded with the visceral awareness of who, where, or what we truly have been missing.

It happened once before for me.

About 22 years ago, my late-in-life 8-year-old son's decision to play baseball brought home my years of separation from the game due to the full-bore thrust of my energies into my professional life and other embraced, but rootless, occupations of my time. My separation from active play and daily following of the game had amounted to a dulling of my feelings for baseball, the singularly passionate activity that had nursed my soul from a southeast Houston childhood into my mid-30s.

In the summer of 1993, my son Neal and I had walked from our house to a nearby abandoned schoolyard to play catch and hit some flies and rollers. On that fine day, I rediscovered that the popping sound of baseballs—as they landed in slap-leather gloves—and the fragrance of summer's cut grass and heat-defiant wildflowers had not changed since my sandlot days in southeast Houston's Pecan Park.

The awareness came upon me instantly that both of these reminders—and the smiling kid throwing the ball to me in 1993 –still felt as they each once did at our "Eagle Field"—only this time, my appreciation of the spell they had cast upon me was even greater. I didn't realize until that moment that all of that rush of life's earliest breath of hope was still residing deeply inside me.

Eagle Field, by the way, was the kids-declared sandlot home of our once alive and shining 1950 Pecan Park Eagles. Most of the time, we simply knew the place more humbly as "the lot."

Visceral reunions sometimes arrive when we least expect them.

On our walk home from this born-again taste of baseball with my son, we saw something entangled deep in a clump of weeds at the edge of the grounds. It appeared to be an old and very dirty brown baseball, so naturally I reached down and wrestled it free, only to find that it was nothing more than an old baseball cover.

I looked at it and smiled, but didn't throw it away. We kept on walking home for a while before Neal finally asked:

"What are you planning to do with that baseball cover, Daddy?"

"I don't know," I answered, but when we got home, I placed the old baseball cover on the kitchen table,

while a poem, calling itself "The Pecan Park Eagle," wrote its way through me the old-fashioned way, by pen and paper, inside of 10 minutes.

For me, the poem personifies my separation and reunion with baseball. It could just as easily have been the same poem I may have written later, with slightly different factual references, to the same kind of reunion I again experienced on that same level with the Astrodome on the occasion of its 50th anniversary party in 2015.

At this moment in time, as we still wait the definitive answer on the future of the Astrodome in 2016, nothing exemplifies my feelings about that venerable domed friend more perfectly than those words that previously have poured their way through my soul for baseball in "The Pecan Park Eagle."

"Eagle" speaks here too for the emotional bond that thousands of us Houston baseball, football, and rodeo fans, especially, each reconnected in our own individually soulful ways to that still frozen-in-time face of tomorrow we all revisited back on the April 9, 2015, the date of the Astrodome's 50th Anniversary.

We had to go back to the future to find her, but we made the trip that day at the party—and we found her waiting for us again. Still strong under the dust and mildew—and still as unique to the history of architecture as she was in 1965—and just waiting for our community's majority to wake up to the world treasure that awaits our decision to redirect her form and energy to some new purpose—and that is always the role of those symbols of tomorrow's wonder.

"The Astrodome still rises as—The Eighth Wonder of the World!"

It is to you, old patient numbered wonder, to whom we today rededicate the experience of transcendent rediscovery that we first found in writing "The Pecan Park Eagle."

That same light came on again for us on April 9, 1965, the date we walked into your gutted interior and found your structure still strong—and your soul still very much in residence.

This time, this play of the same words is for you:

"The Pecan Park Eagle," by Bill McCurdy (1993)

Ode To An Old Baseball Cover I Found While Playing Catch with My 8-Year Old Son Neal In An Abandoned School Yard.

And, yes, that is the actual cover in the

In Rededication to The Houston Astrodome (2015). (Photo courtesy of Bill McCurdy).

above photo that inspired the poem that rests before you as our closing text.

Tattered friend, I found you again,
Laying flat in a field of yesterday's hope.
Your resting place? An abandoned schoolyard.
When parents move away, the children go too.
How long have you been here?
Strangling in the entanglement of your grassy grave?
Bleaching your brown-ness in the summer sun?
Freezing your frailness in the ice of winter?
How long, old friend, how long?
Your magical essence exploded from you long ago.
God only knows when.
Perhaps, it was the result of one last grand slam.
One last grand slam, a solitary cherishment,
Now remembered only by the doer of that distant past deed.
Only the executioner long remembers the little triumphs.

The rest of the world never knows, or else, soon forgets.
I recovered you today from your ancient tomb,
From your place near the crunching sound of my footsteps.
I pulled you from your enmeshment in the dying July grass,
And I wanted to take you home with me.
Oh, would that the warm winds of spring might call us,
One more time, awakening our souls in green renewal
To that visceral awareness of hope and possibility.
To soar once more in spirit, like the Pecan Park Eagle,
High above the billowing clouds of a summer morning,
In flight destiny—to all that is bright and beautiful.
There is a special consolation in this melancholy reunion.
Because you once held a larger world within you,
I found a larger world in me.
Come home with me, my friend,
Come home.

NOTES

[1] en.wikipedia.org/wiki/The_Jetsons.

[2] "Astrodome to be Home for Astros," *Silsbee* (Texas) *Bee*, December 24, 1964: 6.

[3] Ibid.

[4] "First Games in Dome, Tickets Come From World-Wide Spots," *Freeport-Brazosport Facts*, January 25, 1965: 5.

[5] Confirmed in interview with Mickey Herskowitz on September 29, 2015. No written documentation is immediately available.

[6] Frank Godsoe, *Amarillo Daily News*, March 29, 1966: 17.

[7] On September 29, 2015, this writer was able to reach Vin Scully by email to ask what he remembered of the time he used the "built in infield fly" quote. I heard back from Mr. Scully the same day via a brief email response from LA Dodgers administrative staff member Jon Chopper. The message was simple and to the point. It read: "Just heard back from Vin and since he can't recall, he said to please credit Mickey (Herskowitz)."—Thanks, Jon (Chopper, Los Angeles Dodgers).

[8] "Love, Death, and the Astrodome," Larry McMurtry, *The Texas Observer*, October 1, 1965: 1.

[9] Confirmed in Interview with Mickey Herskowitz on September 18. 2015. The author's precise quote appeared in his column for the *Houston Post* on an unspecified date, sometime between 1972 and 1974.

[10] Bob Hulsey, "The New Era Begins," *Astros Daily*, April 9, 1965. astrosdaily.com/history/19650409/.

[11] First football game in the Astrodome: bill37mccurdy. com/2013/09/25/sept-11-1965-first-astrodome-football-game.

[12] Judy Garland performance, en.wikipedia.org/wiki/Astrodome.

[13] Rodeo, Elvis, en.wikipedia.org/wiki/Astrodome.

[14] Muhammad Ali, en.wikipedia.org/wiki/Muhammad_Ali.

[15] Game of the Century, UH-UCLA basketball, wikipedia.org/wiki/ Game_of_the_Century_%28college_basketball%29.

[16] Battle of the Sexes, en.wikipedia.org/wiki/Astrodome.

[17] First official NFL game in the Astrodome, box score, pro-football-reference.com/boxscores/196811280kan.htm.

[18] NBA All-Star Game, en.wikipedia.org/wiki/1989_NBA_All-Star_Game,

MLB All Star Games, en.wikipedia.org/wiki/List_of_Major_League_Baseball_All-Star_Games.

[19] Only rainout in Astrodome history, June 15, 1976, chron.com/news/houston-texas/article/The-only-rainout-in-Astrodome-history-occurred-6327953.php.

[20] The Katrina Refuge, 2005, houstonpublicmedia.org/news/10-years-since-katrina-when-the-astrodome-was-a-mass-shelter/.

[21] Foamer Homers, *Port Neches* (Texas) *Mid-County Chronicle Review*, June 2, 1974: 6.

[22] The Long Road Home, crawfishboxes.com/2012/7/25/3177586/astros-history-the-wild-wild-road-trip-of-1992.

[23] Mad Dog and *The Houstonian*, 1980 UH Yearbook, Pages 177, 190. digital.lib.uh.edu/collection/yearb/item/21601/show/21434

digital.lib.uh.edu/collection/yearb/item/21601/show/21444.

[24] "Houston Needs 2 Days, A&M Turnovers to Post 17-13 win," *Joplin Globe*, October 13, 1980: 12.

An All-Star Team of Contributors

MARK ARMOUR is the founder and director of SABR's Baseball Biography Project (BioProject) and is a prolific writer on baseball topics. He lives with Jane, Maya, and Drew in Oregon's Willamette Valley.

JOHN BAUER resides with his wife and two children in Parkville, Missouri, just outside Kansas City. By day, he is an attorney specializing in insurance regulatory law and corporate law. By night, he spends many spring and summer evenings cheering for the San Francisco Giants and many fall and winter evenings reading history. He is a past and ongoing contributor to other SABR projects.

FREDERICK C. "RICK" BUSH, his wife, Michelle, and their three sons, Michael, Andrew, and Daniel, live in northwest Houston, and he teaches English at Wharton County Junior College in Sugar Land. Though he is an avid fan of the Astros, his youth has also left him with an abiding affinity for the Texas Rangers and Pittsburgh Pirates. Rick has contributed articles to SABR's BioProject, the Games Project, and numerous SABR books. Currently, he is co-editing a book about the 1948 Birmingham Black Barons and Homestead Grays for SABR.

ALAN COHEN has been a SABR member since 2011, has written over 30 biographies for SABR's BioProject, and has contributed to 13 SABR books. His first game story, "Baseball's Longest Day—May 31, 1964," has been followed by several other game stories. He is the datacaster (stringer) for the Hartford Yard Goats of the Double-A Eastern League and the Connecticut Tigers of the Class A New York-Penn League. He lives in Connecticut with his wife, Frances, two cats, and two dogs.

RORY COSTELLO had one opportunity to see a major-league game at the Astrodome. It came when a Houstonian friend from college got married. As a Mets fan, he remembers the troubles that the Mets had at the Dome over the years—and the excitement of the 1986 NLCS. Rory lives in Brooklyn, New York, with his wife, Noriko, and son, Kai.

RICHARD CUICCHI joined SABR in 1983 and is an active member of the Schott-Pelican Chapter. After retiring as an information-technology executive, Richard authored *Family Ties: A Comprehensive Collection of Facts and Trivia About Baseball's Relatives*. He has contributed to several SABR BioProject efforts. He does freelance writing and blogging about a variety of baseball topics on his website, TheTenthInning.com. Richard lives in New Orleans with his wife, Mary.

LARRY DIERKER debuted for the Houston Colt 45s on his 18th birthday in 1964. In his 14-year big-league career, the two-time All-Star right-hander originally from Californian went 139-123, spending all but his final campaign with Houston. After retiring, he served as color commentator on Astros radio and television broadcasts from 1979 to 1996. In 1997 he left the broadcast booth for the dugout, and guided the Astros to the NL West Division Crown. In 1998 he was named the NL Manager of Year. In his five years skipper, the Astros finished in first place five times. As of 2015 he served as Special Assistant to the Astros.

GREG ERION is retired from the railroad industry and currently teaches history part-time at Skyline Community College in San Bruno, California. He has written several biographies for SABR's BioProject and is currently working on a book about the 1959 season. Greg is one of the leaders of SABR's Baseball Games Project. He and his wife, Barbara, live in South San Francisco.

DAN FIELDS is a manuscript editor at the *New England Journal of Medicine*. He loves baseball trivia, and he regularly attends Boston Red Sox and Pawtucket Red Sox games with his teenage son.

Dan lives in Framingham, Massachusetts, and can be reached at dfields820@gmail.com.

T.S. FLYNN is an educator and writer in Minneapolis who has published short fiction, essays, reviews, and articles. His blog, *It's a long season*, is a hobby and habit, and he is currently working on his first book-length project, an excavation of Tom Sheehan's baseball career.

JAMES FORR is a past winner of the McFarland-SABR Baseball Research Award, and co-author (with David Proctor) of *Pie Traynor: A Baseball Biography*. He lives in Columbia, Missouri. He was the fact-checker for the articles in this book and is one of the leaders of SABR's Games Project

GORDON J. GATTIE serves as a human-systems integration engineer for the US Navy in Virginia. His baseball research interests involve ballparks, baseball records, and statistical analysis. A SABR member since 1998, Gordon earned his Ph.D. from State University of New York at Buffalo, where he used baseball to investigate judgment/decision-making performance in complex dynamic environments. Originally from Buffalo, Gordon learned early the hardships associated with rooting for Buffalo sports teams. Ever the optimist, he now roots for the Cleveland Indians and Washington Nationals. Meanwhile, Lisa, his lovely bride, who also enjoys baseball, continues to challenge him by supporting the Yankees.

PAUL GEISLER serves as pastor of Christ Lutheran Church in Lake Jackson, Texas, where he lives with his wife and their three children. For his entire life, Paul has enjoyed all aspects of baseball—playing, watching, coaching, researching, and writing.

CHIP GREENE, the grandson of former Brooklyn Dodgers pitcher Nelson Greene, joined SABR in 2006. He has contributed to multiple SABR book projects, including as the editor of *Mustaches and Mayhem*, the story of the three-time champion Oakland Athletics. A project management profes-sional, Chip lives in Waynesboro, Pennsylvania, with his wife, Elaine, and daughters, Anna and Haley.

MATT HENSHON practices law in Boston. When not attending "little league" games (his three sons played a combined 200 small-diamond (both 46/60-feet and 50/70-feet) game schedule in 2015), he watches the Red Sox play 60/90.

BRENT HEUTMAKER has been a member of SABR's Halsey Hall chapter for nearly two years. Brent resides in the Minneapolis-St. Paul metro area and works in the litigation support industry.

SABR member **MICHAEL HUBER** is professor of mathematics at Muhlenberg College in Allentown, Pennsylvania, where he teaches an undergraduate course titled "Reasoning With Sabermetrics." He has published his sabermetrics research in several books and journals, including *The Baseball Research Journal, Chance*, and *Base Ball*, and he genuinely enjoys con-tributing to SABR's Baseball Games Project. He has been rooting for the Baltimore Orioles for close to 50 years.

CHUCK JOHNSON has been a SABR member since 1991 and is a co-founder of the Arizona Flame Delhi Chapter. He has written for the BioProject and Games Project as well as *Bleacher Report, SB Nation*, and MLB.com. A member of the Minor League Alumni Association, he lives with his wife, Migdalia, and daughter, Kelsey, in Surprise, Arizona.

A SABR member since 2010, **NORM KING** lives in Ottawa, Ontario. His baseball research focuses on his dear departed Montreal Expos. He has written biographies of numerous Expos players and person-nel, including Bob Bailey, Warren Cromartie, Steve Rogers, and Hall of Fame broadcaster Dave Van Horne. Norm thought he was crazy about missing his team until he met people from Brooklyn who are still unhappy that the Dodgers moved to Los Angeles. He was the editor of the SABR book *Au jeu/Play Ball: The 50 Greatest Games in the History of the Montreal Expos*, published in 2016.

Justin Krueger is currently a Ph.D. student in Social Studies Education at The University of Texas at Austin. His research interests include critical geography, cultural and public memory, curriculum, outdoor education, museums, and maps. He has also recently contributed to the website Behind the Tower: New Histories of the UT Tower Shooting which can be found at *behindthetower.org*.

BOB LEMOINE was born in Maine and has never been to Houston, but couldn't resist contributing to another baseball history book. He recently was co-editor with Bill Nowlin on the SABR book *Boston's First Nine: The 1871-1875 Boston Red Stockings*, and has contributed to other Red Sox and Boston Braves publications. He lives in New Hampshire, where he works as a school and public librarian.

LEN LEVIN has been the copy editor for most of SABR's recent books. A retired newspaper editor, he lives in Providence, Rhode Island.

BILL MCCURDY is the operator of his own website, The Pecan Park Eagle. As a longtime SABR member, this former board chairman and executive director of the Texas Baseball Hall of Fame is a previous article writer for SABR. He also has co-authored published biographies on Jimmy Wynn (*Toy Cannon*) and Jerry Witte (*A Kid From St. Louis*) since 2003.

BILL NOWLIN has helped edit lots of books for SABR. A Red Sox fan, he started out writing only books that were Red Sox-related but that kind of went by the wayside when he combined efforts with Jim Sandoval on the December 2011 book *Can He Play? A Look at Scouts and Their Profession*. That was the first book in the so-called SABR Digital Library. He's combined with other dedicated SABR members to help build the library into something substantial.

CHAD OSBORNE is a public-relations writer at Radford University in Virginia. He works with the SABR Games Project and writes about baseball and inclement weather at The Rainout Blog. In midsummer, Chad regularly attends Bristol Pirates (Appalachian League) games with his wife, Tina; daughter, Gracie; and son, Ty. They live in Marion, Virginia, two miles from the site of Nolan Ryan's first professional pitch.

THOMAS RATHKAMP is a senior technical writer who counts baseball and baseball writing as his prime passions and is anxiously waiting for his Milwaukee Brewers to reach their second World Series in 46 years. He has contributed to books by other SABR members, has covered local, Milwaukee-area sports, and wrote an online sports column for the *Greenwich Village Gazette*. His first book, *Happy Felsch: Banished Black Sox Center Fielder*, was published by McFarland and Company in May of 2016. Tom lives in Cedarburg, Wisconsin, and can be reached at thomas_rathkamp@yahoo.com.

ALAN REIFMAN is professor of human development and family studies at Texas Tech University and is a SABR member. He is the author of the book *Hot Hand: The Statistics Behind Sports' Greatest Streaks* (Potomac Books) and also contributed to the SABR-published book *Detroit Tigers 1984: What a Start! What a Finish!* Among his many sports blogs is one devoted to the history of the 1968 UCLA-Houston college-basketball "Game of the Century" played in the Astrodome (gameofthecentury.blogspot.com).

RICHARD RIIS is a librarian, writer, and researcher from Long Island, New York. A former magazine writer and editor as well as a lifelong baseball fan and historian, Richard has contributed to the SABR Baseball Biography Project and to books about the Yankees, Tigers, Pirates, and Brewers.

RICK SCHABOWSKI, a retired machinist at the Harley-Davidson Company, is currently an instructor at the Wisconsin Regional Training Partnership in the Manufacturing Program, and is a certified Manufacturing Skills Standards Council instructor. He is president of the Ken Keltner Badger State Chapter of SABR, treasurer of the Milwaukee Braves Historical Association, and president of the Wisconsin Oldtime Ballplayers Association, and is a member of the Hoops Historians and Pro Football Research Association.

MARK S. STERNMAN works in Boston and, though a diehard fan of the New York Yankees, holds a partial season-ticket plan for the Boston Red Sox. A SABR member since 1990, he roots for the Astros when the team takes on the Sox. With a fondness for ballplayers who have good gloves, speed, and little power, Sternman continues to consider Terry Puhl as his all-time favorite Houston player.

JIM SWEETMAN is a lifelong Phillies fan, despite growing up on the edge of the New York media market in central New Jersey and living for the past 25 years just outside Washington, D.C. Since 1994, he's operated www.broadandpattison.com, a website providing daily slices of Phillies history, for which he has conducted extensive reviews of contemporary press accounts. He holds bachelor's and master's degrees from Rutgers University and an MBA from James Madison University. He is a senior official with the US Government Accountability Office, where he manages efforts to evaluate the efficiency and effectiveness of government programs.

JOSEPH THOMPSON currently is a Ph.D. student at the University of Houston. His research focuses on baseball's drug, gambling, and vice culture. His first book project was as co-author of the Larry Dierker SABR Chapter book *Houston Baseball: The Early Years, 1861 -1961*. He is wrapping up research for his second book, *Mexican American Baseball in the Gulf Coast Region*. He currently writes on baseball films and literature. In his spare time, he writes fiction.

ROBERT C. TRUMPBOUR is associate professor of communications at Penn State Altoona. He is the author of *The Eighth Wonder of the World: The Life of Houston's Iconic Astrodome* (Nebraska University Press) and *The New Cathedrals: Politics and Media in the History of Stadium Construction* (Syracuse University Press). He has taught at Pennsylvania State University, Southern Illinois University, Saint Francis University, and Western Illinois University. Prior to teaching, Trumpbour worked in various capacities at CBS for the television and radio networks.

STEVE WEST and his wife, Marian, attended the final regular-season game played in the Astrodome. Marian's parents, Marie and Alex Broussard of Beaumont, Texas, attended the first ever game played in the Astrodome. This makes the family an unusual set of bookends to the eighth wonder of the world.

TAL SMITH spent 54 years working in Major League Baseball front offices. In three separate stints with the Houston Colt .45s/Astros that spanned a total of 35 years, he held positions as the franchise's Farm System Director, Vice-President of Player Personnel, General Manager, and President of Baseball Operations. As an assistant to Judge Roy Hofheinz, the president of the Houston Sports Association, Tal helped to oversee the construction of the Astrodome and later was responsible for finding the stadium's synthetic playing surface that came to be known as AstroTurf. As General Manager, he assembled the Astros' first playoff team, for which he was recognized as *The Sporting News'* Major League Executive of the Year in 1980. Tal and his wife, Jonnie, reside in Houston; they have two children, Valerie and Randy. Randy followed in his father's footsteps and, at age 29, became the youngest general manager in MLB history when he took the reins for the San Diego Padres in 1993.

Upon realizing that he couldn't hit a curveball, **MIKE WHITEMAN** took to reading and researching about the national pastime. He enjoys nothing more than sitting on his porch in Lancaster, Pennsylvania, listening to ballgames on the radio. His home team includes his wife, Nichole, and two daughters.

A lifelong Pirates fan, **GREGORY H. WOLF** was born in Pittsburgh, but now resides in the Chicagoland area with his wife, Margaret, and daughter, Gabriela. A professor of German studies and holder of the Dennis and Jean Bauman Endowed Chair in the Humanities at North Central College in Naperville, Illinois, he edited the SABR books *That's Joy in Braveland! The 1957 Milwaukee Braves* (2014), *Winning on the North Side. The 1929 Chicago Cubs* (2015), *A Pennant for the Twin Cities: The 1965 Minnesota Twins* (2015), and *From the Braves to* *the Brewers: Great Games and Exciting History at Milwaukee's County Stadium* (2016). He is currently working on a project about Sportsman's Park in St. Louis and co-editing a book with Bill Nowlin on the 1979 Pittsburgh Pirates.

KENNETH WOMACK is dean of the Wayne D. McMurray School of Humanities and Social Sciences at Monmouth University, where he also serves as professor of English. He is the author or editor of numerous books, including *Long and Winding Roads: The Evolving Artistry of the Beatles* (2007), the *Cambridge Companion to the Beatles* (2009), and

The Beatles Encyclopedia: Everything Fab Four (2014). Womack is also the author of three award-winning novels, *John Doe No. 2 and the Dreamland Motel* (2010), *The Restaurant at the End of the World* (2012), and *Playing the Angel* (2013). He serves as editor of *Interdisciplinary Literary Studies: A Journal of Criticism and Theory*, published by Penn State University Press, and as co-editor of the English Association's *Year's Work in English Studies*, published by Oxford University Press.

SABR BioProject Team Books

In 2002, the Society for American Baseball Research launched an effort to write and publish biographies of every player, manager, and individual who has made a contribution to baseball. Over the past decade, the BioProject Committee has produced over 6,000 biographical articles. Many have been part of efforts to create theme- or team-oriented books, spearheaded by chapters or other committees of SABR.

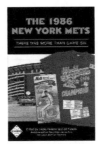

THE 1986 BOSTON RED SOX:
THERE WAS MORE THAN GAME SIX
One of a two-book series on the rivals that met in the 1986 World Series, the Boston Red Sox and the New York Mets, including biographies of every player, coach, broadcaster, and other important figures in the top organizations in baseball that year. .
Edited by Leslie Heaphy and Bill Nowlin
$19.95 paperback (ISBN 978-1-943816-19-4)
$9.99 ebook (ISBN 978-1-943816-18-7)
8.5"X11", 420 pages, over 200 photos

THE 1986 NEW YORK METS:
THERE WAS MORE THAN GAME SIX
The other book in the "rivalry" set from the 1986 World Series. This book re-tells the story of that year's classic World Series and this is the story of each of the players, coaches, managers, and broadcasters, their lives in baseball and the way the 1986 season fit into their lives.
Edited by Leslie Heaphy and Bill Nowlin
$19.95 paperback (ISBN 978-1-943816-13-2)
$9.99 ebook (ISBN 978-1-943816-12-5)
8.5"X11", 392 pages, over 100 photos

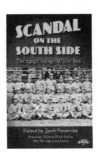

SCANDAL ON THE SOUTH SIDE:
THE 1919 CHICAGO WHITE SOX
The Black Sox Scandal isn't the only story worth telling about the 1919 Chicago White Sox. The team roster included three future Hall of Famers, a 20-year-old spitballer who would win 300 games in the minors, and even a batboy who later became a celebrity with the "Murderers' Row" New York Yankees. All of their stories are included in Scandal on the South Side with a timeline of the 1919 season.
Edited by Jacob Pomrenke
$19.95 paperback (ISBN 978-1-933599-95-3)
$9.99 ebook (ISBN 978-1-933599-94-6)
8.5"x11", 324 pages, 55 historic photos

WINNING ON THE NORTH SIDE
THE 1929 CHICAGO CUBS
Celebrate the 1929 Chicago Cubs, one of the most exciting teams in baseball history. Future Hall of Famers Hack Wilson, '29 NL MVP Rogers Hornsby, and Kiki Cuyler, along with Riggs Stephenson formed one of the most potent quartets in baseball history. The magical season came to an ignominious end in the World Series and helped craft the future "lovable loser" image of the team.
Edited by Gregory H. Wolf
$19.95 paperback (ISBN 978-1-933599-89-2)
$9.99 ebook (ISBN 978-1-933599-88-5)
8.5"x11", 314 pages, 59 photos

DETROIT THE UNCONQUERABLE:
THE 1935 WORLD CHAMPION TIGERS
Biographies of every player, coach, and broadcaster involved with the 1935 World Champion Detroit Tigers baseball team, written by members of the Society for American Baseball Research. Also includes a season in review and other articles about the 1935 team. Hank Greenberg, Mickey Cochrane, Charlie Gehringer, Schoolboy Rowe, and more.
Edited by Scott Ferkovich
$19.95 paperback (ISBN 9978-1-933599-78-6)
$9.99 ebook (ISBN 978-1-933599-79-3)
8.5"X11", 230 pages, 52 photos

THE TEAM THAT TIME WON'T FORGET:
THE 1951 NEW YORK GIANTS
Because of Bobby Thomson's dramatic "Shot Heard 'Round the World" in the bottom of the ninth of the decisive playoff game against the Brooklyn Dodgers, the team will forever be in baseball public's consciousness. Includes a foreword by Giants outfielder Monte Irvin.
Edited by Bill Nowlin and C. Paul Rogers III
$19.95 paperback (ISBN 978-1-933599-99-1)
$9.99 ebook (ISBN 978-1-933599-98-4)
8.5"X11", 282 pages, 47 photos

A PENNANT FOR THE TWIN CITIES:
THE 1965 MINNESOTA TWINS
This volume celebrates the 1965 Minnesota Twins, who captured the American League pennant in just their fifth season in the Twin Cities. Led by an All-Star cast, from Harmon Killebrew, Tony Oliva, Zoilo Versalles, and Mudcat Grant to Bob Allison, Jim Kaat, Earl Battey, and Jim Perry, the Twins won 102 games, but bowed to the Los Angeles Dodgers and Sandy Koufax in Game Seven
Edited by Gregory H. Wolf
$19.95 paperback (ISBN 978-1-943816-09-5)
$9.99 ebook (ISBN 978-1-943816-08-8)
8.5"X11", 405 pages, over 80 photos

MUSTACHES AND MAYHEM: CHARLIE O'S THREE TIME CHAMPIONS:
THE OAKLAND ATHLETICS: 1972-74
The Oakland Athletics captured major league baseball's crown each year from 1972 through 1974. Led by future Hall of Famers Reggie Jackson, Catfish Hunter and Rollie Fingers, the Athletics were a largely homegrown group who came of age together. Biographies of every player, coach, manager, and broadcaster (and mascot) from 1972 through 1974 are included, along with season recaps.
Edited by Chip Greene
$29.95 paperback (ISBN 978-1-943816-07-1)
$9.99 ebook (ISBN 978-1-943816-06-4)
8.5"X11", 600 pages, almost 100 photos

SABR Members can purchase each book at a significant discount (often 50% off) and receive the ebook edtions free as a member benefit. Each book is available in a trade paperback edition as well as ebooks suitable for reading on a home computer or Nook, Kindle, or iPad/tablet.

To learn more about becoming a member of SABR, visit the website: sabr.org/join

THE SABR DIGITAL LIBRARY

The Society for American Baseball Research, the top baseball research organization in the world, disseminates some of the best in baseball history, analysis, and biography through our publishing programs. The SABR Digital Library contains a mix of books old and new, and focuses on a tandem program of paperback and ebook publication, making these materials widely available for both on digital devices and as traditional printed books.

GREATEST GAMES BOOKS

TIGERS BY THE TALE:
GREAT GAMES AT MICHIGAN AND TRUMBULL
For over 100 years, Michigan and Trumbull was the scene of some of the most exciting baseball ever. This book portrays 50 classic games at the corner, spanning the earliest days of Bennett Park until Tiger Stadium's final closing act. From Ty Cobb to Mickey Cochrane, Hank Greenberg to Al Kaline, and Willie Horton to Alan Trammell.
Edited by Scott Ferkovich
$12.95 paperback (ISBN 978-1-943816-21-7)
$6.99 ebook (ISBN 978-1-943816-20-0)
8.5"x11", 160 pages, 22 photos

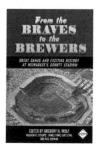

FROM THE BRAVES TO THE BREWERS: GREAT GAMES AND HISTORY AT MILWAUKEE'S COUNTY STADIUM
The National Pastime provides in-depth articles focused on the geographic region where the national SABR convention is taking place annually. The SABR 45 convention took place in Chicago, and here are 45 articles on baseball in and around the bat-and-ball crazed Windy City: 25 that appeared in the souvenir book of the convention plus another 20 articles available in ebook only.
Edited by Gregory H. Wolf
$19.95 paperback (ISBN 978-1-943816-23-1)
$9.99 ebook (ISBN 978-1-943816-22-4)
8.5"X11", 290 pages, 58 photos

BRAVES FIELD:
MEMORABLE MOMENTS AT BOSTON'S LOST DIAMOND
From its opening on August 18, 1915, to the sudden departure of the Boston Braves to Milwaukee before the 1953 baseball season, Braves Field was home to Boston's National League baseball club and also hosted many other events: from NFL football to championship boxing. The most memorable moments to occur in Braves Field history are portrayed here.
Edited by Bill Nowlin and Bob Brady
$19.95 paperback (ISBN 978-1-933599-93-9)
$9.99 ebook (ISBN 978-1-933599-92-2)
8.5"X11", 282 pages, 182 photos

AU JEU/PLAY BALL: THE 50 GREATEST GAMES IN THE HISTORY OF THE MONTREAL EXPOS
The 50 greatest games in Montreal Expos history. The games described here recount the exploits of the many great players who wore Expos uniforms over the years—Bill Stoneman, Gary Carter, Andre Dawson, Steve Rogers, Pedro Martinez, from the earliest days of the franchise, to the glory years of 1979-1981, the what-might-have-been years of the early 1990s, and the sad, final days.and others.
Edited by Norm King
$12.95 paperback (ISBN 978-1-943816-15-6)
$5.99 ebook (ISBN978-1-943816-14-9)
8.5"x11", 162 pages, 50 photos

ORIGINAL SABR RESEARCH

CALLING THE GAME:
BASEBALL BROADCASTING FROM 1920 TO THE PRESENT
An exhaustive, meticulously researched history of bringing the national pastime out of the ballparks and into living rooms via the airwaves. Every play-by-play announcer, color commentator, and ex-ballplayer, every broadcast deal, radio station, and TV network. Plus a foreword by "Voice of the Chicago Cubs" Pat Hughes, and an afterword by Jacques Doucet, the "Voice of the Montreal Expos" 1972-2004.
by Stuart Shea
$24.95 paperback (ISBN 978-1-933599-40-3)
$9.99 ebook (ISBN 978-1-933599-41-0)
7"X10", 712 pages, 40 photos

BIOPROJECT BOOKS

WHO'S ON FIRST:
REPLACEMENT PLAYERS IN WORLD WAR II
During World War II, 533 players made the major league debuts. More than 60% of the players in the 1941 Opening Day lineups departed for the service and were replaced by first-times and oldsters. Hod Lisenbee was 46. POW Bert Shepard had an artificial leg, and Pete Gray had only one arm. The 1944 St. Louis Browns had 13 players classified 4-F. These are their stories.
Edited by Marc Z Aaron and Bill Nowlin
$19.95 paperback (ISBN 978-1-933599-91-5)
$9.99 ebook (ISBN 978-1-933599-90-8)
8.5"X11", 422 pages, 67 photos

VAN LINGLE MUNGO:
THE MAN, THE SONG, THE PLAYERS
40 baseball players with intriguing names have been named in renditions of Dave Frishberg's classic 1969 song, Van Lingle Mungo. This book presents biographies of all 40 players and additional information about one of the greatest baseball novelty songs of all time.
Edited by Bill Nowlin
$19.95 paperback (ISBN 978-1-933599-76-2)
$9.99 ebook (ISBN 978-1-933599-77-9)
8.5"X11", 278 pages, 46 photos

NUCLEAR POWERED BASEBALL
Nuclear Powered Baseball tells the stories of each player—past and present—featured in the classic Simpsons episode "Homer at the Bat." Wade Boggs, Ken Griffey Jr., Ozzie Smith, Nap Lajoie, Don Mattingly, and many more. We've also included a few very entertaining takes on the now-famous episode from prominent baseball writers Jonah Keri, Joe Posnanski, Erik Malinowski, and Bradley Woodrum
Edited by Emily Hawks and Bill Nowlin
$19.95 paperback (ISBN 978-1-943816-11-8)
$9.99 ebook (ISBN 978-1-943816-10-1)
8.5"X11", 250 pages

SABR Members can purchase each book at a significant discount (often 50% off) and receive the ebook edtions free as a member benefit. Each book is available in a trade paperback edition as well as ebooks suitable for reading on a home computer or Nook, Kindle, or iPad/tablet.
To learn more about becoming a member of SABR, visit the website: sabr.org/join

Society for American Baseball Research

Cronkite School at ASU
555 N. Central Ave. #416, Phoenix, AZ 85004
602.496.1460 (phone)
SABR.org

Become a SABR member today!

If you're interested in baseball — writing about it, reading about it, talking about it — there's a place for you in the Society for American Baseball Research. Our members include everyone from academics to professional sportswriters to amateur historians and statisticians to students and casual fans who enjoy reading about baseball and occasionally gathering with other members to talk baseball. What unites all SABR members is an interest in the game and joy in learning more about it.

SABR membership is open to any baseball fan; we offer 1-year and 3-year memberships. Here's a list of some of the key benefits you'll receive as a SABR member:

- Receive two editions (spring and fall) of the *Baseball Research Journal*, our flagship publication
- Receive expanded e-book edition of *The National Pastime*, our annual convention journal
- 8-10 new e-books published by the SABR Digital Library, all FREE to members
- "This Week in SABR" e-newsletter, sent to members every Friday
- Join dozens of research committees, from Statistical Analysis to Women in Baseball.
- Join one of 70 regional chapters in the U.S., Canada, Latin America, and abroad
- Participate in online discussion groups
- Ask and answer baseball research questions on the SABR-L e-mail listserv
- Complete archives of *The Sporting News* dating back to 1886 and other research resources
- Promote your research in "This Week in SABR"
- Diamond Dollars Case Competition
- Yoseloff Scholarships

- Discounts on SABR national conferences, including the SABR National Convention, the SABR Analytics Conference, Jerry Malloy Negro League Conference, Frederick Ivor-Campbell 19th Century Conference
- Publish your research in peer-reviewed SABR journals
- Collaborate with SABR researchers and experts
- Contribute to Baseball Biography Project or the SABR Games Project
- List your new book in the SABR Bookshelf
- Lead a SABR research committee or chapter
- Networking opportunities at SABR Analytics Conference
- Meet baseball authors and historians at SABR events and chapter meetings
- 50% discounts on paperback versions of SABR e-books
- 20% discount on MLB.TV and MiLB.TV subscriptions
- Discounts with other partners in the baseball community
- SABR research awards

We hope you'll join the most passionate international community of baseball fans at SABR! Check us out online at SABR.org/join.

- -

SABR MEMBERSHIP FORM

	Annual	3-year	Senior	3-yr Sr.	Under 30
U.S.:	❏ $65	❏ $175	❏ $45	❏ $129	❏ $45
Canada/Mexico:	❏ $75	❏ $205	❏ $55	❏ $159	❏ $55
Overseas:	❏ $84	❏ $232	❏ $64	❏ $186	❏ $55

Add a Family Member: $15 each family member at same address (list names on back)
Senior: 65 or older before 12/31 of the current year

All dues amounts in U.S. dollars or equivalent

Participate in Our Donor Program!

Support the preservation of baseball research. Designate your gift toward:
❏General Fund ❏Endowment Fund ❏Research Resources ❏_____
❏ I want to maximize the impact of my gift; do not send any donor premiums
❏ I would like this gift to remain anonymous.

Note: Any donation not designated will be placed in the General Fund.
SABR is a 501 (c) (3) not-for-profit organization & donations are tax-deductible to the extent allowed by law.

Name _____

E-mail* _____

Address _____

City _____ ST_____ ZIP_____

Phone _____ Birthday _____

* **Your e-mail address on file ensures you will receive the most recent SABR news.**

Dues $_____

Donation $_____

Amount Enclosed $_____

Do you work for a matching grant corporation? Call (602) 496-1460 for details.

If you wish to pay by credit card, please contact the SABR office at (602) 496-1460 or visit the SABR Store online at SABR.org/join. We accept Visa, Mastercard & Discover.

Do you wish to receive the *Baseball Research Journal* electronically?: ❏ Yes   ❏ No
Our e-books are available in PDF, Kindle, or EPUB (iBooks, iPad, Nook) formats.

Mail to: SABR, Cronkite School at ASU, 555 N. Central Ave. #416, Phoenix, AZ 85004

Made in the USA
San Bernardino, CA
12 March 2017